PEOPLE, MARKETING AND BUSINESS

Business Explained
PEOPLE, MARKETING AND BUSINESS

MALCOLM SURRIDGE
Senior Lecturer and Assistant Director of External Affairs, Great Yarmouth College;
Senior Examiner AEB A Level Business Studies

TONY BUSHELL
Principal Lecturer in Business and Management Studies,
City College, Norwich

PHILIP GUNN
Head of the School of Management, Great Yarmouth College; Assistant Chief
Examiner AEB A Level Business Studies

CollinsEducational
An imprint of HarperCollins*Publishers*

Dedication
To Rosemary, Diana and Sheila, with love

Published by
Collins Educational Ltd
An imprint of HarperCollins Publishers
77-85 Fulham Palace Road
Hammersmith
London W6 8JB

First published in 1993

British Library Cataloguing in Publication Data is available on
request from the British Library

ISBN 0-00-3223124

Typeset by Dorchester Typesetting Group Ltd
Cover designed by Ridgeway Associates
Printed by Scotprint Ltd, Musselburgh

Contents

ACKNOWLEDGEMENTS

A number of people have been of great assistance in the production of this book. We are most grateful to Murray Lauder for reading and commenting upon the whole manuscript. His ideas were invaluable and improved the manuscript in many ways. We are very grateful to Martin Liu of HarperCollins for his thorough and professional work in helping to prepare this book for publication. We also wish to thank David Chell, Clare Gunn and Kevin Gunn for reading and offering comments upon specialist parts of the manuscript. In spite of their help we are, of course, entirely responsible for any errors or omissions which may remain.

We wish to record our thanks to Barbara Francis for her suggestions as to sources for the various materials necessary to write this book. We are indebted to the many businesses, big and small, who offered materials for publication in the book. Without their co-operation the end result would have been much poorer.

Finally, we wish to acknowledge the following examination boards for permission to reproduce questions from past examination papers: Associated Examination Board, Northern Examination and Assessment Board, and Cambridge Local Examinations Syndicate. Any answers or hints of answers are the sole responsibility of the authors and have not been provided by the Boards.

Every effort has been made to contact all copyright holders, but if any have been inadvertently overlooked the publisher would be pleased to hear from them and to make the necessary arrangement at the first opportunity.

Study Skills

▷ ▷ **QUESTIONS FOR PREVIEW** ▷ ▷

1 How can I organize myself to study effectively?

2 How can I become more aware of business that exists around me?

3 What do examiners expect in answers to business studies questions?

4 What other sources of information about business studies exist?

5 How is the Business Explained series organized and how can it help me to study the subject?

Effective Study

MANY OF you who are about to start an A level, BTEC or similar course in business studies will have had relatively little experience of taking more advanced courses where much is expected of the student outside the classroom. It is broadly true to say that the higher the level at which you study the more work the student is expected to undertake outside the classroom or lecture theatre. Do not be daunted! By organizing yourself and your time you can develop the skills and techniques which are essential for success at this level.

Probably the first thing you need to sort out is somewhere to study. You will need a desk or table to work on and possibly some shelves for your books. It should also be somewhere you can work without disturbance – well away from distractions!

You need to organize your week so as to allocate regular times for study. It makes sense to use the same times each week so that you and your family and friends become used to the arrangement. This might seem unnecessarily formal to you but it is essential that you work steadily throughout your course. You cannot expect to do well by leaving everything to the last minute. Indeed, the growing emphasis on coursework will make such an approach impossible.

The actual studying you undertake may take a number of forms. Business studies is a unique subject in that it is going on around you all the time. Pick up a newspaper or magazine and it will inevitably contain a number of advertisements. Similarly, your favourite TV programmes may be interrupted by advertisements. As your knowledge of the subject increases, you will discover that you can learn much about the firm and its competitors from the way and place it advertises. Equally, as you walk down your local high street you will find a lot of evidence of business taking place. Delivery vans and lorries will be regularly seen and many famous retailers such as Marks & Spencer and W H Smith will have branches. Business studies will help you to understand why they have chosen such a location and why some businesses succeed and others fail.

You can learn a lot about business from talking to relatives or friends who are at work. You may care to ask some of the following questions:

- What do you like most and least about your job?
- What does your business (organization) do?
- Where and how does it advertise?
- Do you work mainly with machinery or with people?
- How large is your business? How do you measure the size of it?

- Are there trade unions where you work?
- Has the business changed a lot over the last few years?
- Do you use computers a lot in your work? If so, in which department – production, design, administration?
- With which other businesses do you do business?

Examples of business studies in action are all around you: make the best use of the examples and evidence offered to support your classroom study. You will gain marks in examinations and coursework by being able to quote relevant, real-life examples.

Writing Answers

Your teacher or lecturer will set you essays, case studies and possibly coursework throughout the course. It is important that you do as well as possible when completing this work, particularly where the marks you score contribute to your final, overall grade.

When tackling essays or other coursework you should resist the temptation to leave everything until the last moment. A successful piece of written work requires careful preparation. You will need to research your answer by using class or lecture notes and texts such as this one. You may also follow up references given in the books you read. Finally, but importantly, you may use quality newspapers and periodicals, such as *The Economist*, to give relevant up-to-date examples in support of your answers. Again, examples from the real world around you should prove valuable. With this material to hand, you should carefully plan your answer before you commence writing.

A level in particular requires more than a simple regurgitation of facts. Marks for factual content alone probably represent less than 30 per cent of the total available. It is what you do with your knowledge that will determine how good a mark you score.

Examiners are looking for evidence of *analysis* in your answers. This means that you must be able to apply your factual knowledge to unfamiliar situations presented to you by the examiners. For example, you may be given a case study describing a large firm which is experiencing communications problems. You might be asked to explain why this firm experiences problems and to recommend some solutions. You may use your notes on barriers to communication as a guide but you will also need to *apply* them to the firm in question, thus analysing that firm's particular problems.

Most questions will also require some *evaluation*. This involves judgement or assessment. So, continuing with our example from the previous paragraph, it may be necessary to identify (justifying your choice) the major barrier to communication or perhaps the most likely cure.

Analysis and evaluation are important components of answers to most types of question and not just case studies. Your teacher or lecturer will be able to help you develop the necessary technique to write well balanced answers.

When the piece of work is returned to you it is important that you read carefully your teacher's or lecturer's comments in order to eliminate weaknesses and improve future performance.

Using the Business Explained Series

This series of books comprises three titles:

- *Finance, Information and Business*
- *The Business Environment*
- *People, Marketing and Business*

It is designed to make business studies both understandable and enjoyable. By adopting the language and approach that we have, we aim to provide a rigorous treatment of the subject whilst not confusing you, the reader.

The series has been written for a typical student who is following an A level, BTEC, GNVQ or similar course in business studies. In particular, consideration has been given to students who will be working alone. Much of your studying will take place outside the classroom and these books are intended to act as a support to the teaching that you receive.

The three books in the series can be read in any order. We have deliberately avoided writing the books in any sequence. Not only can you begin with any book, but with any chapter. If you encounter business terms with which you are unfamiliar then simply look them up in the Dictionary at the end of each book.

We recommend two ways in which you may use this book apart from as a class text.

Method A

Reading about business studies in this book and others, as we saw earlier, is an important part of your studies. It will help you to strengthen your knowledge of the subject and its techniques. You may wish to read a topic area prior to your teacher covering it in class. Indeed you may be asked to do so! Alternatively, it could be that you choose to read such an area after you have been taught it.

At the end of the chapters we have included an

Exam Preparation section. This will allow you to practise the skills you are attempting to acquire and to assess how well you understand the subject matter. Because many examination boards are now using case studies most chapters contain at least one to allow you to familiarize yourself with this style of question.

We have also included regular Key Points which act as a summary of the principal elements covered in the preceding section. When you reach the end of each chapter you should reread the points for preview and confirm that you now understand them.

Method B

Throughout your course, your teacher or lecturer will set you essays, case studies or similar questions. You will be able to use this book in several ways to help with such assignments. It will, of course, provide you with much of the information needed to answer questions set on A level, BTEC, GNVQ and similar courses. In addition, you may also make use of the references offered at the end of each book.

Finally, you would be well advised to look at some of the past examination questions and the suggested solutions at the back of the books. This should give you valuable guidance on what your teacher (or the examiner) is looking for when setting questions.

As the examination approaches your studying should become more intensive with the main emphasis on the revision of material covered earlier. In the meantime the best of luck with the course!

CHAPTER 1

Introduction to Business

▷ ▷ **QUESTIONS FOR PREVIEW** ▷ ▷

1 What do we mean by the term 'business'?

2 In what sense are businesses dynamic and how do they interact with society?

3 Why can businesses be described as integrated systems and how should they plan their activities?

4 What forms of business exist in the UK?

What is Business?

A DICTIONARY and Thesaurus give many meanings of the noun 'business':

- A trade or profession – for example, 'What business are you in?'
- The purchase and sale of goods and services – for example, 'Smith and I do business together'
- A commercial or industrial establishment – for example, 'This business employs 400 people'
- Volume of commercial activity – for example, 'Business is good at the moment'
- Commercial policy – for example, 'Overcharging customers is bad business'

Other meanings exist, but they are not relevant here. So you can see the problem that needs to be cleared up before we start a study of business. What do we mean when we use the term 'business' in this book?

It is essential that our study examines all the internal and external pressures that affect the many organizations from which we earn or receive money, and all the organizations with which we spend our money either voluntarily or by compulsion. Therefore, in general we mean 'commercial or industrial establishments' like ICI, Marks & Spencer, Abbey National Building Society or Commercial Union Insurance.

But we cannot exclude local government which places planning and development restrictions on businesses, or national government which passes laws that affect every business, and collects taxes on profits and VAT on purchases. Trade unions influence the pay and conditions that employers provide, and pressure groups can cause firms to alter the way they make or package their products. Similarly, we must consider the impact of international organizations such as the European Community and the International Monetary Fund. This book together with the two others in this series will consider all the forms of business which exist, what comprises these businesses and the external influences to which they are subject.

So when we think about 'business' in this book, we mean commercial and industrial establishments and everything that affects them.

Business studies is not a single, tidy subject with its own body of knowledge and its own language. Rather, it is a blend of many specialist subjects. Economics is the basis of business studies and provides a firm foundation upon which to build. Money (as represented by finance and accounting) is the language of business, and needs to be controlled and kept secure. People make business, and their behaviour must be understood and influenced when possible. Laws control business and protect society from its worst excesses. Communication is the lifeblood of business and pervades every aspect of it. Mathematics and statistics are the key to understanding, describing and solving many of the problems faced by businesses. We do not need to study each of these in as much depth as a specialist might – we need a working knowledge of each, and to understand the interaction of each of them with the others. The good student of business studies understands the components which comprise business studies and the way in which the elements fit together to provide an integrated approach to the subject.

For example, a company thinking about developing a new product or service ought to consider if there will be sufficient demand for it, and whether the level of demand would be affected by price (*economics*). Can the company afford to produce it and make a profit at the price customers would be willing to pay (*finance*)? Has it got people with the right skills and expertise to design and make the good (*people*)? Is the product covered by any special legal regulations as the upholstery or toy industries are (*law*)? Ought the company do some marketing research to find out what people think before they spend too much money (*mathematics* and *statistics*)? In everything mentioned here, the company will be giving and gathering information and ideas all the time (*communication*).

If any one of these activities turns up a problem, it will affect all the others. For example, if the law says that only flame resistant foam may be used in the product, it may put up the costs, the price may have to be raised to cover it, that may mean fewer customers and less income, which may mean the company cannot afford to employ expert staff, so it may have to drop the whole idea.

ACTIVITY 1.1

Your cousin is about to set up in business as a window cleaner. In conversation with him, you mention the elements which make up business and remark that he will be affected by them all once he starts trading. He is surprised and asks for examples which relate to his business.

Using the six headings outlined earlier, give examples of how he will call upon skills or knowledge from these subject areas in running his business.

Classifying Businesses

Another difficulty facing you is the very wide range of activities that can be described as business. If you look at the *Yellow Pages* trade directory, there are over 2 700 trade classifications, starting with 'Abattoir equipment' and ending with 'Zoos'. We need a much more general structure to allow access to the subject.

The most common and accepted classifications take three stages in the production of goods and services:

- Primary activities
- Secondary activities
- Tertiary activities

Primary Activities

Most commodities or goods that we buy start their life as raw materials in the ground, the seas or the fields.

All the activities concerned with extracting ores, oil or other basic materials; growing grain, fruit and vegetables; breeding animals for meat and fishing are called primary activities, and this part of the production chain is called the primary sector. The industries that make up this sector include mining and quarrying, agriculture, forestry and fishing.

Secondary Activities

Converting these raw materials into useful products, either by manufacturing or processing, is called secondary activity. For example, converting iron ore into steel, and then using the steel for manufacturing cars; or purifying water and pumping it to homes for drinking; or milling wheat to make flour, and then baking it for bread – all these are secondary activities, and together these industries constitute the secondary sector.

Tertiary Activities

Distributing these goods to make it convenient for the consumer to buy them – transportation, wholesaling, retailing, direct mail – are tertiary activities. So, too, are all the supporting services to industry: banking, insurance, travel, street lighting, refuse collection and any other supporting activities (such as holidays, health services, education and training). All these make up the tertiary sector.

SUB-DIVISIONS

There are many sub-divisions to these general categories. Farming can be sub-divided into arable (crops) and dairy (cattle), and these can be sub-divided again into types of crop and types of cattle. We could carry on sub-dividing until we are back to the 2 700 classifications found in the *Yellow Pages*. But the three main sectors we have described above are enough for our purposes.

ACTIVITY 1.2

Look in your daily or local newspaper and turn to the pages where jobs are advertised. Select ten advertisements and categorize the firms that placed them according to whether they are in the primary, secondary or tertiary sectors. Why do you think that firms from certain sectors of the economy placed most of the advertisements – particularly if you looked in a national newspaper?

The Size of Businesses

Another difficulty we have to deal with is the variation in the size of different businesses and the scale of their operations. For example, the Ford Motor Company is a business that manufactures cars on a very large scale in many countries of the world. Rolls Royce manufactures a small number of exclusive cars in the UK for a particular type of customer. Dennis Beeston & Co service and repair cars for a small number of customers in Bradwell, near Great Yarmouth. The one thing they have in common is that they are businesses to do with motor cars – but there is little else.

There are many ways to measure the size of businesses. Probably the most commonly used is the value of turnover or sales, although the number of employees is also used on occasions. Can you think of any alternatives?

Look back now at your answers to Activity 1.2. Do you think that there is any relationship between the size (and probable wealth) of firms and where they advertise for employees? Might this have biased your mini-survey?

The Dynamic Nature of Business

Another aspect of business that we must take into account is the fact that it is dynamic. It is always changing in response to changes within it, and in response to changes outside it. It has an energy of its own that affects its environment, just as its environment has energy that affects the business. In other words, businesses and the environment in which they operate affect one another.

A writer on psychology, Kurt Lewin, described this idea as 'a field of forces' that create a balance between opposing forces. Imagine a balloon that has been inflated. It is the shape and size that it is because the pressure (forces) inside are exactly equal to the forces outside. If you increase the forces outside without an equal response from inside, the balloon will get smaller. The opposite is also true. If you increase the forces inside the balloon without an equal response from outside, the balloon will get bigger. This idea is very useful in helping us to understand what might happen to a business, or to businesses in general, as the environment in which they exist changes. We can call this the 'concept of balancing forces'.

The energy inside a business comes from the people who manage and work in it. When a team of people are working together in harmony, committed to the same aims and objectives and all pulling in the same direction, it is likely that it will be creating forces which will affect its environment. For example, if it develops a new and revolutionary product that the consumers want, and none of its competitors have responded to this new 'force', almost certainly it will get larger and the competitors will get smaller as a result. Similarly, if the company invests in new technology, and as a result reduces its costs, it can either lower its prices to gain a bigger share of the market (thus taking business away from its competitors) or it can make more profit to finance further growth.

We will study the various internal forces that make businesses dynamic. Whether a company grows or contracts depends upon its ability to respond to the changes in internal and external forces.

Business Within Society

People in society demand goods and services for a number of reasons. For example, we need food

---

KEY POINTS 1.1

- **'Business' in this book means commercial and industrial establishments and everything that affects them**

- **The study of business calls upon knowledge from many disciplines**

- **Businesses can be classified by describing where they come in the**

    production chain: primary, secondary or tertiary

- **The size of a business can vary enormously even between firms in the same industry**

- **There are a number of ways in which the size of a business can be measured**

and drink in order to survive. It is very difficult nowadays for an individual or family in the UK to provide for themselves all that they want in the way of basic needs. So they depend upon businesses to supply their needs. Also, we need good health care to keep us fit and free from disease. Not many of us are expert enough to do this for ourselves. We also need recreation and leisure pursuits to help us relax and enjoy friendship.

Another reason is because we have very high expectations. As a very affluent society, we do not see our needs in terms of survival, but in terms of our standard of living. And this standard is set not in relation to necessities, but in relation to how much other people have. Today's luxuries become tomorrow's necessities. Televisions and cars are good examples of this. How many people do you know who do not have a television? Politicians and the media make comparisons between what we have and what others have so that our expectations are never allowed to rest.

ACTIVITY 1.3

Make a list of all the goods and services you have used today. Now tick those services which you think you could provide yourself. Why do you choose not to produce for yourself the goods and services which you have not ticked?

In response to this demand, appropriate means of supply develop. These may be businesses which produce goods in response to the demand in order to make a profit, or the government of the day providing the health care required. It is almost certain that if a demand exists, a means of supply will respond. So business is shaped by the demands of society.

However, you can probably quote many examples of business shaping society. For example, do you think that 'Coke is it!' whatever 'it' is? Yet, worldwide, more people buy this soft drink than any other. The power of advertising can and does create expectations that influence our society. The temptation to improve our looks or to become more attractive to the opposite sex, as promised in many advertisements, is too great for many of us, and we buy the product whether or not the promise is realistic. Advanced economies become more advanced. Developing economies try to grow by serving and competing with them. Some will provide raw materials while others, like the textile industries in Korea and Taiwan, use cheap local labour to produce low-price goods. Some of them get into debt to such a degree that they use their new wealth to pay the interest rather than improving the standards of living in their own country. Poland and Mexico actually got to the stage where they could not even pay the loan interest. Western businesses are shaping the societies of the developing nations as well as their own.

Our standard of living is greatly influenced by job opportunities. The more successful business is, the more jobs there will be (if we assume that technology does not take over!). This in turn influences the amount of money that is spent on goods and services. Failure of business can have the opposite effect. When British Steel closed down a major factory at Corby, it had a disastrous effect on the local community because the firm had been the major employer and purchaser in the town.

During the 1980s, many incentives were offered to businesses to start up, grow and become more efficient. The spirit of enterprise was encouraged by the Conservative government under Margaret Thatcher. The philosophy of the free market economy has given businesses a much greater influence in the shaping of society than previously: and, almost inevitably, they shape society to demand more of their goods and services.

As demand grows, more raw materials are used and more waste is generated. Lewin's concept of

KEY POINTS 1.2

- **Businesses shape and respond to their environments**

- **The internal and external environments of business interact with one another**

- **Our society demands a wide range of goods and services, few of which we can produce for ourselves**

- **Our changing demands and rising expectations have implications for businesses**

balancing forces warns us that as one force alters, it affects the other variables in the environment.

Should businesses be allowed to behave in such a way as to risk these undesirable consequences? Is it ethical or not to pursue profit at all costs? It is possible to control some aspects of business behaviour by law, but it is not possible to cover all eventualities. Should some moral responsibility, therefore, be borne by owners and managers? There is no ethical code for managers as there is for, say, doctors and other professions, so how can they be controlled?

Business as an Integrated System

- Which comes first, the chicken or the egg?
- Which comes first, the product or the customer?

CASE STUDY

(The Negative Version)

John returned home from work looking more frustrated and fed up than usual. He hardly said a word to his wife and family, sat down and drank his cup of tea without looking up. Going through his mind were things that had happened at work that day: things like the decision by his boss to change production from 500-gramme packets to 400-gramme packets without consulting him. He could have told the boss that the 500-gramme packets were an urgent run for their best customer, but he had not been asked. It seemed to John that the only way to run the job properly was to run it himself – but how could he with a boss who does not consult.

His wife Jenny sat down beside him and asked him what was wrong. John explained his frustration as he had done many times before, only this time Jenny sensed that it was about time he did something about it.

'Why don't you set up on your own?' Jenny asked. 'You will never be happy working for somebody else. Take the bull by the horns before it's too late. You've got skills and experience and lots of energy. I'll support you.'

'It's not as easy as that,' replied John. 'What could I do? Where would I get enough money? Who would buy from me?' At the same time John found the idea of being his own boss very attractive. Perhaps it would be worth making a few enquiries, he thought.

(The Positive Version!)

John came home from work very excited. He could not wait for the children to go to bed so that he could discuss his decision with his wife, Jenny. At last they sat down with a cup of tea, and John said, 'Jenny, I'm going to set up in business with two of the lads from work. We know we've got the skills and experience, it's just a matter of deciding exactly what we're going to make and sell. How do you feel about joining us and running the marketing side of the business? You'd be brilliant.'

Jenny smiled. She had often thought about running their own business. It seemed a very attractive proposition, but too many people started their own business only to fail within a very short time.

'On one condition,' she said, 'and that is that

we do everything properly: don't rush in and don't take unnecessary risks.'

'That's right,' agreed John, 'we'll take it one step at a time and plan carefully before we take any action.'

The conversation went on into the night, and the main outcome was that they would take the best advice they could find at each step along the way.

QUESTIONS

1 Why do you think that John and Jenny are more likely to succeed with their business in the second case than in the first? You should give as many reasons as you can.

2 If John and Jenny asked for your advice about their intended business in the first case study, what would you advise them to do?

A business can be run by one person. That person can do everything: the production of the good or service, the accounting, the selling, the delivering and any after-sales service. This person will be very busy, too busy to become an expert at any of the tasks in the business. She or he will be talking to a customer one minute, paying a supplier the next, making the product the next minute, answering the phone, trying to find time for a cup of tea and so on. All these jobs are essential to the success of the business, no one being more or less important than another.

In a medium-sized company, there will be enough selling activity to justify the full use of one or more person's time. It will become a specialist department where real expertise can be developed. Similarly, several people may make the product in such a way that it is more efficient and less costly. A specially trained accountant may take care of all financial matters and ensure that the company keeps spending in line with income. Perhaps a special section is set up to employ the right sort of person for each job, train them, make sure that the workplace is safe and that the company looks after its staff well. Each of these *functions* is important to the success of the business.

As with the one-person business, all these activities are going on all the time, non-stop, day-in and day-out. But in the case of the medium-sized business, no one person knows everything that is going on at any one time. There is a need for planning and co-ordination to keep everything pulling in the same direction.

A good example of this need for planning and co-ordination may be seen in your school or college. The National Curriculum requires that certain subjects are taught to all students and that some of those are taught across the curriculum (Information Technology, for example). Teachers and lecturers will attend training days and staff meetings in order to plan how this will be achieved and to ensure that everyone is doing what is required of them.

An example from industry might include every department in a company. If the people doing the selling learn that there is going to be an increase in demand for the company's product, they need to tell production to make more. Production need to buy more raw materials in time to have the goods ready when the customer wants them. If production needs more workers to make the goods, the personnel section will need to find, employ and train enough people. The accountant must ensure that the company has enough money available to pay for the additional raw materials and wages. And someone must make certain that all these interdependent activities happen at the right time to avoid holding anyone else up – particularly the customer.

You can see how complicated business can be in a medium-sized company. Just think how much more complicated it can be in a very large company, with several factories and many different products. Or a multinational company like Ford or Unilever. Or a large government department, or a worldwide charity.

All the various activities that are continuously going on affect each other. We can apply Lewin's concept of balancing forces to these internal activities – as one alters, so it affects others, and they must respond or the business will go out of balance.

A business is like a stewpot. There are a lot of ingredients and each one affects the flavour of the dish. If one is missing, or there is too much of another, the flavour will be different, and perhaps not very nice.

In our study of business, we have to understand how each of the functions operate, how they contribute to the well-being of the whole business, how each one influences and affects the others, and how to keep them all in balance. We must also see the business in its environment. How it affects the environment and is affected by it is very important.

Business Plans

Before starting any business it is essential that plans are drawn up. Small businesses have a very high mortality rate: only 20 per cent survive the first five years. A major reason for this is that the new owners of businesses do not fully understand all the aspects of running a business, or the environment in which their business is to operate, or both!

It is important to research the market to make sure that buyers exist for the good or service that is to be sold and to get some idea of the prices that should be charged. Hopeful entrepreneurs should then calculate carefully the costs of supplying the good or service in order to find out whether a profit can be made.

The process of planning a business is important. It helps to draw attention to aspects of the business which might be unsuccessful or difficult and to skills which the entrepreneur may not possess.

A good business plan will help an entrepreneur to obtain finance. Bank managers are likely to be more impressed by a carefully prepared plan than by a simple expression of a business idea – no matter how great its potential.

A good business plan will contain some or all of the following:

Figure 1.1 – **A Business Plan Checklist**

Objectives:
What are your personal objectives?
What are your business objectives?
Are they specific?
Have you thought of the consequences?

The business:
History if already established.
Accounts for previous years's trading.
Present financial position.

Management:
Experience of proprietors/managers.
Responsibilities of managers.
Is the team complete or is further recruitment necessary?

Market:
How large is it?
Is market research possible/available?
What is the competition?
What advantages do competitors have?
What advantages does your product/service have?

What are the distribution channels?
What advertising or marketing will you need?

Products:
Do they meet customers's needs?
Have they been tested, including production methods?
How have costs been calculated?

Pricing:
How have prices been arrived at?
Are they competitive?

Suppliers:
Are adequate supplies available?
Is quality known to be acceptable?
What credit is available?

Physical resources:
What premises are available?
Are they adequate?
What is the cost?
What machinery/vehicles are required?

Source: Barclays Bank plc

- A full account of the entrepreneur's business experience and qualifications
- A clear statement as to what product or service is to be sold and the intended target market. How is it different from other goods or services that are already being sold on the market?
- An assessment of the costs that the business will incur in starting production and continuing over the first year or so. These should be broken down into monthly payments so that periods of financial difficulty can be identified and planned for
- The amount of capital that the owner of the business has contributed; the amount that she or he has borrowed (or wants to borrow) from others, and the rates of interest that the business is already commited to pay
- Details of the place in which the product is to be produced and sold (this might be a factory, office or shop). Does the business own part or all of it, or is it rented?
- The aims and objectives of the business. What are the intentions of the entrepreneur with regard to her or his business? Does she or he hope for rapid growth or slower growth, concentrating on a particular segment of the market. In other words, what is the overall aim of the business? What objectives will be pursued in order to achieve this overall aim?

KEY POINTS 1.3

- **It is unlikely that one person can carry out all the activities necessary to operate a business**

- **Planning and co-ordination are essential for business success**

- **The many components of business all interact and contribute to the operation of that business**

- **Business plans highlight areas of weakness and can help avoid problems before they occur**

The Types of Business Organization

Companies

Read the Case Study below. In it, Sue thought she faced a choice between forming her clothes shop business as a sole trader or taking a partner. She could, however, have formed a private company to run her clothes shop. Her business could then have been called 'Thomas's Clothes Ltd'. All private companies have the term 'Ltd' (or 'Limited') after their name. It is likely that you know of such a business that trades somewhere near you.

CASE STUDY

Sole Traders and Partnerships

Sue Thomas has just been made redundant from her job as a manageress in a local factory. She has plenty of ideas on how to spend her redundancy payment of £5 000. After much thought she has decided to open a clothes shop for women and children in her home town.

Her cousin Paula Marsh is a manager at a local bank and unsurprisingly Sue has turned to her for advice. They spent a long while together discussing plans for Sue's business and Paula was able to give her some good advice. Paula and Sue chatted about finding a suitable empty shop and how much rent Sue could afford to pay; they also discussed Sue's likely sales. Paula argued that some research was essential to find out whether Sue would have sufficient customers to make her business profitable.

'Are you going to form a company, Sue', asked Paula, 'or will you find someone to join you in a partnership?' Sue was unsure what these terms meant and asked Paula to explain.

'When you walk down the High Street in Wimberly [a nearby town],' began Paula, 'you must notice the names above the shops and other businesses that are there. In the side roads there are little businesses like Jones's Newsagents who deliver your papers each morning. We call this type of business a sole trader or sole proprietor. It is owned and managed by just one person; although, if large enough, there may be other employees. It's very easy and cheap to set up and consequently is a very popular type of business.'

'Sounds just right for me,' exclaimed Sue, 'I'll start my business as a sole trader.'

'Hold on, Sue! There are other possibilities. When you bought your new house you saw it advertised in West, Marsh and Curwen, the estate agents in Morris Street. They are an example of a partnership which exists when at least two people decide to join together to run a business. They usually all put in money and share any profits that are made.'

'Yes,' said Sue slowly, 'I can see that taking a partner would have advantages.'

Task One

Talk to someone (possibly a friend or relative) who runs her or his own business as a sole trader. Ask why she or he decided to set up this type of business. You should also ask whether she or he can think of any disadvantages of running this type of business. Finally, putting yourself in the role of Paula, write a memo to Sue setting out what you have found out.

Two weeks after their first meeting, Paula and Sue went together for lunch in a local pub.

'Thanks for your memo, Paula. I can see that it would make sense to form a partnership because of the difficulties of running a business on your own. I am worried about taking a partner, though. I would have to find someone I could trust and who agreed with my business ideas. What if we argued? I would also have to share my profits with that person.'

Paula was reassuring. 'There are advantages, you know, Sue. It would be much easier for you to have a holiday and your partner could help you with routine jobs like paying bills and ordering clothes from suppliers. It would also help to have someone to discuss your ideas with and, importantly, your partner should have money to invest into the shop. This should make it bigger and allow you to advertise to attract more customers to the shop. It's not all bad!'

Task Two

Using your local *Yellow Pages* or some other local directory, find at least a dozen examples of partnerships. They are recognizable because they will be made up of several names and will not have 'Ltd' or 'plc' after the business's name. What sort of businesses are run as partnerships? Why do you think such businesses choose to operate as partnerships?

Private limited companies offer a number of advantages. Many people can put their money into this type of business, enabling the company to grow and buy more expensive equipment and property to help it trade. People who put their money in companies are called investors or, more commonly, shareholders. They buy a 'share' of the company and, as well as receiving a share certificate, are entitled to some of the company's profits. This extra money allows the business to trade on a larger scale and may also let it employ experts (such as engineers and lawyers) which should help the business develop further.

Possibly the main advantage of forming a company to run your business relates to the term 'Ltd' that follows the name of the business. This tells people who might want to invest their money in the company (in the hope of making a profit), that if the company were to fail, then all that they could lose, at worst, is the value of their investment. This is very reassuring to potential investors because if their liability is not limited in this way then their personal possessions (home, car, etc) could be sold to meet the business's debts if it were to fail. Businesses which are structured in this way so as to protect the people who invest in them are said to have 'limited liability'.

With a few exceptions, it is only companies that can enjoy the benefit of limited liability. If Sue established her clothes shop as a private company (as suggested earlier) then the law would treat the business as separate from her personal affairs. This means that any customer who was unhappy with the clothes they bought from the shop would have to take legal action against the company, not against Sue. As outlined earlier, since the business is legally separate, the owners (or shareholders) are not responsible for its debts.

Surprisingly, it is not expensive to establish a private company and it would be possible for Sue to set up her business using this legal structure. Apart from limited liability, it would offer the major advantage that she could invite other people to put money into the business. By allowing people to buy a share in the shop, Sue would have more capital. However, in return for their funds these shareholders would have the right to say how the business should be managed.

In looking at the establishment of a business, we have met a number of new, and important, business terms. Before moving on you should make sure that you fully understand the meaning of the business language we have introduced in this section. Indeed, it is crucial that you learn to use the business terms that you encounter as you progress through the subject.

Public Companies

Increasingly companies are making headlines in the newspapers. The winning of a major overseas order, the prosecution of directors for fraud, or the collapse of a famous firm because of financial problems are all newsworthy items. Most of the companies who appear in the media in these ways are public companies. They are identified by the letters 'plc' ('public limited company') after the name. You should be able to think of some famous businesses which trade as public companies.

Although public limited companies have similarities to the private limited companies we discussed earlier, there are also some important distinctions, including the following:

CASE STUDY

W H Smith and Boots to join forces in DIY

Boots and W H Smith are to pool their Payless and Do It All businesses into a joint venture. With sales of more than £500 million, the new company will trade from 230 stores under the Do It All banner and concentrate on home improvement.

Payless and Do It All each have 4 or 5 per cent of the DIY market. The new combination will rank alongside or slightly ahead of Texas, owned by the Ladbroke group but behind the largest firm B & Q which has a 13 per cent market share.

Source: adapted from the *Independent*, 6 June 1990

QUESTIONS

1 List the advantages enjoyed by W H Smith and Boots as a result of their joint venture.

2 Can you think of any group(s) of people associated with the new venture who might suffer as a consequence of the merger?

- Public limited companies are entitled to sell their shares on the Stock Exchange. This is a large market in which people can buy and sell shares. Public limited companies can raise extra funds relatively easily since they have an enormous number of potential buyers of their shares

- Public limited companies tend to be much larger

- Public limited companies tend to be owned and managed by different groups of people. Boards of directors run public limited companies. They comprise professional managers who are paid salaries and probably do not own shares in the company. *Public* limited companies are owned by shareholders who have little say in the running of the company. In *private* limited companies it is quite common for the owners (the shareholders) to manage the business

The Public Sector

Some goods and services are provided for which people do not have to pay directly. Many people do not pay for their education: the services of schools and colleges are free to the users. When you visit your doctor you do not have to pay directly for the consultation. Similarly, you do not have to pay tolls to travel on the UK's roads. The reason why these goods and services are apparently 'free' is that the government or local authority provides them by using money taken from taxes. These goods are said to be provided by the public sector.

The public sector of the economy is that range of goods and services which are provided by the government, local authorities or nationalized industries (such as the National Health Service).

As well as providing 'free' goods and services the public sector is also responsible for providing some goods and services for which consumers have to pay. Examples of this latter group include:

- Coal produced by British Coal
- Rail travel provided by British Rail
- Swimming pools and libraries operated by your local authority or county council

Public sector businesses have fallen from favour in recent years and many have been sold to shareholders, thus becoming public limited companies, as part of the government's privatization programme.

People, Marketing and Business – About this Book

Earlier in this chapter, we looked at all the activities that go on in any business, whatever sector it is in, whatever stage it is in the production chain, or whatever its size. In this book we will examine in detail the activities that relate directly to *people*. The two main bodies of people that any organization has are employees and customers. The relevant business functions are called 'human resource management' and 'marketing'.

Human Resource Management

Despite all the advances in technology, and fears about computers or robots taking over jobs, businesses will never be able to do without people. People bring to a business more than just a pair of hands. They bring:

- Their knowledge, ability to think and their ideas
- Their skills, expertise and experience
- Their time and energy
- Their personalities, humour, enthusiasm and expectations
- Their culture, values and beliefs

KEY POINTS 1.4

- **Many small businesses are owned by a single person and they are termed sole traders**

- **Businesses can raise more money if partnerships are created**

- **Companies are owned by shareholders. Shareholders's liability is limited to the amount of money** they have invested in their shares

- **Public limited companies are far larger than private limited companies**

- **Some businesses are operated by, or on behalf of, the state. These businesses are said to be the public sector**

No other source can offer such a variety of gifts in such a small package – not even the microchip.

This variety makes 'people' the most complex of the resources used in any organization. The complexity is a benefit in the main, but it creates difficulties in management. There are two approaches to the problem:

a   The personnel management approach

Firstly, there is the personnel management approach. This tends to focus on the organization's employees and operates in the interest of each individual as well as the entire workforce. The approach is concerned with the techniques and skills of finding the best people for a given job, negotiating their contracts of employment, training them, endeavouring to satisfy their needs at work, and looking after their personal needs as a 'social service'. At the same time, the personnel manager would represent management's policy and communicate each side's view to the other. It has been argued that the role of the personnel manager differs from other managers of other departments in that she or he serves not only the employer, but also acts in the interest of employees.

b   The human resource management approach

Secondly, there is the human resource management (HRM) approach. HRM is much more strategically orientated, and aims to ensure the company has the right number of the right sort of people to fulfil both short and long-term plans. Later in Chapter Three, we will examine the management process and list the activities of managing as planning, organizing, motivating, reviewing, communicating and co-ordinating. This is the general emphasis of the HRM approach. The HRM manager sees the line manager as the day-to-day personnel manager whilst she or he is more concerned with the workforce as a whole, and the direction in which it is taking the firm.

BALANCING THE TWO APPROACHES

These two approaches are not to be seen as competing philosophies which are mutually exclusive – HRM actually evolved through personnel management. In most companies the personnel function contains elements of the two. External factors have a significant influence on the personnel function, as they do with most aspects of business. It can be argued that at a time of high unemployment, attitudes to work change both for the firm and individuals. The Conservative government under Margaret Thatcher set out to restore 'managers's prerogative' – that is, their right to manage the business without being greatly constrained by trade unions. These issues will be considered in Chapter Six, but at this stage, you may be able to see that their influence on the personnel function would result in a move towards a more HRM approach.

Irrespective of the balance between the two philosophies, there are bodies of knowledge and certain activities which are necessary to achieve the objectives of a personnel management.

WHAT A PERSONNEL MANAGER NEEDS TO KNOW

If you were to study for the professional qualification of the Institute of Personnel Management, you would find that there are many subjects that need to be studied. They would include communication, industrial psychology, industrial relations law, organizational change, labour markets, recruitment and selection procedures, training methods and procedures, the design of jobs, payment systems and pensions, computer systems and general personnel procedures.

As this range of specialist knowledge is growing and changing all the time, it is becoming common for a company's personnel manager to call upon consultants in specialist areas as and when needed, rather than try to maintain a comprehensive expertise within the firm. Knowing where to find the information and when to call upon it is becoming an essential skill in personnel.

Our study of the human resource (HR) function will start with some theories of motivation and then consider how these theories might help the practising manager to get the best out of people. We will then look at some ways of finding the best person for a particular job, how to support and develop people, and finally how to reward people for their work and maintain working relationships.

Marketing

In a free market economy, responding to the needs of the market is important if a company is to grow and prosper. That is, it must know who its customers are, what they want, where they are willing to go and buy it, and how much they are willing to pay for it. Then the company needs to set about producing the good or service in the quantity and quality demanded, keeping its costs under control so that the product can be sold at a competitive price, sufficient to create enough profit to stay in business.

THE MARKETING CONCEPT

Any organization that adopts the philosophy outlined above is said to be 'marketing orientated'. It organizes itself around the needs of its customers and potential customers. It is alert to changes in its environment and responds quickly to them.

WHAT MARKETING MANAGERS NEED TO KNOW

Marketing, like HRM, is not one subject. It demands a wide range of knowledge and skills. They would include communication, the design of marketing research, statistical analysis, product (service) design, creativity, consumer psychology, some applied economics, finance, computer systems and general marketing and administrative procedures. There are many specialisms within the scope of marketing. For example, advertising is a complex mix of lots of skills – research, psychology, creativity, art, drama and so on. That is why there are specialist advertising agencies like Saatchi & Saatchi. There are specialist research agencies like MORI, public relations experts, design consultants and so on. The marketing manager will need to know how to select the right specialists for the product or service in question, how to brief them and how to control them.

All this is needed to ensure that the firm is producing the right product range, distributing them through the right channels to the right place, telling their target customers all about them, and charging a price that is acceptable to the user and profitable to the company. The four Ps – product, place, promotion and price – are the four elements of any organization's marketing strategy. Getting the mix of these four Ps right is the result of good marketing.

We will study the subject by first examining some definitions of marketing, considering the communication systems that are important to success, and taking an overview of some important concepts – including the product life cycle and the marketing mix. Then we will take a detailed look at issues related to getting the products that customers want to the place they will go to buy them – the development of new products and how they can be managed throughout their life cycle. Finally, we will consider some of the options open to firms in promoting their products or services, and options about pricing methods.

Altogether, these principles and techniques are what an organization uses to create and maintain satisfied customers.

EXAM PREPARATION

SHORT QUESTIONS

1   Which of the following are businesses: a firm of solicitors, a car manufacturer, a bank, a university, a holiday company, a doctor's practice?

2   Find examples of two well-known firms in each of these categories of business: primary, secondary and tertiary.

3   Give one example of a way in which changes in society alter business activity.

4   List four subject areas which are a part of business studies.

5   Give two benefits that a business may derive from drawing up a business plan.

6   What is meant by the term 'limited liability'?

7   State two differences between a public limited company and a private limited company.

8   Give three examples of businesses which operate within the public sector.

9   Give two reasons why most newly established businesses are set up as sole traders.

ESSAY

1   Why do businesses of different sizes exist? Are there any relationships between the size of the business and the industry in which it trades?

CHAPTER 2

Motivation – Theory and Practice

▷ ▷ **QUESTIONS FOR PREVIEW** ▷ ▷

1   What are human needs? How do they affect people's satisfaction at work?

2   What events at work make people feel satisfied? How do these differ from events that make people feel dissatisfied?

3   How might a manager's beliefs about the attitude of people to work influence the way they treat subordinates? How might subordinates respond to different forms of treatment?

4   To what extent does a manager's own motivational make-up affect the success of an organization?

5   What is the nature of the psychological contract?

Understanding 'People' at Work

IT IS easy to assume that we know all about people. After all, each of us is one! We are surrounded by them most of the time: we socialize, work and communicate with people most of our waking hours. We like some people, and we dislike others. Some we find stimulating, others we find amusing, others we find boring.

These are very important issues when it comes to such fundamental business decisions as finding the right person for a job. One of the biggest mistakes a business could make is putting the wrong person in a job, who either cannot do it to the standard required, or who does not get on with the other people in the organization and creates discord and disunity.

ACTIVITY 2.1

Look around you at the people you work (or study) with. Select a small sample that is roughly representative of the whole group – say ten people.

What things make them all the same?

What things make them different from each other?

Are they all equally good at what they do, or are some better at some things than others?

Do they all have the same enthusiasm and willingness to do what they have to do?

If there are differences, what form do these differences take?

Are they just physical, or are they intellectual and attitudinal as well? Visible or invisible? Internal or external?

That may not have been an easy exercise to do. It was too vague and we did not have any framework or method to help us handle it. People are too complex to analyse in a simplistic fashion.

You probably decided that some of the ways in which they were different included:

- Physical characteristics and appearance
- Background and upbringing
- Intelligence and education
- Attitudes and values

and so on.

Understanding people's behaviour is the special skill of psychologists, behaviourists and sociologists, each of them in a different context. These specialists must study for a long time before they get to the stage where they would claim to understand people's behaviour – so it is quite possible that our 'understanding of people' is superficial compared with the experts. People are one of the main resources of any business and getting the right people doing the right jobs to

Productivity Up at Volvo's Kalmar Plant

New management concepts and new technology have brought immense benefits for the Volvo car company at its plant in Kalmar, Sweden. A new study shows that the factory has reduced the rate of man hours per car by 40 per cent since 1977, and this has resulted in a productivity lead of 25 per cent over the next most efficient Volvo plant.

A number of factors may have contributed to these results, but the most significant seems to be the participation of shop floor workers in establishing production budgets. At the initial stages of the budget cycle Volvo management sets a productivity improvement target, usually in the order of 4 to 7 per cent. At the same time, the MBL committee (a management/labour group set up to follow the application of Sweden's 1976 Co-determination law) is given the company's current financial position and prospects for the future by management.

During the summer months, targets are assessed by management and MBL committee representatives at the company's head office in Gothenburg and at the factory in Kalmar. The budget is prepared through the summer vacation and is usually finalized by the end of October. At this stage, union representatives and foremen participate in developing concrete plans to achieve goals for productivity, number of office employees, inventory, turnover, etc.

Profit centres

To facilitate achievement of these goals, the Kalmar plant has established 'mini factories' within the main factory, and has created results groups or profit centres at the foreman level, each with about sixty employees. The individual groups set their own financial targets for quality, production volume and personnel matters. Hence foremen have ultimate profit responsibility for their group, and feedback is given on results achieved. Part of the advantage of such a system is the increased cost consciousness of the workforce; finances are kept in mind for such things as labour cost per car, consumption of tools and materials, etc.

Information on financial targets and results is openly available to all staff. The philosophy behind the system is that everyone affected should participate in it to reflect a common commitment by the entire organization.

Linked to this profit group system is a payment plan incorporating incentive elements for all employees of the plant. This has been designed to orientate all staff towards the same goals, and relates not only to production costs but also to staff costs, quality costs, delivery times and levels of work in process.

An important feature of the wage system is the results related portion for both office and production workers. This system was instigated in 1978 after discussions between management and unions, and these produced agreement on a scheme incorporating the following:

- Hours worked (for office staff)
- Man hours per car, direct and indirect labour (production workers)
- Spoilage and adjustments
- Consumption of materials and supplies
- Consumption of added materials
- Capital costs for total inventories
- A quality index (based on a point scoring system)

The system covers all employees except the plant manager, and the results portion of the wage is paid out in identical sums of money per hour worked for all staff, providing only positive modifications to pay. The budget values for 1980 are used as a basis for calculations of the results portion; the agreement specifies that employees receive a 25 per cent results improvement over the 1980 base rate. This part of the pay structure resulted in an average 3.50 Swedish kronor per hour for each employee in 1983.

Management regards the wage system as being important in keeping employees's interest and enthusiasm in the company's performance at a peak. It also keeps efficiency at a high level.

QUESTIONS

1 In what ways did the Volvo managers provide a physical and psychological climate to encourage their employees to give of their best?

2 Identify the following:

- Participation by employees in planning
- Joint setting of productivity targets
- Joint planning of activities to achieve goals
- Work groups setting their own targets for quality, quantity and people
- Groups (profit centres) receiving feedback about their performance
- Information about progress being freely available to all staff
- Bonus payments earned by everyone directly and indirectly contributing to achieving standards

the right standards is a key skill for managers to master. Not only that, but keeping them working willingly and well is an ongoing task that every manager must be expert at.

Just because a person is capable of doing a good job does not guarantee that she or he will do a good job. It is up to the business managers to provide a physical and psychological climate in which people can and are willing to give of their best. They need to be motivated to give their energy and expertise willingly to the achievement of the organization's goals, so as to improve the organization's performance and competitiveness.

You may have noticed fellow students, who are quite capable of doing well, wasting their time in the refectory. They lack motivation. Others are more willing to study for long periods at a time. They are motivated to learn so as to achieve the best results they can.

People are not only different from one another, but they are constantly changing as they grow older and gather more knowledge and experience. People are the most complex resource in a business and present the greatest challenge to managers. Dealing with such a multitude of ever changing variables and trying to get the best out of each individual has been the subject of many studies.

We can look to the work of some notable writers, both academics and industrialists, to help us understand more fully the nature of motivation at work. We can then examine how practising managers apply the theories so as to make work satisfying for their employees. But first, read the Case Study opposite which tells us how managers at Volvo's car plant in Kalmar, Sweden, attempt to motivate their staff and improve productivity. We can see from this that productivity was improved by some carefully thought out strategies.

Let us be quite clear about Volvo's reasons for employing these strategies. Volvo management saw each of these as having value in achieving the company's objectives.

Most of what they did is based upon the findings of research into people's behaviour at work. It is a subject that has many aspects and we will spend the rest of this chapter looking at a small selection of these studies. While you are reading, bear in mind the strategies used by Volvo – we will refer to them from time to time.

F W Taylor: The Science of Work

Taylor was an engineer who believed that people worked only for money. In the late nineteenth century he developed work study techniques to allow jobs to be made as simple as possible so that they could be done quickly. All other elements, such as planning the job and checking the work, were to be done by a supervisor.

For example, his best known study was to find the ideal sized shovel for feeding coke into a blast furnace. Workers brought their own shovels, and Taylor noticed that some were large (carrying seventeen kilos of coke) and others much smaller (down to two kilos). By experiment, Taylor found that a man using a seventeen-kilo shovel moved twenty-five tonnes of coke in a day; using a fourteen-kilo shovel he moved thirty tonnes; but using a nine-kilo shovel he moved 'much more'. Therefore, Taylor decided that the scientific approach to efficient shovelling was to employ men who would all use nine-kilo shovels and move X tonnes of coke each day. Believing that financial reward played a central role in motivation, he devised payment systems so that the quicker they worked, or the more they shovelled, the more they earned. Taylor reasoned that in this way the company would earn more profits and the person would earn more wages, and both would be happy.

But this reasoning was wrong. Work people hated his 'scientific management principles' and they did not co-operate, working hard only when they were being watched. This was countered by Taylor who appointed special supervisors – the discipline bosses – to stand over the work people and keep them working.

It is true that money is a major incentive to work, but Taylor relied on it solely. Many work people were satisfied with a certain level of income and did not see the benefit in working harder for some more. Taylor did not attempt to find other ways of satisfying that sort of person. However, some of his principles of work study, quotas and payment by results are still used today, though few experienced and skilled managers would use them in isolation.

Elton Mayo: The Hawthorne Experiments

During the late 1920s and the early 1930s a team of researchers, under the direction of Elton Mayo, were trying to improve productivity in the Hawthorne Works of General Electric Company.

Initially they were applying Taylor's scientific management principles. They were experimenting with the effects on productivity of varying certain physical factors. To do this, they chose a group of ladies who assembled telephones, and put them together in a special room where the experimenters could watch and record their reactions to different changes. The lighting was improved, and productivity went up. Tea breaks were introduced, and productivity went up. Soup, coffee and food were made available at tea breaks – and productivity went up. Shorter working days were introduced – and productivity went up. Shorter working weeks were introduced – and productivity went up again.

In all, ten changes were made. It did not make good sense to the experimenters that such changes should cause the improvements they were getting. Mayo said, 'The itemized changes experimentally imposed could not be used to explain the major changes – continually improved production.' So they decided to test them further. Tea breaks were withdrawn, lighting was returned to its previous level, working hours were increased – all things which normally one would expect to have a bad effect on productivity. You can imagine their bewilderment when output continued to improve. We can see that this highlighted the limitations of Taylor's scientific management, but it did not explain what was causing the improvements.

Mayo and his team studied this 'Hawthorne Effect' for several years. They concluded that the ladies felt important because they had been consulted about each change; they liked one another; relationships in the group were good; they got on well with their supervisor; and it was these things that made work more pleasant, resulting in the desired improvements.

We can deduce from this part of Mayo's research that the way people are treated affects the way they work.

In another department, the Bank Wiring Room, a group of men were observed while they wired and soldered telephone switchgear.

This, too, illustrated the effect of social and group influences on the way people work. But this time the effects were not really in the best interests of the business.

Within the room there were two sub-groups, one working on more complicated equipment than the other. This created a high status group and a low status group and resulted in competition between them. They had their own group rules – 'group norms' – which were not the same as the company's rules. The groups had their own idea of what was a fair day's work and put pressure on all members to conform. Anyone breaking the rules was subjected to varying degrees of pressure from the group until they came back into line. Even the supervisor had to comply. It was a group norm that nobody should 'act officious'.

The company's daily output target was sometimes reached and sometimes not, but the group always reported the same amount each day, excess from one day being 'saved' for days when there was a shortfall. They could have produced more than they actually did but 'restricted practice' to what they thought was a fair day's output.

It appears from this that it is important to try to ensure group norms equate with company norms, and that there is acceptance of these by the people concerned. Volvo achieved this through a planned period of careful consultation to obtain agreement, and then devolved responsibility down to the foremen.

ACTIVITY 2.2

You can consider the findings of the Hawthorne Experiments by looking at your own experiences. At school or college, how do you feel when you are ignored by a teacher or treated as just one of the crowd, compared with when you are treated as an individual and your views are listened to and respected? Which of these two situations would draw the best response from you?

Similarly, if you are a member of a group, and you enjoy being a part of that group, would you risk upsetting your friends to the extent that they would throw you out? To what extent would you prefer to risk upsetting your teacher or parents rather than be ridiculed by your peers?

Abraham Maslow: Hierarchy of Human Needs

Maslow was an American psychologist most famous for his model of human needs which he published in 1943.

The noun 'need' means a requirement; a necessity. We all have needs: we have a need for food, drink and shelter; we have a need for friends; we have a need to be respected for what we are, and so on.

Maslow classified our needs under five headings and put them in an hierarchy – the order in which he believed we satisfy them. He said that we would use our energy first to find food and drink. If we had any energy left, we would then use it to defend our sources of food and drink. When means of satisfying these basic needs had been established and secured, we would make friends, seek recognition and become independent and autonomous. This was the order in which he placed them:

- Physiological or basic needs
- Security or safety needs
- Social or belonging needs
- Status or ego or esteem needs
- Self-fulfilment or self-actualization needs

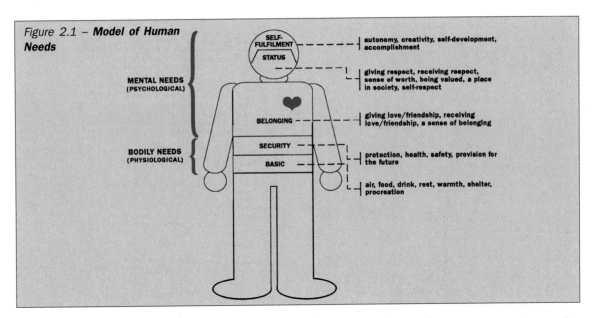

Figure 2.1 – *Model of Human Needs*

SELF-FULFILMENT — autonomy, creativity, self-development, accomplishment

STATUS — giving respect, receiving respect, sense of worth, being valued, a place in society, self-respect

MENTAL NEEDS (PSYCHOLOGICAL)

BELONGING — giving love/friendship, receiving love/friendship, a sense of belonging

SECURITY — protection, health, safety, provision for the future

BASIC — air, food, drink, rest, warmth, shelter, procreation

BODILY NEEDS (PHYSIOLOGICAL)

The model contained in Figure 2.1 will help you to appreciate the different levels of need and what each one might mean.

ACTIVITY 2.3

Spend some time studying Figure 2.1, then draw it yourself in your notes so that you will appreciate the *whole person* as a being that has both *bodily* and *mental* – physiological and psychological – needs to satisfy.

Our lower, or bodily, needs are concerned with preserving life. For example, we get hungry several times a day, and must eat several times a day. If we do not, we will eventually die. If anyone or anything threatens our bodily needs, it is almost certain that we will react to defend them.

The higher needs are enjoyed in the mind. Belonging and status needs can be satisfied fully. But self-fulfilment is insatiable – we can never fully satisfy it. It is our highest level of need and it seems to feed off itself. If anyone is lucky enough to satisfy all levels of her or his needs, Maslow said that person has the capacity to enjoy 'peak experience' – that is, the pinnacle of personal satisfaction.

Maslow did not apply this model specifically to people at work. But it is safe to assume that a person whose needs are satisfied at work will be co-operative and work well. On the other hand, it is highly likely that if one or several needs are threatened at work, particularly the lower needs, a person will react differently, and probably in a way that is not in the best interest of the business.

ACTIVITY 2.4

Just consider how you, or a working adult you know, would react if you were in a job you enjoyed, but you heard that your department was to close down and you might be made redundant.

Jot down how you think you might feel. Consider a range of actions you might feel inclined to take to deal with the threat.

Applying Maslow to People at Work

We can apply Maslow's hierarchy of needs to all people at work, whether they are male or female, young or old, or whether they work in a factory, office or the executive boardroom.

If a manager were to ask the question: 'What facilities or events at work go towards satisfying people's needs?', the answer might include those shown in Figure 2.2 (next page).

Although some occupations have special problems – coal mining is dangerous and dirty, lorry driving can be lonely, assembly work can be tedious and repetitive – Maslow's model is a *starting point* (no more than that!) for business managers who are considering such problems.

We will see as we progress through the people aspects of business that the answers to the question would have an impact upon:

- Pay and fringe benefits
- Recruitment, training and promotion
- Job design and safety
- Employee relations
- Participation schemes
- Leadership styles
- Communication systems

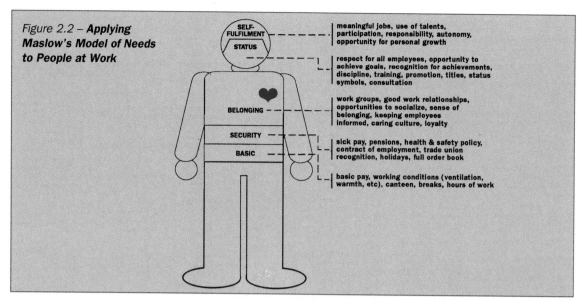

*Figure 2.2 – **Applying Maslow's Model of Needs to People at Work***

SELF-FULFILMENT — meaningful jobs, use of talents, participation, responsibility, autonomy, opportunity for personal growth

STATUS — respect for all employees, opportunity to achieve goals, recognition for achievements, discipline, training, promotion, titles, status symbols, consultation

BELONGING — work groups, good work relationships, opportunities to socialize, sense of belonging, keeping employees informed, caring culture, loyalty

SECURITY — sick pay, pensions, health & safety policy, contract of employment, trade union recognition, holidays, full order book

BASIC — basic pay, working conditions (ventilation, warmth, etc), canteen, breaks, hours of work

Each of these will be examined in detail later in this book.

We can conclude that Maslow takes us much nearer to an understanding of human motivation than Taylor or Mayo. Taylorism does, however, satisfy the basic needs identified by Maslow; similarly, Mayo satisfies the belonging and perhaps status needs.

Frederick Herzberg: The Two Factor Theory

ACTIVITY 2.5

Can you recall an occasion at school, college or at work when you went home feeling very good about your work?

What happened during that occasion to make you feel so good?

Herzberg took this approach. He was interested to know what happened at work to make people feel 'satisfied'. In 1968 his researchers interviewed two hundred white and blue collar employees (accountants and engineers) and recorded 1753 incidents that interviewees claimed made them feel good about their work.

Careful analysis of the interviews revealed that many people felt good when they actually *achieved* something they set out to do. They also felt good when their achievement received *recognition* of one kind or another from the manager. The nature of the *job itself*, if it was intrinsically interesting to the job holder, was another source of satisfaction. Many also found satisfaction in being treated as a *responsible person*, capable of planning and checking their own work, without too much direction from above. Some felt satisfaction at the opportunity for *advancement*, either by promotion or progress within their own discipline. Finally, some enjoyed a job that offered some challenge and allowed for *personal growth* – the development of intellect and skills.

KEY POINTS 2.1

- People are a complex resource and are constantly changing
- Money alone does not satisfy people at work
- Social needs are important, and people respond to the way they are treated
- Group pressure is a powerful influence on people's work performance
- Both bodily and mental needs must be considered if people are to be satisfied at work
- Any event that threatens needs will produce a defensive response

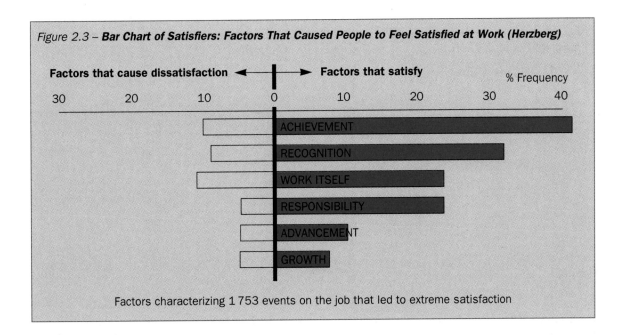

Figure 2.3 – **Bar Chart of Satisfiers: Factors That Caused People to Feel Satisfied at Work (Herzberg)**

Factors characterizing 1 753 events on the job that led to extreme satisfaction

How did your answers compare with that?

- Achievement
- Recognition
- The work itself
- Responsibility
- Advancement
- Personal growth

– these factors, called satisfiers, are illustrated in Figure 2.3.

ACTIVITY 2.6

Consider the opposite from this. Can you recall an occasion at school, college or work when you felt awful – fed-up – about your work, so much so that you considered leaving. What caused you to feel so badly about your work?

Herzberg's researchers gathered 1 844 incidents that made people dissatisfied. The analysis showed, for the main part, that these were markedly different from the causes of satisfaction. They included:

- A company policy and style of supervision that cared more for the tasks than for the people doing them
- Poor relationships with their supervisors or workmates
- Poor working conditions
- Low salaries or wages
- Adverse effect on their personal lives
- Low status given to their jobs
- Lack of job security

Herzberg showed that the factors which might cause dissatisfaction are different from those which cause satisfaction. They are not just the negatives of the latter. (See Figure 2.4, next page.)

He also said that it was essential to minimize or eliminate these dissatisfiers by planning the right levels of pay, the right working conditions and so on, before you can *start* to motivate people. A very useful analogy makes this easier to understand. Herzberg likened them to hygiene factors. Keeping the workplace clean and disinfected makes it fit to work in. In other words, keeping pay levels 'right', keeping relationships good and so on, makes the workplace fit to work in.

If these satisfiers and hygiene factors are put alongside Maslow's model, it becomes apparent that the hygiene factors equate to the lower needs, whilst the satisfiers equate to the higher needs. So it can be deduced that if lower needs are not adequately met, work people will be dissatisfied. If they are adequately met, people will not be dissatisfied.

If people's lower needs *are* met at work, they will *not* be dissatisfied with their jobs. If, in addition, their higher needs *are* met, they will be satisfied with their jobs. It is necessary to meet both lower and higher needs to ensure people enjoy job satisfaction. We can say no more than that.

Applying Herzberg's Theory to People at Work

If a manager had to design a package of incentives to ensure that her or his workers were not dissatisfied, she or he would set about ensuring that lower needs were catered for.

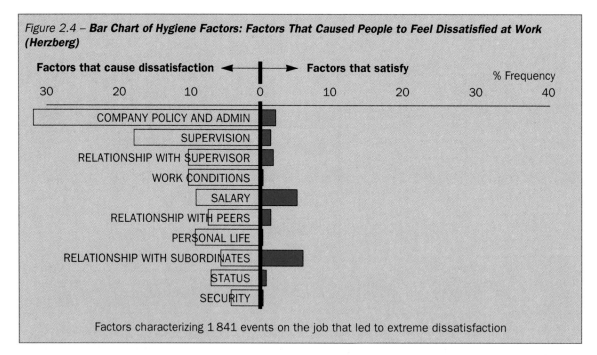

Figure 2.4 – **Bar Chart of Hygiene Factors: Factors That Caused People to Feel Dissatisfied at Work (Herzberg)**

The payment system would be equal to, or better than, other similar companies, and enough to cover basic needs. Working conditions would be good: they would be clean, well lit, well ventilated, not too noisy and as safe as possible. There would be a canteen, and so on.

All these are obvious enough as they happen

Figure 2.5 – *Employee Morale*

Employees' morale shows big decline

A SURVEY on employee attitudes in the UK suggests there has been a significant decline in morale.

The International Research's Survey report, based on interviews with 120,000 people in all types of jobs and industries, shows there had been a change in attitudes between 1977 and 1989.

While job satisfaction peaked in 1987, and most aspects of jobs have remained satisfactory, more than two-thirds of employees are dissatisfied with their pay and only half are satisfied with management.

Employees also feel more insecure in their jobs as they realise management may reduce the workforce as a way of cutting costs.

Source: Independent on Sunday, 11 February 1990

outside the person – they are extrinsic factors. According to Herzberg, whatever is done to make extrinsic factors acceptable will not lead to satisfaction, but only to the absence of dissatisfaction.

It is more difficult to ensure that work people are satisfied because factors like achievement and recognition take place inside the person's mind – they are intrinsic factors.

What can be done is to design jobs so that work people can *achieve* goals, and be given *recognition* for achieving them. The managers have to be willing to *share* decision-making and create an environment in which people are able *to take part* in planning their own work and measuring their own progress, and are *trusted* to act in the best interest of the organization.

ACTIVITY 2.7

Refer back to the Volvo Case Study (page 14). To what extent have the Volvo managers met these requirements? Quote evidence from the Volvo Case Study to illustrate how Herzberg's theory can be applied in practice?

Douglas McGregor: Theory X and Theory Y

We have mentioned several times the importance of how people are treated. McGregor's study focused on *managers* and how they treated their

KEY POINTS 2.2

- People are dissatisfied if their lower needs *are not* met. They cease to be dissatisfied if their lower needs *are* met
- People are satisfied if their higher needs *are* met. They cease to be satisfied if their higher needs *are not* met
- Lower needs are met through extrinsic factors, such as wages and working conditions
- Higher needs are met by intrinsic factors, such as achievement and recognition
- Managers can design jobs that provide extrinsic and intrinsic reward

employees. He was concerned with the views managers held and *assumptions* they made about people's attitude to work.

The questions he wanted answered were: 'How will the views and assumptions which a manager holds about people at work affect the way that the manager treats them?' And then: 'If work people are treated like that, how might they react?'

There is a very wide range of possible views and assumptions. To handle this range, McGregor described two extreme, opposite views.

Theory X

Firstly, let us consider the manager who holds the extreme view that workers are lazy, work only for money, respond best to fear of punishment, cannot think for themselves, need to be told exactly what to do and cannot generally be trusted. McGregor called this extreme Theory X.

McGregor was concerned about the ways in which a Theory X manager might give orders and instructions; the form rewards and recognition would take; the style of relationship that would exist between manager and staff; the amount of freedom to use initiative that would be given to them by this type of manager.

Probably the Theory X manager would be inclined to break jobs down into relatively minor tasks, give instructions and ensure that they are carried out, use authority to maintain control and use money as the main motivation to work. The manager may be pleasant enough and have reasonable relationships with the staff most of the time. But in times of crisis he will probably adopt a dictatorial style of management.

ACTIVITY 2.8

With this picture in mind, imagine how you might react to being treated like that. Would you be co-operative or belligerent? Would you speak kindly of your employer? What would be the main reason you would work at all?

If that is the effect it would have on you, to what extent would it be reasonable to assume that people who worked for the same Theory X manager might feel the same?

It would be safe to guess that they will be inclined to do only as they are told and work hard only if they are being watched or if there is extra money in it for them. They may well feel as though they have no responsibility and it is the manager's job to think – if anything goes wrong it is his or her problem.

Looking at this carefully, we can see that the work people are acting as the manager assumed they would. His views will be reinforced and he will say, 'I told you they were lazy . . . etc' and continue to treat them as such. A vicious circle develops and the consequences for the organization are awful. Yet McGregor wrote that most managerial policy and practice was based on the beliefs that he described as Theory X.

Theory Y

On the brighter side, we can consider a manager who holds the views and assumptions at the opposite end of the range. This manager believes that work people can enjoy their work, will use their initiative to do a good job, will act responsibly and can be trusted to get on with their work without supervision. If anything goes wrong, the manager believes the person concerned will seek guidance and put the organization's best interests first. McGregor referred to these assumptions as Theory Y.

How might a manager who holds Theory Y beliefs treat people at work? Almost certainly she or he will seek views and involve the workers in decision-making; once targets have been set and agreed, the work people will be given a great deal of freedom to get on with their work, the manager becoming involved only when needed. The work people will be kept informed of their progress and be encouraged to use initiative to improve performance. The manager will be on good terms with the work people and will show them a great deal of respect. But the manager will be no push-over; rather he or she will be honest, firm and fair.

ACTIVITY 2.9

In what ways would you react differently to this manager compared with the previous example?

It can be reasonably assumed that work people who are trusted and given scope will co-operate and work well, use their initiative and consider the organization in a good light.

This, too, is a self-fulfilling prophesy. McGregor used the word 'integration' to describe the situation in which managers use their authority to help work people enjoy their job while improving performance and working for the success of the organization.

Theory Y management is not 'soft' management. The Theory Y manager sees the most effective way of achieving organizational objectives as empowering people – that is, giving them enough freedom to use their knowledge, skills and initiative to get work done to predetermined standards of quality, quantity, time and cost. When things go wrong, the Theory Y manager will want to analyse the situation to determine the true *causes*, and then set out to ensure they do not occur again.

It seems that Theory X managers deal only with hygiene factors, while the Theory Y managers consider the whole person.

ACTIVITY 2.10

Look at the Volvo Case Study (page 14) again and identify *evidence* in the text to illustrate which views and assumptions are held by their managers.

What effect might these have on Volvo's performance? How does this relate to the reputation which you think Volvo cars have in the market?

David McClelland: The Motive Patterns of Managers

McClelland, a psychologist at Harvard University in America, was interested, like McGregor, in the way managers think. By using a simple test called a Thematic Apperception Test (TAT), McClelland gathered a large sample of the thoughts provoked in managers by a series of pictures of people in different settings.

ACTIVITY 2.11

Try this test yourself. Look at the picture in Figure 2.6 (opposite) for one minute, then write as quickly as you can, what you think might be going on: who are they? Why are they there? What are they doing? What are they thinking? What might happen next? Do not write for longer than five minutes.

What you see in the picture has been filtered through your own motivational screen, so what you have written will contain clues about your motives. McClelland devised ways of analysing these stories to identify the motives of the writer. He found they fell into three main categories: 'power need', 'achievement need' and 'affiliation need'. All of us have some of these three motives but the mix will be different from person to person. In most of us, one will predominate. McClelland believed that the predominant motive in a manager would influence the way she or he acted, and as a consequence was a key determinant of the success or otherwise of the manager.

You are unlikely to be able to identify your predominant motive from one story. However, if your story refers to good performance, new inventions or success in life, it implies 'achievement need'. References to controlling others, punishment or boss–worker relationships implies

---

KEY POINTS 2.3

- **The views, beliefs and assumptions held by managers about people at work determines, to a large extent, how they treat staff**
- **Theory X assumptions lead to the use of extrinsic factors**
- **Theory Y assumptions lead to the use of intrinsic factors**
- **How workers are treated will determine, to a large extent, how they will behave, thus creating a self-fulfilling prophesy**

Figure 2.6

'power need'. If you have talked about emotional relationships, sadness about broken relationships, consoling others or celebrations, it implies 'affiliation need'. The frequency with which each occurs in your story may give some clues as to your predominant motive, but further evidence would be essential before reaching any reliable conclusion.

In the same way as we considered Theories X and Y, we can consider how the following three managers might act:

- A manager whose predominant need is for power
- A manager whose predominant need is for affiliation
- A manager whose predominant need is for achievement

We could reasonably expect power-driven managers to use a fairly authoritarian approach, with little encouragement for initiative. They would probably give instructions and expect them to be carried out without any argument.

You might see them as being Theory X managers.

The managers high in 'affiliation need' would act quite differently. They will want to keep relationships sweet at all costs, and consequently, may fail to pursue objectives if there is a risk of disagreement or strife. It is often the case that such people find management stressful to the extent that they are ineffective.

It is a little more difficult to imagine how managers high in 'achievement need' might act. It is probable that they will set targets that are reasonably easy to reach so that they enjoy achieving them. They will want to maintain control of their own destiny and may find it difficult to let other people take responsibility. They will surround themselves with other achievers and design organizations that are dynamic and exciting. McClelland said that they must be good entrepreneurs and play an important role if organizations are to succeed. However, McClelland said that their 'high achievement need' must be supported by a fairly 'high power need' if they

KEY POINTS 2.4

- Everyone has a need for power, a need for achievement and a need for affiliation, but in most people, one of these three will predominate

- A manager's motivational make-up will be a major influence in an organization's performance

- Managers with a predominant 'achievement need' appear to be more successful as entrepreneurs than the other two

- Managers with a predominant 'power need' appear to create organizational difficulties.

are to function as effective leaders.

A study by a social psychologist, John Andrews, in 1967 showed how two companies performed differently, and how that difference could be attributed to some extent to the predominant motives of the top managers. The following extract will help us to understand this more clearly:

> John Andrews' study of two Mexican companies is striking in this regard. Both companies had presidents who scored high in Power, but one firm was stagnating whereas the other was growing rapidly. The manager of the growing company, though high in Power, was also high in Achievement and was dedicated to letting others in the organization satisfy their own needs for achievement by introducing improvements and making decisions on their own. The stagnant company, though well capitalized and enjoying a favourable market, was constantly in turmoil and experienced a high rate of turnover, particularly among its executives. In this company, the president's high Power, coupled with highly authoritarian values, led him to make all the decisions himself, leaving no room for individual responsibility on the part of his personnel. A comparison of motivation scores of upper-level managers of the two companies showed that the dynamic company's managers were significantly higher in achievement than those of the stagnant company, who tended to be more concerning with power and compliance than with individual responsibility and decision-making.

Source: Kolb, Rubin and McIntyre (1971) *Organizational Psychology (2nd Edition), Prentice Hall*

A Summary of Motivation Theories

It will help us at this stage to summarize the theories so far in table form (see Figure 2.7).

Taylor's contribution was not helpful to our understanding of motivation at work. His scientific approach to work study and work measurement proved much more valuable.

We learnt from Mayo that social relationships and being consulted and involved can have a greater effect on output than economic incentives alone, but that group pressure can, in some circumstances, work against the company's interests.

We can see from the table in Figure 2.7 that Maslow considered the whole person, and saw needs in the order in which he believed they were satisfied. What he did not tell us is *how* people satisfy their needs, particularly as each individual's needs are forever changing.

Herzberg's Two Factor Theory takes us closer to understanding people at work. There are critics of the questions he asked, however, who point out that people will blame things outside themselves for unpleasant events, whilst accepting personal credit for pleasant events. Repetition of his experiments does not always produce the same results.

Help in understanding why managers treat workers as they do is given to us by McGregor and McClelland.

You might think that McGregor's Theory Y appears to be idealistic, but it does focus our thoughts on people's higher needs.

Similarly, Herzberg's 'satisfiers' attend to higher needs. It seems that allowing work people to use their talents, and to contribute directly to the objectives of the organization, requires a style of management which values participation, shares authority and encourages responsibility.

McClelland believed that entrepreneurs high in 'achievement need' were essential for organizations to succeed. He developed training programmes which successfully increased achievement motivation in managers, thereby showing us that a person's motivational make-up can be modified.

Unless managers treat employees as responsible adults, they cannot complain if they behave

Figure 2.7 – **Summary of Main Motivation Theories**

Whole Person	Maslow's Hierarchy of Needs	Herzberg's Two Factor Theory	McGregor	McClelland
Psychological	Self-fulfilment Status	Satisfiers	Theory Y	Achievement orientation
Physiological	Belonging Security Basic	Hygiene factors	Theory X ↓ ↓	Power orientation ↓ ↓
	People's Needs	Factors of the job	Beliefs held by managers	Forces in the manager

as children – rebellious, emotional and unwilling to become involved in the organization's goals. Characteristics that distinguish adults from children relate closely to the assumptions in Theory Y – whereas Theory X assumptions relate more closely to immaturity and childish behaviour.

It is becoming clearer that the motivation of people to work well is a complex combination of a number of elements. It seems that it is a product of the interactions between individuals, their jobs, their managers and the organization. We are confronted with a problem. Are good employees highly motivated, or do they work for an organization whose managers design jobs that are interesting and challenging? Are poor employees lacking motivation, or do they work for an organization whose managers are insensitive to their needs?

Edgar Schein, writing in 1970, suggested an answer to these questions. He pointed out that their are two types of contract that exist between employees and the organization: a legal contract

Figure 2.8 – **Employees's Attitude to Work**

Volvo workers assemble components of own bank

IN A rare and innovative move, Volvo Group employees plan to start their own co-operative bank. Its main function would be to handle salary payments, which last year amounted to Ecu2.3 billion.

The bank, which has the support of Volvo management and the trade unions, would take control of employee funds, earning interest of seven to eight per cent. This compares with only two per cent paid on conventional salary accounts in banks.

Profits earned by the bank would be returned to co-operative members, the employees, through once- or twice-yearly refunds. The bank would be licensed to lend to members and handle transfer payments.

The scheme worries S-E-Banken and Nordbanken, Volvo's two main bankers in Sweden, who fear a drop in business. It is also an embarrassment for Volvo chief Pehr Gyllenhammar, who is on the S-E-Banken board.

Although trade unions are calling the plan a "financial association" rather than a full-blown bank, bankers argue that the large amounts of capital involved could result in the hiring of professional bankers and investment analysts to provide financial services comparable to, or better than, those offered by the banks.

The Volvo Bank as proposed would offer five basic services to its members, including salary clearing, high-interest, long- and short-term savings accounts, investment advice and giro payments and transfers. Investment counselling services would be geared to the Swedish stocks, bonds and options market.

Source: European, 19 March 1992

that sets out the terms and conditions of work for all to see; and a psychological contract, which is not written down – it is all in the mind as it were.

This psychological contract is based on the expectations the organization has of the individuals, and the expectations the individuals have of the organization. The closer these expectations are to reality, the more likely it is that individuals will work well and be loyal to the organization. Conversely, if the two sets of expectations do not match, it is unlikely that the organization will be happy or productive.

Schein's hypothesis leads us to the notion that if managers want work people to be committed to the organization's goals they must attempt to design jobs that are satisfying to individuals, or seek to employ individuals who are suited to the jobs. This was stated at the beginning of the chapter – it is up to the business manager to create a physical and psychological climate in which people can, and are willing to, give of their best. Volvo managers were attempting this in the previous Case Study. The article contained in Figure 2.8 (previous page) illustrates the latest development in Volvo's employees's attitude to work.

In 1988, Professor Keith MacMillan of Henley Management Centre suggested that 'investing in the quality of its psychological contract with employees could greatly improve an organization's performance'.

In the next chapter we will examine recent research and consider practical ways to apply the theories we have looked at to the problems of getting the best out of people at work.

KEY POINTS 2.5

- **No single theory of motivation provides a satisfactory answer to the question of how to get the best out of work people**

- **Creating 'motivated' work people seems to be a result of interactions between individuals, group members, their jobs, their managers and their organizations**

- **Most theories have weaknesses that should be appreciated when using them in practice**

- **Treating work people as responsible adults is an attractive generalization**

- **Work people have expectations of organizations, and organizations have expectations of work people which together make up a psychological contract**

- **If the expectations of each other are in balance, job satisfaction may be experienced**

- **The organization's managers can attempt to create this balance in order to improve work performance**

EXAM PREPARATION

SHORT QUESTIONS

1   List Maslow's physiological needs.

2   Distinguish between hygiene factors and satisfiers.

3   What is meant by 'scientific management'?

4   Name McClelland's three motives.

5   What is meant by the 'psychological contract'?

DATA RESPONSE QUESTION

1   Read the following extracts adapted from *Quality Circles in Action* by M Robson and answer the questions below.

'Though Quality Circles first developed in Japan during the late 1950s and early 1960s, the approach is based on Western theories of management, notably Douglas McGregor's Theory Y . . .'

'Firstly Quality Circles is an approach which allows people to become more involved, but puts no pressure on them to do so; in other words the approach is entirely voluntary at all levels of the organization . . .'

'Secondly people who join in are encouraged to solve their own job-related problems . . .'

'Thirdly members solve their problems in an organized way; in other words they are given training in the skills of systematic problem solving and of working together effectively in a group . . .'

'A Quality Circle consists of a group of 4 to 10 volunteers who work for the same first-line supervisor and who meet regularly to identify, analyse and solve their work problems . . . '

' . . . the group does not need to consist of the entire workforce from that section'; only those that volunteer.

' . . . the group meet regularly once a week, for an hour and in paid time . . .'

' . . . the groups at their meetings do not stop at the identification of problems for passing on to management for solution, they utilize the training they receive to analyse and solve them and then present their own findings to management . . . '

' . . . there are 3 main possible goals: staff involvement, people development and the generation of tangible benefits . . .' for the organization and people in it.

(a) As the Training Manager for Alpha Components Ltd write a report to the Managing Director, outlining **four** possible benefits for the company of introducing Quality Circles. (*10 marks*)

(b) Consider and explain **five** problems the company might encounter in establishing and operating Quality Circles. (*10 marks*)

(c) What evidence is there to suggest that 'Quality Circles' is based on McGregor's Theory Y (lines 2-3)? (*5 marks*)

(N.B. Quality circles are examined in Chapter Three)

(AEB June 1988)

ESSAYS

1 Are all attempts to motivate workers merely gimmicks, or are they based on established motivational theories? (AEB June 1989)

2 Examine critically the statement that effective motivation of employees arises as much from an understanding of their needs as from the application of standard textbook methods. (AEB June 1985)

CHAPTER 3

The Design of Jobs That Satisfy

▷ ▷ QUESTIONS FOR PREVIEW ▷ ▷

1 Are the popular theories of motivation relevant to today's businesses?

2 What are the principles of job design that would create fulfilling jobs? How are these applied in practice?

3 What forms of job design are possible? What are the strengths and weaknesses of each?

4 Can organizations consider the logical division of work rather than the capacity of one work person?

5 What is the job of 'managing'?

BEFORE MOVING on to examine how managers might set about designing satisfying jobs, let's look at two recent Case Studies that provide up-to-date views expressed by work people relating to job satisfaction.

CASE STUDY

Perks at Luncheon Vouchers

'Perks' are non-salary, extrinsic work benefits. Luncheon Vouchers Ltd have been in business providing perks for a very long time. Their forward-looking managing director wanted to know how employees and potential employees valued perks alongside intrinsic motivational factors. He commissioned Professor Keith MacMillan to find out.

Using a sample of five hundred managers and workers from five industrial sectors, the researchers asked each one of them to put into order of personal importance, a list of twenty perks *and* motivational factors.

As we would expect from the theories we have examined in the previous chapter, when asked in this fashion, the result showed that most people placed intrinsic factors highest. The top ten factors were:

1 Opportunities for further education
2 Health care
3 Job training and development
4 Clear career progression
5 Recognition for my contribution
6 Clearly defined expectations
7 Opportunities to be innovative
8 Financial services/assistance
9 Good communications
10 Opportunity to perform effectively

Professor MacMillan said: 'Employees most highly value the non-material benefits, which derive from how they are treated in the workplace and the quality of interpersonal relationships there, particularly the extent to which they feel valued as individuals by their employers.'

Further analysis of the data gave researchers reason to believe that most of the people questioned were not satisfied with their present job. MacMillan found that 'present job' fell short of 'realistic expectations' and a long way short of 'ideal job'.

One of the things highlighted by this piece of research was that 'motivation' seemed to be viewed differently by people who worked in different industrial sectors. For example, manufacturing industries tended to be more concerned with extrinsic rewards than non-manufacturing.

(Contd.)

The researchers suggested that individual companies should do their own research, identify the needs of their own workforce, and put together a tailor-made package – rather like Volvo – of both intrinsic and extrinsic factors. The benefits to the company would be reaped in improved performance.

Source: K MacMillan (1988) *Perks in Perspective,* Luncheon Vouchers Ltd

QUESTIONS

1 Put the ten motivational factors into higher (psychological) needs and lower (physiologically) needs.

2 How does this fit in with Herzberg's Two Factor Theory?

3 Comment upon factor 8 in the light of Volvo's employees latest actions (see Figure 2.8).

CASE STUDY

Involving Employees

The Industrial Society promotes the practice of employee involvement in the organizations which use its consultancy services.

In 1986 The Industrial Society set up a working party, under the chairmanship of the chief executive of Inchcape plc, to examine its present role and its role in the 1990s. The working party commissioned Market & Opinion Research International (MORI) to carry out a national survey of the attitudes, perceptions and values of work people in relation to job satisfaction, and to evaluate the effect of job satisfaction on company success.

MORI interviewed 1 063 managers, skilled employees and unskilled employees, representing a broad range of manufacturing and service industries. As in the previous Case Study, a questionnaire containing a long list of factors was given to each individual in the sample of workers. Each person had to choose the six factors that most mattered to her or him. All the individual choices were collated and analysed. The result was as follows:

1 Interesting job
2 Job security
3 Able to accomplish something worthwhile
4 Basic pay
5 Chance to learn new skills
6 Opportunity for advancement

The report also highlighted the following:

- Managers and clerical staff chose 'interesting job' as one of their six factors, but few manual staff did

- Half the manual employees said they could do more work without much more effort

- Nearly half the people interviewed thought management communicated only one-way. They were *told* rather than being *listened* to

- One-third of manual employees had no interest in the company – it was just a job

- Half the sample thought their company's products were better than competitors's, but they did not think their company looked after their employees better

The report pointed to the fact that people who feel they are well informed and involved in the decisions that affect them tend to be more motivated and feel better about their company. (We can relate this to Mayo's theory.) It also claimed evidence that companies which plan to create more motivated employees eventually benefit in financial terms, through lower costs, better quality and improved overall efficiency.

But it also highlighted the many opportunities missed by business managers to obtain greater commitment from their employees. McGregor's comment that most managerial policy and practice was based on Theory X beliefs (see page 21) would seem to be reflected in this report.

Source: The Industrial Society (1989) *Blueprint for Success: A Report on Involvng Employees in Britain*

QUESTIONS

1 Relate the findings of MORI to Maslow's Hierarchy of Needs. Note which needs may be satisified by these factors.

2 Consider which are intrinsic factors and which are extrinsic factors.

3 What do they suggest about Herzberg's Two Factor Theory?

Jobs That Satisfy

As we have seen from the theories and the research, ensuring that people enjoy some satisfaction at work, and willingly give of their best, is the result of many things.

It is complex mix of variables that are ever changing, so there is no single answer. Many of the variables are outside the control of the average business manager and some are even outside the control of the business itself.

Job satisfaction may be affected by an individual's values; by the social context of the job; by the individual's private life; by the attitude of managers to their employees; by the wider economic environment and the ability of the business to respond to it; or by competition in the organization's market.

However, one area where business managers can use the theories and the information from research is in the design of jobs. Getting that right will go a long way to making the organization successful.

A job is a set of tasks that constitutes the work of one person (see Figure 3.1). A task is a specific element within a job. No matter which department the job is in – production, finance, marketing or personnel – or whether it is a manual job or a clerical job, designing it so as to make it meaningful and satisfying is important in order to improve efficiency. There is nothing soft or sentimental about it; it is good business sense.

We know that before attempting to create 'satisfaction', it is essential that an organization's managers get the hygiene factors right (see Chapter Two). Until they do, all other efforts and costs may be wasted.

There is a great deal of choice open to a business in deciding the individual tasks that should be allocated to a job, and how these tasks should be performed. Each task is made up of three elements: 'plan', 'do' and 'check' (see Figure 3.2).

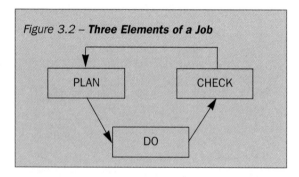

Figure 3.2 – **Three Elements of a Job**

Someone has to 'plan' how a task will be done, what materials and tools will be used, when it will be done and how often. This is most often decided by the supervisor.

Someone has to 'do' the task, usually the employee.

Then someone has to 'check' that the outcome is what was planned in terms of quantity, quality, time and costs. Once again, this is most often done by the supervisor.

ACTIVITY 3.1

Apply this model to your course of study. Who 'plans' what you study? Who 'does' the studying? Who 'checks' that you have learned what was planned for you to learn?

Consider the difficulties in designing your course so that you 'plan', 'do' and 'check' yourself.

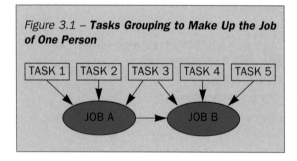

Figure 3.1 – **Tasks Grouping to Make Up the Job of One Person**

Taylor, you will recall, would have a job made as simple as possible with all other elements undertaken by the supervisor. Herzberg would argue that jobs should be made meaningful – as much responsibility should be given to the job holder as possible.

The questions that have to be answered are:

- How should tasks be allocated to individual jobs so as to achieve the organization's objectives?
- How should they be performed to give satisfaction to the person doing the job?

Motivational factors have to be translated into job characteristics, but in a general way so that they can be applied to any job, and meet the needs of most people.

This was done to good effect by Hackman and Oldham. They examined a large number of jobs to establish the relationship between the way a job was designed, the effect it had on the job holder, and the result in terms of what the organization got out of it.

The model contained in Figure 3.3 is a simplified version of their findings. Using this as a guide, we can include intrinsic factors in the design of jobs.

Forms of Job Design

Herzberg was one of the earlier people to study job design, and he described three broad ways of dealing with it:

- Job rotation
- Job enlargement
- Job enrichment

Job Rotation

In a situation where several work people are involved in monotonous, repetitive tasks, it might be possible to rearrange the layout of the workplace to enable them to swap jobs with each other, thus adding a little variety to their work.

For example, in a large canning factory in Suffolk, one person removes cans of vegetables from a conveyor belt, four at a time (this is quite a skilful job – you try lifting four cans in a straight line – the ones you are holding supporting two in between), and places them in a cardboard carton holding twenty-four cans, twelve on the bottom layer and twelve on the top. Another person standing opposite takes a flat carton, makes it into a box, and places it ready to be filled. When it is full, the same person tapes it and slides it

---

*Figure 3.3 – **Characteristics That Make Jobs Meaningful***

Characteristics of Job	How job-holder feels as a result	What effect it has on company
• A variety of skills	• Feels work is meaningful	• Highly motivated staff; good morale
• Clearly defined tasks	• Enjoys responsibility for outcomes	
• Important tasks		• High quality work
• Can make own decisions	• Knows how she/he is getting on – and the value of work outcomes	• Staff enjoy job satisfaction
• Receives feedback about achievement against targets		• Low staff turnover and absenteeism, and high co-operation

---

KEY POINTS 3.2

- **Designing meaningful jobs is within the scope of every business**

- **Decisions about the make-up of individual jobs will be influenced by the values and beliefs of the business managers**

- **Job characteristics that contribute to satisfying work include variety, discretion, achievable goal and contribution**

down a runner to a third person, who puts the carton onto a pallet.

These three people change jobs every half hour so that each has a little variety added to an otherwise limited task.

When this rotation was first introduced, productivity improved. Whether this was because of the variety or because the group of three could socialize more easily, or because of some other factor, is not clear. However, absenteeism and staff turnover reduced markedly. It was a very worthwhile exercise for all concerned and did not involve the company in any significant additional costs.

In this case, there was no resistance to the changes by the work people involved. Other attempts to introduce job rotation have met with resistance, either because people quite liked being good at a particular task, or because they feared being unable to cope with new training and new tasks.

Some managers believe that variety itself is not a motivator, but just relieves boredom and makes tedious jobs tolerable. We might ask why jobs are designed that are boring and tedious in the first place!

Job Enlargement

Job enlargement relates to situations where a job can be extended laterally. For example, several people may be working alongside each other on an assembly line, the first adding item A to an assembly, passing it to the second person who adds item B, passing it to the third who adds item C and so on, until the finished product is ready for packing (see Figure 3.4).

This job could be *enlarged* by changing the

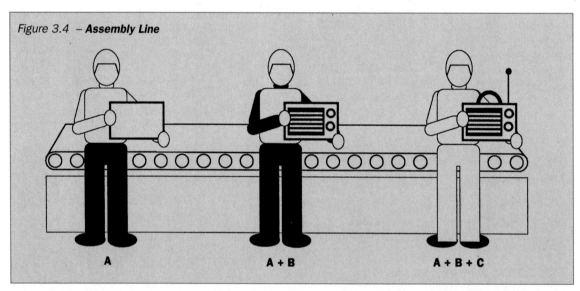

*Figure 3.4 – **Assembly Line***

A   A + B   A + B + C

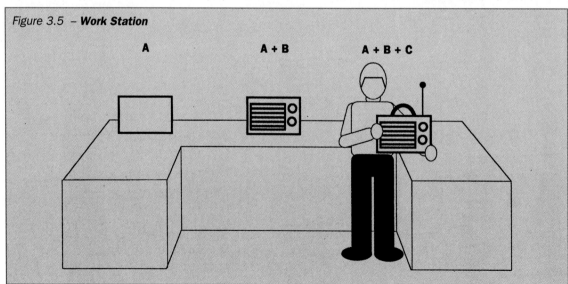

*Figure 3.5 – **Work Station***

A   A + B   A + B + C

assembly line layout to a work station where one person adds all the items and completes the finished product (see Figure 3.5).

This may result in an increase in variety of skills and a greater contribution to the finished product – thus making the job appear more important. Targets for quantity and quality may be agreed with the employee so that achievement can be measured and rewarded.

Some reports of job enlargement schemes show a greater improvement in quality than quantity, and others show frustration with the enlarged job as it may consist of *several* meaningless tasks rather than just *one* meaningless task. It may be that the change has reduced socializing without significant compensation.

Enlarging jobs can be costly in terms of new equipment and training. It can sometimes meet resistance from trade unions. Unless the redesigned job can be seen as likely to meet Hackman and Oldham's characteristics, thus giving greater satisfaction and increased efficiency, it is probably wise not to attempt it.

Job Enrichment

Job enrichment refers to situations where a job can be extended vertically – that is, some of the

---

CASE STUDY

Enriching the Jobs of Cleaners

In a large manufacturing unit, cleaners employed were of low educational status, were poorly paid, closely supervised and treated less well than other employees. There was staff turnover of 400 per cent per year among the cleaners, and their effectiveness in keeping the factory and offices clean was 65 per cent.

A job enrichment programme was planned which would organize the cleaners in small teams, give them a pay rise to the same scale that other employees were on, and seek their participation and involvement in raising standards and thinking of better ways of keeping the place clean.

The team members supported each other, checked each other's work, dealt with their own supplies and could requisition new products or machines that would improve their performance. Some of the teams designed faster and more efficient cleaning methods, and then taught other teams how to do the same. They urged the people who worked in the premises to work tidily and use waste bins for their rubbish.

After two years, effectiveness in keeping the factory and offices clean had risen to 85 per cent; staff turnover had dropped to 40 per cent per year; and the number of cleaners needed had dropped by 40 per cent.

QUESTION

1 Have Hackman and Oldham's characteristics been applied in this case? Show evidence to support your decisions.

KEY POINTS 3.3

- **The three basic forms of redesigning individual jobs are: job rotation, job enlargement and job enrichment**

- **Job rotation involves minor alterations in tasks and jobs, and provides for people to swap jobs on an organized basis so as to enjoy limited variety and some socializing**

- **Job enlargement involves considerable alterations in the scope of an individual's job by extending the range of tasks laterally. It is thought to create frustration in some work people**

- **Job enrichment extends the range of tasks vertically, adding some 'planning' and 'checking' to the 'doing'. Supervisors's roles change and care is needed to ensure their support and co-operation**

'planning' and 'checking' is added to the 'doing' of the task (see Figure 3.2 on page 30). Some of the tasks usually done by the supervisor are undertaken by the operator. This can be applied to all sorts of jobs, but it can require a little bit of imagination on the part of the job designer. The Case Study on the previous page provides an example of job enrichment in a large manufacturing unit.

A Wider Perspective

Each of these three methods tends to look at individual jobs in isolation. In 1973, however, a piece of research was commissioned by the Department of Employment (DoE) which resulted in a move towards the notion of 'organization design', taking in the overall view of all jobs contributing to an organization's efficiency. It saw each job as a single piece of a jigsaw, of little value in isolation, but essential as a part of the whole picture. Business managers, it suggested, should concentrate on the whole picture, not on individual pieces.

The report, *On the Quality of Working Life*, highlighted the necessity to consider the *context* in which jobs are performed. In essence, all the careful design of individual jobs will be to no avail if the present state of the company is poor, or industrial relations are poor, or the payment system is unfair, or communications are inadequate, or the workplace is unhealthy and unsafe, or management's attitude to work people is Theory X-ish.

To assist business managers in implementing organizational changes which would improve efficiency and enhance the Quality of Working Life (QWL), a small unit, called the Work Research Unit (WRU), was set up within the DoE to give information and advice. In 1985 it was

---

CASE STUDY

Borg Warner Automotive

The motor transmissions division of Borg Warner Automotive is situated at Kenfig, South Wales. During the late 1970s and early 1980s, the company's business was declining and all efforts to revive it seemed to have failed. The South Wales plant was to close in 1984. However, it was saved by the US parent company who decided that all its marine and industrial transmissions would be manufactured in Kenfig, for distribution worldwide. This offered an opportunity to reorganize the way jobs were done, and, with union agreement, it was decided to introduce autonomous work groups. It was carefully planned and a great deal of training took place to prepare people at all levels for the change.

Each work group consisted of fifteen work people with a wide range of skills. The duties of each work group were:

- Allocation/rotation of tasks
- Materials movement and controls
- Safety and housekeeping
- Cost monitoring and control
- Tooling and gauge measurements
- Statistical process control (individuals are responsible for quality)

- Minor maintenance and services
- Basic administration

You can see that the range of skills in each group was great, and members were able to extend their levels and ranges of skills within the group. Imagine the difficulties that might arise in such major change. Borg Warner tried to ensure that there was adequate support and training at all levels at all times.

It is too early to assess the effectiveness of the reorganization, but the company is enjoying a high level of success in its market. The change in management style no doubt played a major part.

Source: reported in *QWL News and Abstracts*, No. 97, March 1989

QUESTIONS

1 In what way does 'a wide range of skills' provide for more satisfaction from jobs?

2 Justify these statements:

(a) 'The Borg Warner management hold Theory Y beliefs'

(b) 'The Borg Warner management was achievement-orientated, backed by sufficient 'power need' to get the job done'.

transferred to the Advisory, Conciliation and Arbitration Service (ACAS). (The role of ACAS is examined in Chapter Six.) WRU organizes conferences, carries out research, monitors efforts by businesses who are introducing QWL techniques and publishes a bi-monthly journal, *QWL News and Abstracts,* free of charge to any business that requests it.

As a result of this philosophy towards the design of jobs, some organizations now tend to look at *wholes* rather than *parts*. Examples of this are Autonomous Work Groups, Quality Circles and Total Quality Management.

Autonomous Work Groups

Autonomous work groups are a development of job enrichment. Rather than looking at the work capacity of one person, it takes the whole process and divides it into logical sub-divisions of work. Then a group of work people, who together possess all the skills needed to complete the work, is assembled.

This approach to job design sets out to give the work group all the decision-making power it needs to complete a whole product or a major part of a product, without having to refer to the manager or supervisor. The group members plan the work, they do the work and they check the work; in fact they do all that Hackman and Oldham suggested.

All the skills needed are located within the group, either by training the members in a broader range of skills, or by bringing together people with all the special expertise needed in one group. The group's supervisor takes on the role of 'facilitator' rather than 'boss'.

A surgical operation is a good example. The surgical team includes surgeons, nurses, anaesthetists, technicians and so on, all of whose skills are essential for the success of the operation and are all interdependent. The surgeon may be the key person, but is only able to carry out the operation if all the others play their parts as well.

You might have recognized that the Volvo Case Study at the beginning of Chapter Two is an example of this approach taken from the manufacturing industry. Another example is Borg Warner Automotive which is outlined in the Case Study opposite.

Quality Circles

There is often a wide gap between senior managers and the people who carry out the operational work of the organization. There can be good reasons for this – for example, the firm has many sites or just large numbers of products or people. If it is the belief that 'managers solve

problems', then delays are likely to occur, and in many cases, remotely taken decisions are not always best. There is sense in letting the people who experience problems, and probably understand them better than anyone else, solve them.

One way of organizing this is through quality circles. Here, workers are encouraged to volunteer to meet in small groups, called quality circles, to identify problems in their day-to-day work, and to propose solutions to them. The proposals are presented to management, and if approval is given, the circle implements the solution it recommended.

Perhaps you can consider how this concept might improve the quality of working life. Each individual, and the circle collectively, will be able to use their knowledge, experience and skills to ensure that problems that may cause them to put in a poor job are dealt with in an appropriate manner.

They will need training in problem-solving techniques and communication skills and to be given access to information and advice. People who previously took the decisions now passed to the circle should be trained in new skills to support and guide the circle, and not to see it as any form of criticism or demotion. Great care will be needed to avoid resentment or antagonism, frustration or apathy.

Reports from companies who use quality circles claim that quality and productivity improve as a result. To ensure their effectiveness, circles must have the commitment and support of senior management who must be willing to allow decisions to be taken and implemented at operational level. Not only must they claim to support it, they must be seen to support it or it will fall into disrepute and cause more harm than good.

Total Quality Management (TQM)

The idea of TQM originated in Japanese industry. It simply sets out to make quality everybody's responsibility in a business.

From the switchboard operator – who is a caller's first contact with the firm – through every department and at all levels, each person is encouraged to pursue *continuous improvement* in all that they do. It takes the concept of autonomous work groups and quality circles a little further and includes everyone in the business in being a party to providing 'Quality' (with a capital 'Q'). Quality becomes the primary consideration of everybody in the organization, whatever their job. It pervades every decision and action of every person in everything they do.

It is a cultural revolution in any organization that embraces it. The success of such a scheme rests entirely upon commitment from all levels of management. If their assumptions about people, motivation and control are in any way X-ish, TQM is unlikely to be effective.

If the QWL benefits are to be enjoyed by businesses, a key skill that managers must develop is the ability to manage change. Badly handled change will always incur resistance, much of which would not arise if it was handled sensitively and in a professional way. Managing change is a topic that will be considered in Chapter Five.

CASE STUDY

Implementing TQM

From some research by Susan Whittle of Sheffield Business School, three approaches to implementing TQM were identified, each reflecting different management beliefs. They are: the visionary model; the planning model; and the learning model.

The visionary model of total quality (VTQ) is based on the belief that people are 'programmable pawns'. It tends to be a top – down approach and has the limitation that if managers do not gain commitment at lower levels (fails to programme them), then it stays at the top and is rejected as manipulative by workers.

The planning model of total quality (PTQ) is based on the belief that people are 'productive resources'. It tends to have its origins in technology and relies upon regulation, specifications for all activities, information gathering and analysis, measurement of perceived value and waste. BS 5750 and ISO 9000 would be evidence of this approach. Its weakness is that its concentration on measurement makes it unreliable in areas where objective measurement of core activities is not possible – teaching is a good example of this problem. It also ignores the behavioural dimension in the belief that people will comply with specifications just because they are being measured. The human characteristic to try to 'beat the system' is ignored despite evidence from other areas of business that it is a game people love to play.

The learning model of total quality (LTQ) is based upon the belief that people are 'willing participators'. It has its origins in human resource management (HRM), and relies upon training, education, skills and attitude development, performance appraisal, recognition and reward. Its weakness is that its HRM origins do not always gain acceptance, recognition and commitment from other functions. It is therefore a bottom–up process which does not have the influence to correct deficiencies that require decisions to be made at very senior levels – for example, problems resulting from product design or manufacturing processes.

Each of these approaches has limitations which may cause the drive for total quality to become stale and to be abandoned. And that would be a pity. Each of the limitations seems to result from deeply entrenched beliefs and assumptions held by the businesses's managers.

To counter this risk of failure, Susan Whittle points to the experience of an American multi-national textile company, Milliken. Milliken operated TQM for over twelve years. During that time, it had changed its approach to TQM many times. It seemed that if it left things the same for too long, TQM tended to become less effective. Therefore, Milliken developed ways of changing the organization and the way things were done so as to ensure continued quality improvements. Managers were trained to ensure that changes could be implemented without too much resistance from the people that were affected by them. The managers also had to ensure that changes produced a greater return on investment by shifting away from TQM activities that were becoming ineffective.

QUESTIONS

1 Discuss the differences in beliefs that might exist between the managers of each of the three models. How do these differences in beliefs account for the differences in their approach to TQM?

2 Consider an organization that is operating the PTQ model which is now becoming stale. By applying principles from VTQ and LTQ, what changes might be introduced to revitalize TQM?

KEY POINTS 3.4

- An approach to job design is to consider the total process and sub-divide the work into logical units rather than the capacity of one person

- Autonomous work groups contain all the skills needed to complete a unit of work, including decision-making and administration

- Passing decisions down as close to operational level as possible is enriching for the work group

- TQM is a cultural change that enriches all the jobs in an organization, encouraging the pursuit of continuous improvement

- The primary skill of managers in this environment is the management of change

The Job of Managing

Perhaps the people who have the most effect on the success or otherwise of any organization are its managers. We have already used the words 'managers', 'management' and 'managing' many times, but what do they actually mean? This is probably an appropriate place to consider the work of these particular people.

What is Meant by Managing?

Economists refer to resources in very broad terms: land, labour and capital. These are the sources of economic wealth. It is through *enterprise* that they are converted into desirable products or services to generate new wealth (see Figure 3.6).

Every organization, be it a business, a charity, a school or whatever, needs resources to achieve its

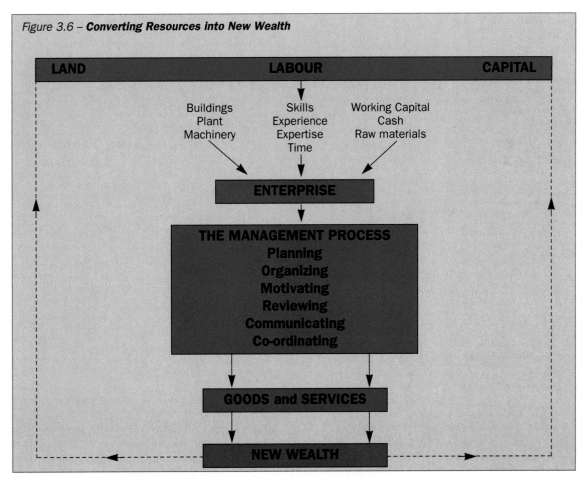

Figure 3.6 – *Converting Resources into New Wealth*

goals. These will include land, buildings, plant, machinery, raw materials, people, skills, experience, expertise, cash, capital and time. Many of these appear on the balance sheet of a business.

ACTIVITY 3.5

Name the resources needed by your school or college to achieve its goal of developing well educated and trained people?

Name the resources needed by Cadbury's to make its chocolate products.

Name the resources needed by Abbey National Building Society to provide its financial services.

You should find that in each case the resources you named fit into the general categories listed above. It is the job of managers to manipulate these resources so as to achieve the organization's goals. Managing is not so much about doing, it is more about getting things done through other people.

There are six main activities that managers carry out to achieve their organization's goals (see Figure 3.7). These activities are:

- Planning
- Organizing
- Motivating
- Reviewing
- Communicating
- Co-ordinating

Planning

A plan is a design for achieving some specific objective(s). Plans can relate to short, medium or long-term intentions. Short-term plans (often referred to as 'tactical plans') are more likely to contain precise objectives and can be more detailed schemes than long-term plans (often called 'strategic plans'); the further it looks into the future, the less certain it can be. However, there is little point in pursuing activities if the business does not know what the intended outcome is. 'If you don't know where you are going, how do you know when you've got there?'

The first step in planning is to state as clearly as possible the desired outcome – that is, the objective. A fundamental skill of managing is the ability to set and communicate objectives.

Next, it is usual to look at the period over which the plan is to take effect and to set specific, measurable targets for quality, quantity, time and costs. This is to allow the plan to be monitored.

In any planning activity, the managers never have all the information they need to make decisions. *The Business Environment* title in this series looks at some of the external pressures and in Chapter Seven in this book we will discuss some of the non-controllable variables that affect the prosperity of a business. They cannot be ignored at the planning stage. Managers have to make forecasts about the effects that factors outside their control may have on their objectives.

During this stage of the planning process, some decisions may be made about how the plan is to be executed, but only in the broadest terms – the detailed activities are the next stage.

Organizing

A plan on its own is a sterile thing. Nothing happens until the plan is turned into actions.

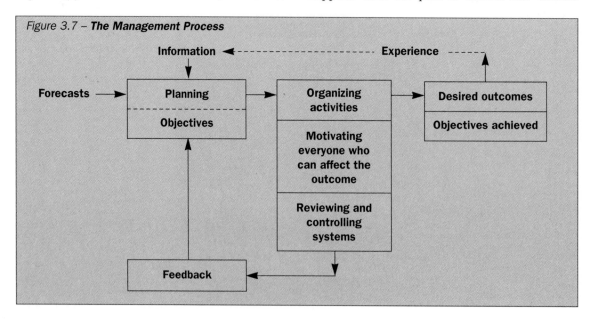

Figure 3.7 – *The Management Process*

That is what organizing is about. A manager is organizing when deploying the resources that are available for a particular job or project:

- People will be allotted tasks according to their knowledge, skills and experience
- Time will be allowed in the form of programmes
- Money will be made available in the form of budgets
- Materials will be scheduled
- Plant and machinery will be allocated

This part of the process is about getting the job done and the objective achieved according to plan.

Motivating

We have already examined this topic in detail. However, from the manager's point of view, motivating relates to any activity that attempts to obtain the co-operation of everyone who can affect the achievement of objectives, and to make jobs as satisfying to the job-holders as possible. It is not just the people who work for a manager who need motivating. The outcome might be influenced by suppliers, or by the boss, or by colleagues in other departments. To achieve the objective the manager will have to communicate plans, targets and progress. She or he will have to build teams and keep them working effectively. The ability to delegate is a key skill used by successful motivators.

DELEGATING

When delegating a task to someone, it is important that the manager lets her or him have enough authority to get the job done. The manager should:

- Give the resources that are needed to complete the task
- Give the necessary authority
- Give clear-cut lines of responsibility
- Let her or him get on without interference
- Have planned review meetings where progress can be monitored

When a manager encourages staff to share in taking the decisions that affect them at work, people involved will almost certainly give greater commitment to their work.

There will always be some decisions that cannot be shared because of their technical or financial complexity: some will be shared decisions, with the manager and the person equally involved in the process; and on occasions, the manager will consult the staff about their views, and then make the decision.

AUTHORITY

The thing that is *delegated* is *authority*. Authority is the right to use up an organization's resources for the purpose intended. No manager has authority to do otherwise with a firm's resources – it could be fraud or stealing to do so. If that authority is delegated to a supervisor, the supervisor can give staff work to do, spend money within the budget, use up materials and so on, to achieve the objective.

ACCOUNTABILITY

Although the manager may have delegated authority for a specific purpose to a supervisor, she or he is *still* accountable to the owner of the resources or the senior manager for achieving the desired outcome from the use of the resources. The supervisor is accountable to the manager and the manager is accountable to the senior manager. There is no question of being able to blame the supervisor if things do not work out. At the same time, the manager will get rewarded if things work out well. If they have been wasted or misused, it becomes a possible disciplinary matter.

Authority belongs to the job, not to the person in the job. The job holder exercises the authority that the job brings with it, but if she or he leaves the post, the authority stays behind and is given to the next holder of the job.

Consider how this notion of the nature of authority is viewed by a manager who holds Theory X beliefs compared with a manager who holds Theory Y beliefs. The contrast between Robert Maxwell, the disgraced tycoon who owned the Mirror Newspaper Group, and Anita Roddick, the founder and inspiration behind The Body Shop, is an example.

RESPONSIBILITY

Bear in mind, it is *authority* that is delegated. However, the person given the authority to use resources is *responsible* for ensuring that the resources are used *only* for the purpose intended. And that person is *accountable* to the boss for the outcome of their use. (See Figure 3.8, next page.)

Reviewing

Having made a plan and put it into action, a manager must constantly review progress to ensure that the plan is working properly – that is, if the activities continue as at present, the desired outcome will be achieved. If not, then the manager can modify the activities so as to ensure that the outcome is achieved in the time available for its completion.

Many other writers describe this as 'control'. The word 'control' has so many meanings that it

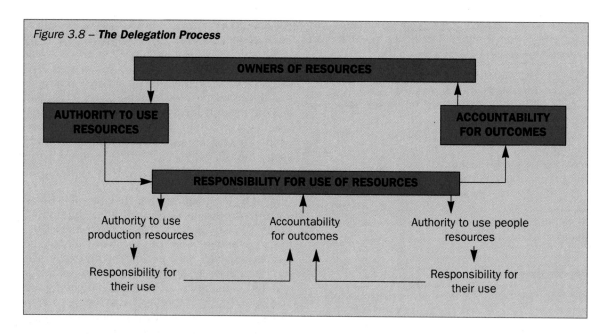

Figure 3.8 – ***The Delegation Process***

can be misunderstood. The *Collins English Dictionary and Thesaurus* lists ten – five for the verb and five for the noun. Many people see control as 'to command, direct or rule'. From our earlier discussions about motivation, this would be a formula for low morale or worse. 'To check, limit or regulate' is what is really required. The word 'review' is much less ambiguous and serves our purpose very well.

The reviewing process depends upon feedback of accurate and timely information relating to the targets set during the planning phase. Managers depend upon clear, understandable information to aid their decision-making.

The system that provides this sort of feedback is often called the Management Information System (MIS). We will discuss how it aids marketing decisions in Chapter Seven. Depending upon the information the manager is receiving from the MIS, things may be left to continue as they are; or some changes may be made in the activities; or, in some circumstances, it may be necessary to modify targets.

There can be incidents of such severity that the plan itself may have to be modified or even abandoned. An example of such an incident might be the Gulf War of 1990–91 that sent oil prices into a spiral and affected nearly every business in the EC.

Communicating

This word keeps cropping up. In all aspects of managing, and in all functions of the organization, the degree of success is directly related to the quality of communication. Communication is the 'nervous system' of managing.

It is both formal and informal. Management Information Systems, meetings, instructions, notice-boards, memos and so on are examples of formal communication. They are usually planned and specific.

Informal communications can be planned to some degree. If it is important that certain people speak to each other regularly, it may be arranged that their offices are close to one another. In this way, the people concerned will meet in the corridor or in their offices and chat.

The 'grapevine' (the channel for gossip) is the sort of informal communication that managers should try to keep to a minimum as it is almost certainly inaccurate and can even be mischievous. It often arises through lack of proper communication. We are information-seeking animals. We need information to help us make decisions about our environment. If we have only partial information, we still constantly make decisions about what is going on around us, only we 'make up' the information we are lacking.

Communication can be verbal, written, drawn or non-verbal. It can take many forms: letters, reports, memos, news-sheets, charts, graphs, blueprints, forms (invoices, orders); meetings, discussions, interviews, chats, presentations; smiles, frowns, relaxed or tense posture, stressed or anxious behaviour.

When thinking about communication, we should remember that it is impossible to divorce meanings from feelings. Whatever is written or said has a meaning that the communicator intended to transmit. But the choice of words, the tone and the timing, together with facial expressions and body posture, will generate feelings in the person receiving the message.

ACTIVITY 3.6

Consider a scene where you are sitting at your desk trying to finish an important piece of work before lunch. If uninterrupted you will achieve it. However, as luck would have it, Andy perched on your desk and enthusiastically started to tell you about last night's film. You wish to transmit the message 'Please go away'. You say: 'Oh for heaven's sake, Andy, can't you see I'm busy?'

Describe how you think Andy may feel as a result of receiving that message to 'go away'?

Or you could have said: 'Oh Andy. I was hoping to see you to hear about the film. I'll just finish this and then you can tell me all the gory details over lunch. I'll come and get you in about ten minutes. OK?'

Will this message to 'go away' conjure a different feeling from the first one?

Communications generate relationships – good, neutral or bad. If managers are trying to get the best out of people, it will probably help if they set out to develop good relationships.

Co-ordination

The *Collins English Dictionary and Thesaurus* defines 'co-ordinate' as: 'to integrate diverse elements in a harmonious operation'.

During the 'organizing' phase, you will recall the manager deployed all available resources to the different tasks that were needed to reach the objective. Provided all the different tasks are completed successfully, their combined results will achieve the overall objective.

The purpose of co-ordination is to ensure that all the pieces fit together to produce the planned outcome – to make sure everyone is pulling in the same direction.

Can you imagine a plan to launch a new product, where the advertising and promotion was going out and creating a demand, but the product had not been distributed to the shops? Co-ordination is achieved through the feedback from the MIS, through carefully designed committees and formal meetings. Communication is the essence of good co-ordination.

Most managers are involved in all the activities of managing all the time. Top managers tend to spend more time planning for the medium and long term, and supervisors tend to spend more time reviewing and motivating. But they are all carrying out each of the six activities to a greater or lesser degree all the time. Management is not a tidy series of discrete activities. It is more like a stewpot. There are many ingredients swimming around in the organizational gravy, each one essential to the final flavour, but none would create a dish on its own.

Many of the issues raised in this brief section on managing will be dealt with in other parts of this book. But this is not a management textbook, it is a business studies textbook. Further reading about management can be found under Dewey ref.658 in your library. It is a fascinating subject.

KEY POINTS 3.5

- **Management is about manipulating resources to achieve business objectives**
- **Planning is designing a course of action for achieving an organization's objectives**
- **Organizing is designing activities and deploying resources according to the plan**
- **Motivating is all those attempts by a manager to ensure the full co-operation of everyone who can** affect the outcome of the plan
- **Reviewing is monitoring the progress of the plan and making amendments to keep on course**
- **Communicating is ensuring that everyone who needs to know, knows and understands**
- **Co-ordinating is the task of getting everyone pulling in the same direction so as to achieve objectives on time and within budget**

EXAM PREPARATION

SHORT QUESTIONS

1 Name three variables outside the control of a business manager that may affect the job satisfaction of an individual employee.

2 List three characteristics of a job that would contribute to job satisfaction.

3 State two forms of job design.

4 What is meant by autonomous work group?

5 State four main activities of management.

DATA RESPONSE QUESTIONS

1 The board of directors of your firm has expressed an interest in various types of worker participation which might be introduced into your organization. As personnel manager, you have been asked to produce a report to assist the board in reaching a decision.

The report *(format: 3 marks)* should explain:

(a) the ways in which worker participation is being achieved in other firms

(*6 marks*)

(b) the problems which might be encountered by management in establishing a system of worker participation   (*8 marks*)

(c) the advantages and disadvantages of an established worker participation scheme to the organization. (AEB November 1990)   (*8 marks*)

ESSAYS

1 **(a)** Why is 'job enrichment' considered an important part of motivation?

(*15 marks*)

(b) How can the concept of 'job enrichment' be effectively applied to production workers on an assembly line? (UCLES June 1990)   (*10 marks*)

2 Why might information technology reduce the effectiveness of communication within an organization? (AEB November 1989)

Employee Resourcing

IN CHAPTER One, we looked briefly at the work of the personnel specialist in an organization. People are a complex resource to manage, but it is *people* who will determine whether an organization is successful, mediocre or a failure. What is more, people represent a major investment for any organization, and in some businesses they represent the greatest cost.

Employing the right people to ensure an organization's success is obviously important. But how can we be sure that one person is 'right' and another is not? The answer to that question, if we are honest, is that it is not possible to be certain, but great care and skill can be used to minimize the risk of employing people who cannot contribute to success.

In this chapter, we will examine ways of attracting the right people into the organization and assessing their suitability for the job. It is of primary importance to employ a person who can do the job to the required standard, but it is equally important to employ someone who will fit in with the existing work group. With these twin objectives, the personnel specialist must plan a strategy and put it into action. The total strategy is illustrated in Figure 4.1 (next page).

There are many parts of the recruitment and selection process which require specialist knowledge and training that the average manager may not possess. Hence the wisdom of having a personnel specialist in the organization, or bringing in a consultant to help.

Human Resource Planning

It has been necessary for several years to take positive action to avoid sexism in life generally, and in business particularly. It is a part of the duties of a personnel manager to ensure, as far as is reasonably practicable, that an Equal Opportunity Policy is enforced.

Hence you will find some topics in personnel using more acceptable titles. Human Resource planning is one such topic – it used to be called manpower planning, but you must be sure to call it by this more appropriate title – HR planning.

The external factor referred to as the 'demographic time bomb' is dealt with in *The Business Environment*, another title in this series. It has been estimated that the number of people leaving school and going into work will fall by 37 per cent during the 1990s. What are businesses going to do to get enough of the right kind of staff? The answer to this question, and other questions like it, would be considered by the personnel specialists in their HR planning exercises.

HR planning is defined by G Stainer as:

'The achievement of corporate objectives through the development of strategies designed to enhance the contribution of people at all times in the foreseeable future' (*Manpower Planning*, 1971).

Others say, very simply, that HR planning sets out to:

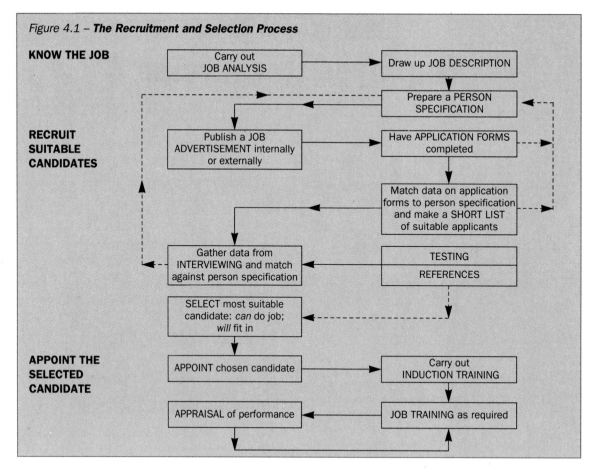

Figure 4.1 – *The Recruitment and Selection Process*

- Employ the right number of people with the right skills and ability at the right time

- Monitor how people are used now and will be used in the future, and to improve their utilization

- Improve people's performance by training, development and by providing satisfying work

The Case Study opposite is an example of the integrated nature of business. The chairperson talks about all the functions of business and many of the disciplines that go to make it up. It is a realistic example of the sort of data that a personnel specialist would use to begin a HR planning exercise.

The HR planners look at four things:

- Internal factors
- The internal labour market
- The external labour market
- Other external factors

Internal Factors

HR planning starts with the organization's corporate objectives. The numbers of people and the types of skill it will need in the future depend, amongst other things, upon:

- The company's plans for capital expenditure
- Any new technology it intends to use
- The new products or services it intends to introduce
- The new markets it intends to enter
- Any acquisitions it intends to make
- The state of the economy and its likely effects on the business

These objectives will be analysed by the HR planners to estimate the number and types of people that will be required to carry them out.

The Internal Labour Market

When they have calculated what their future needs are, the HR planners will analyse their existing workforce (the internal labour market). The business will want to get the best out of its existing people before it considers employing others. The questions to be answered include:

- What skills have we got?
- How many of each do we have?
- What levels of performance are we getting ?
- Can people transfer their skills to other jobs?
- Are trade unions concerned about this?

CASE STUDY

The Annual Report

In her annual report the chairperson of Prodon Electronics Ltd said that 1992 had been a good year all round. Profits had risen by 19 per cent and a dividend of 12p per share had been paid. Despite high interest rates, its market had remained buoyant and the company was planning to expand its market share in the next three years from 9 to 12 per cent. This objective would be achieved by replacing the present production machinery with state-of-the-art technology, most of which will be financed from reserves. Plans have been made to increase production capacity by 25 per cent and reduce unit costs by 18 per cent through economies of scale.

A major reassessment of employment policy will be undertaken, and a retraining programme will give all staff the opportunity to upgrade their skills and enjoy greater job satisfaction in a hi-tech environment.

Four new products are being developed and it is intended to introduce them to the market to replace declining products over the next two years. This will maintain its reputation of being the most innovative and forward looking company in the industry.

The chairperson thanked all the staff for their dedicated service and said she looked forward to the present prosperity of the company continuing, and everyone sharing its fruits.

QUESTIONS

1 Read the definitions of HR planning again. How do you think this annual report may affect the need for people in the firm? Might it have to employ some or make some redundant?

2 Discuss your notes with others and decide what effect the changes outlined in the annual report will have on employment in the firm.

- Have we got people who can be promoted to management jobs?
- What is the age distribution of the staff?
- Have we got a balance between the sexes?
- Are we catering for minority groups?
- How many people leave each year?
- How many are due to retire?

The External Labour Market

If there is an insufficient number of people employed at the moment, the planners will examine the supply of potential staff (the external market). Whether or not there will be enough people with the right knowledge, skills and experience depends upon several factors, including:

- The availability of young people leaving education with the relevant training
- The competition for staff from other British and European organizations
- The level of unemployment
- The acceptance levels of wages
- The state of the economy
- The influence of trade unions
- The state of technology
- The availability of facilities for training and retraining
- Particular skills which are in short supply

Other External Factors

HR planners will also need to take account of environmental factors including:

- Availability and quality of housing
- Local transport services
- Schools
- Recreational facilities
- Social and cultural opportunities and pleasant surroundings

These issues relating to the quality of life have taken on a much greater importance in recent years (see Figure 4.2, next page). Many skilled and specialized people do not want to work in poor conditions and a firm might find it hard to recruit key staff if it cannot satisfy them.

Knowing the number of people they will need, what they already have and what is available in the job market, will allow the planners to calculate how many people they will have to find, how many they will have to retrain, how many they will have to move into other jobs and, if necessary, how many will have to be dismissed. The diagram in Figure 4.3 (next page) summarizes this process.

*Figure 4.2 – **Quality of Life is Important Too***

The parks that bring in the business

BUSINESS PARKS have helped to encourage companies to relocate. Now competition among the parks themselves has produced a more sophisticated approach and the emphasis is on amenities and location rather than the bare buildings.

Jeremy Williams, a director at Redrow, which has developed a business park in northeast Wales, says: "You have only got to queue for a car parking space to know what convenience is about".

St David's Park is in Clywd, six miles across the border from Chester. Its capacity will be 500,000 sq ft, of which 125,000 sq ft are booked and 50,000 sq ft are already operational. Tenants have come from nearby towns.

Alex Robinson, the managing director of UK Land Developments, which is building Northampton Business Park on 54 acres only a mile from the town centre, is another executive who does not scorn the humble parking lot. He says: "Parking is still the single most important factor. The big attraction is that there is room for visitors and staff." The Northampton park has 1,000 spaces.

Motorways have been another factor determining location. A prime example has been the regeneration of South Wales. The M4 provides a fast link with London, and particularly Heathrow. Bedfordshire, with the M1 and M11, and its own airport at Luton, has seen business parks proliferate.

Many of the employees recruited locally for companies moving to business parks are mothers returning to work. Crèches and day-care facilities are now regarded as important.

Hotels and conference and leisure facilities are highly rated by incoming companies.

Source: Times, 1 November 1990, Rodney Hobson. © Times Newspapers Ltd. 1990

*Figure 4.3 – **HR Planning Process***

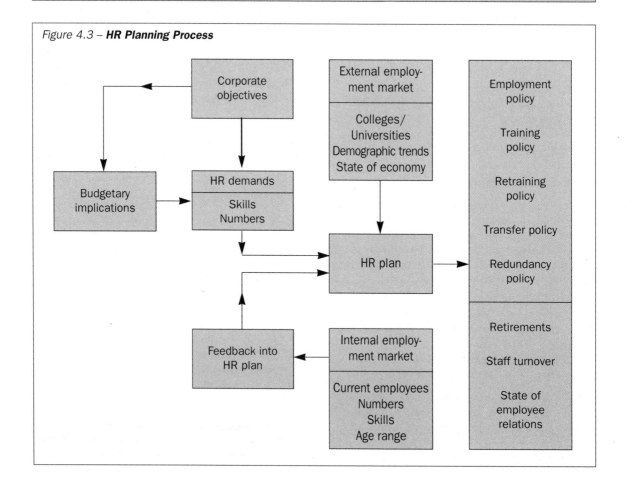

KEY POINTS 4.1

- HR planning ensures that the organization maintains the correct employee levels

- Such planning is based upon an analysis of the organization's corporate objectives in order to determine the changes in numbers and skills

- External factors that will influence the availability of people must be taken into account when planning

- Training and retraining are ways of improving employee utilization

Recruitment

We have already stressed that getting the right people in the right jobs is fundamental to the success of the organization.

If an unsuitable person is employed it will result in less efficiency or possibly having to go through the whole selection process again. The time that the organization's managers take to avoid this is time well invested.

We will examine the process of finding the right person for the job by a series of short activities based on the following Scenario.

Scenario: The Personnel Manager

Working quietly in your office, you are interrupted by a flustered and irate colleague – the sales office manager. 'I'm fed up with the quality of sales staff we get nowadays. Can't the personnel department do something about it? Our newer recruits want to be spoon-fed, have no work to do and be paid a fortune for not doing it!'

Concerned at her frustration, you suggest that she sits down and has a cup of coffee while you discuss the problem. Once she has calmed down, you try to consider the problem rationally. 'What we've got to do,' you say, 'is to find a way that helps us to choose people that can do the job we want, to the standard we want, and to fit into the workgroup.' The sales office manager agrees but adds doubtfully, 'If there is such a process!'

Job Analysis – Know the Job

Creating a new post, or replacing someone who has left, gives an opportunity to analyse the job that has to be done. Rather than just 'replace' the person who has left the post, it is often a chance for the manager to consider other and better ways of getting the work done.

Perhaps the job has changed gradually, or the departing person had 'bent' the job slightly to suit her or his own strengths. Indeed, the manager should consider whether the answer lies in reorganizing the work among existing staff. Or maybe a part-time person is the best solution. The use of more up-to-date machinery should also be considered. In some cases the use of temporary agency staff or overtime will be what is needed. If none of these is suitable, then the solution will be to employ someone full-time or on a fixed-term contract.

The simplest and most common methods of analysing jobs are talking to and observing the job-holder at work. The data is carefully recorded and analysed. Usually the job holder's manager is able to give additional information, although it tends to be rather general and would not normally be sufficient on its own. There are several different ways in which jobs can be analysed, but they are beyond the scope of this book.

ACTIVITY 4.1

Through your observations of your Business Studies teacher at work, make a list of all the tasks that go into the job of teaching (see Chapter Three). What mental processes are required to do the job? Who is she or he accountable to, and what responsibilities does the job carry?

Discuss your list with others in your group and make as comprehensive a list as you can. Then show it to your teacher and get her or him to comment about things that may be missing or that are not within a teacher's job.

In the Scenario above, it might be a good idea for the sales office manager to consider exactly what the job entails: she needs to be absolutely clear about the tasks that the job-holder will have to perform and the standard of work required.

She should describe the responsibilities of the job:

- What tasks have to be completed by the job-holder?
- How often is each one done and how important is it?
- Is there machinery involved that requires special skills?
- Is the job-holder required to take decisions and use initiative?
- If so, what are the limits of her or his authority?
- Is the output from the job a part or a whole?
- Does the job-holder have to work with others or control the work of others?
- What are the required standards and how will they be measured?

Job Descriptions

When all this information has been gathered, it should be analysed and written down in a summary report of what the job entails. It is called a job description and one of its uses is to assist in finding the right person for the job.

We have a language difficulty with this topic. Although many companies and respected personnel textbooks use the term 'job description' as the sole name for the document which records everything about a job, the Department of Employment has published a *Glossary of Training Terms* which splits it into two: job description and job specification. The DoE's definitions are:

- *Job description:* a broad statement of the purpose, scope, duties and responsibilities of a particular job
- *Job specification:* a detailed statement of the physical and mental activities involved in the job and, where relevant, of social and physical environmental matters. The specification is usually expressed in terms of behaviour – ie, what the work person does, what knowledge she or he uses doing it, the judgements she or he makes and the factors the job-holder takes into account when making them

In other words, the job description describes the tasks of the job, and the job specification describes the behaviour necessary to actually do

---

*Figure 4.4 – **Job Description for a Salesperson***

JOB DESCRIPTION

Name of post:	Salesperson.
Responsible to:	Sales Office Manager.
Responsible for:	No direct staff.
Relationships with:	Sales clerks; warehouse personnel; customers.
Job summary:	To call upon existing and potential customers according to the prescribed call schedule. To collect repeat orders, introduce new lines, open new accounts, arrange deliveries and returns, and collect overdue accounts. Keep customer records.
Job responsibilities:	The salesperson is responsible for selling the company's range of pharmaceuticals. S/he must know and keep up to date with the complete range of goods so as to inform and advise chemists of latest developments. S/he must behave in a professional manner and exercise care and security with samples and products. S/he must deal sensitively with complaints and errors. S/he must follow schedules and report daily on shortfalls.
Working conditions:	The salesperson will drive a company van, keep it clean and roadworthy, and ensure that any accidents or faults are reported immediately to the sales office manager.
Standards:	All calls must be made to schedule. Complaints and errors must be dealt with within 24 hours. Orders must be processed on the day they are taken. Records must be completed immediately after call. Sales targets must be met.

the tasks. There is a good case for keeping these two perspectives together in one document. In this text we will use the term job description to mean the two together.

When the sales office manager in our Scenario has completed the analysis, she should write it down in a job description. This information will be most valuable in trying to decide what sort of person might be able to do the job satisfactorily. Figure 4.4 contains such a job description.

Person Specification

A person specification (sometimes called a 'personnel profile') describes the human characteristics that are required in order to do the job to the standards set.

ACTIVITY 4.2

Read the job description in Figure 4.4 carefully, then try to imagine the ideal person for the job. (To help you do this, think of someone you know who is a salesperson in a shop or a sales representative for a firm.) It is important to remember that people can operate only within the limits of their ability, present knowledge and experience. To operate beyond this requires education, training and development.

What sort of personal presentation would you see as appropriate to this job? Smart? Clear speaking voice? Or does it not matter?

What educational or trade qualifications, if any, are essential to the job? How intelligent does the job-holder have to be?

And what about the ability to get on with the job – will there be constant supervision? Or must the person be able to get on with it without being told what to do all the time?

Are there any special interests that would help the person do the job? Will the person be working under pressure and have to cope with people who are difficult? Are the hours unsociable? Is there a lot of travelling? How flexible do you want the person to be in this respect?

When the sales office manager knows precisely what the job is, and has written it down in a job description, she can go through the process that you have just completed and describe the ideal person for the job.

There are several useful models available to help with this. The one you have been using in Activity 4.2 is Alec Rodger's Seven Point Plan. It simply describes the person you are looking for under seven broad headings:

- Physical make-up
- Attainments
- General intelligence
- Special aptitudes
- Interests
- Disposition
- Circumstances

Using this Seven Point Plan, the person specification for a salesperson may look like that in Figure 4.5.

There is a great similarity between this and a photofit picture used by the police in hunting suspects. They gather information, analyse it and come up with an idea of what the offender might look like. The difference is that we are hunting for an ideal employee who will help to make our business prosper, not rob us by failing to do the job to the required standard.

There are other models available. Some experienced personnel specialists design a 'person specification' especially relevant to their own organization's needs.

Figure 4.5 – **Person Specification for Salesperson**

PHYSICAL MAKE-UP
Well groomed; smartly dressed. Clear grammatical speech.

ATTAINMENTS
Four GCSEs grade C, including Chemistry or a science. Formal sales training preferred. Clean driving licence.

GENERAL INTELLIGENCE
Above average. Quick on the uptake. Agile mind.

SPECIAL APTITUDES
Ability to listen. High in social skills. Accuracy and clear handwriting.

INTERESTS
Any team sport or social responsibility.

DISPOSITION
Pleasant and happy. Ability to cope with customers who are upset.

CIRCUMSTANCES
Preferred stable, settled home life. Able to work occasional Saturdays. Lives on territory.

Recruiting Suitable Candidates

ACTIVITY 4.3

If you were searching for the person described in the person specification, where would you look? Would you find her or him reading the *Times* or the *Daily Express*, or visiting the Job Centre? In your library, look at the job advertisements in a tabloid like the *Daily Mail* and at a 'quality' like the *Daily Telegraph* until you find the size and layout of advertisement that you think would be appropriate for the person you are looking for. How big is it?

Then ask the librarian if you can see the directory called '*British Rates and Data*', (*BRAD* for short). This useful directory gives prices for advertising in most of the media. Look up the cost of placing a job advertisement the size that you have chosen. How does this compare with the same advertisement in your local newspaper?

Find out how much the Job Centre charges for finding a suitable employee for a firm and compare this with a local employment agency. If you cannot visit these places, enquire by phone.

When a company is looking for suitable applicants, it can be sure that there are people looking for suitable jobs. The art of recruiting is to attract those who fit the company's person specification, and no others. The first stage of the recruiting process is to identify, accurately, where the ideal people can be found. The process is very similar to the targeting skills of the marketing manager which we will examine in Chapter Seven.

They may be found within the company itself; or within the families and friends of present staff; or they will be found reading the *Daily Telegraph*, or the *Daily Mirror*. If the post is a very technical one, or is highly specialized, there will be specialist journals which these people read or specialist agencies who are in contact with them. Perhaps someone straight from school or college, or on a Youth Training programme, would be ideal.

Research by Derek Torrington and Laura Hall, both lecturers at the University of Manchester Institute of Science and Technology (UMIST), suggests that the most popular sources of new employees are through internal advertising and local newspapers. For specialist and management jobs the most popular source is through professional and trade journals.

The decision about which media to use in order to contact your target audience is very important for the success of any recruitment campaign. It can be very expensive to advertise in national newspapers and journals, and agencies charge substantial fees. The expenditure would be justified only if the right sort of people are applying for the job.

The sales office manager in our Scenario has the task now of deciding how to communicate

her job needs in such a way as to attract suitable candidates. She may put an advertisement in the local newspaper or a notice on the notice-boards in the firm, or both. The problem which she is trying to solve is that her staff are unsuitable. This is her chance to use careful wording to attract only suitable candidates. It might even be worth using a recruitment agency to design and word the advertisement and also to place it in the most suitable media.

Research suggests that there are four things that most applicants look for in a job advertisement. They are:

- Details about the organization
- A clear description of the job
- The location
- The salary scale

'Who would I be working for, what would I be doing, where would I be doing it and what reward would I get?'

The advertisement should also make it quite clear how any interested person should apply. Our sales office manager may decide to ask for a letter of application and a Curriculum Vitae (CV). Or she may simply ask them to write or phone for an application form.

ACTIVITY 4.4

Examine the two advertisements below and judge which will attract the right sort of person. Why? Now sketch an advertisement for our salesperson based upon these reasons.

The Coach House
RUN ROAD, OXFORD

Due to maternity leave the following
permanent positions are now available

PART-TIME NIGHT STAFF
(2 nights)

FULL AND PART-TIME DAY STAFF
We work to a shift rota which includes weekends.
Experience is not essential as training will be given.

Tel. Oxford 66676
for further details

Job Advertisements

You will have found out in Activity 4.3 that advertising can be expensive. A national daily can cost over £80 per single column centimetre, which means a two column by 14cm advertisement would cost £2 240. You will want a good return on that investment, so writing a clear, precise advertisement that will attract the right people makes good economic sense.

It seems sensible for a company to provide the four pieces of essential information in its job advertisements. Equally important is the image that the advertisement gives the business. The organization's marketing policy will set out the sort of image that should be created by all the publicity the firm puts out. These job advertisements must carry that image and attract the sort of people that would be happy to be part of it. The objective is to attract people who will fit in. So, for example, the messsage should indicate that the firm is looking for people who are sombre and serious, or bright and ambitious. There should be a positive attempt to create a good impression of the firm.

There are legal constraints to bear in mind. The Race Relations Act 1976 (as amended), The Equal Pay Act 1970 and the Sex Discrimination Act 1975 and 1986 (as amended) make it unlawful to discriminate against persons, directly or indirectly, on the grounds of race, gender or marital status. The Disabled Persons (Employment) Act 1944 and 1958 provides that an employer of more than twenty people has a duty to employ a quota of disabled people who are registered under the Act. The Employment Act 1990 makes it unlawful to discriminate or appear to discriminate against union members in a job advertisement.

The penalty for a breach of these laws can be severe, not only in terms of the fines imposed and the legal costs involved, but also in terms of management time in answering any charges, the stress it imposes upon those who must answer to the courts for the breach, and the adverse publicity that it will attract.

The two advertisements in Figure 4.6 won

Figure 4.6 – *Award-Winning Advertisements*

THE FINEST TOYSHOP IN THE WORLD

Action man needed to protect Teddy from the forces of evil.
Security Guards
£8,800 pa plus benefits

Hamleys enjoys a unique reputation as the finest toy store in the world and they're looking for Security Guards who can uphold that reputation.

You will be working in shifts from 7.00am to 7.00pm. Ideally you have experience of working in a retail environment and you have an in-depth knowledge of P.A.C.E.

You are smart in appearance, you have good references and even better eyesight. Hamleys is a very busy store, so rest assured that Teddy, the Cabbage Patch Kids and Masters of the Universe will keep you on your toes.

If you're interested in being a Security Guard with Hamleys, write enclosing relevant details to The Personnel Department, Hamleys, 188-196 Regent Street, London W1R 6BT. Telephone: 01-734 3161.

This position is open to Wonder Women as well as Action Men.

WE'LL HELP YOU STAND OUT FROM THE CROWD

You only have to look at the shops in your local High Street to know that retailing these days is a constantly-changing business full of ideas and opportunities.

As the world's most famous store, our ideas have to be that bit better, and that bit more adventurous than anyone else's! So join us as a retail trainee and we'll give you more than just a taste of everything retailing has to offer.

In some of the best and most varied training in the business, we'll develop, and encourage your imagination too! You could deal with anything from toys to leather goods, the finest food to designer fashion. You could be involved in specialist areas such as personnel or customer services. There are practical work-related projects where you can show your initiative right from the start, backed up by college release courses to study nationally-recognised qualifications.

After training your career can take off in any number of exciting directions. You choose an area that best uses your talents . . . and can then progress as quickly as your abilities allow. There are 20 acres of sales floor and more than 200 departments. With no limit to your imagination, who knows where you'll end up!

For further details please write to the Retail Training Co-ordinator, Prospects at Harrods, Harrods Limited, Brompton Road, London, SW1X 7XL.

KNIGHTSBRIDGE

awards for their quality. When you have studied them, consider what sort of images they project, and why Harrods did not mention salary.

ACTIVITY 4.5

How might the personnel manager evaluate the cost effectiveness of the recruitment campaign?

Application Forms

The purpose of an application form is to gather data about the candidate that will give definite clues about personal attributes, qualifications, experience and so on. This should help to determine whether she or he matches the person specification. It should be designed in such a way as to make the matching relatively quick and straightforward. By matching the data given on the application form or in the CV with the person specification, it should be possible to create three piles: 'unsuitable', 'maybe suitable' and 'suitable'. The next step is to re-examine the 'maybe' pile and decide which they are – 'suitable' or 'unsuitable' – and put them in the appropriate pile.

Sales office managers and other executives are busy people. Interviewing unsuitable people is both a waste of their time, and it unnecessarily raises the expectations of the people who will not be offered the job. So selecting these two piles is worth a good deal of care. The suitable candidates should be invited to attend for interview.

The completed application form of the successful candidate will form a part of her or his contract of employment. Any deliberate misinformation could render the contract void, resulting in dismissal.

*Figure 4.7 – **A Part of the Standard Application Form***

Standard Application Form (SAF)		Name of Employer		1
Please complete this form in BLACK ink or typescript. Check employer literature or vacancy information for correct application procedure	AGCAS/AGR approved form			
		Vacancies or training schemes for which you wish to apply Job function(s) Locations(s)		
Current/Most Recent University/Polytechnic/College				
First names (BLOCK LETTERS)		Surname (Dr, Mr, Mrs, Miss, Ms) (BLOCK LETTERS)		
Out of Term address (BLOCK LETTERS); give dates at this address		Term address (BLOCK LETTERS); give dates at this address		
Postcode Telephone		Postcode Telephone		
Date of birth	Age	Country of birth	Nationality/Citizenship	Do you need a work permit to take up employment in the UK?

Secondary/Further Education Name(s) of Schools(s)/College(s)	From	To	Subject/courses studied and level (eg GCSE, O, A, AS, H, IB, BTEC) Give examination results with grades and dates	
First degree/diploma University/Polytechnic/College	From	To	Degree/diploma (BA, HND, etc)	Class expected/ obtained	Title of degree/diploma course

Main subjects with examination results or course grades to date, if known		

Postgraduate qualifications University/Polytechnic/College	From	To	PhD/MA/ Diploma etc	Title of research topic or course
				Supervisor:

KEY POINTS 4.2

- Recruitment is an analytical process that improves the chances of finding the right sort of people to invite to the selection process

- Job analysis is a detailed study of the tasks and responsibilities of a job

- A job description is a written statement deriving from the job analysis, plus a description of the behaviour needed to carry out the job to the standard required.

- A person specification is a structured description of the human characteristic thought necessary in any person that would be able to do the job described

- Recruiting refers to targeting a message to the people described in the person specification

- Application forms are designed to gather information about the applicant that can be matched to the characteristics in the person specification. Those that match closely can be invited to interview

ACTIVITY 4.6

How does the information given in answer to questions on an application form help the personnel specialist to choose candidates for interview? Look at the first part of the Standard Application Form (SAF) contained in Figure 4.7. Use Rodger's Seven Point Plan as your model. Against each question on the SAF, note which of the seven points is/are likely to be covered by the answer. For example, the 'Out of Term Address' might give some idea of 'circumstances' if used in conjunction with ACORN or PIN or SAGACITY (see Chapter Seven). 'Vacancies.... for which you wish to apply' can give some indication of 'interests'.

Selection

The initial stages have been designed to determine precisely the sort of person needed to do the job to the required standard, and then to attract such people to apply for the job.

The next stage sets out to 'measure' the characteristics of each candidate against the desired characteristics for the job. There are several techniques for achieving this. We will consider various forms of interviews, testing, taking up references and assessment centres.

Selection Interviews

An interview can be described as a planned discussion with a specific purpose.

Interviews are used in many different circumstances for many different purposes. Although we are concerned only with selection here, it is worth noting that others include counselling, grievance and discipline interviews.

ACTIVITY 4.7

Carefully consider how an interview differs from a conversation. What would a personnel specialist do in order to make a selection interview differ from a chat about a job?

We have mentioned several times that the business manager needs to gather information that provides evidence about the applicant's ability to do the job, and to fit in with the work team.

But interviewing is a mutual exchange of information. It is an opportunity to give applicants as much information about the job as possible so that they can decide whether or not they want to take it if it is offered. Torrington and Hall reported that nearly 40 per cent of candidates who were given a job offer did not take them up.

A company wants people who accept jobs to be *motivated* to work for the business. Treating them with respect at interview is an important example of nurturing this motivation. It is important that all applicants see the way the process was handled was legal, fair and just.

Reliability of Interviews

There is a great deal of research evidence to show that interviewing is a very inexact procedure. Many researchers have shown that different interviewers given exactly the same information will form very different opinions of the same candidate.

One of the authors of this book has experienced this phenomenon on many occasions when simulating interviews for management training. Different managers will select different candidates for a job and set out elaborate arguments to justify their decisions. The fact that the simulation was designed to provide only one ideal applicant sometimes fails to convince them that they might not have chosen the best person. The great danger is that it will never be known if the best candidate is not spotted, and is rejected.

Some research conducted in 1964 by E C Webster of McGill University, Canada, provides some interesting conclusions that are as valid today as then:

- Interviewer's first impressions arise from the application form, and from their first sight of the interviewee. Evidence shows that they seldom change this opinion
- Interviewers make their decision about a candidate in the first few minutes of the interview, then spend the rest of the interview gathering evidence to support their early decision
- Most interviewers look for reasons why candidates are *not* suitable more than they look for evidence that they *are* suitable
- If an interviewer has made an early decision, this is communicated to the candidate by the interviewer's body language, and the interviewee will respond accordingly

Despite these serious weaknesses, which seem to be reasonably well proven, interviewing is still the most common selection technique used by businesses today. Perhaps it is a problem of the skill of the interviewer as much as it is weaknesses in the process itself. Such complex interpersonal situations require a level of knowledge and experience to handle them that we should not expect to find automatically in most managers. While it is often difficult to get managers to accept it, study and practise are essential if the potential values of interviewing are to be exploited.

Preparing the Interview Questions

The interviewer's questions set out to get the candidates to talk about their work experiences and their lives in general. The answers can reveal whether they can do the job, plus their motivation and adjustment, and give some indication of how they cope in a variety of situations – including those where they are likely to be under pressure and stress.

The questions that are most effective in this regard are 'open ended questions'. The soldier and poet, Rudyard Kipling, wrote:

> I keep six honest serving-men
> (They taught me all I knew);
> Their names are What and Why and When
> And How and Where and Who.

All these words help to keep questions open. 'How did you do your stock-taking?' should get a much different answer from 'Did you do stock-taking?' Phrases such as 'Tell me about . . .' or 'Can you explain . . .' should give a great deal of useful information. Questions should not imply the answer. 'I expect you were very busy in your job' will almost certainly get the answer 'Oh yes! I was'.

Where an answer leaves doubt, or raises an interest, it should be probed further. 'I was responsible for the stock' may mean that the candidate kept the records up to date, or it could mean that full budget responsibility rested on that person's shoulders. Probing for clues is a part of the interviewer's skill.

If interviewees are to reveal their ability, experience, motivation and adjustment, they, not the interviewer, must do most of the talking. A ratio of 60:40 is what the interviewer should aim for. That is quite difficult for the interviewer to achieve without careful preparation.

Once again, it is important to avoid asking any questions that may discriminate against any person or group of people.

Types of Interview

There are two schools of thought about interviewee's behaviour. One school assumes that adult's personalities have formed and stabilized, and that their future behaviour can be predicted from their past behaviour. People will be more inclined to respond honestly and openly if they are relaxed and in a friendly atmosphere. The interviewers who hold this view will create a congenial atmosphere and seek to learn from the interviewee how she or he coped with a variety of situations by discussing past experiences and behaviour. This, they believe, will provide some insight into how she or he may behave in the future.

The second school assumes that people will exaggerate their strengths, and minimize their weaknesses, even though this may be done unintentionally. In order to predict future behaviour, therefore, the only evidence is that which the interviewee shows during the interview. So the interviewers who hold this view will set up a variety of situations which they believe will provoke the candidate to exhibit their true behaviour. This, they assume, is how the candidate will behave in a similar situation in the future.

ONE-TO-ONE INTERVIEWS

Some organizations are happy to rely upon one trained specialist to conduct all the interviews and select the most appropriate applicant. Other organizations will use more than one interviewer to try to reduce the risk of error.

The one-to-one interview is popular because it demands less management time, and is preferred by most interviewees. They seem to cope more easily when they need only relate to one person, and where the questions follow a logical pattern.

SUCCESSIVE INTERVIEWS

Where more than one interviewer is used, the advantages of one-to-one can be maintained by having successive interviews each with a different manager. However, it has been found that candidates tend to become bored with the same questions being asked time and again, or they become better at answering them as the interviews proceed. It also takes a lot of their time. In addition, a bad impression can be created if the interviewers are of differing views about the job or organization.

TANDEM INTERVIEWS

Often, a firm will use a line manager in tandem with a personnel specialist in the hope that each will bring special knowledge and skill to the situation. This can be economical, acceptable and an efficient use of time. Only one interview is conducted, and the two interviewers plan in advance what role each is to play. Some lessening of rapport with the interviewee is experienced, but overall, the results are considered to be satisfactory, though it is difficult to evaluate as it will never be known if the best candidate was not appointed.

PANEL INTERVIEWS

Panel interviews are often used in the public sector. Up to five people will sit on a panel and the candidate will be interviewed once only, but by the whole panel. For most people it is quite daunting. It is more like a tribunal sitting in judgement than an interview. Often, a panel member will appear hostile to the candidate. Unless the panel member is consistently hostile to all the candidates, it will cause an aberration. Questioning can be repetitive and disorganized and create a situation where some candidates are unable to give a good account of themselves.

Quite often, disagreement among panel members as to who should be appointed leads to a compromise candidate being offered the job with all the risks that that involves. It may also be the case that one or two members of the panel holds more sway than others, which results in 'their' candidate being appointed. This merely satisfies their power need rather than the organization's personnel need.

BOARD INTERVIEWS

Board interviews are conducted by groups of more than five people. It has been known for as many as thirty people to sit on an interviewing board. It is hard to justify the effectiveness of this procedure, but the fact that they are used suggests that some organizations feel a need for them. Some feel that it is satisfying the political aspirations of the board members, rather than providing the applicants with a fair and realistic opportunity to give an honest account of their suitability to perform the requirements of the job to the standard specified.

Rapport is impossible. Often, some board members are not expert interviewers, and may be more interested in projecting their own image than gathering evidence about the candidates. Co-ordinated, logical questioning is unlikely, and control of the proceedings is a headache for the chairperson.

Possibly, some members of the board will have a different perception of the job than was implied in the job description. Extraneous and irrelevant issues, like political affiliations (which may have no bearing on ability to do the job), may take on significance. Achieving agreement among thirty people as to who is the most appropriate person to appoint could prove difficult.

In its favour, it could be claimed that many people can see the candidates on one occasion, and would be able to observe their behaviour under stress. Variations of this method, (using closed circuit television, for example) can lessen the stress for some candidates. However, as different people react differently to being televised, it puts an unfair pressure on some to their disadvantage, whilst others may blossom because 'they're on TV'. Unless 'being photogenic' is a characteristic important to the job, it can give a biased picture.

Perhaps these explanations highlight one reason why some businesses seem not to have very good staff whilst others have excellent staff. The efficiency of a business, and its ability to compete in its markets, reflect the quality of its employees.

ACTIVITY 4.8

Consider each of these five ways of conducting an interview. If you were an interviewee, which one would you prefer and why? How might you prepare yourself for an interview if your aim was to give a good account of the qualities you would bring to the job.

Testing

Interviewing may not give enough information about various aspects of an applicant's ability, experience and personality. Additional data can be gathered by different types of test.

Some people consider testing an invasion of privacy, while others simply doubt its value. However, one thing is clear. If tests are to be used, there is a strong moral obligation on the user to ensure that the tests chosen are valid and *reliable* for the purpose for which they are being used. They should be conducted by a person who is trained and qualified in their use and the interpretation of the data collected.

VALIDITY

Tests must be *valid* – that is, they must test what they are intended to test. If a personnel specialist is using a test to predict future performance in a job, then there must be valid data to support the claim that a high score means a future high performance in the job being offered. Otherwise the test cannot be described as a good predictor.

RELIABILITY

Tests must be *reliable* – that is, they must be consistent in measuring what they are supposed to measure whenever they are repeated. There must be data to show how reliable a test is. The more reliable it is, the more weight it can carry in the selection process.

Statistical techniques are used to show the value of tests. If the correlation coefficient (r) is equal to 1, then the test is a perfect predictor of future performance. If r=0 it does not predict anything about future performance. To give you some idea of their value as predictors of future performance, r=0.4 is accepted by personnel specialists as being helpful in the selection process.

TYPES OF TEST

a Aptitude tests

These help a business to select people who have no experience of a particular job (for example, apprentices). There are many tests which are designed to indicate that the applicant has the basic mental and physical qualities which are required for success. A business that invests in training such people is taking less of a risk if it uses this sort of test than if it did not use any. Tests exist for mechanical aptitude, numerical aptitude, spatial aptitude and verbal aptitude.

b Achievement or attainment tests

These are used to measure skills already learned.

For example, people applying for a secretarial post may be asked to do a typing test. All those that achieve a certain standard in the test will be considered further; those that do not will be rejected. Many types of job lend themselves to work-sampling tests which are easily devised by the business itself.

c Intelligence tests

These are plentiful and can be used to help with the creation of a shortlist. They measure a person's Intelligence Quotient (IQ). People whose scores fall below a known minimum IQ for the job being filled would not be interviewed. It is important that intelligence tests are used precisely as directed, and that they should always be given under the control of a trained psychologist.

d Personality tests

These assess a person's emotional make-up. They attempt to predict an individual's behaviour under different circumstances. Personality is described by plotting an individual's score on a series of factors.

One of the most popular is the Cattell Sixteen Personality Factor Test (16PF). The following is a sample of six of these factors:

SERIOUS	_ _ _ _ _ _ X _	OUTGOING
AFFECTED BY FEELINGS	X _ _ _ _ _ _ _	EMOTIONALLY STABLE
SUBMISSIVE	_ _ _ _ _ _ X _	DOMINANT
GROUP DEPENDENT	_ _ _ _ X _ _ _	SELF-SUFFICIENT
CONSERVATIVE	X _ _ _ _ _ _ _	EXPERIMENTING
TRUSTING	_ _ _ _ _ X _ _	SUSPICIOUS

The candidate completes a questionnaire, which when analysed by the expert, shows where she or he falls on each of the scales. For example, the individual shown on the scale above is very outgoing, emotional, very dominant, quite self-sufficient, very conservative and quite suspicious.

Some tests are designed to focus on individuals, whilst others compare a group of individuals against a norm for a particular occupation.

Although there seems to be a growing tendency to use personality tests in selection and development of managers, there is a need for more reliable research data to relate personality types to different occupations. For example, what sort of 'personality score' would indicate likely success as a teacher? In the meantime, their use should be handled with care and only skilled experts should be allowed to analyse and interpret the outcomes.

Figure 4.8 – *Psychometric Testing*

Psychometric tests – do they work?

IN THE current economic climate of recession and associated cost controls, many companies are starting to take a closer look at psychometric tests as a means of helping them find and retain the best staff and hence reduce their staff turnover costs.

All organisations need to assess individuals, whether they are existing employees or potential employees. In this respect psychological testing has an established role to play in selection – both for preliminary screening and later, in the final stages of decision making – and in the development of individuals and teams within organisations large and small.

No-one claims that psychological tests replace traditional selection methods. However, when properly used, personality tests can and do help improve the quality of decisions affecting recruitment and throughout the subsequent career. In terms of cost-affectiveness, even a slightly better choice of candidate will bring financial benefits which far outstrip the extra costs involved.

Values

The growing use of psychological tests in selection and assessment has, to some extent, outpaced the level of sophistication and knowledge about them and even experts fail to agree about the relative values of rival sets of tests.

The problem for the layman lies in knowing how to distinguish between the good and the bad tests and in knowing which tests will best suit a given purpose.

In many cases, the choice of test is determined more by sales hype than on the qualities of particular tests. Anyone contemplating buying a test, specially any that appear to need minimal training, should be aware that many of the claims made about performance may be extravagant. You should also check that the organisation selling the test should at the very least have a fully qualified psychologist on the staff.

Source: Anglia Industry & Business, January 1991

ACTIVITY 4.9

Using the six factors (from Cattell's Sixteen Factors) given above, compare the desirable characteristics of a police inspector and a social worker. How different are they? If you were to test a group of people without knowing their occupations, would the results help you to decide whether they would make better police inspectors or social workers?

Using tests will give the personnel specialist additional information to that gleaned from the application form and gathered at the interview upon which to base the selection. But that is all they will do. There is no test so accurate that it can predict success in any job. At best, they may provide information that suggests someone is unsuitable or unlikely to succeed under certain circumstances.

References

A reference is an opinion, usually in writing, of a person's character, ability, honesty and reliability in support of a job application. A business may take up references to confirm that information given by an applicant is true, and to seek additional information that may have been hidden by the applicant.

The problem with references is that it is usually impossible to obtain a detailed report on how candidates are performing their present jobs from their current employers. It would be unethical to contact a present employer who may not be aware that an employee had applied for another job.

For those employers who do give references to current employees, such as teachers and local government staff, it is hard to know if there is bias. Perhaps personal relationships may influence some referees more than job performance, even to the extent of helping to get rid of someone they do not like!

Past employers are often cautious when writing references. There is no legal obligation to provide references on request, but most employers do. References must be accurate. Any fake information, or any omissions that might cause a candidate to fail to be offered a job which she or he would have been offered had the correct or whole information been given, may make a case for damages against the writer. Therefore, some references are so bland that they are of little value. Often, to speak to a referee and ask carefully worded questions will produce more relevant information. Interestingly, it is often what is *not* said that gives the best clues to what to follow up. For this reason, many references are taken over the telephone.

Selecting the Right Person

Selection is based on matching the person with the person specification. It is about gathering as much evidence as possible to help decide whether the candidate is likely to perform the job to the standard required.

The application form will have given a lot of clues; the interviews will have added to these and filled in some gaps; tests may have provided more data and confirmed previously gathered information. It is for the personnel specialist and the relevant manager to analyse all the data for all the applicants and decide which one most closely meets the person specification. Then they must decide if that person will fit in with the work team. If the answer is that an individual meets both criteria, then it is reasonably safe to select that person and offer her or him the job.

ACTIVITY 4.10

Organizations invest large sums of money in plant and machinery. They have sophisticated techniques for evaluating and comparing investments, and decisions to spend capital are usually taken at the highest level of management. On the other hand, decisions to invest in people tend to be taken lower down in the organization, and less time is spent taking the decision.

Calculate the total investment that a firm makes in a person who joins the organization on a salary of £7 000 per annum, receives a pay rise each year of 5 per cent, and remains with the organization for thirty years.

Appointment of Selected Person

In the entire process of recruitment and selection, it is illegal to set any standards, or ask for qualifications, experience or personal qualities that would discriminate unfairly against minority racial groups, the disabled or one sex. Keeping a record of reasons for appointing or rejecting candidates may be important in this regard. As we saw earlier, the law protects such groups.

The selected candidate will be offered the job, and presumably will accept it. At this stage the other candidates should be informed and thanked for their time and interest.

A detailed examination of the contract of employment appears in Chapter Five. It is sufficient to say at this stage, that within eight weeks of starting work, an employee should receive written details of the main terms and conditions of the contract.

If the sales office manager in our Scenario were to follow this process, do you think she would stand a good chance of solving her staffing problem? If you answer 'yes' to this, would you also agree that people are worth looking after once they have joined a company, in the ways discussed in Chapters Two and Three?

Assessment Centres

Many of you seeking a career in a large or medium-sized organization may find that the selection process is carried out by means of an assessment centre. WH Smith and English China Clay are firms that have developed their own very successful assessment centres.

The name is a little deceiving – it is not a place, it is a series of events that are intended to provide evidence of competence in people for selection to the firm or for promotion and transfer within the firm.

Throughout this chapter, the importance of getting the right person in the right job has been stressed, and the weaknesses of traditional methods of selection have been pointed out. The same applies to progression and development of individuals for future roles.

Assessment centres usually last several days during which a group of candidates are exposed to a series of interviews, discussions, tests, written exercises and role plays; and social situations, such as having dinner with the senior managers, dressing for different types of event, socializing with peers and so on.

Each of these is carefully designed to provide relevant evidence about the individual's competence across a wide range of assessment criteria.

You may recognise that many of the criteria have their origins in the things we examined in Chapters Two and Three. For example, evidence is sought relating to skills and competence in:

- Oral and written communication
- Openness in dealings with others
- Sensitivity to other people
- Leadership and persuasiveness
- Decision-making
- Assertiveness
- Planning and organizing
- Analysis and judgement

Besides these, note will be taken on the use of initiative, common sense, energy, ability to 'come back after a fall' and particularly the degree of achievement motivation.

Assessment is usually along a scale, say one to eight, for each of the above criteria. One is dreadful and eight is amazing.

Assessors are carefully trained in observation skills, and are drawn from HR specialists, line managers and senior managers. There is usually one assessor for every two candidates.

The focus of the assessment centre is on people's strengths, in the belief that there is immediate return from exploiting our strengths. Weaknesses that are identified are fed back to the candidate for attention, but not in a critical way. We all have weaknesses.

Firms that use this process, and there are more and more of them, claim that it reduces the incidence of error markedly. Desite its expense and use of time, if results are that good, then it is a wonderful investment.

Conclusion

The success of a business depends very much on getting the right person in each job. It is important that expertise and experience should be deployed to achieve it. Any one of the methods or techniques available for this purpose is not guaranteed to produce accurate results. Therefore, the wise firm will gather information by a variety of means, from application forms to testing, and weigh the evidence very carefully against the person specification before arriving at its decision to appoint. Better still, it will move towards a full assessment centre process.

After appointment, the same thoughtful process continues, so as to help the newcomer to settle down quickly, and to willingly give of her or his best. That is the subject of the next chapter.

Review and Control

Any management activity sets out to achieve an objective. The achievement of the objective provides a means of measuring the cost effectiveness of the manager's actions and decisions. (See Chapter Three.) In the case of recruitment and selection, control can be exercised by asking and answering the following questions:

- Are all job vacancies analysed and considered?
- Are the job descriptions up to date and accurate?
- Are the person specifications a true reflection of the job needs?
- Are the standards we are seeking too high, too low or just right?

- Are the sources of recruitment appropriate; could new, less expensive sources be found?
- Are advertisements receiving sufficient responses?
- Does the application gather the information needed; is it user friendly?
- Are all candidates given equal opportunity?
- Are selection methods producing acceptable results?
- Are people appointed staying with the firm?

Besides these questions which everyone involved in recruitment and selection should ask, H T Graham (formerly Principal Lecturer at Croydon College) and R Bennett (a management consultant) in their book *Human Resources Management* (Macdonald & Evans, 1992) suggest some ratios to help monitor the efficiency of those personnel specialists who recruit on a large scale:

- Average time that job posts are vacant
- $\dfrac{\text{Number of applicants to an advertisement}}{\text{Number of applicants interviewed}}$
- $\dfrac{\text{Number of applicants interviewed}}{\text{Number of job offers made}}$
- $\dfrac{\text{Number of job offers made}}{\text{Number of acceptances}}$
- $\dfrac{\text{Number of new employees}}{\text{Number performing up to standard}}$
- $\dfrac{\text{Number of new employees}}{\text{Number still employed after one year}}$
- $\dfrac{\text{Cost of recruitment and selection}}{\text{Number of new employees}}$
- $\dfrac{\text{Number of vacancies}}{\text{Number filled internally}}$

Graham suggests that these ratios will monitor efficiency – if they rise, efficiency is falling; if they fall, efficiency is improving. This kind of practice, in any organization, public or private, will highlight complacency or incompetence.

KEY POINTS 4.3

- Interviewing is the most commonly used selection method, but it is not particularly reliable

- Testing can be used to add evidence to that gathered at interview. There is a wide range of tests available

- Tests must be valid and reliable. Most tests should be administered and interpreted by specialists

- References are unreliable and are usually available only after selection

has taken place. They can be used to confirm data gathered in other ways

- To minimize the risk of putting an unsuitable person into a job, assessment centres are becoming more popular. These use a variety of methods of gathering data over several days to reduce the incidence of error

- Businesses can monitor the efficiency of their recruitment and selection procedures by using a series of ratios

EXAM PREPARATION

SHORT QUESTIONS

1 List two sources of recruitment a firm might use when attempting to fill a vacancy. (AEB November 1989)

2 List three factors that might influence a firm in planning its manpower needs. (AEB November 1990)

3 Give three possible consequences of unsatisfactory recruitment procedures in a business enterprise. (AEB June 1990)

DATA RESPONSE QUESTIONS

1 Read the information and answer the questions which follow:

A job description

Job Title:	Office Services Supervisor.
Department:	Administration.
Main purpose of job:	To ensure the provision of efficient typing, reprographic and switchboard services to company personnel.
Scope of job:	Responsible to administration manager. Responsible for: five staff, equipment to value of £300,000.

Main duties:

1 To allocate suitable personnel to switchboard, telex, offset printer and photocopiers, as required.

2 To ensure the provision and maintenance of an accurate and efficient typing and reprographic service.

3 To ensure the maintenance and upkeep of equipment.

4 To collate control information on departmental costs, etc.

5 To order stationery, reprographic chemicals and other materials, recording use and maintaining suitable stock levels.

6 To train and assist in selection of new staff.

A person specification
Seven Point Plan

Essential	**Desirable**
Physical make-up Good health record. Acceptable bearing and speech.	Pleasant appearance, bearing and speech.
Attainments GCSE English language. Ability to type, and to operate office machines. Experience of general office work.	GCSE maths or equivalent. RSA II typing. Experience of using simple statistical information and experience of staff supervision.
General Intelligence Above average.	
Special aptitudes Reasonable manual dexterity. Facility with figures.	

Interests	Social activities.

Disposition

Persuasive and influential.	Good degree of acceptability,
Self-reliant.	dependability and self-reliance.
	Steady under pressure.

Circumstances

No special circumstances

(Adapted from *Recruitment and Selection*, ACAS)

(a) Using examples given in the data, distinguish between a Job Description and a Person Specification   (*2 marks*)

(b) How might a firm recruit for this post?   (*4 marks*)

(c) What factors might be important in the conduct of an interview?   (*5 marks*)

(d) The firm has appointed someone to fill the post without interview, what information might they have used in making their selection?   (*6 marks*)

(e) Outline **four** pieces of legislation that might be taken into account during the recruitment and selection process.   (*8 marks*)
(AEB June 1991)

2   A company has recently moved from its traditional site in the centre of a town to a newly opened industrial estate on the outskirts of the town. Following the move there has been a sudden increase in the level of labour turnover.

(a) As personnel manager, write a report to the managing director, using a suitable format (*6 marks*), to cover the following areas.

(i) How labour turnover may be calculated.   (*2 marks*)

(ii) Why the company should be concerned about the recent increase in labour turnover.   (*7 marks*)

(iii) Possible reasons for the increase.   (*6 marks*)

(b) What steps would you, as personnel manager, need to take to establish clearly the nature of the problem?   (*6 marks*)
(AEB June 1987)

ASSIGNMENT

1   Many employees face recruitment difficulties in the 1990s as a result of changes in the structure of the working population. Select a trading organization which employs over 200 people and

(a) examine the effects of these changes on its particular situation

(b) assess its responses to the problems identified in (a).
(SEB June 1992)

ESSAYS

1   In what ways might the functions of a firm's personnel department be affected by falling levels of unemployment?
(AEB June 1989)

2   In the 1990s, population trends will reduce the number of young people entering the workplace. How might a firm respond to this situation?
(AEB June 1991)

CHAPTER 5

Human Resource Development

▷ ▷ **QUESTIONS FOR PREVIEW** ▷ ▷

1 *What is the nature and content of the contract of employment?*

2 *What is the purpose of induction training, and how might it benefit a business?*

3 *Why is health and safety at work important?*

4 *How does performance appraisal motivate people to work more*

effectively, and how is it linked with training?

5 *How should a business handle promotions, demotions and transfers so as to make the best use of the human resource?*

6 *How does organizational culture influence leadership and communication?*

Appointment

IN MOST situations, the person who has been selected as a result of all the evidence is offered the job. In the first instance, this offer may be verbal, and if it receives a verbal acceptance (which is not always certain), a formal, written offer is prepared. Great care is needed to ensure that what is written represents accurately what has been agreed; it will form a part of the contract of employment once it has been accepted. Perhaps this is another indication of the value of a personnel specialist.

It is also usual that the selected person is asked to write a letter of acceptance of the terms set out in the written offer.

Both of these documents may be important in the event of any future disagreement between the two parties. A dilemma occurs if the selected person declines the offer. There is a classic case where a candidate was selected after a stress interview, having come through it with flying colours. (A stress interview is the sort of event you would expect from an interviewer of the second school of thought mentioned in Chapter Four on page 54. His response was that he had no wish to work for an outfit that treated applicants in such an inconsiderate way!

Does the firm then offer the position to the second choice? Or does it start at the beginning again? The answer is 'it depends'. The original questions still apply. Can the person do the job to the standard required, and fit in with the work team? If the answer to both questions is 'Yes', then offer the job to that person. If the answer to either is 'No', then start again or put up with the consequences – as the sales office manager in the Scenario in Chapter Four (page 47).

ACTIVITY 5.1

Assume that you are a personnel specialist who has just experienced the sort of difficulty outlined above – the applicant who most nearly fitted the requirements of the job declined the offer and withdrew, and the remaining candidates were not suitable. Your managing director has called you and told you the vacancy must be filled quickly, and to offer the job to one of the others.

Your task is to prepare a case to put to the managing director that sets out the disadvantages of taking the route he has ordered. You should include the financial as well as the job performance implications. It should also include a short-term solution to the problem whilst you are pursuing a more permanent one. You must *not* in any way cause the MD to lose face, even if he is wrong.

Contract of Employment

Basically, a contract is an agreement between two parties. The essence is *agreement*. This is examined in detail in another title in this series, *The Business Environment*.

A contract of employment, in its broadest sense, is an agreement between an employer and an employee, that the employee will carry out the legitimate work of the employer in return for the payment of wages.

It all stems from the old master/servant relations of long ago. The word 'servant' still survives in some situations – for example, a civil servant, and until about twenty years ago, railway workers were considered as 'railway servants'. The master contracted the servant for services in return for some consideration, in kind and/or in cash. Since then, changes in the culture and laws of our society have complicated the matter considerably (see Figure 5.1).

---

*Figure 5.1 – **Contract of Employment***

Sikh priest not an 'employee'

THE COURT of Appeal rules in *Santokh Sing v Guru Nanak Gurdwara* that a Sikh priest in charge of a temple is not an employee within the statutory meaning of that term. He is employed under a contract for services rather than under a contract of service.

Source: IRS, *Industrial Relations Legal Information Bulletin 407*, 21 August 1992

Today, the legal relationship between employer and employee rests solely upon the contract of employment. But the contract is not a single, written document such as one might find in a commercial transaction. It is a complicated combination of both express and implied terms, and may be verbal as well as written. (An exception to this is a contract for apprenticeship which must be in writing.) We will examine the nature of the contract by first looking at express terms and then implied terms, including some statutory rights.

EXPRESS TERMS

As mentioned earlier in this chapter, the letter of appointment is a very important document. Because it sets out the details of the agreement between the two parties in writing, and is usually accepted in writing, it is the cornerstone of the contract and may be called upon in the event of a dispute between the employer and employee about the nature of the agreement. In the event that a verbal offer and acceptance takes place, the agreement is based upon what was said during the interview and what was agreed during the discussions. Similarly, any additional detail about what the job contains – such as a job description, work rules or employee handbook – may also be called upon to clarify the details of the contract. So what is written, or what is said, which the two parties intend to be binding upon them, is part of the contract of employment.

Fundamental rights of employees were first set

---

*Figure 5.2 – **Extract from EP(C)A 1978***

Employment Protection (Consolidation) Act 1978

1978 CHAPTER 44

An Act to consolidate certain enactments relating to rights of employees arising out of their employment; and certain enactments relating to the insolvency of employers; to industrial tribunals; to recoupment of certain benefits; to conciliation officers; and to the Employment Appeal Tribunal.
[July 1978]

BE IT ENACTED by the Queen's most Excellent Majesty, by and with the advice and consent of the Lords Spiritual and Temporal, and Commons, in this present Parliament assembled, and by the authority of the same, as follows:

PART I
PARTICULARS OF TERMS OF EMPLOYMENT

Written particulars of terms of employment

1.—(1) Not later than thirteen weeks after the beginning of an employee's period of employment with an employer, the employer shall give to the employee a written statement in accordance with the following provisions of this section.

(2) An employer shall in a statement under this section—

(*a*) identify the parties;

(*b*) specify the date when the employment began;

(*c*) state whether any employment with a previous employer counts as part of the employee's continuous period of employment, and, if so, specify the date when the continuous period of employment began.

Source: HMSO. © Parliament

---

out in statute law in 1963 and 1971. Parts of these two Acts were consolidated into The Employment Protection (Consolidation) Act 1978 (EP(C)A 1978) where the right to receive written particulars of the terms of employment is set out (see Figure 5.2, previous page).

Under this Act, most employees were entitled to receive a written statement of the main terms and conditions of their employment within thirteen weeks of starting work. However, in April 1993 an EC Directive reduced this time period to eight weeks.

The written statement must include:

• The employer's and the employee's names
• The date upon which employment began, including any previous employment that is to be considered continuous
• The job title
• The payment scale or rate and the frequency of payment
• Hours of work
• Holiday entitlement and holiday pay
• Sick pay and allowances
• Pension scheme
• The amount of notice to end the contract
• Disciplinary and appeal procedures, and grievance procedures

If an employer fails to provide a written statement, it could result in the employee exercising her or his legal right to ask an Industrial Tribunal to decide what ought to have been in the written statement. This is then imposed upon the employer. Hardly a way to begin a mutually satisfactory and productive relationship! And costly too!

IMPLIED TERMS

If you think about the many eventualities that could occur in the relationship between an employer and an employee, it is probably impossible to predict them all, or to put them in a form that could be scrutinized and agreed by both parties. To overcome the difficulties that this complexity creates, the courts will read into contracts implied terms that are necessary to allow the contract to work.

Some implied terms are reasonably straightforward. For example, all contracts of employment will be deemed to include common law duties, such as the duty of care, each party for the other.

Others are less clear. In the case *Shell UK Ltd v Lostock Garage Ltd 1976,* Lord Denning suggested the test should be:

'Has the law already defined the obligation or the extent of it? If so, let it be followed. If not, look to see what would be reasonable in the general run of such cases, and then say what

the obligation shall be.'

Can you imagine the difficulties this creates for a company in trying to decide whether or not an employee is in breach of an implied term in her or his contract? It is probably beyond the average manager and would require a lawyer to examine case law and advise the firm.

As a general guide, however, there will be implied terms in all contracts relating to the following:

• A duty to act with good faith towards the employer
• A duty of care, each party for the other
• A duty to maintain confidence and trust between the employer and the employee
• A duty of the employer to provide work, and a duty of the employee to carry it out conscientiously
• A duty of the employer to give reasonable support to all employees so that they can carry out their work
• Similarly, the employer has a duty to support its managers in their managerial duties

There will, of course, be some contracts into which particular implied terms are read. For example, a skilled craftsman would be expected to know her or his craft and to practise it to an acceptable standard. This does not only apply to crafts, but to professional people as well. For example, a person claiming to be a marketing specialist would impliedly be expected to know and practise marketing to an acceptable standard.

There will also be firms that have negotiated agreements with unions – collective agreements. These usually relate to wages and conditions of work. Whilst these agreements are not legally binding between the firm and union, once they are incorporated into an employee's contract of employment (for example, your wages will be that agreed with the XYZ trade union during the annual pay negotiations), they are binding upon both the employer and the employee.

Finally, there may be occasions when 'custom and practice' is considered to be an implied term in the contract. Custom and practice is hard to establish and courts do not like it. However, if a practice is reasonable, if it is certain and if it is well known, then it may be deemed part of the contract. The case *Devonald v Rosser 1906* gives us a precedent: 'A custom so universal that no workman could be supposed to have entered into this service without looking to it as part of the contract'.

STATUTORY RIGHTS

In order to clarify matters, and to ensure that employee rights are protected from abuse by employers, Parliament has passed numerous laws in the past thirty years. It is not possible to waive these rights, so they are read into every contract of employment.

There are too many to list here, but the main ones, some of which are subject to length of service – usually two years – are:

- Not to be discriminated against on grounds of race, sex or marriage
- To receive equal pay for work of equal worth
- To receive a written statement of the main terms of the contract
- To be a member of a union or not, as the individual wishes
- To receive notice of termination of employment
- To be paid redundancy payments depending upon age and length of service
- To work under safe conditions
- To receive sick pay
- Not to be unfairly dismissed
- To be given a written reason for dismissal

All of these have been or are being amended or supplemented to meet EC Regulations or Directives. Personnel specialists from now on must take a European perspective.

So a contract of employment is made up of many parts: the offer and acceptance of the job; the written statement of the terms and conditions; any other written and agreed documents; common law duties and rights; other implied terms; collective agreements; sometimes custom and practice; and both UK and EC statutory rights.

Collectively, this has an impact on the business in that the law restrains managers in how they treat their work people. The notion of 'British Justice' applies as much in the workplace as it does in any other walk of life.

ACTIVITY 5.2

Look again at the 'whole person' approach to motivation in Chapter Two and consider how the contract of employment might satisfy some human needs.

Look also at McGregor's Theory X and Theory Y, and consider how a manager holding Theory X assumptions might view a contract of employment differently from a manager holding Theory Y assumptions.

In Chapter Six we shall consider how a contract can be altered to allow a company to grow or change with minimum constraints, at the same time being as fair as possible to those employees affected by the changes. We shall also examine breach of contract by each of the parties, and the right not to be unfairly dismissed.

Induction Training

Induct means: 'To bring in formally; to install in an office'. Induction training is the way of achieving this. The Americans have another word for it. They call it 'orientation' training – that is, helping people to get to know their new surroundings, environment and colleagues.

ACTIVITY 5.3

If you were preparing to welcome someone – say an uncle whom you had never met but who is reputed to be a good guy – who will be staying in your home, who is a complete stranger to the people and the area, what sort of things could you plan to do to help him settle quickly and feel as though he belonged?

KEY POINTS 5.1

- **All the agreements and documents of the recruitment process form the basis for the contract of employment**

- **It is not necessary for the contract to be in writing. It is made up of express and implied terms**

- **A written statement of terms must be given to each employee within eight weeks of starting work. This is not the contract, it is only evidence that a contract exists**

- **All employment laws, and all negotiated agreements between recognized unions and the employer are included in the contract**

Now put yourself in the stranger's position. How would you feel if you were left to sort yourself out and no-one offered a welcoming, friendly, helping hand? Make brief notes of what might be: (a) your immediate reaction (b) your longer-term reaction. Share your reactions with your group, and make a list of the range of reactions that might occur.

Having spent a great deal of time, expertise and money in finding an ideal employee, an employer will want that person to settle quickly and become productive as soon as possible. That will satisify two needs:

- The business will start to benefit as soon as possible from its investment in the employee
- The person will begin to feel useful and a part of the team, and will enjoy a sense of worth

Research shows that the majority of people who leave an organization within six months of joining, make the decision to go within their first few weeks. The effect on the business is twofold:

- The employee does not feel inclined to give of her or his best
- The costs incurred in recruitment and selection

have been wasted and further expenditure will be necessary to put it right

If in Activity 5.3 above you considered details such as where he will hang his coat, preparing his room and having it ready for him, showing him where the amenities are, deciding who to introduce him to immediately (that is, the people most likely to be his main contacts), then you were thinking good induction strategy. You might even introduce him to the dog in such a way that the dog will accept him and not eat him, thereby keeping him safe. All these efforts will be rewarded when your Uncle says: 'I'm glad I came. You've made me feel at home. Thank you. I'd like to do something for you in return.'

To help new employees settle quickly they need to know three things:

- How their basic needs will be met?
- How their security needs will be met?
- How their belonging needs will be met?

Later on they can be introduced to things from wider fields relating to their status and self-fulfilment needs. In the first few hours and days, they need these three things to survive comfortably.

The answers to the following three questions will help in the design of a progressive induction programme:

- What must they know?
- What should they know?
- What could they know?

From the answers will come the priorities for the induction training programme.

It is probable that among the essential data that the new employee will need immediately are answers to the following questions:

- Where is my territory? Where do I hang my coat? Where do I eat/drink? Where do I work? Where do I socialize? Where is my private space? (Maslow's basic needs)
- When do I get paid? How do I get paid? How much will I be paid? (Maslow's basic needs)
- Who do I work for? Who do I work with? What is expected of me? (Maslow's belonging needs)
- What rules must I obey? How safe am I? Who do I turn to for help? Who looks after my interests? (Maslow's security needs)

The way each business designs the programme is entirely up to them; there is no formula that will meet all needs. Each will be influenced by their culture and beliefs about how employees should be treated.

Once a new employee feels that these lower needs are being met, she or he will be ready to listen to those things that the firm wants them to know, including:

---

*Figure 5.3 – **ACAS Stresses Why Good Induction is Important***

WHY IS IT IMPORTANT?

Starting a new job is an anxious time for anyone. No matter how eagerly a recruit looks forward to a new job, there is bound to be concern about some aspects of it.

Will the recruit:
    get on with fellow workers
    make a good impression with the boss
    get to know the way about the place of
      work
    know what to do
    look silly by making mistakes?

Helping a new employee to settle down quickly is not just a question of kindness – it also makes good business sense and benefits the organisation as a whole. It is just as important to the small as to the large company. Whatever the job, induction will be beneficial to the individual and the company. Good induction need not be costly in time or money, but poor or forgotten induction can prove to be expensive.

Source: ACAS, Booklet No 7, Introduction of New Employees

- The organization's history and policies
- The full range of products or services
- The total organization: what goes on elsewhere
- How jobs and departments relate to one another
- Training policy, opportunities for promotion, personal development
- Employee benefits, personnel services, recreational facilities and so on

The timing and pace of an induction programme is important. It is essential to keep the objectives clearly in mind all the time: to settle the new employee in the job as quickly as possible and help them to become productive as soon as possible.

ACTIVITY 5.4

Do you recall your first day at your present school or college? What was it like? How did you feel? Identify if you can, any special efforts made to welcome you and help you to settle into your course of study.

Is there anything that you think might have been done that would have helped? Was there anything that was done that you now feel should not have been done? Why?

When you have thought it through, design a short induction programme for next year's intake of new students. Show how it would help new students settle into their course of study quickly, and become productive in terms of their learning.

Health, Safety and Welfare at Work

No doubt, an early topic in any induction programme would be health, safety and welfare. As we mentioned earlier in this chapter, all employers have a common law duty to look after the health and safety of all their workers – wherever they work and whatever they do.

Health relates to the general condition of body and mind.

Safety relates to freedom from danger or risk of injury.

Welfare relates to all those things provided by employers to ensure the well-being of their employees.

ACTIVITY 5.5

Identify one feature in your school or college that may be detrimental to health. For example, is the lighting bright enough for you to read without eyestrain? Are there any safety hazards in or outside the buildings – for example, holes in the footpaths that could cause a fall? What welfare facilities are there – for example, toilets, first-aid room? Why should an organization like your school or college worry about such dangers?

What Causes Accidents and Ill Health at Work?

There is a temptation to answer 'careless employees'. But to be careless implies a need to be careful. One only needs to be careful if there is a risk of injury; if there is no risk, there is no need to be careful.

So it is what the risk relates to – the hazard – that causes accidents; employees are the potential victims. In any case, if fumes from a degreaser or a paint shop can cause lung damage, is it reasonable to describe someone as careless for breathing? Also is it reasonable to say that an injured employee 'was not paying attention'? How long can you concentrate for? Is it reasonable to expect a person to concentrate throughout an eight-hour working day? No. We must look more deeply for the causes than simply to blame the victims.

KEY POINTS 5.2

- **Induction training settles the newcomer into the organization and makes her or him feel wanted and valued**

- **Its purpose is to make the newcomer productive and able to contribute as quickly as possible**

- **Each business will design its induction programme to suit its own needs. It can use Maslow's hierarchy as a guide to the content of the initial part of training**

*Figure 5.4 – **Accidents at Work***

Cormorant Memorial Service

A MEMORIAL service for the eleven people who died as the result of the helicopter incident near the Shell Cormorant Alpha platform 70 miles east of Shetland on Saturday 14 March was held in the Kirk of St Nicholas in Aberdeen on 3 April 1992.

Six of our colleagues died and five other men also lost their lives, three of them were from subcontractors of Press, Bet Plant Services, BPS. The other two being the Bristow's co-pilot and subcontractor of McDermotts. Our thoughts go out to their family, their friends and their colleagues.

As soon as the news was heard in Aberdeen, Press made sure that all the families of those who lost their lives were visited by a member of the management team and each family was given a personal contact within Press to whom they could turn to if the need arose.

General Manager's Comments

Both myself and my fellow directors were absolutely devastated by the tragic helicopter incident in the Cormorant field on 14 March that claimed a total of 11 lives, six of whom were colleagues of ours.

Our thoughts go out to the loved ones and close friends of those who died. Our company has done, and will continue to do, all it can to aid and comfort them as they struggle to come to terms with their terrible loss.

The company is progressing the insurance claims as a matter of urgency and the setting up of the Cormorant Trust Fund is a tangible expression of our personal support for the families. But money can in no way compensate them for their loss.

We have not forgotten our two survivors – we are providing help and support to them and their families to see them through the aftermath of an horrific ordeal.

The incident was a cruel reminder – if one was needed – of the harsh environment in which we work. We can never be too careful; never become complacent about the dangers; we must always have a high safety awareness.

We must dedicate ourselves to strive even more to ensure the safest possible working conditions for ourselves and everyone offshore so that loss of life – or even simple injury – becomes a thing of the past.

MIKE STRAUGHEN General Manager

Source: AMEC Offshore Developments Ltd's newsletter, *Inpress,* April 1992

In the late 1960s and early 1970s, as a result mainly of trade union pressure, a committee under the chairmanship of Lord Robens examined this question most thoroughly. *The Robens Report* is full of tables and statistics that highlighted a need to improve safety in British industry. It is well worth a look if your library has a copy.

Despite the fact that various Factory Acts had been enacted since the 1830s (the latest being 1961), and an Offices Shops and Railway Premises Act 1963 was in force, accidents and ill health resulting from work were horrifyingly high. About twenty people were being killed at work each week. Ten thousand were being injured each week.

Think of the suffering and distress caused to the victims, their dependants and their relatives. Think of the cost to the Health Service, insurance companies and the state. Think of the effect on the victim's colleagues, of losing a workmate and having to continue working in the unsafe environment. Figure 5.4 highlights these points.

Accidents resulted in over 20 million working days per year being lost to British industry. There are no figures available for the cost of these tragedies, but it must be many, many millions of pounds.

Assuming that the average job requires a person to work forty-seven weeks a year, five days each week, a total of 235 days:

$$\frac{20\,000\,000}{235} = 85\,106$$

that is the equivalent of 85 106 people's work lost through accidents every year. The national average income is about £13 000 per year. The wage cost would therefore be £1.1 billion.

You can obtain up-to-date figures from your Health and Safety Executive Regional Office – it will be in the telephone directory.

Besides the morality of making people work unprotected amidst hazards, it is economically unsound. Safety is an important management issue that requires a positive approach and an active policy.

ACTIVITY 5.6

What are the main businesses in your area? You can obtain an analysis of occupations from your local government Economic Development Officer free of charge. Other information is available from your local Job Centre and your local Training and Enterprise Council (TEC).

What are the working conditions like in these businesses? Are they clean or dirty? Is there a lot of noise or dust or fumes? Are people working at heights, below ground or in very cramped, confined spaces? Are chemicals used, or radiation, or toxic substances? Are people using VDU screens or photocopiers? Parents, relatives and friends are useful sources of this kind of information.

When you have determined what conditions may be like, think about the hazards that could be present in the workplace. If possible, ask the personnel officer from a local firm to show you their 'Safety Policy' and arrange a visit to the workplace to see how it works. Your school or college will have a 'Safety Policy'. Ask to see it and have it explained to you.

*Figure 5.5 – **Safety at Work***

Work starts on safety

A PUBLIC awareness campaign has been launched to reduce the toll of accidents and injuries at work.

Accidents currently cost the European Community Ecu20 Billion a year in compensation payments alone. Billions more are lost in reduced productivity.

European Year of Safety, Hygiene and Health at Work aims to reduce the volume of accidents and occupational illnesses which affect ten million workers in the EC every year.

The European Commission says the campaign will focus on reducing air pollution and improving safety and general well-being.

It will concentrate on workers perceived to be at risk, such as young trainees, those working in small businesses and people in high-risk sectors. This last group includes construction, farming and fishing.

A Eurobarometer poll for the Commission found that 42 per cent of employees feel their health is, or could be, affected by their work, and 40 per cent fear they run the risk of accidents at their work place.

A massive 94 per cent of those poled were in favour of common EC legislation on health and safety.

However, the Commission still faces staunch opposition from some countries, including Britain, over plans enshrined in its 1989 Social Charter.

That document included a whole raft of new legislation on health, safety, social and labour legislation.

Source: European, 19-25 March 1992

Health and Safety at Work Act 1974 (HSWA 1974)

As a result of the *Robens Report*, the government of the time decided that it could no longer be left to employers to exercise their common law duties of care. Moreover, the current legislation was not doing its job – the figures showed that it did not adequately protect employees. New legislation was needed to enforce standards for all employers to follow.

The HSWA 1974 was the result. The function of this Act was to protect everyone at work, wherever they worked and whatever their job. It also offered some protection to other people (for example, visitors to a workplace), who might be affected by the actions of the people at work.

The HSWA 1974 is an enabling act. Briefly, this means it gives power to the Secretary of State for Employment to make Regulations relating to health and safety without having to pass a new Act of Parliament. She or he prepares a Regulation and places it before Parliament for a specified length of time. During that period, any Member of Parliament can ask questions about it. After that period of time, if there have been no objections to it, it becomes a Regulation under the Act, and as such, has the same weight as the Act itself. Over 140 such Regulations have been passed since 1974.

Section 2(1) of HSWA 1974 says:

> 'It shall be the duty of every employer to ensure, so far as is reasonably practical, the health, safety, and welfare at work of all his employees and trainees.'

Section 2(2) goes on to say:

> 'Without prejudice to the generality of an employer's duty under the preceding subsection, . . .'

There can be no doubt in this wording that the law clearly puts the employer at the centre stage as far as health and safety at work is concerned. The phrase 'as far as is reasonably practical' means that an employer, having evaluated the risk and calculated the costs of eliminating it, makes a judgement: Is the risk high enough to warrant that expenditure? In the event of an accident, a court may ask to see the evaluation and the cost calculation to decide if the employer acted reasonably. If a solution is 'practical', a court would normally expect the employer to use it.

But it does not stop there.

The HSWA sets out to ensure that whoever creates the hazard is responsible for the safety of the people the hazard puts at risk. People who may create hazards include designers of equipment and substances, manufacturers (or importers of machines and substances from overseas), installers, employers, managers, supervisors, and employees.

For example, a designer of a bacon slicer is required by the HSWA 1974 to ensure that safety features are included in the original design – guards to keep people's fingers away from the blade and electrical cut-out switches, for example. The manufacturer must build the bacon slicer as specified by the designer, and include all the safety features. The servicing manual and the user manual should give clear instructions about how to use it and clean it safely. Businesses which use bacon slicers must buy only equipment that is as safe as is reasonably practicable, and have it installed correctly, with safety considerations given a high priority. Managers must design jobs involving the use of the bacon slicer in such a way as to ensure that there is no risk to the people using it. They must be trained in its safe operation, and the supervisor must ensure that the staff always follow safe practices.

The Act has as its theme, that safety is everyone's responsibility, and co-operation and consultation are the keys.

There are sweeping powers given to the Health and Safety Inspectorate to enforce the provisions of the Act, and businesses that are prosecuted and found guilty can receive heavy fines. It is possible in certain circumstances, for individual managers and supervisors to be fined, or in extreme cases, to be sent to prison.

Trade unions have the right to appoint their own safety representatives in workplaces where they are recognized, and to call for the setting up of a safety committee. The committee is constituted under the Safety Representatives and Safety Committees Regulations 1977, and is not an employer-controlled body. Safety representatives have the right to inspect the workplace regularly and report any hazards or potential hazards to management for action. They have a right to be consulted on matters of health, safety and welfare, but that does not lessen management's overall responsibility.

The HSWA 1974 applies only to employees, not consumers. Consumer protection is provided under different legislation, and is discussed in Chapter Nine.

Some employers might argue that having to include safety in their decisions about work methods, equipment and substances puts them at a competitive disadvantage. Besides the moral weakness of this arguement, all countries in the EC and most countries in the developed world have to abide by similar laws.

Each of us has to decide for ourselves the extent to which putting other people at risk is 'justified'. It is probably impossible to make any job completely safe and healthy. An interesting issue relates to management style which was discussed briefly in Chapter Three. If the manager puts her or his staff under pressure to the extent that they suffer from stress (a dangerous health hazard), is that permissible? Or do you think that managers should be held accountable for such matters?

The law is quite clear. Employers have a statutory duty to ensure the health, safety and welfare of all their employees.

ACTIVITY 5.7

Have you ever had the opportunity of looking at an Act of Parliament? It is not as daunting as you might fear. The Health and Safety at Work Act 1974 is an excellent example of a well laid out report and is not full of legal jargon. If you can, get a copy from your library, find Section 2, headed 'Duties of Employer to Employees'. Read it down to Section 3 and list all the things that the law requires of employers. Sections 3, 4, 5 and 6 refer to the other parties mentioned above. Section 7 relates to duties of employees. List their duties. Now draw some conclusion as to the scope of the law. In the main, who does the law consider the most responsible for the health and safety of employees? Why?

ENFORCEMENT OF HSWA

There would be little point in having such an extensive piece of legislation if there was no-one to ensure that employers and others obeyed it. The people who police this Act are the Health and Safety Inspectors. They receive their power under Section 20 of the Act and they can take action which is intended to prevent accidents and ill health resulting from work.

There is little point in only acting after an accident when someone has been injured. Health and Safety Inspectors are very experienced and expert and they take a very positive attitude to safety. It is not their primary intention to prosecute employers; they would sooner work in co-operation and ensure that accidents do not occur.

However, if they visit a workplace and find a situation that is unsatisfactory, they can immediately take action to have it rectified. This action can be of two types:

- They can issue an *improvement notice* which calls upon the employer to correct the unsatisfactory matter within a specified time
- Where a situation, in the opinion of the inspector, is so dangerous as to risk imminent danger to health or safety, she or he can issue a *prohibition notice* ordering the unsafe practice to cease forthwith

Under Section 26 of the Act, the inspector can order something in the above category to be seized and rendered harmless. Such powers are to be welcomed in view of the Robens findings. However, there are too few inspectors to visit all businesses regularly and some businesses will not see an inspector from one year-end to the next. It is said that some businesses will receive only one visit every five years.

One regulation requires employers and self-employed people to report to the inspectors by the quickest possible means, any serious injury caused by an accident at work. There is a long list of injuries to which this applies. In some cases, even if no-one is injured, the inspectors must be informed. An example of this would be a crane toppling over or a lift crashing.

Every business must make available an Accident Book in which anyone can record any accident or injury to any person. This can range from a cut finger to an injured back. One of the purposes of these records is to make factual information available to managers and safety representatives where they exist, so as to permit accountability relating to this important aspect of manager's responsibility for their employees.

Control of Substances Hazardous to Health (COSHH) Regulations 1988

As modern technology is applied in factories, shops and offices, more and more sophisticated processes are being introduced. It is hard to keep up with them all. The worry is that some of the substances introduced will not have been tested for their effect on people's health. It is said that there are over 4 000 substances used by various industries that are carcinogenic – that is, they can cause cancer. And it does not have to be heavy industry or chemical manufacturers. For example, some photocopiers can emit ozone, carbon monoxide, nitrogen oxide or selenium. Some of these, particularly in combination with other substances, can be toxic and should not be inhaled. The COSHH Regulations were brought in to deal

with this ongoing and growing danger.

COSHH applies to all substances used in an organization that are toxic, harmful, corrosive or irritant, whether they are single substances, compounds or mixtures. It also applies to micro-organisms, many more of which are appearing in industrial processes.

Every business is obliged to undertake a comprehensive assessment of the effects on employees of all the substances used anywhere in the organization for any purpose. It ranges from a sophisticated catalyst in a blast furnace to a hair dye in a hairdresser's salon. The assessment must be recorded in a register. This is to be an ongoing assessment and must not become out of date – any new substances must be added to the register as they come into use.

Employers are obliged to eliminate or minimize any risk to the people who come into contact with the substances or their outputs.

*Figure 5.6 – **COSHH***

EC State of Play

Article 118A CARCINOGENS
(Ref Directive 90/394/EEC)

Aim:
On the protection of workers from the risks related to exposure to carcinogens at work.

UK Implications
There have been no fundamental disagreements with the proposals. The proposals will amend the COSHH Regulations to give greater emphasis on the prevention of exposure to carcinogens at work by means of substitution and enclosed systems of work. COSHH assessments would have to be regularly reviewed. Health surveillance records would have to be maintained for 40, rather than 30 years. The Directive provides for carcinogens and for substances classified 'R45' ('may cause cancer') to be automatically subject to its provisions. Otherwise, most of the provisions are covered by the COSHH Regulations. The Health & Safety Commission's (HSC) carcinogens code lists more substances than those specified in the Directive. Main requirements of the Directive include: assessment of the risk of exposure; replacement of carcinogen with a harmless or less dangerous substance, or reduction of risk to as low a level as possible; emergency procedures; monitoring and health surveillance; information and training provision.

Source: IRS, Health and Safety Information Bulletin 198, June 1992

They should do this by keeping people away from the hazard – perhaps by using engineering controls. If this is not reasonably practical, they should provide the employee with suitable protective equipment that will adequately limit their exposure to the substance. Thereafter, the employer is required to monitor the workplace to ensure that precautions are effective, and to exercise control over the processes to keep them safe. Certain maximum exposure limits have to be observed, and people working with substances listed in Schedule 5 of COSHH are required to be examined by a doctor appointed for the purpose at least once every year.

In all matters of health and safety, the employer is obliged by law to ensure that safety equipment, protective measures and protective clothing are maintained in good working order. The cost of all the equipment that they are legally obliged to provide must be borne by the employer, as must be the cost of maintenance and replacement.

Implications for Businesses

The implications of all this for a business are quite far reaching. To meet its moral and legal obligations, the business will incur costs that do not add value to its products or services. Most businesses will attempt to keep these costs as low as possible – some might even cut corners on the basis that 'it will never happen to us'.

If an accident does occur, there might well be adverse publicity that could affect the firm's standing in the community; it might find it harder to recruit good quality staff, and to keep them. It could end up in court and face heavy fines. The managers concerned may suffer the stress and worry of having to give evidence, and perhaps be shown as negligent. A good barrister can be a formidable interrogator. Civil action may be taken by an injured person who could claim large sums in damages. Most businesses are required by the Employers' Liability (Compulsory Insurance) Act 1969 to insure against liability for

---

*Figure 5.7 – **Hazardous Substances***

Mexican gas disaster

RESCUE workers and sniffer dogs continued their search for more victims from Wednesday's deadly gas explosion as an eerie calm descended on the streets of Guadalajara yesterday.

Reports on the casualties varied greatly, but Mexican Red Cross officials had put the number of dead at more than 200 by yesterday morning, mainly women and children, and said there could be as many as 1 000.

Thousands more were injured when the Reforma district of the city was rocked by a series of at least 20 explosions, bringing down one- and two-storey buildings and small shops in a 30-block area. Almost 20 blocks were reduced to rubble, apparently when hexane gas trapped in a sewer ignited, sending cars flying into the air and carving a 20ft crater the length of the street.

At a meeting at City Hall yesterday morning, local officials warned that there was still a danger of more explosions. The smell of gas continued to linger in the air. In some parts of the city the odour was so strong that rescue efforts had to be put off, and many bodies could still be buried there.

The cause of the explosion, meanwhile, still remained a mystery yesterday, and people were demanding to know how the tragedy was allowed to happen. Local officials say that hexane gas, a hydrocarbon used as a solvent in food processing, was mistakenly leaked into the sewerage system's storm drains.

Industries are not obliged to install their own waste disposal systems, so dangerous substances can find their way into the main drains. The law on this is about to be changed, but it has come too late for Guadalajara.

Officials of the state-owned oil company, Pemex, are also being investigated. But some people have already expressed fears that any inquiry will be kept secret and Wednesday's gas explosions are a prelude to other accidents waiting to happen unless industrial safety standards are enforced.

Pemex has been involved in several past explosions in Mexico, including three during the 1980s. In 1984, a gas explosion in San Juan Ixhuatepec just outide Mexico City, killed more than 500 people and forced the evacuation of 200 000.

Pemex has issued a statement, however, saying that the source of the gas leak was a privately-owned cooking oil factory, La Central.

According to local residents, gas could be detected in the air as early as Tuesday morning. Hours later, a series of explosions with the force of a powerful earthquake was to rock the neighbourhood.

President Carlos Salinas de Gortari, who arrived in the city on Wednesday night, has ordered the Attorney-General to lead an inquiry and bring criminal charges if necessary.

Source: Independent, 24 April 1992

injuries or diseases suffered by employees as a result of their work. Should such a claim be successful, it is probable that the insurance premium will go up for that employer.

Safe working should be a part of the organization's culture, and any person, at whatever level, who causes the standards to slip should be subject to the firm's disciplinary procedures.

The Health and Safety Inspectors would not look kindly upon a management which blamed employees for being unsafe. The courts have always taken the view that the person controlling the resources is answerable for their use, and many more managers are prosecuted and found 'guilty' than work people.

EC Directives

The UK must now comply with all the EC standards for health and safety at work. At the beginning of 1993, seven Health and Safety Directives had been agreed which had to be implemented by all twelve member states. Some amendments to UK legislation was needed to meet EC requirements, mainly in the area of prevention of accidents and ill health through the prior analysis of risks and workplace design.

All EC countries will be working within the same constraints, and no competitive advantage should be gained by any member.

HIV, AIDS and Work

People with Human Immune Deficiency Virus (HIV) are capable of continuing work for many years. The disease cannot be spread by social or work contact and there is no need for precautions in normal circumstances.

Some people whose job may involve handling blood will have very special precautions in place, as will police, firemen, ambulance staff, undertakers and so on.

Performance Appraisal

The dictionary definition of 'appraisal' is: 'an assessment of the worth or value of a person or thing'. Performance appraisal could be defined as a judgement of the worth or value of a person's performance. Think of the motivational impact of 'being valued'.

ACTIVITY 5.8

How do you feel about your work or your sporting skills being 'judged'? If it causes you concern, what is it that actually concerns you? If you welcome it, what is it that happens which you find valuable?

If you fall into the 'concerned' category, find a colleague who falls into the 'valued' category and share your feelings about it. Having done this, are there ways in which 'being judged' becomes more acceptable than other ways? List the things which would make it acceptable.

Appraisal is a formal process of monitoring and measuring people's performance against agreed work standards. It is described as 'formal' because we are appraising everyone and everything around us informally all the time.

For example, you may say: 'Pat is best at taking corners, so Pat will take all corners in the match this afternoon'. That is a judgement about Pat's performance.

Such appraisals are *ad hoc*. They happen every day and are a part of the rich fabric of life. Unfortunately, we are influenced in our everyday judgements by subjective issues and biases, such as our liking for the person, whether our intention is to help them or condemn them, and whether our knowledge of their performance is accurate and complete or not. Some of these judgements would be difficult to support with hard evidence.

KEY POINTS 5.3

- **Hazards cause accidents; people are the victims**

- **Businesses have to comply with a common law duty of care, statute law and EC Directives in matters of health and safety**

- **All businesses in Western Europe, and most of the industrial world, have similar obligations**

- **Everyone who causes hazards, from designer to user, is constrained by the law, which is constantly updated by regulations**

- **Enforcement is by the Health and Safety Inspectorate, who have powers to prevent accidents and to prosecute companies and individuals**

That is why a formal appraisal is useful; one which has been planned by both the manager and the employee. It should be a discussion based on the *facts* relating to a person's performance over a realistic period – say, one year. Most of all, it must be fair, and must not be used as a threat to a person's security.

You will recall that there were two questions that had to be answered at recruitment and selection: could the person do the job to the required standard, and would the person fit in with the work team? The formal appraisal process will give managers some feedback about the selections they make. Do the people they selected come up to expectations against both criteria?

Appraisal also helps with HR planning. A clear knowledge of the abilities and potential of the present staff will be part of the input.

The greatest benefit of appraisal, however, is that it allows people's strengths to be recognized and built upon, and their shortcomings to be overcome through education, training and development.

Some business managers also use appraisal as a means of deciding what pay awards to give on the grounds of merit. This is a controversial issue because very few people are wholly responsible for their job performance. In some jobs, the quality of performance may rest mainly on external influences, or the efficiency of management, or the adequacy of resourcing. The Volvo Case Study in Chapter Two is a good example, where the company recognized this and paid merit awards to the whole group rather than to isolated individuals.

The article in Figure 5.8 should be read with this thought in mind, and you should use your knowledge of appraisal *and* teaching to judge whether the teachers' argument is well founded.

Appraisal Interviews

An organization uses a system of appraisal or performance review that suits its needs; there is no one correct way of structuring a formal performance appraisal scheme. Most take the form of

---

*Figure 5.8 – **Performance Appraisal***

Teachers at odds on appraisal policy

DELEGATES at the National of Union Teachers' conference in Blackpool were poised to deprive the union of a clear policy on teacher appraisal after an inconclusive debate yesterday.

Under new rules teachers will have to be appraised every two years starting in September, with each teacher having been appraised for the first time by September 1994. At present appraisal records cannot be used directly to determine pay, promotion or disciplinary decisions, but the rules allow schools to take appraisal records into account.

Next year, however, the Teachers' Pay Review Body has promised to deliver a plan for performance-related pay which is likely to include appraisal. The union's position is widely seen as crucial, because the Government, and the Teachers' Pay Review Body are certain to press ahead with these plans to link individual teachers' performance to their pay.

All the teacher unions support appraisal, but only for the purpose of professional development. They are firmly opposed to any direct link being made with pay, promotion and discipline.

Left-wing delegates at yesterday's conference proposed a ballot of NUT members on non-cooperation with any appraisal schemes unless the appraisal record became the teacher's sole property and teachers had complete choice over the person making the appraisal. This is not the case with the appraisal schemes now being put into practice.

John Berry, from Stevenage, Hertfordshire, said that appraisal would be used by 'unscrupulous headteachers, desperate governors and authorities desperate to lose jobs'. Shaun Doherty, from Islington, north London, argued that the Government would use appraisal 'to make individual teachers the scapegoats for failures of the system'. The NUT executive attempted to amend the proposal, arguing that a non-cooperation policy would put it out of step with other teaching unions, and expose individual NUT members to disciplinary action for refusing to take part in appraisal without having the protection of their colleagues. The NUT executive argued that the union should stick to its existing policy of taking 'appropriate measures up to and including industrial action to support and defend members' in areas where unacceptable appraisal schemes are imposed.

Malcolm Horne, for the executive, said that the union's policy on appraisal had ensured that no local authorities had yet introduced unacceptable appraisal schemes. But he warned that a non-cooperation tactic would make martyrs of some teachers, 'pave the road to hell for our members', and isolate the NUT from its allies.

Source: Independent, 20 April 1992

an interview between the person being appraised – the appraisee – and that person's manager – the appraiser.

An appraisal interview should be a mutual exchange of views about actual job performance and how future performance may be improved: even good performances can be made better.

ACTIVITY 5.9

Consider the sort of relationship with your teacher that would permit an open and honest discussion about your performance? If the teacher was a fierce authoritarian, would you be willing to listen to advice? How would your feelings differ if the teacher was a good listener and interested in your point of view?

If you feel inhibited by the authoritarian, and feel open with the listener, you can judge how effective each would be as an appraisal interviewer. Would you be able to state pride in your strengths and admit your weaknesses to an authoritarian?

Organization culture and leadership style will be determinants of how successful or otherwise an appraisal scheme might be.

APPRAISAL METHODS

Although there are many different variations of appraisal methods, they can be placed into three main types: ranking, grading and rating.

a Ranking

This is a simple and crude method of appraisal. The appraiser is required to place each person who works for her or him in rank order, with the 'best' at the top and the 'least good' at the bottom. Its virtue is that it is easy to do and seems to be reasonably accurate. Several appraisers who each know the group, working independently, will reach a similar conclusion. But it does not provide much information. How much better is the 'best' from the 'least good'? Is the 'best' ready for promotion? How will the individuals in the group perform in the future? What training needs are exposed? Should one person be paid more than others, and if so, how much? None of these questions would be answered by this method.

b Grading

Several key job criteria are chosen for a particular group of staff. For example: quantity of work produced to standard; quality of work after rejects and reworks; use of time; planning ability; co-operation with supervisor; relationships with colleagues; attendance or absences and so on.

Each appraisee is graded against each of these criteria along a four or five-point dimension – for example:

1   Awful
2   Not very good
3   Good
4   Very good
5   Excellent

A problem with this method is that managers who 'want to be liked', (McClelland's Affiliation need in Chapter Two) will tend to overstate people's performance. They may be tempted to designate everyone who works for them 'good' or above, whether it is accurate or not. The tendency is called 'centring'. To avoid centring, some appraisal systems require the manager to distribute all five points on each dimension among her or his staff. For example, poor 10 per cent, not very good 20 per cent, good 40 per cent, very good 20 per cent, excellent 10 per cent. This is intended to cause managers to think objectively about the relative performance of staff and not to take an easy way out. The Civil Service appraisal system uses a four-point grading scale to make centring impossible.

Grading may indicate some areas of training need, and may suggest that some staff should get a better pay rise than others, but it is still very difficult to quantify how much the 'best' is better than the 'least good'.

c Rating

This is the most common method used. It requires the appraiser to make a choice of one from five statements relating to job criteria and personal characteristics for each individual member of her or his staff, along the following lines:

- Jumps three-metre wall in one bound
- Requires run at three-metre wall, then jumps it
- Scrambles over three-metre wall after several attempts
- Fails to clear three-metre wall
- Misses wall

This system helps the appraiser to be more definite in the assessment of each criterion, although it would be difficult to claim and prove that it is more accurate. However, it should provide enough information to answer the three questions relating to performance, pay and prospects.

All of these methods fail to exploit the motivational potential of appraisal. In each case it is quite possible that the appraisee may not agree to the decisions of the appraiser – that can actually create low morale.

ACTIVITY 5.10

Review Herzberg's motivators (Chapter Two). How might each of these appraisal methods give people a sense of achievement and recognition? If you find that it is unlikely, how could the method be modified for it to be possible?

PROBLEM-SOLVING APPROACH

Appraisal is most productive when the appraisee feels that she or he has been involved, listened to and allowed to influence the decisions about future actions and training. This is not dissimilar from a selection interview where the candidate is encouraged to do most of the talking. Only, in this case, the appraisee is encouraged to talk openly about her or his actual performance in the job.

Questions like: 'What pleased you most about your work this year?' will get the appraisee talking about her or his own achievements, strengths, weaknesses, ambitions, training needs and so on.

There will be a need for the appraiser to bring things that are not up to standard to the attention of the appraisee, but not in a threatening way, more in a problem-solving way – always with the offer of help and support.

This creates a sense of responsibility in appraisees, in that they are active in recognizing their own achievements, proposing how they can improve their performance, choosing or agreeing training programmes that will build on their strengths and tackle their weaknesses, and taking more ownership of their jobs. If you refer again to Herzberg in Chapter Two, you will see how these factors meet people's higher needs, make their work more satisfying and create a culture where people can grow and give of their best.

Appraisers

Who should appraise whom? It is most common that people are appraised by their immediate boss. However, there are some who feel that the closeness of the two can create anomalies. Besides, some managers feel that they are appraising their staff all the time and fail to see any advantage in one formal effort once a year. Many managers do not have the social skills nor the time to conduct problem-solving interviews, so they revert to an annual pantomime approach, which brings appraisal into disrepute.

However, those who treat it as a logical conclusion and drawing together of all the mini-appraisals that have been going on all year, can put it to good use in improving performance in their departments.

Self-Appraisal

One possible solution to this problem is self-appraisal. Each member of staff completes a prescribed form, which requires them to rate different aspects of their own work relative to other aspects of their own work. That is, they consider their own strong points and weak points without any reference to colleagues or standards. It seems that individuals do this quite objectively, although some will be reticent if they think their self-appraisal will become public in any way.

In some self-appraisal schemes, this form is compared to a similar form completed by the manager, and the differences between the two are the subject of a discussion. The aim is that agreement is reached, but if it is not, each signs that they agree to disagree.

In many schemes, appraisal forms are seen and signed by the manager's boss. The boss will see all the other managers's appraisal forms as well,

KEY POINTS 5.4

- **Appraisal is a formal judgement about a person's performance. It is concerned with strengths more than weaknesses**

- **Appraisal interviews are a two-way discussion between the appraiser and appraisee based on facts relating to a whole appraisal period, and conducted fairly**

- **There are three main types of appraisal: ranking, grading and rating. None is perfect. A problem-solving approach is the most motivational, though it is more demanding of the appraiser than the others**

- **Appraisal should result in an agreed plan for the next period – usually twelve months – with performance targets and training needs stated clearly** so it gives a little bit of quality control; but mostly, it keeps the boss informed and offers approval for the process from the top.

There are a few schemes where the appraisal is completed by the peer group, and others where the subordinates appraise their managers. There is insufficient data to establish their value, and it is unlikely that either will ever become popular.

Appraisal is necessary to keep an 'asset register' of the organization's human resource. It is a very inexact process, and the personnel specialist has a duty to make the scheme as fair and as just as possible. It could be a great motivator, or it might be a cause of lowered morale. It depends to a large extent upon the nature of the organization's culture.

Training

If appraisal identifies areas where a person could build on strengths and correct weaknesses, then training is one way of achieving the desired outcomes.

Training is a method of changing behaviour. If new technology requires a change in the way people operate, this change can be brought about by training so that operators learn how to use the new technology. If someone is performing a job in an unsatisfactory manner (unwanted behaviour) training is one way of changing that to a satisfactory manner (desired behaviour). If someone has potential, training will help them to realize their potential.

Learning takes place all the time, whether we are conscious of it or not: it is not the exclusive product of school or of formal teaching. Sir Richard Livingstone said that people who assume that learning stops after school 'behave like people who would try to give their children in a week all the food they need for a year: a method which might seem to save time and trouble but would not improve digestion, efficiency or health'.

Who Needs Training?

Newcomers to the organization, whose first need is for induction training, are the most obvious candidates. People like apprentices, trainee managers or transferees to different jobs will have clear training needs which can be met by conventional training methods.

But based upon the above definition, anyone in an organization who has to respond to changes, however those changes arise, will need to undertake some form of behaviour modification. This may be brought about by a formal training programme, some self study or experimentation. In the extreme case, it may be that trial and error results in the learning that is needed – one hopes that the error element is not too damaging.

It also follows that people at all levels of an organization will require training from time to time – from the chief executive to the car park attendant.

ACTIVITY 5.11

You may leave school or college with good qualifications – A levels, BTEC National – or you may go on and be awarded a degree. Prepare an argument to support the view that learning begins all over again when you start work.

Benefits of Training

An efficient and competent staff creates satisfied customers. Training is one way of helping people to be efficient and competent.

Whether the customers are students in a college, the community of a borough council, the consumers of food or the industrial users of machinery or raw materials – their satisfaction with the outputs of the organization will be closely related to the degree of proficiency of every member of the organization.

Training will enable:

- Employees to do their jobs to the required standard
- People to improve their performance and make progress in the organization
- People to become confident in the job that they are doing, which is likely to lead to greater job satisfaction and lower staff turnover and absenteeism
- Costs to be kept as low as possible through less scrap, fewer accidents, better productivity and more efficient use of equipment
- Management to spend more time on developing the organization, rather than constant trouble shooting

Training Needs and Training Programmes

Training can be designed for a whole organization, for a department or for individuals. It can also be designed for a specific discipline – for example 'customer care' training, total quality management (TQM) training, management training and so on. Organization-wide training needs may have been highlighted in the HR plan, whilst individual needs may have come out of the appraisal process.

Many companies use Training Needs Analysis (TNA) as a way of exposing areas of work that would benefit from training. This employs very similar methods to HR planning, but it focuses on training rather than the recruitment of people.

TNA asks the following questions:

- What are the organization's short and medium-term goals?
- What range of tasks and how much of each will be needed?
- To what extent are they present in the current workforce?

And from the answers, some estimate of the amount of training needed will be made.

Training policy is drawn up by personnel specialists, and put to senior management for approval. Sufficient resources, usually in the form of a budget, are made available to carry out the policy. Line managers are responsible for the efficient job performance of all their staff, and will be involved in planning, delivering and evaluating training. They may have the services of a specialist training officer to help and advise them on the best methods of achieving the overall aims.

The objective may be broad – to improve performance. Or it may be general – to ensure that all staff are familiar with the latest safety regulations. At an individual level, it may be to improve her or his accounting skills, or to prepare for promotion or a new role.

There are other issues that may come under the heading of Organization Development (OD), as we mentioned in Chapter Three, which can incorporate elements of training. The objective may be to create a more open communication style or to develop team working.

Once the objective is clear, careful consideration can be given to the training options that are likely to achieve, or help to achieve, it. A systematic approach is the most efficient way to use training as an agent of change in an organization. The alternative, piecemeal approach tends to be ineffective and can give training a bad name. It can also be a waste of money.

Designing a training programme for individual job performance is a fairly logical process, and H T Graham and R Bennett offer a useful mnemonic to help us remember it. Each letter of the word APPROACH stands for one of the key steps:

- **A**nalyse job
- **P**erformance standards
- **P**erformance attained
- **R**equirements of training
- **O**riginate training programme
- **A**dminister training
- **C**heck results
- **H**ow can training be improved next time?

Training of this sort can be given in a local college or on the job. Each has its benefits and drawbacks. On-the-job training is always more relevant, and the trend in training in recent years has been to credit people with what they learn at work. We will return to this in a moment.

Most colleges and polytechnics offer a wide range of vocational courses, and personnel specialists can make maximum use of the relatively cheap facilities they offer. It is possible for personnel specialists to get on to advisory committees at the local college where they can influence the types of course that are on offer.

Very often, local colleges welcome specialist people from industry to teach on a part-time basis. Some personnel specialists use this as an opportunity to develop their staff and improve individual manager's training skills. This has two benefits for the firm:

- The person concerned will become even more expert at her or his speciality through having to teach it
- The firm will know that if they put some of their staff on the course as students, it will be relevant and up to date because it is being taught by a practitioner

Costs of Training

Training is a specialist function, and firms that undertake their own training may need to employ a trainer. There are many fine courses for training trainers, and it might be in the firm's interest to promote one of their experienced staff and have them trained to train. The salary and training of the trainer is one of the main costs.

Buying places on courses for their staff is another cost. In 1992, the cost of a one-day course in an hotel in London was anything between £100 and £200. A one-year part-time course in supervisory management at a local college was about £250 to £400 depending upon content. A distance learning course (study at home with tutorial support) in middle management was about £1 300 to £2 000.

Interactive video training programmes in a wide range of topics are increasingly becoming available, though they are quite expensive at this early stage in their life cycle, and their effectiveness has not yet been thoroughly evaluated.

The use of a training room and hire of materials (like videos and computer software) also has to be considered.

One of the less obvious costs of training is the opportunity cost of releasing someone for a day a week to attend a course.

In calculating the costs of training, one should, however, also take into account the cost of *not training*:

- What is the cost of scrap caused by poorly trained staff?
- What is the cost of losing a customer because goods were faulty or were not delivered on time?
- What is the cost of an accident that could have been prevented by safety training?
- What is the cost of poor staff morale caused by awful management who lack interpersonal skills?

If you think training is expensive, you should cost out ignorance and incompetence!

Politics and Training

The political parties in the UK are united in their insistence that levels of skills in UK industry must be improved if it is to compete on equal terms with EC and international competitors in the twenty-first century. Where they differ is in how that should be achieved. The three main parties place training high in their priorities, but they differ in the ways it will be supported and financed.

In the late 1980s and early 1990s, the government made some major changes in the provision for vocational training. The main emphasis was to set up bodies of employers whose function was to define what their actual training requirements are now and will be in the years ahead.

The Employment Act 1989 reformed Industrial Training Boards (ITBs), virtually privatizing them, and required the majority of board members to be employers in appropriate industries. There are now only eight ITBs left. Several of them make levies against employers, then give grants to firms for training initiatives. Others provide training services specifically tailored to their particular industry and make a charge for them. In Northern Ireland, the Training Development Agency has sole responsibility for vocational training within industry.

The personnel specialist would know these things, and be aware of grants and support for training that might be obtainable. The Planning Exchange in Glasgow publishes a directory of sources of grants for training.

In 1989 the government set up The National Training Task Force (NTTF). It is a high powered body made up of leading industrialists and businesspeople which advises the Secretary of State for Employment about training matters and organizes research and initiatives to bring training up to the same level in the UK as it is in Europe and elsewhere. The NTTF establishes and watches over Training and Enterprise Councils (TECs), a subject which is discussed in another title in this series, *The Business Environment*.

Management training is important in every organization. It is unlikely that any organization with untrained management will be very efficient. Charles Handy's report, *The Making of Managers*, began a great debate about the UK's poor performance in management education and training compared with USA, Japan, France and Germany. One of the results of this debate was the establishment of a Management Charter Initiative, (MCI) which was to set out clearly the competencies needed to be efficient managers at various levels in any organization – industrial, commercial or public sector.

In 1990, the MCI launched the first of three sets of national standards aimed at first line managers and supervisors. Late in 1991 it issued its second set of standards relating to middle managers, and in the future the MCI will publish its third level programme, a Masters Degree.

The Institute of Management (IM) – formerly the British Institute of Management – has developed qualifications based on these standards: the Certificate in Management and the Diploma in Management. It will later produce a Masters Degree based on level three.

These qualifications will become the 'gold standard' for managers in the future. Managers do not have to attend college or sit exams. Instead, they must produce evidence of competence to the MCI standards through their own work. To do this successfully, a manager working towards a qualification will be guided by a 'mentor' within her or his own company. Once a manager has qualified for the certificate, she or he can automatically progress to the diploma, again through their own work.

The rapid move towards 'competence' is driven by a body called the National Council for Vocational Qualifications (NCVQ).

NCVQ

The government set up the NCVQ to reform and rationalize vocational qualifications in the UK. There was, and in some vocational areas still is, a plethora of different qualifications, but with no common standard to compare levels of achievement. The NCVQ should put an end to all that. In future, a personnel specialist will be able to look at a qualification, see that it is, say, NVQ Level 2 in catering, and know exactly what the holder is capable of. Not only in the UK, but any employer in the EC will be able to compare UK vocational qualifications with their own national qualifications. This is a great step forward in rationalizing what has been, up to now, a free-for-all between awarding bodies. From now on, RSA, City and Guilds and all other awarding bodies must comply with the NCVQ standards in their courses in

*Figure 5.9 – **NCVQ Annual Report***

Statutory Report and Accounts

Report of the Council members

The Council members, who for the purposes of the Companies Act 1985 are the directors of the company, have pleasure in presenting their report and the accounts of the National Council for Vocational Qualifications for the year ended 31 March 1992.

Principal activity, business review and future developments

The National Council was set up by the Government to promote, develop, implement and monitor a comprehensive system of vocational qualifications throughout the United Kingdom (excluding Scotland). Its sponsoring Departments are the Department of Employment, the Department of Education and Science, the Welsh Office and the Northern Ireland Office. Grant-in-aid from these Departments was the main source of finance, accounting for 59.4% (1990/91 48.9%) of gross income in the year ended 31 March 1992.

During the financial year the National Council continued to work towards its objectives. The number of qualifications accredited as NVQs rose from 249 to 285, and NVQ certification fees yielded income of £463,781 arising from the issue of 104,530 certificates.

The National Record of Vocational Achievement (NROVA) was discontinued at the end of the year, following the sale or issue of 265,774 copies during the year producing gross income of £1,326,155. The majority of the sales were to the Employment Department for use on the Employment Training and Youth Training programmes. It was announced by the Prime Minister at a national conference on 23 January 1992 that the NCVQ would become responsible for the management and development of the National Record of Achievement (NRA), within which the functions of NROVA would be integrated and which would cover both academic and vocational achievement. This responsibility was undertaken early in 1992/93.

The period of this report saw important work continuing in the fields of quality assurance, research and development and communications. The National Database of Vocational Qualifications was launched for general use at the beginning of last year: over 1,000 subscriptions to it were sold during the year, producing income of £471,815.

Financial results for the year

The deficit for the year amounted to £129,845 (1990/91 surplus of £68,720) which is taken to reserves. It resulted from the decision to discontinue NROVA and the allocation of funds arising from the liquidation of NROVA stocks to revenue expenditure supporting the achievement of the National Council's objectives.

Share capital and constitution

The National Council is incorporated as a company limited by guarantee and without share capital.

The National Council's governing instruments are its memorandum and articles of association.

Fixed assets

The movements in fixed assets are shown in the notes to the accounts.

Council members

Twelve Council members served throughout the whole year and there was one new appointment and one resignation. Full particulars are given in the list of Council members at the head of this report.

Auditor

A resolution to reappoint the auditor, Coopers & Lybrand, will be proposed at the Annual General Meeting. Until 1 June 1992 the Firm practised in the name of Coopers & Lybrand Deloitte.

By order of the Council.

John Hillier, Secretary
222 Euston Road, London NW1 2BZ
25 June 1992

Source: National Council for Vocational Qualifications, *Annual Report 1991/92*

KEY POINTS 5.5

- Training is one means by which a business can improve the performance of its work people. It is an investment in people

- Everybody who has to respond to change needs training of some sort

- The costs of training should be set against the wide range of benefits to an organization

- Training needs can be identified

- from TNA and from the appraisal system

- The NCVQ has created a structure for vocational training that sets out occupational standards for every job

- This standardization will simplify recruitment, encourage people to gain vocational qualifications and allow comparison between all EC countries

order to have the NVQ endorsement. Without it, they will not be recognized as currency in the job market.

The extract in Figure 5.9 from NCVQ's Annual Report shows the nature and scope of its work.

Like every innovation, NVQs will have teething problems. But the concept is very attractive and one which will bring some order to the jungle of vocational qualifications that has baffled students and employers in the past.

The advantage to businesses is that recruitment will be much simpler. An employer wanting a certain level of skill can restrict applications to only those holding, say, NVQ Level 3 qualifications in the required occupation. And they know exactly what someone holding that qualification should be able to do. Additionally, they can train their own staff to a national standard and issue qualifications that are transferable from company to company. In time this will improve the level of qualifications held by people working in the UK.

Promotion

As we mentioned briefly in Chapter Two, the opportunity to gain promotion will motivate some people. However, what of those who do not want promotion, or those who would like it, but are unlucky or unsuitable.

There are many fine people in organizations who do not want to leave their chosen craft or specialism. If the only route to more money and status is by giving up what one is good at and dedicated to, and moving into 'management', the organization could be missing opportunities with human resources.

Possibly an example of this is in the teaching profession in the UK, where a good teacher is promoted and as a result does less teaching. So

someone who loves teaching, but wants to progress their career, must give up some or all of their teaching to achieve it. This might increase satisfaction with salary and status, but reduce satisfaction with content and intrinsic interest in the job.

Herzberg's theory (Chapter Two) might imply that this is not the right way around. McClelland, on the other hand, might suggest that 'power-oriented' people will attempt to progress in this way to satisfy their power need, irrespective of their likely competence in the job. It is quite difficult to distinguish between ability and ambition!

The implications for the personnel specialist are profound.

The promotion process has to be rigorous and fair in selecting the best person for the new job. However, there should also be a way of giving recognition and reward to those who do not wish to be promoted but have reached a high state of excellence in their work. The latter could be handled within a good appraisal scheme, and the former through an open and cogent promotion process.

Two errors are to be avoided at all costs:

- Promoting someone who turns out to be incompetent. Lawrence J Peter, an American University professor, suggests that many people are promoted to their first level of incompetence and then left there. This is known as 'The Peter Principle'. The organizational implications are horrifying

- Promoting someone in such a way that their appointment is not accepted by colleagues and subordinates, and is seen as some sort of favouritism or corruption

Every person who is promoted or brought into an organization at a senior level has to establish her or his own credibility with peers and sub-ordinates. No-one else can do it for them. It is not theirs by right. Poor promotion procedures can make the job very difficult for the newly appointed person, and it can be very costly for the organization if she or he does not perform efficiently.

Demotions

Sadly, there will be occasions when a person must be moved to a job with less status and lower pay. Two reasons why this might happen are:

- New technology or reorganization may cause certain skills or activities to reduce or disappear
- A person may genuinely be no longer capable of doing the job

A counselling approach may help the person to come to terms with the situation. However, people suffer a loss of self-esteem and will look for ways to defend their status. This is often in the form of blaming others, moaning about the company or the management, and justifying their own contribution. If work mates believe that she or he has been treated badly or unjustly, it will cause discontent and lower morale.

Transfer Policy

Moving people around within an organization can broaden their knowledge of the way it operates, and develop their potential use to the firm. It is one way that the personnel specialist can manage the human resource effectively in the best interests of the firm. This policy relates closely to the HRM approach discussed in Chapter One.

There is a risk that a transfer policy might be abused; it could become a way of transferring the problem of a useless member of staff to someone else instead of dealing with it properly. To avoid this sort of buck-passing, a clear and public process for advertising transfer opportunities, applications and selection should be followed. If all staff know and respect the process, transfer will be seen as a means of progressing and be a part of the organization's motivation policy.

Once again, before putting anyone into a job, an objective selection procedure is needed to ensure that the successful applicant will be able to do the new job to the required standard within a reasonable period of time.

In the case of transfers that are intended to develop the person, all parties must agree that a period of planned learning is an integral part of the package:

- The transferee should be selected carefully
- The purpose of the transfer should be defined
- The transferee and the manager should both be in agreement with the purpose, and how success will be measured
- The transferee must not be less well-off as a result

If this approach is taken for those who are unlikely to be offered promotion, the organization will be opening up a wide range of opportunities to a large number of its staff. Many of the UK's competitors use this approach for keeping people motivated. Not everyone can be, and not everyone wishes to be promoted to the role of manager. There are many other routes to advancement besides the management ladder that people find satisfying. An organization which adopts this approach, and places value on other roles, has the advantage that it can move people to new positions without having to call it 'promotion', thus giving greater flexibility in the use of its human resource.

KEY POINTS 5.6

- **The promotion process should be similar to, and as rigorous as, the recruitment and selection process**
- **It is essential that it should be seen to be scrupulous, unbiased and fair. The Peter Principle must be avoided if the business is to prosper**
- **Demotions, if they are necessary, must be handled in a sympathetic way**
- **Transfers between departments can be a useful training and development method for many organizations**

Organizational Culture

The idea that each organization has a distinct 'culture' that comes from the beliefs and values held by its senior managers has become a very important issue in personnel management. From it derives the way the business treats its employees, how it develops and implements strategy, and how it determines 'how things will be done around here'. It is an integrating force that moulds all the organization's goals into a cohesive whole. Modern management writers like Rosabeth Moss Kanter suggest that there is evidence linking culture with success.

Defining Culture

Culture is very difficult to define. A working definition is provided by Allan Williams, Paul Dobson and Mike Walters in their book, *Changing Culture: A New Organizational Approach* (IPM, 1989):

> Culture is the commonly held and relatively stable beliefs, attitudes and values that exist within the organization.

Other definitions focus on the fact that culture is nebulous, invisible, unmeasurable and sub-conscious. They are all very true but not very helpful. However, the two together should allow us to study the topic briefly.

Douglas McGregor's Theory X and Theory Y (see Chapter Two) dwelt on the beliefs held by managers and how those beliefs might influence the way they treat the people who work for them. Their beliefs and values would have developed through their up-bringing, education, background, family and friends; and also as a result of the national culture.

In turn, employees can respond only as their manager's style allows. This is irrespective of the values and beliefs that they hold which may or may not be the same as the managers. As we saw in Chapter Two, it is a major influence upon their attitudes to work which may or may not be for good.

These two elements form the cornerstone of an organization's culture.

However, organizations do not exist in a vacuum. The internal culture develops in the context of an external environment. That environment imposes pressures on the organization – legal, social, technical and so on. The organization has to respond to these pressures, and the way in which it responds is determined by its culture, but would also influence its culture. The culture determines the response and is itself affected by the response.

And lastly, the purpose of the organization has a bearing on its culture. A college has a different culture from a prison; or a department store has a different culture from a coal mine.

From all these influences, both inside and outside the organization, the culture develops and settles down. The circle is completed when this settled culture determines how the organization, its managers and its staff will respond to the environment and to each other. It almost becomes a filter through which everything flows, and some things pass while others are held up. Some things are important, and other things are not. Over time, it becomes well established 'how things are done around here'.

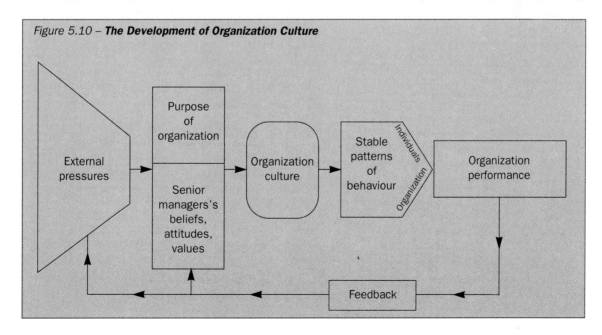

*Figure 5.10 – **The Development of Organization Culture***

Change and Culture

Going back to our definitions, the culture is 'stable' beliefs operated at a 'sub-conscious' level. So the worry is that a strong, well established culture may mean that things will be done the same way 'around here' whatever is happening in the environment, and the organization may fall behind its competitors.

The realization that a culture could be so ingrained as to prevent or hinder changes taking place is quite important to those who see the need to change in order to compete and survive.

As a result of the European Single Market, many UK firms will have to change from a belief that the home market is safe, to a belief that Europe is the home market and that survival is not a right, but a consequence of being efficient within a healthy economy.

Others may need to change their belief that their technical competence will create a demand for their products, to one where the customer's needs are paramount and a policy of 'customer care' is the most important thing.

Most firms will need to alter their belief that 'quality' refers only to its products and come to accept that quality will only result from everyone in an organization producing their particular job outputs to the highest standards – that is, total quality.

To implement fundamental changes of these sorts goes to the roots of the organization. Such changes will not happen unless the culture, too, is changed. How can something that is sub-conscious and ingrained be changed?

Changing the Culture

Some of the human aspects of implementing changes at work are considered later in this

---

CASE STUDY

Sir Desmond's Private Life at Littlewoods

Sir Desmond Pitcher's departure next spring as chief executive of Littlewoods leaves Britain's biggest private company no closer to stepping into the public arena than when he joined ten years ago.

Sir Desmond was brought in by the Moores family to turn the stores group around in 1983.

Since then profits have risen ten-fold to £97 million as Littlewoods has been dragged up to date.

But the failure to sell its mail-order operation earlier this year puts paid to any dwindling hopes that the company might opt for the stock market in the near future.

As Sir Desmond points out, the group's three main retail operations, Littlewoods stores, the mail-order operation and Index, the catalogue stores, are now completely separate.

The Liverpool group headquarters has been hugely scaled down and each division has its own separate management, with the directors reporting direct to Sir Desmond.

The lack of synergy between the three businesses, which had collective sales of £1.8 billion last year, would make it extremely difficult to float them as one vehicle.

The younger members of the family are likely to want to float the company or sell off parts when they get control, as their wealth is tied up in trusts, but for the foreseeable future Littlewoods is unlikely to move out of private hands.

Meanwhile, strict control of working capital has thrown up cash for expansion when Sir Desmond is succeeded by Barry Dale, his finance director, who is 'very much in my mould'.

Source: Evening Standard, 28 July, 1992

QUESTIONS

1 Identify evidence in the article which shows Sir Desmond changed the organization culture at Littlewoods.

2 List the business successes that resulted.

3 The 'younger members of the family' seem to have different values from Sir Desmond. What might these be, and how might they alter the organization's culture 'when they come to power'?

4 Speculate upon Barry Dale's task as far as organization culture is concerned.

chapter. Taking account of the human aspects of change is most important if people are to co-operate and accept changes. The personnel specialist is the one who adds the human dimension to the change process.

Changing an organization's culture, however, is about a profound change that will affect everybody, from top to bottom – from the chief executive to the newest apprentice. It is about changing their beliefs and values so that they think and act in new ways in response to events in their environment.

In the past, this sort of thing only happened as the result of a crisis: the company slipping slowly or quickly into terminal decline. Often, the catalyst for the change was the appointment of a new chief executive to 'save the company from extinction'.

Nowadays, it is becoming apparent that the best managed companies are conscious of their culture and its strengths and limitations, and see the constant monitoring of their culture as the key to keeping efficient and ahead of competitors. This is almost certainly a main benefit of having a HRM approach with an expert personnel specialist advising the senior managers of the firm.

Based on the belief that organizations are made up of people and will only be as good as the people in them (that is a cultural statement), the HRM specialist will use all the techniques of selecting the right people, training them, motivating them and so on that we have discussed in the chapters on people.

The most important thing, though, is that they are not separate techniques for specific purposes, they are each a part of a corporate jigsaw, the final picture being the achievement of the organization's overall aims and objectives in its ever-changing environment.

Change is happening all the time, in every organization. Some changes are minor, day-to-day matters, and require little thought for how they will affect those involved. Others go right to the heart of the organization and require an overall strategy that takes into account every aspect of its operation and every one of its people. Managing change effectively is a key management skill, and is directly related to survival and success.

The timescale of change varies greatly with the nature of the change. Some can be planned, implemented and evaluated in a matter of weeks. An example might be altering the layout of an office. Others require complex planning, detailed organizing and a long period of implementation. An example would be the switch from coal to gas powered electricity generation, or the building of the Channel Tunnel rail link.

The problem with complex changes is that they do not occur in isolation. The whole environment in which the change is taking place is changing, too. Plans which seemed perfectly practicable this year, may be untenable next year because of parallel changes in the economy, or international competition, or whatever. Changes of this magnitude have wide ranging impact upon individuals, groups, organizations, communities, the nation and even the world. Managing change, whatever the timescale or magnitude, is a key management skill, and is directly related to survival and success.

Human Aspects of Change

Businesses must have change. They have to respond to competition, new technology, laws and regulations, social pressures, growth and so on.

Most people fear or resist change. They may fear loss of jobs, not being able to cope with new demands, having to work with new people, loss of status, being given work that they do not like and so on. These reasons can be linked directly with Maslow's hierarchy of human needs.

You can see that there is nothing wrong with a business having to change, but it is equally reasonable to expect resistance – it's only human. Analysis of the reasons given above shows that the reasons for change are mainly technical, whilst the reasons for resistance are mainly social.

It is in a business's interest to be able to implement changes without too much resistance – there will always be some – and so it must take into account the genuine human reasons for it. To do this, it must accept that it is perfectly reasonable for those affected by the change to want an answer to the 'great change question': 'How is it going to affect ME?'

In planning changes, therefore, it is good sense for a business to include social issues as well as technical issues. Participation by those most affected by the change will help to reduce resistance. It is important to give as much information as possible to reduce uncertainty – give guarantees of job security if it can, state that the company will provide retraining, job transfers, keep groups together where practical, and create means of answering individual questions about 'how it will affect me?'.

Where the answer is favourable, resistance will turn into support. Where the answer is unfavourable, it is reasonable that there should be fear and resistance, so managers should set out to minimize the hardship. Figure 5.11 (next page) illustrates this.

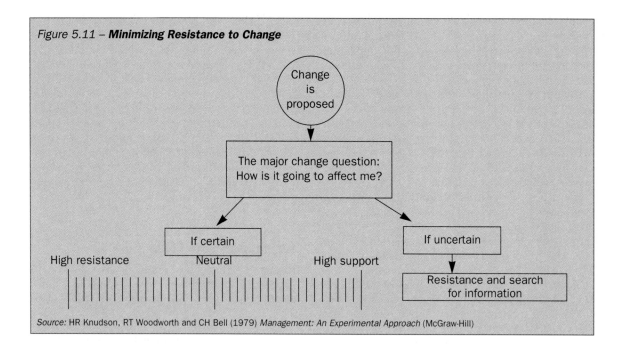

Figure 5.11 – *Minimizing Resistance to Change*

Source: HR Knudson, RT Woodworth and CH Bell (1979) *Management: An Experimental Approach* (McGraw-Hill)

Leadership at Work

In our discussion about culture, we suggested that an organization was an entity in its own right, but it was made up of individuals. Bringing them all together so that they shared the same values did not make them any less individual, it just helped to make the organization whole. The management activity that brings them all together so that they can pursue the common goals of the organization is leadership. It is a relationship through which one person influences the behaviour of other people.

The verb 'to lead' has several meanings: 'to cause to act, feel, think or behave in a certain way' or 'to guide, control, direct: to lead an army' (*Collins English Dictionary and Thesaurus*). Many would agree that there are elements of each needed to lead people in an organization. However, leadership is broader than that, and exists both inside and outside the context of work and organizations. Some leaders are not seen as managers, whereas all managers are expected to lead.

We will examine leadership in the context of work, and consider it as an activity of management.

Concepts in Leadership

Leaders have authority that has been delegated to them by the organization. The authority is limited to the job, and if the leader leaves the job, the authority stays behind with the job. It is not personal property. The authority relates to the right to use the organization's resources to achieve specific goals. The leader is responsible for seeing that the resources are used efficiently, and only for the purpose intended. She or he is then accountable to the delegator of the authority, for how efficiently the resources were used and whether the goal was achieved.

These three concepts, 'authority', 'responsibility' and 'accountability' are important aspects of leadership and were discussed in Chapter Three.

'Power' is a difficult concept in leadership at work. We discussed power need in Chapter Two. The word implies that people can be forced to comply with orders and instructions, either by force or by sanctions. However, the contract of employment, the law, trade unions and human nature limit the amount of naked power that any manager has. There has to be a certain amount of acceptance or consensus if the manager's use of authority is to be effective. We have implied in the discussion on culture that shared beliefs and values are important to an organization, if it is to be successful.

There is no leadership without followership! Acceptance of the manager's power by the staff can result from four things:

- *Tradition*: for example, the family firm where the children of the owner are accepted in senior positions whether they are competent or not
- *Rational-legal*: the process or procedure for selecting people that is seen to be fair and receives the consent of the majority. In organizations, the process has to be seen to be used fairly, and the notion of fairness extends to the belief that the abuse of power, or the

incompetence of the leader, will result in her or him being removed by legitimate means

- *Charisma*: there are some people who are able to lead others purely by the nature of their personality. Some managers can develop tremendous loyalty in their staff, maybe because they set an example that is admired or create a role model that others are willing to emulate
- *Rational-expertness*: when someone is perceived as expert or competent in their job, their authority is easily accepted, even if they are not particularly well liked

One thing is sure: if the leader's power is not accepted by members of the organization the business is unlikely to be efficient.

Leadership Styles

There has been a great deal written about different leadership styles.

TRAIT (or QUALITIES) THEORY

Trait Theory suggested that leaders were born, rather than made. If you had certain characteristics and came from a certain background, you were expected to be a leader. Many studies set out to define these magic characteristics, but when someone put all the studies together, and compared the so-called 'leaders's traits', there were very few that were found to be common to all leaders. Two traits that featured more often than others were 'individuality' and 'originality'. So that approach to understanding leadership was abandoned.

STYLE THEORY

Style Theory is based on the notion that there are two extremes: leaders have either an autocratic (or authoritarian) style or a democratic style. A third style of *laisser-faire* is sometimes included, but it does not often relate to managers as leaders.

Autocratic style is where the manager makes most of the decisions and all power rests in her or him.

Democratic style is where the manager relates more closely with the group, which has a much greater say in decision-making.

Laisser-faire style is where the group works independently of the manager and simply calls upon the manager as a resource when needed. By letting them 'get on with it', there is, however, a risk that this would lead to non-leadership.

Respected researchers, such as Likert, Tannenbaum, Schmidt, Vroom and others, examined the effects on performance of different styles of leadership. Although there was evidence that people enjoyed more job satisfaction when working under a more democratic style of leadership, the difference in productivity levels was only marginally higher than under autocratic leadership. There is no empirical evidence to show that the difference was due solely to the style, and there are other variables that should be considered.

Tannenbaum and Schmidt produced a range of leadership styles along a scale from autocratic to democratic, as illustrated in Figure 5.12.

CONTINGENCY THEORY

Contingency Theory is based on the degree of association between variables.

F E Fiedler, author of *A Theory of Leadership Effectiveness* (McGraw-Hill, 1967), is the best known of the contingency school. He was interested in the relationship between:

- The type of task being carried out

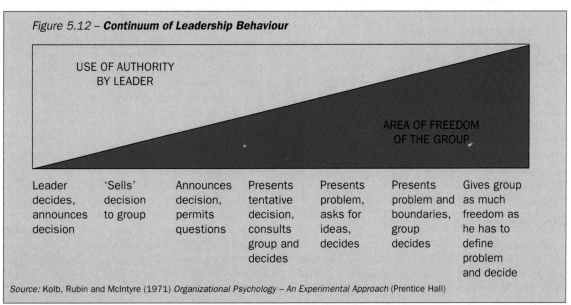

*Figure 5.12 – **Continuum of Leadership Behaviour***

USE OF AUTHORITY BY LEADER

AREA OF FREEDOM OF THE GROUP

| Leader decides, announces decision | 'Sells' decision to group | Announces decision, permits questions | Presents tentative decision, consults group and decides | Presents problem, asks for ideas, decides | Presents problem and boundaries, group decides | Gives group as much freedom as he has to define problem and decide |

Source: Kolb, Rubin and McIntyre (1971) *Organizational Psychology – An Experimental Approach* (Prentice Hall)

- The relationship between the leader and the subordinates
- The leader's position of power

In essence, he suggested that, where the leader is powerful, has a good relationship with the group and the task is structured, then a task-centred, authoritarian approach would be most effective. A task-centred approach would also be most effective where the leader had little power, poor group relations and an unstructured task.

In all other situations a participative, democratic approach would be most effective.

Critics of Fiedler's theory note that the way he measured the relationship with the group was only from the leader's point of view. There may have been other variables that created a situation where the leader's concern with relationships was less important to her or him than other issues. Later, with other researchers, Fiedler examined three variables: the task, the leader and the subordinates.

This has become a commonly used model for investigations into leadership.

'BEST FIT' APPROACH

There does not seem to be one best leadership style. The research points to there being a need for managers to analyse situations and to make a choice of the wide range of styles available to them. The variables to be considered are:

- The leader's power
- The structure of the task
- The relationship between the manager and the staff
- The situation that has to be dealt with at the time

When the manager has analysed these variables, she or he must decide whether to tell, sell, consult or join in this situation. If the situation changes, then a new analysis will be necessary, and a fresh choice of style made.

Communication

We have discussed one aspect of this topic in Chapter Three, and we will discuss it from another angle in Chapter Nine under marketing. It permeates every aspect of business life. It is the nervous system that keeps all the parts of the organization in touch with each other and with the centre.

Just as a leadership style can be chosen, so can a communication style. The ways in which communication takes place in an organization will be a consequence of its culture.

If management believe that people need to be told what to do, they will adopt a one-way, telling style, and a bureaucratic administration. If managers believe that people have a contribution to make and will add richness to decisions if they are allowed to take part, managers will use a more open, two-way, listening style, and administrative systems will be flexible and adaptable. But like leadership styles, there are times and places for both.

Communication is about transmitting meanings accurately. But it also creates feelings and affects morale. It is possible that, as a result of communication, people feel confident or not, depending upon whether they believe they have understood.

Communication also takes time, and most managers will claim that they are busy and do not have enough time. The quality of the communication will also impinge upon accuracy. If the communication was good, and the correct meanings were received, then using that information will result in accurate outcomes. The converse is tragically true as well.

One-Way

The one-way, verbal communication style can be described as the boss telling subordinates what to do, with minimal opportunity for checking that they have understood. This takes relatively little time and the manager is not harassed by staff asking questions. In effect, the boss's status is intact – no-one challenges anything he or she says, which is taken as confirming that she or he is right and reinforcing belief in one-way communication.

However, the receiver of one-way communication may have missed a point, or not understood something, but there is no way of going back and hearing it again or asking for an explanation. Therefore, the information may not be accurate and there may be no channel for checking.

This can lead to a loss of confidence, and a feeling of frustration or anger with the communicator. The most disturbing thing about it, though, is that if that person now uses the information to make decisions, those decisions could be based on poor quality data. Any poor and inaccurate work that results is the fault of the person concerned, because the boss had told them what to do!

Two-Way

The two-way style can be described as the boss explaining what is to be done and answering all questions as and when they arise. When she or he is certain that the message is correctly understood, the staff get on with it. In effect, the boss will be sharing information with the subordinates and dealing with misunderstandings.

However, it takes anything between three and five times as long as the one-way style. But everyone has accurate information, and the staff feel more confident about it. Decisions will be based on good quality information. Some frustration may be experienced between group members but not usually with the boss. The fact that the work is very accurate is probably attributed to the organization's systems, rather than the manager.

There is a place for both styles of communication. If the room is on fire, a discussion about which way to exit the building would be daft. It needs a bit of firm, one-way communication. The investment in time may not always be justified, in which case, one-way will do fine. On the other hand, some things might be of such import, that spending as much time as is needed to ensure that everyone has understood and is clear about what actions to take is a very worthwhile investment. The manager must consider the situation and make her or his choice.

KEY POINTS 5.7

- Organizational culture is the product of all the beliefs and values held by the senior managers of the business, and is a powerful influence on 'how things are done around here'

- As the environment in which the organization exists changes, it is essential that the organization changes too, in order to meet new challenges and survive. This may involve a change in culture, so that 'things are done differently around here'

- Changing culture starts at the top, and takes time and care

- The style of leadership adopted in the organization will reflect its culture, and will have an effect on performance. The 'best fit approach' is a useful model that helps us to understand the topic

- Communication style also reflects an organization's culture and is influenced by it

- Choice of communication style will have an impact upon accuracy, confidence and morale

EXAM PREPARATION

SHORT QUESTIONS

1 State two purposes of induction training. (AEB November 1992)

2 Distinguish between autocratic and democratic styles of leadership. (AEB November 1989)

3 The Health and Safety at Work Act 1974 provides for the law to be updated by regulations produced under the Act. Give two examples of such regulations. (AEB June 1992)

4 List three different methods of performance appraisal.

5 State three indirect costs of training.

ESSAYS

1 'Management training is little more than a reward or a mark of approval. It is not a cost-effective contribution to a company's efficiency.' Critically examine this view. (AEB November 1987)

2 How far does the style of leadership adopted by management make any significant difference to the way people work? (AEB June 1992)

3 It is often said that managing people in a firm which is growing rapidly is more difficult than in one which is growing slowly. Explain why this might be so. (AEB November 1990)

CHAPTER 6

Reward Management and Employee Relations

▷ ▷ **QUESTIONS FOR PREVIEW** ▷ ▷

1 In what ways can pay be structured?

2 How are unlike jobs evaluated so that pay is fair?

3 Who are the parties in employee relations, and how do they work?

4 What is collective bargaining?

5 How are discipline and grievances handled?

6 What records of personnel are needed?

Wages and Salaries

IN CHAPTER Two it was suggested that wages were a very important element of the total reward received in return for work. It is the main reason most people are willing to work under another person's direction. According to Herzberg, of itself, money has limited motivational effect – it is very short term. If pay is inadequate, or compares unfavourably with the other firms in the same industry or in the locality, it will cause dissatisfaction and contribute to low morale. On the other hand, if it is adequate, it will simply remove dissatisfaction; it will not cause satisfaction.

ACTIVITY 6.1

In groups of (say) six, divide into two: those who would say that money is a motivator; and those who say that money has a very limited motivational value. Prepare an argument to support each view.

It has also been mentioned that the wages agreed for the job with the employer, either by an individual or through collective bargaining with a trade union, are a part of the contract of employment.

There are laws that affect wages in three ways: levels of pay; calculations of pay; and deductions from pay.

Some laws relate to specific minimum levels of pay in certain occupations: the Wages Councils Act 1979; the Wages Act 1986; the Equal Pay Act 1970. Other laws relate to methods of calculating a week's pay, to deductions an employer may make from an employee's pay and to rights to certain payments: the Employment Protection (Consolidation) Act 1978; the Wages Act 1986; the Employment Act 1988; the Attachment of Earnings Act 1971. In 1990, there were over 8 000 complaints to ACAS alleging unlawful deductions by employers from people's pay.

Finally, other laws relate to how much should be deducted for tax, National Health and so on: the various annual Finance Acts; the Finance (No 2) Act 1987.

Direct government intervention in wage levels has not occurred since the early 1970s, but there is little to stop a government from interfering if it considers it wise to to do so. However, by indirect means, governments do affect wage levels (which is discussed in another title in this series, *The Business Environment*). The EC favours a legally enforceable minimum wage, and although the present UK government opposes it, we might well see moves in that direction in the course of time.

It is not new, however. As long ago as 1968 the

*Figure 6.1 – **Reducing Costs***

Freelance oil workers forced to take pay cut

HUNDREDS of workers in the oil industry were forced to take a 10 per cent cut in their wages yesterday because of demands by the oil companies for offshore contractors to cut costs.

The cuts, for freelancers who find work through agencies, hit workers on the design and maintenance side of the industry. But they are being seen by many as the start of a pay squeeze that could move into all areas on and off-shore.

Self-employed workers form between 60 per cent and 70 per cent of the design side of the industry, which is responsible for maintenance and modifications of platforms. They range from chartered engineers, who can demand up to £350 a day, to clerks, who command about £8 an hour.

The Manufacturing, Science, Finance union, which has several thousand members in offshore oil, estimated that up to 75 per cent of the 30,000 employees in the industry would eventually be affected by the calls for cuts. But an Aberdeen-based agent said only 600 faced an immediate drop in pay.

Jimmy Inglis, Aberdeen regional officer for MSF, said talks had been taking place between the oil companies – primarily Shell Expro and BP Exploration – and contractors such as Brown and Root, Amec Engineering, John Brown Engineering, and others, aimed at cutting costs in a market where production has fallen from 117 million tonnes in 1987 to 83.1 million last year.

'At the moment, agency workers are the ones being affected, but inevitably, the contractors' own employees may be hit,' Mr Inglis said. 'The oil companies are pushing for 10 per cent cuts in return for the promise of longer contracts, from two years to five.'

The agent, who asked not to be named, said only 600 workers from design specialist companies were likely to be affected, but he added: 'The oil companies are looking for ways and means to cut costs. It could well be that other people are in line for wage cuts.'

Shell confirmed that it was holding discussions about 'the cost-effectiveness of services' provided by the contractors, but refused to discuss cuts. BP said it had told several dozen freelance chartered engineers last Friday that it intended to drop their rates from £350 to £325 a day, but it denied pressing contractors for 10 per cent cuts in costs.

However, one oil company said: 'We expect sacrifices in the bad times just as we are happy to see them prosper in the good times.'

Source: Independent, 4 August 1992

Department of Employment rejected minimum wage levels because it considered them an unsatisfactory way of dealing with low pay generally. Advocates of a minimum wage point out that several of the UK's European partners have a legal minimum wage level, and it does not appear to make them less competitive.

Internally, wages are a *cost* which must be affordable, and will be reflected in prices of the organization's goods or services. If prices are higher than competitors's as a result of wage levels, then demand may fall and jobs may be lost to reduce the proportion of costs that results from wages. Figure 6.1 provides an example of this point.

Pay has also been the cause of the majority of disputes within firms, whether unions are involved or not, and can influence the organization's reputation with its customers in terms of delivery, quality and reliability. Getting the right pay structure and system is therefore important to a business.

ACTIVITY 6.2

Obtain a copy of the latest ACAS annual report. (You can find out your regional ACAS address from your local Job Centre.) There will be a table showing the completed conciliation cases and analysed by cause of dispute. What proportion of disputes was caused by 'pay and terms and conditions of work'? How does this compare with previous years?

Sketch a diagram that shows the proportion of ACAS involvement in each cause during that year. Sketch another diagram that shows the comparison between years for the same cause.

Wages and Salaries Policy

Many of the considerations for human resource planning and recruitment discussed in Chapter Four apply to developing a wages policy. The main issues are:

*Figure 6.2 – **Pay Causes the Majority of Disputes***

Gas staff threaten to strike over pay

British Gas clerical workers are threatening to strike after union leaders rejected a 4.3 per cent pay offer.

If unions win a yes vote to the strike ballot it will be the first national industrial action by gas staff since 1986.

Unions representing the 45,000 white-collar workers say the improved offer is an insult compared to recent high pay rises for senior management at British Gas.

'What will anger our members is how a company faced with so many financial problems can justify the increases in salaries and executive share options which it has recently given to its top managers,' said Nalgo national gas officer Dave Stirzaker.

Nalgo, which represents 35,000 of the workers, has demanded a substantial improvement on the offer.

It pointed to last year's 50 per cent profit rise and recent salary increases for chairman Robert Evans.

This year Evans received a rise to £450,000, in line with inflation.

A Nalgo spokeswoman said it was confident members would back action.

British Gas has increased its offer three times after opening talks with a 3.7 per cent offer.

The result of the strike ballot is due to be announced around 25 August.

Source: Personnel Today, 14 July 1992

- How much must be paid to attract and retain the right number of the right quality of people?
- How should it be paid? All basic pay? Piece-work? Payment by results?
- What proportion of total costs is wages?
- How should the cake be divided between different jobs and different grades?
- On what basis should decisions be made about pay rises and additional awards?
- What fringe benefits, such as sick pay and pensions, should be offered and to whom?
- What is needed to ensure that the pay policy is consistently applied throughout the organization?

The answers to these questions will lead an organization to a policy that can then be applied by managers to all their staff. It may be that the personnel specialist co-ordinates all matters of wage awards to ensure that the policy is controlled. With this information and the human resource plan, the financial accountant will be able to set up a wages budget to feed into the master budget.

Interestingly, it is unlikely two organizations will produce the same answers to these questions. You will deduce that the reasons for this lie in the type of product or service, the nature of the firm's market, the technology and the organization culture. For example, if wages represent, say, 70 per cent of total costs, as in teaching, there will be less ability to pay a high wage compared with chemical processing where wages represent a much lower percentage.

It might follow that teachers are paid a basic wage with no additions, whereas chemical process workers may stand to earn high bonuses for higher productivity. The most important thing is that the organization chooses the system that suits it and provides as much incentive as possible to its employees.

Some employers may be considered 'good payers' and others 'poor payers'. The good payers may not necessarily be considered good employers, but it is pretty certain that the poor payers will be considered poor employers.

Productivity

Before we look at the many ways in which wages and salaries can be structured, it is important that we are clear about what is meant by productivity.

It must not be confused with 'production'. Productivity is the relationship between the physical output of a product or service and the inputs which have gone into producing that output. Input is measured in the amount of people, machines, materials and money put in, and output is measured in the volume, quality and costs (*not* price!) of products or services produced as a result of those inputs. A firm may be producing very few goods but be very efficient and productive, whilst another may have a massive output of goods or services, but have poor efficiency and productivity.

ACTIVITY 6.3

Consider a service like banking, and a product like a television set. Research the inputs required for each. List as many ways as you can think of for improving productivity – that is, how can you get more output for the same input; or the same output for reduced input?

Wage Structure

Pay can be made up of many elements, including:

- Basic pay
- Overtime
- Shift allowances
- Special additions
- Merit awards
- Payment by results (PBR)
- Profit sharing

BASIC PAY

Basic pay is usually expressed as a rate per hour, and calculated by multiplying the number of hours worked by the rate. For example:

£4.80 per hour, 38 hours per week
£4.80 × 38 = £182.40

This is probably the simplest method to calculate and administer pay. It gives the employee a regular, constant income which is easily understood. Many people like it for these reasons. However, it does not reward extra effort or increased productivity.

OVERTIME PAY

Most hourly paid workers are paid extra for working over and above their contracted hours. (Many contracts of employment require employees to work reasonable overtime if requested.) Usually, overtime is paid at a higher rate than basic. For example, the first three hours of overtime in any week may be paid at time and one quarter; the next three hours may then be at time and a half. Saturday or Sunday working may be paid at double time.

For example, a person works six hours's overtime, plus three hours on Sunday:

3 × 1¼ × 4.80 =	£18.00
3 × 1½ × 4.80 =	£21.60
3 × 2 × 4.80 =	£28.80
Total overtime payment	£68.40
Plus basic rate	£182.40
Gross pay	£250.80

Overtime is useful to a firm to increase production or cope with extra work for a short period, without having to employ more staff. In some industries, maintenance of production machinery can only be done when it is not being operated. It might have to be done at weekends. This is true of oil refineries, car plants and food processing plants.

SHIFT ALLOWANCES

High technology production machinery costs a great deal of money. It is a major investment decision and depends upon sophisticated analysis of the returns that might be expected. (This is discussed fully in another title in this series, *Finance, Information and Business*.)

In order to gain a reasonable return on investment, modern, expensive production machinery, like computers and robots, needs to be producing goods or services for more than just 'normal' working hours. Ideally firms would like them to produce non-stop.

If the machines have to run all hours, some of the people who run them must work all hours, and to do this they are organized into 'shifts'. And if people have to work all hours, they need to be compensated for the inconvenience – that is, they need to be paid shift allowances.

The day may be split into three eight-hour shifts which cover the full twenty-four hours non-stop. There are all sorts of systems for achieving this, the most common being the Continental Shift System. There are four work groups, A, B, C and D. The day is divided into three shifts, say, 6.00am to 2.00pm; 2.00pm to 10.00pm; and 10.00pm to 6.00am. The work pattern for group A looks something like this:

Day of the week

	Mon	Tues	Wed	Thur	Fri	Sat	Sun
Week							
1	6am	6am	2pm	2pm	10pm	10pm	10pm
2	off	off	6am	6am	2pm	2pm	2pm
3	10pm	10pm	off	off	6am	6am	6am
4	2pm	2pm	10pm	10pm	off	off	off

While group A is working this pattern, groups B, C and D are covering other shifts. Four groups are needed, because at any one time, one group is 'off'.

The company gains a great deal of additional production as a result of this shift pattern, and it is reasonable that some extra payment is made to the people who make it possible. There are a multitude of different ways that these extra payments are made up.

To give you some idea of the differences for the same work between dayworkers and shiftworkers we can look at straight percentages. Research during the late 1970s showed the following:

- Unskilled shiftworkers earned an average (mean) of 42 per cent more than their daywork equivalents. The range in ten industries was 23 per cent to 63 per cent
- Craftsmen shiftworkers earned an average 37 per cent more than their daywork equivalents. The range was 19 per cent to 64 per cent

These figures are an indication only; some include paid breaks, some are for longer days than others; some may include cost of living allowances and so on. There is no standard way of collecting or calculating this data.

Disadvantages of shiftwork

There are disadvantages to shiftwork for both the employer and the shiftworker:

- The company needs to train supervisors to operate and take decisions at night in the absence of managers, who tend to work conventional hours
- All welfare facilities (canteen, first aid) must be available
- Public transport may not be available at the start and finish of the night shift
- Machine breakdowns are more difficult to cope with at night. Also, breakdowns may be more frequent as the machinery is in constant use
- Communication between shifts can be a problem. Some scapegoating can take place where incoming shifts blame outgoing shifts for things that go wrong. Or outgoing shifts can leave their problems for the incoming shift to deal with
- Shiftworkers have to adjust to the constant changes to their bio-rhythms (circadian rhythms). Some people, as many as 25 per cent, seem to be unable to cope with these changes and have to revert to daywork
- Shiftwork can affect the health of some people. Scientists are unwilling to 'blame' shifts for illnesses as it is difficult to prove the direct link. But there are many recommendations as to how shiftwork might be organized to minimize any possible adverse effects
- Shiftwork can affect social and family life. There is some evidence that those with high financial needs adjust to the inconveniences of shiftwork better than those with lower financial needs

SPECIAL ADDITIONS

These payments tend to relate to specific features of the job. Danger money, height money, dirty money or wet money are agreed with the people in question and tend to be either a weekly lump payment or an additional few pence per hour.

MERIT AWARDS

These payments are in addition to the rate for the job, and usually result from performance appraisal (see Chapter Five). Many people do not feel awards made in this way are justified. They believe that pre-determined and published work standards are the only fair way of judging 'merit'. They fear that many merit awards are made on the basis of 'your face fitting' rather than on the true value of better work. However, it is a method of recognizing achievement, and provided it is conducted in an objective and fair fashion, can act as an incentive for some.

PAYMENT BY RESULTS (PBR)

This relates to all those payment schemes that set out to provide an incentive to increase productivity. They usually rest on the estimated time it should take to complete a job; the value of any 'time saved' is shared with the person or people concerned.

The estimate of how long a job should take, usually called the 'standard time', is made by a Work Study Engineer using both work measurement and method study. If it relates to office or administrative work, it is carried out by an Organization and Methods (O & M) specialist. The British Standards Institution (BSI) has produced standards of measurement for the purpose of calculating bonuses. These are widely used in manufacturing jobs, but not so in administrative jobs.

The following are examples of PBR:

a   Piecework

This rather primitive incentive system dates back to the time of Fredrick Taylor (see Chapter Two). It is based upon a price for each unit produced, for example, £1.00 will be paid to the employee for every unit she or he produces. If the person produces 180 units in a week, the following will be paid:

$$\text{Units produced} \times \text{Rate per unit} = \text{Earnings}$$

$$180 \times £1.00 = £180.00$$

There are variants of this system which *guarantee* a portion of the payment, to offer a little stability and security to the employee. Not being certain of income can have a detrimental effect on morale – a state of dissatisfaction.

b   Premium bonus

There are several versions of this system, named after the person who developed them. Each is based upon time saved:

$$\text{Time allowed (TA)} - \text{Time taken (TT)} = \text{Time saved (TS)}$$

Halsey:
$$\tfrac{1}{2} \times \text{TS} \times \text{Basic hourly rate}$$

Halsey-Weir:
$$\tfrac{1}{3} \times \text{TS} \times \text{Basic hourly rate}$$

Rowan:
$$\frac{\text{TT}}{\text{TA}} \times \text{TS} \times \text{Basic hourly rate}$$

There are many versions of 'straight proportional schemes'. The principle is the same in each of them, though there are some differences in philosophy. The ACAS Advisory booklet No. 2

gives a good overview of them. It, along with other ACAS booklets, is free from your local Job Centre or ACAS Regional Office.

c Measured daywork

Because many PBR schemes cause earnings to fluctuate from period to period, which can bring hardship to people with regular financial commitments, measured daywork gives the rewards of PBR without the constant fluctuations.

The Work Study Engineer will set levels of performance which the employees, usually through their trade union, agree to maintain over a period of, say, six months. Pay is usually set at a rate for this higher level of performance, and guaranteed for that six-month period irrespective of actual performance.

Performance is monitored throughout the period, and the time period will be extended for those who achieve the agreed level. Where someone consistently fails to achieve the agreed level, extra training will be given; and if performance still fails to reach the required level, she or he will be moved off measured daywork.

Once again, there are many variations of the system, including 'stepped measured' daywork which allows people to move within bands of rates for differing levels of performance.

d Group bonus schemes

All of the systems we have looked at so far have been for individual production work people. That excludes many from the opportunity of earning more for more effort.

For example, the stores people may have to work a lot harder to keep supplying raw materials to those on the bonus scheme, or the forklift truck driver may be essential to the success of the scheme by keeping goods moving around the factory to where they are needed next, but they do not earn the same as the people they serve.

If this is ignored by management, it may result in hold-ups or disputes between sections in the workplace. In the worst situation, overall production levels could fall. The Volvo Case Study in Chapter Two illustrated the principle that all who contribute to success, either directly or indirectly were entitled to share the reward for the success.

There are as many schemes for achieving this as there are companies using it, so it is difficult to describe a set system. Many are based on volume of output, others on the sales value of what is produced, and others on the 'value added' to materials and services purchased by the firm.

Doubts about the effectiveness of PBR

In recent years, research into incentive schemes has revealed some interesting findings. Since Taylor's Scientific Management in the late nineteenth century, despite its known weaknesses in motivating people at work, managers seem to have been seeking the ideal incentive scheme that would cause people to work their hearts out with minimum supervision. None has been found. Indeed, it is hard to find any bonus scheme that has actually achieved its objectives. More often than not, the scheme's 'rules' are seen as a game, and the two 'sides' play at imposing the rules and avoiding the rules respectively. Most often, the employees concerned find ways of earning the bonuses without the related increase in productivity.

Herzberg's Two Factor Theory suggests that schemes of this nature will not, on their own, cause satisfaction. It is important to see it only as a part of an overall package of benefits, both physiological and psychological. We are back to the 'whole person' approach to motivation.

An explanation of why managers might persist with incentive bonuses might be found in McGregor's Theory X and Theory Y. The research discussed in Chapter Three, *A Blueprint for Success*, tended to the view that there was still a Theory X approach towards production people. A Theory X set of beliefs would incline the manager towards bonus schemes.

The movement in the 1990s is towards a much more 'whole person' approach. Organization culture, as we discussed in Chapter Five, is at the root of everything, and efforts to get the culture right (whatever 'right' is) are seen as the most valuable.

PROFIT SHARING

Another way of rewarding everyone in a company for its overall success is profit sharing. Obviously, there is no incentive in offering a share of the profits if no profits are being made, and so most of these schemes are found in quoted companies with good track records.

The main requirement is that a profit or loss figure should be made known to the staff at regular intervals. The element of profit to be distributed can be in cash or shares, and in schemes where there is a choice, it seems that about 80 per cent opt for cash.

The notion of profit sharing is popular in the European Community, and some political parties favour it. In the UK, the Finance (No. 2) Act 1987 allows for income tax relief to be received by employees on that part of their pay which is profit related. The regulations are stringent, and a company has to register its scheme with The Profit Related Pay Office, Inland Revenue, St Mungo's Road, Cumbernauld, Glasgow G67 1YZ for approval. A leaflet explaining the rules for such schemes can be obtained from this address.

*Figure 6.3 – **Examples of Cash Profit-Sharing Schemes***

Organization	Scheme	Eligibility	Formula for allocation	Distribution of bonus
Boots	Cash/shares	Permanent (including part-time) staff with 6 months' service at 31 March. New members receive $1/12$ share for each month following qualifying period to end of financial year (31 March)	8.85% of pre-tax profits paid into profit earning bonus fund (PEB). One PEB share equals total fund divided by total members' entitlements	PEB shares allocated according to weekly wage multiplied by a service factor of up to 8 × 2.85 for more than 30 years' service
British Nuclear Fuels	Cash	All adult permanent employees, (pro-rata payment for those under 18 and part-timers)	£50 for achievement of annual company profit target plus £5 per £1 million above this level up to a further £50. Additional £50 for achievement of half-yearly profit target. Maximum total for year: £150	Equal distribution for all fully eligible employees
Kodak	Cash/shares	All permanent staff in post at 31 December. Employees with less than four years' service eligible for cash only	At discretion of board	Percentage of current salary. Employees with less than 5 years' service receive $1/60$ of payment for each month's service over one year
Rowntree Mackintosh	Cash	All employees with 52 weeks' continuous service at start of financial year. Pro-rata payment for those completing 52nd week of employment during year	At board's discretion	1. Wage earners in proportion to average weekly wage; 2. Salaried staff in proportion to salaried earnings during year

Source: IRS, *Pay and Benefits Return Bulletin 262,* 21 August 1990

Advantages and disadvantages of profit sharing

Profit sharing has its drawbacks, like any other incentive scheme:

- The link between an individual's job and the final profit figure is difficult to make
- People who do not pull their weight receive the same reward as those who do
- The details of how the final figure is arrived at are complicated and can give rise to mistrust if the figure fluctuates between payments
- A drop in profits may be related more closely to market forces than employee effort
- Poor management can affect profits as much as or more than employee effort

The advantages of profit sharing are:

- Employees become aware that everyone's contribution to the enterprise is important
- Individual efficiency is seen in the final results. This, it is believed, encourages a sense of responsibility, and helps to make everyone cost conscious
- Management comes under greater scrutiny from the work people and are more accountable for their performance
- People who receive a share of the profit feel more ownership of their company and develop greater loyalty

*Figure 6.4 – **Profit-Sharing Payouts***

Organization	Last profit payout
Boots	Each Profit Earning Bonus (PEB) 'share' for each year to March 1990 was worth £3.36. Employees could take their service-related PEB allocation as cash or use it to buy shares at concessionary price of £2.86. Approximately 94% of eligible employees took cash
British Nuclear Fuels	£100 paid in November 1989 for profits in year to 31 March 1989 plus £50 for attaining half-yearly target for the year ending 31 March 1990
Kodak	8% of salary paid in cash or shares in March 1990 for 1989 calendar year, 93.8% of staff received cash
Rowntree Mackintosh	4% of salary paid in March for 1989 calendar year

Source: IRS, *Pay and Benefits Return Bulletin 262,* 21 August 1990

Salary Structures

Compared with wages, salaries are clear and simple. Salaries are usually quoted as annual amounts, £12 500 per year, for example, paid in equal periodic payments, generally monthly.

They are usually paid to non-manual work people, and do not normally have additions (like danger money).

The concept of salary is much more stable and permanent than wages. People who receive it are even called by a different name from wage earners – 'staff' as opposed to 'workers'. They are expected to think like the management and to hold the company's interest at heart.

The Institute of Management recognizes four main groups of salary earners:

- Senior and middle managers – those at director and head of department level
- First level managers and supervisors – those with responsibility for day-to-day operations and accountable to the people mentioned above

- Technicians and specialists – those with technical or professional qualifications, who do not have line responsibility
- Administrators and clerical staff – those whose jobs do not involve manufacturing

The salary scale for each group may be different. They may be structured in steps so as to encourage people to seek promotion or to reward experience. Teachers, nurses, civil servants and local government officials's salary structures are a good example of this approach. Figure 6.5 illustrates this.

ACTIVITY 6.4

The perceived difference between workers and staff has its origins in history. Prepare a reasoned argument to the question: 'Is the difference real? Is it helpful to perpetuate divisions in such a fundamental way, or would it improve performance to treat everyone equally?' Support your argument with facts that have been given to you in this book.

In the mid-1970s, the new managing director of Hotpoint in North Wales noticed that some men were having to clock in, while their 'young daughters' walked in to the office building without clocking in. When he asked why this should be, he was told: 'They are workers, these are staff!' He could not understand this explanation and he asked his managers to choose between everybody (including himself) or nobody clocking in. The result was that nobody clocked in, and lateness and absentism was reduced.

Job Evaluation

How do you decide how much to pay a machine operator in the workshop who spent two years training, compared with a clerk/typist who also spent two years training? Or a qualified nurse compared with a qualified accountant? Or a teacher with direct responsibility for the education of one hundred children, compared with a head teacher with responsibility for thirty staff and a £1 million budget? How can you work out what each job is 'worth' to the organization, and set up a pay structure that is fair and orderly? A partial answer can be obtained through job evaluation techniques.

Job evaluation is defined in the Equal Pay Act 1970. The law allows for men and women employed on 'like work' or 'work of equal value' to receive equal pay. In order to avoid pay discrimination on the basis of sex, a method of assessing the relative demand of different jobs is

---

*Figure 6.5 – **Salary Structure***

HEALTH SERVICE (GB)

	1.12.91	1.4.92
Student nurse (1st year)	£6 440	£6 820
Student nurse (3rd year)	£7 450	£7 900
Clinical grades		
A e.g. nursing auxiliary, (6 increments)	£6 605 to £8 100	£7 000 to £8 570
B e.g. nursing auxiliary, (4 increments)	£7 845 to £8 930	£8 300 to £9 450
C Minimum for those with second level registration, enrolled nurses (5 increments)	£8 930 to £10 570	£9 450 to £11 180
D Minimum for those with first level registration (4 increments)	£10 230 to £11 720	£10 820 to £12 400
E Nurse regularly in charge of wards (4 increments)	£11 720 to £13 570	£12 400 to £14 350
F Minimum for sister/charge nurse (5 increments)	£12 995 to £15 920	£13 750 to £16 830
G District nurse, health visitor, community midwife (4 increments)	£15 320 to £17 735	£16 200 to £18 750
H Minimum for senior nurse i.e. supervision/ deployment of staff (4 increments)	£17 130 to £19 565	£18 100 to £20 700
I Minimum level for clinical tutors	£18 955 to £21 470	£20 050 to £22 700

Source: IDS Report 613, March 1992

KEY POINTS 6.1

- Pay is an extrinsic factor. If the rates are too low, people will be dissatisfied; if they are too high, the organization will risk being uncompetitive. More industrial disputes arise over pay than all other reasons put together

- Companies will design a pay policy to suit their individual circumstances. The law is concerned mainly about how wages are calculated and paid, and not generally about the level of pay

- Pay can be made up of many elements according to the type of work and working hours

- Payment by results is a popular way of linking pay to productively, but it has limitations as an incentive

- Profit sharing is popular with the EC, and receives tax concessions, but it is not very popular with many employees

- There is a distinction drawn between direct people (workers) who are paid wages, and indirect people (staff) who are paid salaries. This distinction is not helpful in developing good human relations

needed. Dissimilar jobs may be compared by examining the knowledge, skills, physical and mental effort, responsibilities, decision-making, seniority, and working conditions of each. From this, it might be possible to design a pay structure that is fair and orderly, and that allows all jobs in an organization to be rewarded in relation to their actual difficulties and value to the firm.

It is the job that is evaluated, not the person who does the job. It is intended to be as objective as possible, although there is no truly scientific method available. Because of this, it is important that everyone whose job is being evaluated should see the process as fair and free from bias. Job evaluation schemes are often set up by outside consultants, such as ACAS, who are seen as unbiased, and the scheme will probably include appeal procedures for those who feel hard done by, to allow justice to be seen to be done. (See Figure 6.6.)

The starting point is the preparation, or updating, of job descriptions for all the jobs being evaluated. It is important that these are accurate and detailed because they will be the source information for later decisions about where the job fits on the pay scale.

Methods of Job Evaluation

There are many methods of evaluating jobs, with many variations of each, but they can be put under three main headings:

- Job ranking
- Job grading
- Points rating

JOB RANKING

This is a quick, simple and inexpensive method. Job descriptions are examined by a panel who simply put them into the order they judge to be their worth. A sort of league table is prepared, and then arbitrary divisions – called 'job grades' – are drawn. It is from these grades that pay levels for each grade are decided.

This approach is acceptable where the jobs

Figure 6.6 – *Justice Must be Seen to be Done*

No constructive dismissal where job evaluation reviewed

IN *Sangarapillai* v *Scottish Homes*, the EAT holds that an employee who resigned when he suffered a loss in status and a potential loss of salary as a result of a job evaluation exercise, had not been constructively dismissed. This was because the employer had promised to undertake a complete review of the exercise, and the employee's existing salary was to be protected in the meantime. There had therefore been no actual or anticipatory repudiatory breach of contract by the employer.

Source: IRS, *Legal Information Bulletin 450*, June 1992

being compared are reasonably similar and where members of the panel are familiar with the content of each one. There is no attempt to analyse the content of the jobs. They are looked at as a whole.

The Court of Appeal in *Bromley v H&J Quick Ltd* decided that job evaluation, which is non-analytical, cannot be used as a defence under the Equal Pay Act 1970.

It can lead to dissatisfaction simply because the views of the panel may not be understood by the job holders – there is no concrete evidence to support their decisions. An appeal procedure tries to take care of these disputes.

Some of the 'hit and miss' can be reduced by using paired comparisons. Every job is ranked in turn against every other job. Note: if there are N jobs to be compared, one with each of the others, then N(N – 1)/2 comparisons have to be made.) Each will be awarded either 0 if it is considered less important than its comparator, 1 if it is equal, or 2 if it is judged more important. Several judges will be involved and all their results will be collated – the total scores for each job places them in a ranked order. You can see that this is slightly more satisfactory, and new jobs can be added in at any time without disruption.

JOB GRADING

This starts at the other end. A set of specifications are prepared for a range of grades of job before any jobs are looked at. The lowest grade might be for unskilled work which requires no decision making and close support from supervisors. The next grade will include jobs which require more knowledge and skills, with some responsibility for decision making. And so on up to jobs that require a high level of training and little supervision, and carry a lot of responsibility.

When this grid of specifications has been agreed, each job description is examined and matched to the criteria in the grades, until the nearest grade is found. The job is then allocated to that grade.

Because some attempt is made to analyse each job, this method is considered to be semi-analytical, although probably not enough to be admitted in discrimination cases.

POINTS RATING

This method, and its many variations, is the most acceptable because it involves a detailed analysis of each job description. The knowledge, skills, effort and so on of each job are carefully analysed and recorded. These factors are often broken down further – for example, knowledge could be sub-divided into education and experience; skills into training, dexterity and experience; and any other relevant criteria for the jobs concerned.

Points are awarded to each of these factors. The number of points given to each will depend upon how important that factor is to the organization concerned. For example, an organization which prefers to train its own staff will give more weight to dexterity than it will to actual training received.

It is possible to build bias into the factors unwittingly. For example, it might be discriminatory to award more points to a characteristic that is found more in males than females – physical strength rather than dexterity.

Although this method is more objective than the other two, it still contains a degree of subjectivity that would be impossible to eliminate. Also, it takes a lot of time and expertise to set the framework, and then to complete the initial ratings. Keeping it up to date can also be costly.

With all systems of job evaluation, the end product is a list of jobs, in rank or grade order, that allows them to be slotted into the pay structure. The aim is to ensure, as far as one can, that the pay given for each job is fair compared with other jobs in the same organization, and the decisions about pay are orderly and just.

Effective Job Evaluation

As with all things, if job evaluation is not done efficiently and kept up to date, it can do harm as well as good to the company.

It adds to costs, and if the advantages are not reaped in terms of 'more satisfied, productive staff', it could affect costs, influence prices, damage competitiveness and ultimately have an impact on profitability.

The job evaluation department must not become self-perpetuating within the organization – it must serve a very definite organizational purpose, and be accountable for it.

During the 1980s, the managers of many organizations sought greater flexibility in payment structures to allow for changes in their markets. Coal miners used to be the wage leaders in industry, but the decline of coal as an industrial fuel has caused them to fall behind many other industries that are growing. The Health Service used to be measured in terms of level of care, but now it is measured by economic criteria for performance and efficiency. Job evaluation must be flexible enough to take account of and respond to these and other changes.

The effectiveness of job evaluation will be distorted if there is government intervention in pay policy, or if the state of the economy is poor.

The fact that there is a skill shortage or surplus may influence pay levels more than job evaluation; so might the fact that the employer is in financial difficulties or highly profitable.

KEY POINTS 6.2

- Job evaluation is a technique for establishing the worth of different jobs so that an orderly and fair pay structure can be set up

- There are three main methods of job evaluation: ranking, grading and rating. Each has weaknesses, and only rating would be accepted by an industrial tribunal in an equal pay case

- Fairness is maintained through an appeals procedure

Computer-assisted job evaluation is becoming more popular. It has the advantage that it can process more data more quickly and efficiently. Questionnaires designed for direct input reduce some of the subjectivity, though safeguards against 'insensitivity' may be needed. The potential advantages are greater efficiency and consistency. Changes can be effected with less demand on resources, and 'what if' techniques can be used to predict long-term financial implications of changes.

Computer-assisted applications in the personnel field can be linked. For example, job evaluation details may be linked with recruitment, performance records, competency records (appraisal perhaps), career planning and so on, to give a co-ordinated, coherent picture relating people to jobs to performance and success. While this might sound a little futuristic, it is beginning to happen in the UK, and is more widespread in the USA.

Employee Relations

Any society where people have to live and work together in close proximity develops rules and codes to allow its members to live in peace and harmony. Some are informal practices (like good manners or etiquette) whilst others are formal (like laws and regulations). Various bodies and institutions grow up to ensure that the laws are observed, and that law breakers are dealt with.

So it is in employment. People have to work together, doing work imposed on them by an employer. People and organizations are under all sorts of pressures: economic, domestic, social, legal and competitive. Change is constantly affecting them: technological, environmental, political, organizational, social and emotional.

Authority and power, and the culture of the organization, influence the quality of relationships, motivation and morale of employees. It is a complex web of human interactions, where a certain amount of control and direction is necessary if the organization's objectives are to be achieved. At the same time, individuals are less powerful than organizations and may be vulnerable to abuse of various sorts by the more powerful employer. Employers may be subjected to disruption if employees band together and use their unity to make demands that are not in the best interest of the organization.

People hold different views about these issues. Some believe that there is an inevitable conflict between 'them and us' – the owners or managers and the work people, and that class conflict will only be resolved through solidarity, conflict and strife at work. The validity or otherwise of this belief has been brought into focus with the collapse of Marxism in countries throughout the world.

Others believe that it is possible to generate a sense of belonging and loyalty to the organization. The goals are commonly shared and everyone is united in making the organization successful, because it is from that success that everyone involved will be rewarded.

Understanding the parties, rules, laws and procedures is a good basis for studying employee relations. We will look at each of these in turn. Then it will be helpful to see how they are applied in practice, and how institutions emerge to assist and control the process.

Independent Trade Unions

A trade union is defined in the Trades Union and Labour Relations Act (TULRA) 1974 as:

Any organization that consists mainly of work people, and whose principal purpose is the regulation of relations between those people and their employers.

Trade Union members pay a subscription from their pay – if agreed, it can be deducted at source by the employer under a 'check-off' arrangement and paid by the employer to the union in one lump sum. These subscriptions fund the activities of the union.

To be recognized as a trade union and enjoy what legal protection there is, it must be independent of any employer or employers. 'Independent' means, not relying upon financial or material contributions from other than their members. The Certification Officer for Trade Unions and Employers' Associations requires evidence of independence before the status of 'trade union' is given. Once registered, a trade union does not have to pay tax on its income from subscriptions, and is indemnified from liability in certain circumstances.

Building up members and keeping them is therefore very important to the viability of a union. There have been a large number of mergers in recent years, because increased unemployment tends to mean less members's subscriptions. Smaller unions could not survive and give their members a reasonable service, and so they were

*Figure 6.7 – **Union Membership***

Union membership drops below 10 million

TRADE UNION membership in the United Kingdom fell by 211,000 to 9.9 million during 1990, its lowest level since 1961, according to the latest figures from the Department of Employment. This is the eleventh consecutive fall in union membership since the 1979 peak of 13.3 million.

The total number of trade unions at the end of 1990 was 287 – 22 fewer than the previous year and a fifth of the peak number of 1,384 recorded in 1920. Of the 287 unions, 61% had fewer than 2,500 members and together accounted for just 1% of total membership, while the nine largest unions accounted for 58% of the total.

The DoE also reveals that women comprised 38% (3.8 million) and men 62% (6.2 million) of all union members. The reduction in trade union membership was almost entirely a result of a decline in male membership. Total male membership fell by 3.3% whereas female membership remained unchanged.

Source: IRS, *Employment Trends 512*, May 1992

swallowed up by bigger ones. In 1900 there were over 1300 unions; in 1950 there were half that number; in 1990 there were fewer than 300. Membership numbers have fallen from 13 million in 1978–79 to less than 10 million in 1990 (out of a working population of about 25 million).

ACTIVITY 6.5

Assume that you are beginning your career with a large organization like the Health Service, British Rail or ICI. Outline three reasons why it would be an advantage to join an appropriate trade union, and three reasons why it would not be an advantage. Make sure that you are constructing a balanced argument, and not one based upon prejudice or bias. How might your argument change if you were joining a small company?

Trade unions have to keep accounts like any business, and are required to submit audited accounts to the Certification Officer each year. The National Union of Mineworkers was taken to court in 1991 because it was alleged to have failed to keep proper accounts. In the event, the charges were dropped.

There are four types of unions:

- Craft unions
- General unions
- Industrial unions
- Staff (white collar) unions

a Craft unions
Craft unions provide membership for people with craft or trade skills. They guard their skill levels jealously. In some trades, they have a say in the appointment of apprentices, the training programmes apprentices follow, and the assessment of their skills. Only if they complete the apprenticeship successfully are they admitted to full union membership. The largest craft union is the Amalgamated Engineering Union (AEU) with about 800 000 members. The next is the Electrical, Electronic, Telecommunication and Plumbing Union (EETPU) with about 400 000 members. These two merged in 1992 to form the Amalgamated Engineering and Electrical Union (AEEU) which is now the largest craft union in the country.

b General unions
General unions accept a wide range of people – semi-skilled and unskilled. They do not restrict entry at all and tend to be quite large. The Transport and General Workers' Union (TGWU) is the largest in the UK with over one and a quarter million members. Next is the General Municipal Boilermakers and Allied Trades Union (GMB) with over three-quarters of a million.

c Industrial unions

Industrial unions are found in specific industries, such as coal mining. The one union offers membership to the whole range of employees in a particular industry – from unskilled to crafts and trades people, and some include supervisors and managers. The Union of Democratic Mineworkers (UDM) and the Civil and Public Service Association (CPSA) are examples.

d Staff unions

Staff unions offer membership to any white collar employees: clerical, managerial, scientific or technical. As the traditional industries's unions are declining, so these are growing. The Manufacturing Science and Financial Union (MSF) has 650 000 members and the Royal College of Nursing has nearly 300 000.

There are many small unions that cater for very specialist groups, like the Headmasters's Conference and the Association of Magisterial Officers. The largest twenty-five unions represent about 90 per cent of all trade union members.

Trade Union Recognition

Unions can only have influence in an organization if they are formally 'recognized' by the management to represent a certain class or classes of employee. Since the Employment Act 1980, there is no obligation on management to recognize trade unions. It is voluntary, no matter how many employees might be members of the union. If the union is not recognized, it cannot act on behalf of its members. If it is recognized, it can take part in collective bargaining on behalf of those it represents. It is wise to draw up an agreement that clearly states the limits of the trade union's rights to act for its members. It does not automatically have a free hand – it may be limited to matters of discipline only, for example.

ACTIVITY 6.6

You will find a classification 'Trade Unions' in the *Yellow Pages*. Note the unions that have offices in your area. Which type of union are they, and in which local industries do they have members?

If it is possible, invite an official from one of the unions to your school or college to talk to your group. Ask her or him to explain their function and how the union operates. If this cannot be arranged, then in all probability some of the teachers in your school or college are members of the NUT or ASM&WT or PAT or NATFHI and they will have a branch secretary. Ask that person to tell you about her or his role.

Trade Union Officials

If an employer gives recognition to a union, the union members will need to organize themselves so that they can negotiate and bargain with management.

Within the company, the members of the union elect their representatives from their own number, by majority vote. The elected representatives are normally called 'shop stewards'. They are still full-time employees of the organization, and will carry on their usual job; but they now add the responsibility of representing their fellow employees to the management. The law allows them to claim 'reasonable' time off with full pay to carry out their new task.

Shop stewards have a dual role. They consult with their members and take any grievances and difficulties to management. The usual issues that are handled by shop stewards are pay, overtime, work allocation and change, health and safety, victimization and discrimination.

On the other hand, while negotiations are going on, and when agreements are reached with management, the shop steward has to report back to the membership and advise them of progress and decisions. Whilst the shop steward is not a communication channel for management, it is important that she or he keeps the members well informed, otherwise there is a risk that they will lose interest, and the shop steward may not have the support needed when the going gets tough in negotiations.

Besides these primary roles, the shop steward will try to recruit new members, collect union dues, communicate with the regional officer of the union, attend meetings, and attend training courses in negotiation and collective bargaining skills.

It is a busy and at times thankless job which is often hard to fill. But it is a key role in industrial relations.

There will be times when a matter arises that the average shop steward cannot handle. Sometimes more than one union will be involved. It may be wise at that stage to call in the district or regional officers. These officers are full-time employees of the trade union, and are accountable to the union. They are usually experts in all industrial relations issues and are skilled negotiators. They act on behalf of the union's members who work for companies within their district. When a union or a group of unions are in dispute with an employer, it is usual for the officers to be kept well informed at all stages of the procedure, and to intervene if and when it becomes too complicated for local shop stewards to handle.

Figure 6.8 – NATFHE

The longest strike ends in victory for NATFHE

NATFHE'S longest running and most successful strike to date ended at noon on Monday 1 June, when members in four Inner London Branches, meeting in Lambeth Town Hall along with NALGO, NUPE, NUS and APEX members, voted to return to work.

The strike followed an official ballot for 'escalating strike action'. It closed Brixton, South London and Vauxhall Colleges for 13 days, and involved more than 300 lecturers as well as support staff and students.

The campaign began in February, when Lambeth Council announced a cut of £1.2 million (11 per cent) in the FE budget for 1992/3.

Some 50 redundancies were threatened, a massive reduction in courses offered, fee increases, etc. – devastation to a service which teachers and support staff colleagues laboured to build over many years.

The action saw off all threat of redundancy, and secured guarantees against course closures and fee increases.

Source: The Lecturer, No 6, August 1992

Single Union Agreements

The problems of having to deal with several different unions within one workplace has always been a criticism of the UK system of employee relations. Some years ago, the management of British Leyland had to negotiate with nearly thirty unions. The logistical problems of dealing with so many vested interests, together with inter-union squabbling, caused great difficulties.

In recent years, a lot has been said about the advantages of 'single union agreements' (SUAs). Some Japanese firms have made it a condition of opening a factory in the UK, that it should have a SUA. Three-fifths of inwardly investing Japanese firms have established SUAs, whereas only two-fifths of inward investors from other countries, mainly the United States, have made such arrangements. It seems to depend upon the company being a green field operation or a continuation of an existing business.

Most unions do not like it, though a few see it as an opportunity to grow and prepare for a future that is going to be different from the past.

The firms ask unions to make proposals about the services they will offer to members, the negotiating procedures they would use, and the methods they would follow in resolving disputes with management. No strike agreements are usually required. Upon receipt of proposals, management study them and choose one union to represent all grades of workers in the company. The unions liken this to a beauty contest, and several refuse to take part, seeing it as a dilution of union power.

In circumstances where it is not possible to insist on SUAs (for example, where a firm already exists and has traditionally had several unions) 'single negotiating table' agreements are sought to ensure that there is minimum rivalry and inter-union competition. All unions sit at the same table to negotiate pay and conditions of work.

This is not the same thing as a 'closed shop', which we will discuss next. No-one can be discriminated against for being or not being a member of a union (Employment Acts 1982 and 1990). Employers can be fined heavily for refusing to employ, or for dismissing, a person because of trade union membership or non-membership.

Closed Shop Agreements

The term 'closed shop' refers to union–management agreements that all employees *must* be members of a certain union or unions, either before they join the company or immediately after they start employment. Failure to become a member used to lead to dismissal. The concern for individual liberty in such matters caused much debate, but it gave the unions great strength, and weak management allowed themselves to be forced into agreeing to such arrangements.

The Employment Act 1980 killed off closed shops without making them illegal. No-one can be discriminated against in relation to trade union membership, as mentioned above. Trade unions would become liable for damages if they tried to force an employer to employ or to sack someone for being or not being a trade union member. So the closed shop is now unenforceable, although it is not outlawed.

Rights of Recognized Unions

Management has the right to recognize a trade union or not. It is voluntary. But once it does recognize a union, that union has some rights under the law:

• Its officials need time to carry out their industrial relations duties. They are entitled to 'reasonable' time off with pay. What is considered 'reasonable' is for negotiation between the parties

- Its members are entitled to time off, without pay, to attend meetings and other essential trade union activities
- Its members can elect, or its officials can appoint, Safety Representatives who have rights under the Safety Representative and Safety Committees Regulations 1977
- Its officials have a right to company information that is necessary to allow them to plan their negotiations. An example of this might be the company's financial status, and its plans for the future. As the company uses these for human resource planning, it seems reasonable that the unions would need them for planning wages and bargaining positions
- Its officials have a right to be consulted if redundancies are likely to be necessary, and to be notified in writing if redundancies are to be made. If more than one hundred are to be made redundant, then ninety days's notice must be given; ten to ninety-nine, then thirty days's notice must be given: under ten will require 'as much notice as possible'
- If the firm is likely to be transferred or sold to new owners, officials are entitled to be informed and consulted

No strike agreements

When we discussed the contract of employment in Chapter Five, it was pointed out that agreements between unions and employers were not binding on those parties unless it was expressly stated that they were to be so. However, the same agreement became an implied term in every employees's contract and as such *was* binding upon the employer and each employee.

No strike agreements are an exception. They are not included in every individual contract of employment unless they are in writing, and are incorporated into each contract of employment expressly or impliedly. It is a difficulty for courts to 'order' someone to work. The value of a no strike agreement is that an employer would be able to seek an injunction which would force the union to keep to all the procedures before a strike could even be threatened.

No right to strike

In most walks of life, if one person causes damage to another, a court may find liability and award damages. In business, if a union calls its members out on strike and damages the employer's business, the employer could sue the union for damages.

There is no legal 'right to strike' in the UK's industrial relations laws. However, immunity from this liability will be granted to trade unions in all cases where:

- There is a secret ballot of those directly involved, in which the majority votes for strike action
- Where action is taken only against the employer with whom the strikers have their contracts of employment

Any employees who go on 'unofficial strike' have no protection and could be dismissed. If shop stewards in a company call for strike action without going through the correct procedure, the union is deemed to be responsible unless it repudiates the action in writing to every member involved in the unofficial action.

Picketing is the traditional way for people in dispute with an employer to try to convince other work people to join them. They do this by standing outside their place of work and giving

---

*Figure 6.9 – **Recognized Unions Bargain for Better Pay and Conditions***

Television staff reject pay offer

UNIONS representing BBC workers are expected to refuse this year's 3.7 per cent pay offer.

Broadcasting union BECTU will write to the BBC this week with its formal response.

The BBC says its first offer, covering 25,000 staff, is designed to tackle low pay, with a guarantee of a minimum rise of £300.

'The BBC believes this is a reasonable offer bearing in mind the retail price index and the fact that following improvements last year BBC pay is generally competitive,' a spokeswoman said.

But unions say the offer, which is below inflation, is not as good as the prevailing rate for the industry. They had asked for 3 per cent above the rate of inflation.

Journalists' union the NUJ has also demanded a minimum salary of £7,500.

National officer at BECTU, Roger Bolton, said the offer was disappointing after the union's two-year battle to improve pay levels.

'After the 1989 industrial dispute we got an 8.8 per cent increase, then an additional 5 per cent last October,' he said.

'But pay is still almost 10 per cent below the norm.'

Unions will meet BBC managers in two weeks' time.

Source: Personnel Today, 2 June 1992

information to those going in. In all matters of industrial action, picketing is only lawful if it is peaceful, at or near the person's place of work, and in furtherance of a legitimate trade dispute.

On 1 May 1992 a revised Code of Practice on picketing came into force. It states that 'there is no legal "right to picket" as such', but that 'attendance for the purpose of peaceful picketing has long been recognized to be a lawful activity'.

Trade Union Congress (TUC)

Most big unions are members of the TUC. It is a focus for trade union thinking and reflects trade union philosophy. Its annual congress (or conference) is a policy-making forum, and the TUC is expected to represent the decisions of congress both inside the trade union movement and to the world at large.

The TUC is not in any way associated with business, though it is probably operated along business lines itself. All affiliated unions maintain their autonomy, and it is they that relate directly with businesses and employers.

Indirectly, the TUC acts as a pressure group and tries to influence government and others on economic and social issues in line with the resolutions of Congress.

The TUC also represents UK trade unions in Europe through membership of the European Trade Union Confederation. Although this body has no powers of its own, it represents trade union views on a number of important committees in the EC and ensures that employee rights are considered in all their decisions.

ACTIVITY 6.7

You can obtain a great deal of up-to-date information about trade union affairs by writing to:

(SCOTLAND)
Scottish Trades Union Congress
12 Woodlands Terrace
Glasgow G3 6DE

(WALES)
Wales Trades Union Council
1 Cathedral Road
Cardiff

(ENGLAND)
Trades Union Congress
Congress House
23–38 Great Russell Street
London WC1B 3LS

Employers's Organizations

An employers's association is any body that consists mainly of employers or proprietors whose principal function is to regulate relations between those employers and trade unions.

There are 86 such associations listed in the back of the *Kompass Directory* – from the British Adhesive Manufacturers' Association to the British Whiting Federation.

Most employers do their own negotiating with trade unions. However, for those that wish it, there are many employers's associations, covering every area of occupation, which provide national negotiating services to their members.

For example, The National Farmers' Union is not a trade union, it is an employers's association which negotiates basic pay and conditions on behalf of all farm workers with the agriculture arm of the Transport and General Workers Union.

The Engineering Employers' Federation negotiates basic wages and conditions on behalf of all its member companies with the Amalgamated Engineering Union and others. It seems that employers' associations have grown up to mirror the structure of trade unions in their area of occupation. There are many other examples of this mirroring.

The agreements reached form a minimum standard for those industries, but most employers then negotiate locally with their own shop stewards, using these standards as a starting point. So there are National Agreements that form a basis for Local Agreements.

This service is particularly helpful to small firms who do not have the time or skill to do the whole thing from scratch. Their associations also provide advisory services in matters of employment law and legal advice to those who are in dispute with unions. They gather statistics about employment matters and distribute it to those who request it.

The Confederation of British Industries (CBI)

The CBI was formed by Royal Charter in 1965. It was deemed necessary to have one body that would talk for all employers, and for business in general.

Like the TUC, the CBI does not negotiate with anyone, but it is a focus for business thinking. Through its twenty-five standing committees it can represent business views on a wide range of matters, including industrial relations, to a very wide audience. It is influential at government level, particularly when there is a Conservative government in power, in economic matters as well as industrial relations.

CASE STUDY

ACAS Gets Busier Than Ever

Britain's independent arbitration service was busier than ever last year, despite an all-time low in the number of working days lost to industrial disputes.

The increased workload was partly the result of the rising number of redundancies caused by the recession and employers' efforts to rationalise production, says the 1991 annual report for the Advisory, Conciliation and Arbitration Service (ACAS)

Requests for conciliation in collective disputes rose by 10 per cent and in individual cases by 12 per cent. Disputes arising from redundancy accounted for almost one in five (19 per cent) of all collective cases completed by ACAS, while those relating to pay and conditions fell to 41 per cent of the total from 50 per cent.

Employers, trade unions and individual workers are now keener to ask for conciliation from ACAS than to pursue confrontation, said ACAS chairman Sir Douglas Smith.

'Redundancy cases are the sort of issue which in the past could have produced industrial action; the parties were readier in 1990 and 1991 to bring their problems to us and see if we could help them resolve them. The other factor is that with the extension of employment rights, more and more trade unions have been ready to back their members' complaints to a tribunal,' he said.

Industrial tribunal cases concerning unfair dismissal and sex discrimination were the fastest-growing subjects for individual conciliation, with the latter more than doubling to 3,500. Issues such as promotion were far more common causes of sex discrimination disputes than sexual harassment.

In all, ACAS succeeded in settling or making progress towards a settlement in no less than 86 per cent of the completed collective conciliations it dealt with. Only a third (43 per cent) of individual cases needed to go forward to industrial tribunals for decision.

ACAS also responded to a record 467,000 enquiries for information on statutory employment rights and entitlements and on other employment matters — a rise of 12 per cent.

Demand for ACAS services is forecast to continue rising steeply in the coming year, based on figures for the first quarter of 1992.

ACAS statistics

	1990	1991
Requests for collective conciliation received	1,260	1,386
Conciliation successful or progress achieved	964	1,056

Completed conciliation cases by cause of dispute:

Pay and terms and conditions	570	496
Recognition	159	174
Changes in working practices	67	46
Other trade union matters	50	91
Redundancy	109	233
Dismissal and discipline	147	144
Others	38	42
Total	**1,140**	**1,226**

Individual conciliation – cases received:

Unfair dismissal	37,564	39,234
All discrimination cases	3,516	6,214
Wages Act	8,114	11,763
Other employment protection provisions	2,877	3,394
All jurisdictions	**52,071**	**60,605**

Source: Employment News, June 1992

QUESTIONS

1 Sketch a diagram that shows the growth in activities shown in the ACAS statistics

2 Why is it important to the users of its services that ACAS should be independent?

3 Discuss three business reasons why 'employers, trade unions and individual workers are now keener to ask for conciliation from ACAS than to pursue confrontation'.

Advisory, Conciliation and Arbitration Service (ACAS)

ACAS is an independent body that offers unbiased help to employers, trade unions and individuals in matters of employee relations disputes. It guards its reputation for impartiality very jealously so that any party in a dispute will feel able to turn to it for help.

The forms of help it can offer are in its name. As well as resolving disputes, it can offer advice on a wide range of employee relations issues. For example, it can help with setting up a job evaluation system or advise on appraisal schemes. It can conciliate between the parties in dispute by listening to both sides of the argument and bringing them closer together.

ACAS can also be called in to arbitrate where two disputants are so far apart that they are unlikely to find enough common ground to reach a peaceful agreement. ACAS will listen to both sides of the argument, consider them carefully, and come up with a solution that both sides must accept. ACAS insists, where it is an arbiter, that both sides agree in advance to accept its decision.

Besides these services, ACAS undertakes research into all aspects of employee relations, particularly in matters of employee participation and involvement. It publishes statistics on matters relating to disputes and case loads of industrial tribunals. It monitors trends in employee relations and publishes many booklets and reports to assist in good practice.

In its 1990 annual report, it outlined the pressures of the recession and the European Single Market on companies in matters of employment practice. The trend away from national and company-wide bargaining towards local agreements was highlighted. In the report's conclusion, ACAS said:

'We saw welcome evidence, for example, that employers might be becoming more aware of the need to consult and inform employees and to involve them more fully in discussions about developing business needs. Trade unions were increasingly ready to discuss what might need to be accepted or avoided to secure the viability of enterprises and jobs. At the same time the challenges are considerable. Much remains to be done.'

Collective Bargaining

The form of negotiation found in employee relations is known as collective bargaining. It is the cornerstone of a trade union's function and the right to bargain is defended fiercely by the senior officers of the trade union movement.

Collective bargaining can be defined as:

A technique for controlling the basic power relationships which underlie the conflict of interest in the industrial relations system.

This definition brings the 'power conflict' difficulty to the fore. Though the two parties –

KEY POINTS 6.3

- Opposing objectives are held by the different parties in business, which leads to conflict. The business can accommodate this conflict by agreements and procedures, thus avoiding disruption

- The parties are employers, employees, trade unions, employers's associations, ACAS and the law

- Employees may be represented by trade unions. The unions must be 'independent'. There are four types: craft unions, general unions, industry unions and staff unions

- Employers are not obliged to 'recognize' unions, but, if they do, unions have certain rights in representing their members to the employer. Shop stewards are elected by the members for this purpose

- The closed shop is now ineffective. No strike agreements and single union agreements are the current vogue. British work people have no legal right to strike. Immunity from liability can be had by unions under certain circumstances

- Employers's organizations exist to mirror the trade union structures, and act on behalf of member companies

managers and shop stewards – are dependent upon each other, and co-operation would appear to be the most beneficial approach, the fact that they are pursuing different objectives (profit v wages in its crudest form) creates competition for a share of the rewards and resources, and bargaining power will affect the outcome in terms of who gets what. Ideally, each party should be as powerful as the other and respect each other's rights in the process.

One way to provide some sort of stability in which bargaining can take place is to have mutually accepted rules and procedures that will provide a framework in which to negotiate.

However, the negotiators may be happy to follow the rules and have the stability to create a balanced use of power, but those for whom the bargaining is taking place – the employees – may not. This will add pressure on one side to alter the rules, and conflict will result unless the other side is willing to be flexible. If this were to happen, the framework would no longer offer stability, and therefore the likelihood of competition and conflict would increase.

During the 1970s, industrial relations law and political influence gave trade unions a power advantage over employers. In the 1980s, this imbalance was redressed and 'the right to manage' was restored.

The influences of the law and government determine where the power lies. The use of 'disputes' to show where the power lay, or to redress a balance of power in the relationship, has been drastically altered by laws passed during the 1980s. These external influences should seek to ensure a balance that provides for harmony, but the values of the law makers will dictate what 'harmony' means!

Perhaps the most realistic scenario is one suggested by Peter D Anthony, Senior Lecturer at University College, Cardiff:

'It would be better to regard collective bargaining as a process in which representative groups involved in employment, seek temporary accommodations of their different interests. The accommodations are not final; at any time they are likely to reflect a distribution of power between the groups which may change and which may then result in a demand for a new accommodation. For this reason, the rules arrived at in collective bargaining may be of a particularly fragile kind.'

Whatever happens, however much harmony or conflict might exist in collective bargaining, the parties will eventually have to reach some kind of agreement. Anthony puts it clearly, that bargaining is about negotiating the distribution of scarce resources, money, status or power; and to achieve their individual objectives, negotiators can choose to collaborate or compete.

ACTIVITY 6.8

Can collective bargaining work in a free market economy in the 1990s? Consider three arguments to support collective bargaining, and three arguments to oppose it.

If it can be organized within your group, set up a formal debate with a proposer and seconder, and an opposer and seconder to consider the motion: 'This house believes that industrial work in the private sector is hindered by collective bargaining.'

KEY POINTS 6.4

- **Collective bargaining is a means of reducing or resolving the inherent conflict that exists between the parties in business**

- **So that all parties know the scope and rules, agreements about procedures are made**

- **Whether disputes are resolved by agreement or conflict will be influenced greatly by the parties's cultures and perception of power balance**

- **As the business environment changes, procedural agreement may have to be modified**

Procedure for Discipline and Grievances

Discipline is defined in the *Collins Dictionary and Thesaurus* as 'a system of rules for behaviour'. Disciplinary action, then, is taken against people who do not follow those rules.

The EP(C)A 1978 requires that all organizations employing over twenty people have a written procedure for discipline and grievances, irrespective of whether trade unions have been recognized. It must be made available to every employee.

It is the responsibility of the management of an organization to produce a written procedure. If trade unions are recognized, they will doubtless want a say in its structure and content (though they would probably steer clear of agreeing policy), but the legal responsibility rests with management.

ACAS has produced a Code of Practice – *Disciplinary Practice and Procedures in Employment* – to act as a guide to those preparing procedures. Of itself it is not a legal requirement, but employers would be expected to conform to the spirit of the Code.

The essence of this procedure is 'fairness':

- Fair and equal treatment of all individuals
- Fair methods of dealing with people
- Fair standards of work that apply to all jobs
- Fair expectations – people know what is expected of them
- Fair decisions – all people are treated similarly, based only on the facts
- Fair outcomes – the right of appeal is given to people who cannot agree with the decision on sensible grounds

Managers should be concerned with discipline all the time – not just when someone breaks the rules. They should be monitoring the behaviour of work people in three areas – attendance, performance and co-operation – and taking minor corrective actions all the time. The action may be in the form of additional training or counselling and its purpose is to ensure that people are giving of their best. It is unlikely that morale would be high if one or two people were allowed to get away with things that resulted in other people having to do their work or cover for them. Good, fair, consistent discipline is important in building high morale. Once again we see that a culture that values fairness will support self-discipline rather than coercive disciplines.

The punishment must be in accordance with the procedure, and usually includes:

- One verbal warning
- A first written warning
- A final written warning
- If all of these fail to correct the behaviour complained of, then the person may be dismissed

Throughout the duration of the procedure (it may be weeks or months) such support and training as may be needed to correct the behaviour must be made available.

If an employee commits an act of gross misconduct, the employee may be dismissed without warning or notice – this is termed summary dismissal in consequence of gross misconduct. Matters that are considered gross misconduct should be specified in the procedure. Violence, drunkenness, theft and dangerous practices may be examples of gross misconduct.

Appeals

Anyone who feels that they have been unfairly treated has a right of appeal to a manager other than the one who awarded the punishment. This is usually a senior manager specified in the procedure. The appeal should be heard quickly after the event – that seems reasonable. All the facts of the case should be put before the senior manager, and she or he should consider them impartially. Usually, the senior manager's decision is final.

ACTIVITY 6.9

For this exercise you must take the role of a personnel officer. It is your job to see that all disciplinary hearings follow the rules of fairness outlined above.

Adel Makram, a brilliant young programmer in the accounts department, has been given a verbal warning by his head of department for frequent lateness. His punctuality has not improved, however, and you are now responsible for conducting the next disciplinary hearing. You have no information as yet, and you are just about to start your preparation for the interview. Set out the steps you will take before the interview to make sure that everything is fair to the company and to Adel.

Grievance procedure

Every employer, irrespective of size, must provide each employee with details of the grievance procedure (EP(C)A 1978).

Grievances range from the usual grumbles about pay, or the boss, to serious aspects of the contract of employment that an individual feels is being breached by the employer. It may be about pay or bonuses, the way the supervisor treats people, discrimination of one sort or another, or any other genuine concern felt by an employee.

It is quite difficult for an employee to bring a complaint against her or his boss, or the organization generally. Besides the impact it may have on future relationships, the employee may not want to rock the boat. But it is important that an organization should care about feelings of injustice felt by its employees. Loyalty and harmony are unlikely to grow in an uncaring culture. So providing them with the means of securing justice is good motivational policy.

As with discipline, managers should be sensing grievances and dealing with them before they can cause any lasting harm to the organization. It should also be part of the culture that grievances should not be allowed to simmer but be brought into the open and dealt with.

A grievance procedure should provide people with the assurance that grievances can be brought into the open, and that they will be dealt with professionally without rancour or reprisal. They should almost be welcomed – because the alternative is not in the organization's best interest.

A formal grievance procedure may have three stages:

- First, any grievance is taken to the immediate manager and discussed with a view to resolving it quickly. Usually three days is considered sufficient at this stage
- Second, if it is not resolved to the complainant's satisfaction, it is passed in writing to the next level manager, who should deal with it within five days. The complainant can seek help from a colleague if she or he wishes
- Third, if it is still not resolved, a senior manager, probably at director level, will meet the complainant and any other people involved and make a final decision about the matter being complained of. Again, this should be within five days

In settling grievances satisfactorily, a company is signalling its concern with justice. If its procedure is perceived as fair it will be accepted and used.

ACTIVITY 6.10

Put yourself in the position of a relatively new, young female member of staff who is receiving mild sexual harassment from a junior manager. His approaches are unwanted but he won't take 'no' for an answer. You feel that you would like to do something about it but you are worried about the consequences. List the pressures on this person to not 'rock the boat'.

Examine your list, and decide how the company's grievance procedure could be set up to ensure that

those pressures do not stop people with a genuine grievance from using it.

Dismissal

Every contract of employment comes to an end. It may be because the contract was for a specific term, and the term has ended; or that the employee has reached retirement age; or that the employee has found another job and resigns. Or it may be that the employer terminates the contract of employment with or without the employee's agreement.

The EP(C)A 1978 sets out reasons for dismissal that are fair in law:

a Capability

If an employee fails to do the job to the standard required because of lack of ability or skill, the employer can invoke the disciplinary procedure discussed earlier. After a reasonable amount of training and support, if the standard is still not achieved, the employee can be dismissed.

b Ill health

This is a sensitive issue and needs careful handling. If a person suffers a long-term illness that keeps her or him off work, and the job must be filled, the employer should go through a process of careful consultation with the employee and the medical advisors, and if a return to work is unlikely in a reasonable time, the employer may dismiss. In such a case, the employer must give the employee the statutory notice and pay full wages during the period of notice, whether sick pay is being received or not.

c Conduct

In the disciplinary procedure, gross misconduct, and the process for establishing that misconduct has taken place, is set out. It is fair for an employer to dismiss an employee for gross misconduct without notice, and without pay in lieu of notice. For ordinary misconduct, such as persistent lateness, it will be fair if the disciplinary procedure has been used to its full extent.

d Some other substantial reason

It would be impossible to list all the reasons that would be 'fair' in all circumstances. An industrial tribunal has power to decide what is substantial.

For example, if, in order to protect its business, an organization needs to make some essential changes in an employee's contract and that employee will not accept them, it may be fair to dismiss. Every effort should be made to persuade the employee of the necessity to accept the changes, but if this fails, the employer has little option but to dismiss.

Another example is if an employee is closely associated with a person who is in serious competition, and that employee could give information that would damage the employer, then it is probably fair to dismiss.

e Redundancy

People are not redundant – jobs are redundant. The sad thing is that if the job disappears, there is no work for the job-holder, so she or he has to be dismissed. Redundancy occurs if the employer ceases the business in which the employee was working, or if a particular kind of work is reduced or ceases.

The resulting dismissal is fair if the people to be made redundant are chosen according to agreed criteria. Seeking volunteers for redundancy or 'last in first out' are often used, but both of these can create an imbalance in the remaining staff. Choosing by levels of performance, or by attendance levels, or some other criteria are fair only if people who may be affected by them are aware of them.

Alternative work must be found if possible. If someone is being made redundant whilst another person is being appointed to a job that the redundant person could have done, then the redundancy is unfair.

Recognized trade unions must be informed in writing and consulted about any redundancies. The employer has to inform them of plans for redundancies, and listen to their comments and advice – but there is no obligation to act on them.

Both the Department of Employment and the unions are to be given notice according to the numbers being made redundant:

10–99 = 30 days's notice
100+ = 90 days's notice.

Many companies will have redundancy agreements with recognized unions. Redundancy payments are set by law, but unions will try to get a better deal for their members. The calculation is based upon age and length of service. For any employee over eighteen and having at least two years's service with the employer:

- Half a week's pay for every year's service between the ages of 18 and 22
- One week's pay for every year's service between the ages of 23 and 41
- One-and-a-half week's pay for every year between the ages of 42 and 64

The Department of Employment sets the upper limit for redundancy pay each year. In 1991–92 it was £198 per week. Employers can pay more if they wish, but that is the maximum that they can claim from the redundancy fund.

Good human resource planning may help to minimize the number of redundancies, but economic cycles and innovations in new technology make it very difficult, if not impossible, for employers not to make some redundancies.

Unfair Dismissal

People who have been employed by the employer for two years have a legal right not to be unfairly dismissed. Any reason for dismissal not listed above may be unfair.

It is automatically unfair to dismiss someone because of:

- Membership or non-membership of a trade union
- Pregnancy
- Sex or race
- A spent conviction under the Rehabilitation of Offenders Act 1974

Besides the reason for dismissal having to be fair, the method of the dismissal must also be fair. Someone might be dismissed for a fair reason under the EP(C)A 1978, but claim unfair dismissal because the method of the dismissal was unfair.

---

*Figure 6.10 – **Redundancies***

Disclosure necessary despite derecognition

IN *Ackrill Newspapers Ltd* v *National Union of Journalists* the CAC upholds the union's complaint that the employer failed to disclose sufficient financial information in relation to its decision to implement redundancies. The fact that the employer had later derecognised the union did not negate its duty to disclose at the relevant time.

Employers who recognise trade unions for collective bargaining purposes have a statutory duty to disclose to union representatives certain information without which the union would be materially impeded in the collective bargaining process, and where disclosure is in accordance with good industrial relations practice (s.17 of the Employment Protection Act 1975 – the EPA).

A complaint by a union that an employer has failed in this duty can be taken to the Central Arbitration Committee (CAC). Where the matter is not settled by conciliation, the CAC can hold a formal hearing and, where appropriate, make a declaration determining the issue.

Source: IRS, Industrial Relations Legal Information Bulletin 452, July 1992

A person who wants to claim unfair dismissal must do so to an industrial tribunal within three months of being dismissed. ACAS will be asked to try to conciliate, but if a settlement is not reached, the case will go to tribunal.

Constructive Dismissal

There are cases when the employer takes actions or behaves in such a way that an employee feels it is impossible to continue working there and walks out.

Examples would be where the employer does not provide for safe working conditions, or where the employer over-rules a senior manager without good reason and makes that manager's position untenable.

The remedy in such cases is to claim unfair dismissal because the employer's behaviour showed that she or he did not intend to be bound by the contract of employment.

The procedure is the same as for unfair dismissal.

Industrial Tribunals (ITs)

Industrial tribunals are full members of the UK legal system. They are unique in having people on them who are chosen because they understand the work environment in matters relating to employment law.

Each tribunal has a chairperson who is a barrister or solicitor with at least seven years's experience, plus two lay people, one of whom was nominated by the CBI and the other by the TUC. Each member of a tribunal has an equal say in their decisions, and a majority verdict is sufficient.

The ITs are more accessible to ordinary people than other courts. A complaint to an IT by an employee or past-employee is written on a very simple form – an IT1 – and sent to the tribunal office. There is no need to engage a solicitor or be represented at any hearing, although there is nothing to stop a person doing so if she or he wishes.

An IT is conducted in a very ordinary room, and there is no pomp or ceremony. The chairperson will help either party to state their case, and conducts affairs at lay-person level, in as non-threatening a way as possible.

There are no court fees, and only in very exceptional circumstances may costs be awarded against a person who loses a case. So it is easy and cheap to take a case to an IT.

ITs are probably best known for their powers to hear complaints of unfair dismissal. It is relatively easy for an ex-employee to bring a complaint against the ex-employer. But to avoid wasting the tribunal's time, every complaint is vetted by ACAS who use their offices to conciliate between the parties and try to reach a settlement.

In 1990, 24 000 complaints of unfair dismissal were lodged (nearly 25 per cent more than the previous year). ACAS were able to settle 8 400 out of tribunal. 6 000 complaints were dropped, and only 6 400 went on to be heard at tribunal. That means that nearly 75 per cent of complaints were dealt with before they got to the tribunal. That is an impressive performance.

Altogether, only about one-third of complaints for unfair dismissal are upheld by tribunals. However, it is no victory for employers to win. They should be asking themselves: 'What went wrong to cause a complaint to be made to a tribunal?' If the answer shows that all the procedures were operated by the managers in the intended fashion, and that the procedures themselves were sufficient, then it may be put down to a difficult employee. But in most cases, there will be evidence of some need for a reappraisal of the way an organization handles these difficult matters.

The stress imposed on managers who have to justify their actions to a tribunal is considerable. The management time it takes up, that could be spent on more productive matters, has an unacceptable opportunity cost in most cases. The cost to the company in time and expenses is considerable. The effect of bad publicity is impossible to measure.

Someone whom an IT has found was unfairly dismissed has a right to compensation, reinstatement or re-engagement.

Compensation is made up of several parts. There is a basic award of up to £5 940. To this can be added compensation for loss of earnings, pension and so on of up to £10 000.

Figure 6.11 – EAT

Perverse tribunal decision overturned

IN *Brian Sherriff Ltd* v *Grant** the EAT holds that an industrial tribunal's decision that a dismissal was unfair, despite its findings of 'a formidable list of misdemeanours relating to conduct', was perverse. In applying the established case law tests as to reasonableness, it had 'lost sight of the requirements of the Act'.

Source: IRS, *Industrial Relations Legal Information Bulletin 415*, December 1990

KEY POINTS 6.5

- Every business employing more than twenty people must have written procedures for discipline and grievances, which must be made available to every employee

- The essence of these procedures is fairness and justice. To this end, each must include appeal procedures

- The contract of employment can be ended by dismissal. There are five circumstances where dismissal is fair – capability, ill health, conduct, some other substantial reason and redundancy

- Complaints of unfair dismissal may be made by an employee of two years's standing for any reason not listed above. Where an employer breaches the contract in such a way as to make the job-holder's position untenable, the employee may walk out and claim to have been constructively dismissed, which, if proven, is also unfair

- ITs are special courts set up to hear a wide range of complaints relating to employee relations law. ITs are a full part of the British judicial system

---

Additions may be made for refusal by the employer to reinstate or re-engage of up to £5 148; or if discrimination for sex or race was the reason, an addition of up to £10 296.

Employment Appeals Tribunal (EAT)

An appeal may be made on a point of law against a decision by a tribunal to the EAT (see Figure 6.11).

The EAT is made up of a High Court judge and two lay people. They can uphold or over-rule the findings of an IT. In rare cases, appeals to the Court of Appeal, and then to the House of Lords, can be allowed.

Personnel Records

In any organization, large or small, public or private, efficient use of resources is one of the key responsibilities of managers. The human resource is no exception. Records represent the basic information to enable managers to plan their people needs for the future; to organize the present use of their people and their training and development; to monitor the labour content of unit costs; to monitor lateness, absenteeism, staff turnover; and to record incidents like accidents, sick leave, discipline and personal matters.

Some records are required by law, such as PAYE records for income tax. Others would help in the event of a matter reaching an industrial tribunal. But the best reason for having accurate personnel records is to ensure that people receive the right pay, holidays, pensions and other benefits; and that they are considered for promotion, training and development when suitable opportunities arise.

Each organization will design its own particular record system. Some will be simple and inexpensive, others elaborate and costly. Provided they produce the information that will enable managers to achieve the above purposes efficiently and cost effectively, it matters little. Information that is personal must be treated with respect, and privacy should be safeguarded. Only those people in the organization who have a right to know should have access. Certain safeguards are provided by law to those whose personal details are held in computer systems.

Data Protection Act 1984

Organizations that hold people's personal details on computer files must register with the Data Protection Registrar.

The following data protection principles apply:

- The data must be obtained fairly and lawfully
- The data should be held only for specified and lawful purposes
- The data should be used for those purposes only
- Only relevant and sufficient data for the purpose should be held.
- The data must not be held once the purpose has ceased
- The data must be accurate and up to date
- The data must be held securely

Anyone whose data is held in this way is entitled:

- To ask and to be informed if data is being held about her or him
- To have access to the data for a fee not exceeding £10
- Where appropriate, to have incorrect data put right or erased

- To compensation for damage caused by inaccurate data held

Any personnel records held on computer files are subject to these principles and steps must be taken by the personnel specialist to ensure that they are met.

EXAM PREPARATION

SHORT QUESTIONS

1 What courses of action are available to a trade union when wage negotiations break down? (AEB June 1991)

2 What factors might be taken into account when preparing a wages budget? (AEB June 1991)

3 State two factors which might influence the basic hourly wage paid to a manual worker in the construction industry. (AEB June 1990)

4 State two situations where an employer can declare redundancies.

5 State the main functions of ACAS. (AEB June 1988)

DATA RESPONSE QUESTIONS

1 Haywood engineering employs 250 workers. In the past there were few union members and little union activity, however, as the number of employees has increased, so too has union membership. There are at present three unions representing employees in the company and discussions are going on about whether to ballot for a closed shop.

The owners of this small and traditional firm are unfamiliar with this new situation regarding trade unions in the workplace. As Personnel Officer, write a formal report (format *4 marks*) to the Managing Director including the following points:

(a) The advantages and disadvantages of trade unions to
   (i) the employees (individually and collectively)   (*8 marks*)
   (ii) the employer   (*8 marks*)

(b) The meaning of a 'closed shop', and the advantages and disadvantages of introducing one   (*5 marks*)
                                                                 (AEB June 1989)

2 Read the following extract and answer the questions below

CBI SPURNS PAY-PROFITS PLAN

1 'British industry has given a universal thumbs-down to the government's scheme to link a proportion of pay to profits . . .
Industry's big 'No' is the outcome of a consultative exercise involving over 1,000 companies, just completed by the Confederation of British Industry (CBI) . . .

6 Most companies have said they favour more profit-sharing. But they regard the scheme that the Treasury has outlined . . . as hopelessly theoretical.
The Treasury scheme envisages that pay might be divided into two components: base pay (say 80%) negotiated in the normal manner, and profit-linked pay (say 20%) which would vary as profits varied.

11 Tax inducements could be provided to encourage participation, perhaps worth as much as £5 a week to the average employee. The objective is to make pay more flexible in response to changing economic conditions so as to protect employment . . .
Companies' main objections to the scheme are:

16 – Employees, except those in the relatively few companies enjoying steadily growing profits, will regard it as far too risky.
– Demand for labour is not very responsive to changes in pay but is determined by many other factors. Really large changes in pay in the event of a recession would in most cases be needed to make employers review the size of workforce they require for operational reasons.

22 – A firm's existing workforce would resist new recruits, preferring to share profits among themselves.
– The definition of profits at the level of operational units, as required for the Treasury Scheme, would be an 'accountancy nightmare', leading to endless disputes about fairness.

27 – Negotiating profit-linked pay would require discussion of profit prospects. That would draw unions into all aspects of company planning.
Most of these criticisms are not thought to apply to the traditional methods of seeking to relate employee remuneration to profit, which generally involve bonuses or add-ons that are not considered part of basic pay . . .

32 A variant which the CBI and other groups that have been consulted . . . regard with some favour, would involve relating pay increases each year to profit increases

Source: adapted from an article by Christopher Smallwood, *Sunday Times*, 6 July 1986

(a) Explain the reason why making 'pay more flexible in response to changing economic conditions' (line 13) may protect employment   (*4 marks*)

(b) State and explain two factors, other than the level of pay, that determine a firm's demand for labour   (*4 marks*)

(c) 'the CBI and other groups . . . regard with some favour . . . relating pay increases each year to profit increases' (lines 32 to 34).
Outline **one** financial advantage and **one** financial disadvantage this would have for each of
(i) a firm   (*4 marks*)
(ii) its employees   (*4 marks*)

(d) Describe briefly how the Treasury's scheme might, if implemented, alter the traditional union-employer bargaining relationship.   (*6 marks*)
(AEB June 1988)

ESSAYS

1   A number of trade unions have reached 'no strike' agreements with some employers. How do these unions justify such agreements and why do some other unions dislike these agreements?

(AEB June 1990)

2   Outline and evaluate the factors which will determine the success of a trade union in negotiating with an employer.

(AEB June 1992)

Businesses Need Customers

Introduction

CUSTOMERS are people who buy the products and services of producers. They may buy for themselves or on behalf of the organization they work for. But because they are *people*, they set out to satisify their needs through the things they purchase. For example, a person may be hungry – she or he has a basic need to satisfy – and wants a salad to satisfy it. Maslow's model of human needs is as useful to the marketing specialist as it is to the personnel specialist.

Organization's Products and Services

When we consider the activities of any organization, we usually think about the products or services it offers. If we think of Norwich Union, we probably think of insurance. If we think of Hoover, we probably think of vacuum cleaners or washing machines. We might consider who buys these products or services and what purposes they serve or what use they are.

Insurance, for example, may compensate for any financial loss if a certain event happens – it probably satisifies a security need. Or it may provide financial help for dependants in the event of death – it satisifies a belonging (love) need. The vacuum cleaner keeps the home clean and hygenic – it possibly satisfies a health (security) need, or a love need, or even a status need ('Look at my beautiful home!').

ACTIVITY 7.1

What products does Sony offer? Who buys them from Sony? Who uses them? What needs might they satisfy? List as many services as you can think of which are offered by Barclays Bank. Who uses each of these services? What needs might they satisfy?

What 'services' does your school or college offer? Who uses them? What needs do they satisfy for their users and others in the local community?

This raises a chicken and egg issue. Which comes first, the product or the demand for that product? Does a company make a product and then convince people they want it, or does it find out what people want and then set out to supply it? Or is it a bit of both?

Successful businesses seem to know what their customers want and provide it at a price they are willing to pay. These firms seem to get their message across to customers and make their products available at a time and place convenient for their customers. They know their market.

A market is a group of people or organizations

who have a need for a product or service and have both the money and the desire to buy it. Getting to know the market and telling the market what you can do for them is the job of the marketing specialist.

ACTIVITY 7.2

You may notice that in Chapter Eight, when discussing supply and demand, there is a different definition used which relates to the place where buyers and sellers meet to set a price.

Use a good dictionary and look up the meanings of the noun 'market'. Now do the same for the verb. How many are there? In what ways are they different? What are the implications of this for you as a student of Business Studies?

Marketing

In the early 1980s Prime Minister Thatcher said that UK firms were not as good at marketing as their international competitors. The reasons for this may be cultural and lie in the history of the UK's industrial development. But it was evident that marketing was not regarded highly by academics or institutions.

Since her remarks, however, marketing as a subject in its own right has gained greater respectability and credibility. Many universities and polytechnics now offer degree courses in marketing. The Institute of Marketing has been granted its own charter which raises its status to that of other chartered institutes like accountancy and engineering. As well as commercial firms, all sorts of organizations now place much greater emphasis on customers: colleges, local authorities, solicitors and so on. In a free market economy, careful study of the market is essential, not optional.

What is Marketing?

The Chartered Institute of Marketing defines marketing as:

The management process of identifying, anticipating and satisfying customer needs profitably.

This is worth examining more closely. In practice it means:

- *Identifying*: researching the market and gathering information
- *Anticipating*: innovating, developing new products, producing them, holding sufficient stocks, distributing them, and publicizing and promoting them
- *Satisfying*: good quality products, that perform as expected, are easily available, are at a price customers are willing to pay, with adequate after-sales service
- *Profitably*: controlling costs, operating efficiently, being dependable, keeping up-to-date, professionally managed

The Marketing Concept

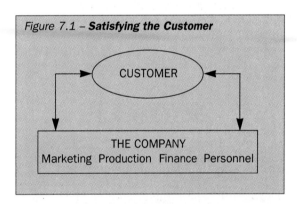

Figure 7.1 – *Satisfying the Customer*

CUSTOMER

THE COMPANY
Marketing Production Finance Personnel

When looked at like this, marketing is a company-wide commitment to create satisfied customers. Everyone who works in the organization is a marketer, from the top-most boss to the lowliest worker. It is a concept that puts the customer in the centre of the stage, sets out to understand her or his wants and needs, and then strives to satisfy them efficiently. This is claimed by the Chartered Institute of Marketing as a 'key to prosperity'.

The American Marketing Association's (AMA) definition follows similar lines:

KEY POINTS 7.1

- **Marketing is identifying, anticipating and satisfying customers's needs profitably**

- **The marketing concept puts customers at the centre of the stage, and everybody in the business is involved in satisfying them**

'Marketing is the process of planning and executing the conception, pricing, promotion, and distribution of ideas, goods, and services to create exchanges that satisfy individual and organizational objectives.'

Marketing as a Communication System

In order to gather information that will help an organization to know what customers's needs are, to interpret those needs and turn them into a product or service, and then to tell customers the organization can meet their needs, a well organized and effective communication system is required. Figure 7.2 illustrates this.

We will be referring to the diagram in Figure 7.2 several times so it may be worth copying it into your notes. In this diagram, the producer sets out to offer *value*. That is an important word in marketing. A customer will perceive good value if the product or service meets her or his needs in terms of performance, availability, quality, price and supporting services. It is this perception that will create sufficient motive for the customer to buy the product or service.

ACTIVITY 7.3

What factors might cause the users of the following products or services to perceive value: a Mars Bar, a pair of shoes, a wrist watch, a visit to the doctor, a bank account, a Rover Mini, a Rolls Royce? In what ways are they similar, and in what ways do they differ?

Communicating Value

The five main ways in which a producer may attempt to communicate this value are:

- Advertising
- Personal selling
- Sales promotion
- Publicity
- Direct marketing

We will consider each of these communication methods in turn.

ADVERTISING

Advertising is a means of sending a carefully planned message to a target audience via the media that the target audience is known to use. The media owners charge a fee for carrying this message to its readers, viewers or listeners.

None of us can avoid the impact of advertising. It is going on all around us all the time. It can be either informative or persuasive. Its purpose is to raise awareness of the advertiser's product or service in the minds of potential customers. This, it is intended, will increase sales and ultimately improve profits.

ACTIVITY 7.4

Identify ten advertisements that set out to inform potential customers about a product or service. Now do the same for advertisements that set out to persuade them to buy. Can you distinguish between the two types of product? It is said that products whose worth and value can be assessed before they are purchased need informative advertising, while

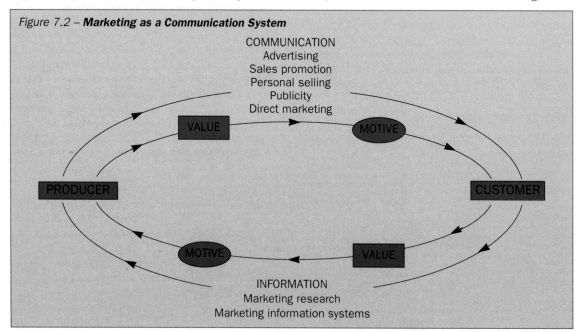

Figure 7.2 – *Marketing as a Communication System*

COMMUNICATION
Advertising
Sales promotion
Personal selling
Publicity
Direct marketing

VALUE

MOTIVE

PRODUCER

CUSTOMER

MOTIVE

VALUE

INFORMATION
Marketing research
Marketing information systems

products that can only be assessed after purchase need persuasive advertising. Is this true of the advertisements you chose?

Advertising is used to bring a business's message about goods or services to the attention of the people or organizations who are its target market – that is, the group of people or firms that it has designed its product or service for. They may be a small, select group – for example, fossil finders in Flintshire or widget makers in Wigan. They may be a very large group – for example, coffee drinkers in the UK or engineers in the EC.

A key skill of the marketer is to define the market clearly and to identify the mass media – newspapers, television, radio, journals, hoardings and directories – that are read, watched or listened to by the target market. The owners of those media are willing to carry a firm's message to their readers, listeners or viewers for a fee. For example:

- Anglia Television covers an area containing 3.2 million adults. About 567 000 of those watch *Coronation Street*. It will carry a thirty-second message to those viewers for £4 000 (or 0.7p per viewer)
- The *Daily Mirror* will carry a message on a whole page to their 3 141 000 readers for £24 600 (or 0.8p per reader)
- The *Great Yarmouth Mercury* will carry a half-page message to their 30 000 readers for £420 (or 1.4p per reader)

You can look up these prices and readership figures in *British Rates and Data* (*BRAD*) as mentioned earlier.

Although the cost of advertising per person is relatively low, the total cost is high and many firms cannot afford to use it. Also, it is very difficult to measure the effectiveness of advertising in increasing sales. In many cases it is a long time before results can be seen.

Target markets – consumers
In Chapter One we classified businesses according to where they came in the chain of production – primary, secondary and tertiary. We can use the same principle for describing people or firms that form different target markets.

Targeting is very important in marketing. If an organization fails to get its message to the people for whom the product was designed, it may lose potential sales income. If it spreads its message so wide that a lot of inappropriate people also see or hear it, the organization is wasting money. It is therefore important to understand how good targeting can be achieved.

ACTIVITY 7.5

An excellent classification system is the Dewey system in your library. Ask your librarian to explain how it works. Find out how you can pinpoint this book on its shelf among the thousands of other books all around it.

As you can target a single book out of thousands by using a methodical targeting system, so you can target groups of like people, or even specific individuals, through systems designed for that purpose.

There are several different classification systems that allow us to target specific types of people.

JICNARS social grading
The Joint Industry Committee for National Readership Surveys (JICNARS) suggests a social grading system that uses six categories:

- Social group A – upper middle class
These are exceptionally successful business and professional people who have become very wealthy. Many of them buy expensive status symbols, such as yachts, Porsches, and villas abroad so as to impress people with their success. They represent 3 per cent of the population.

- Social group B – middle class
In this group will be found the solicitors, doctors, teachers and senior managers. Their careers are important to them and they value education and cultural activities. They encourage their children to take advantage of higher education so as to build secure, professional careers. They are a good market for quality furniture, clothes, household appliances, cars and the like. They represent about 15 per cent of the population and are

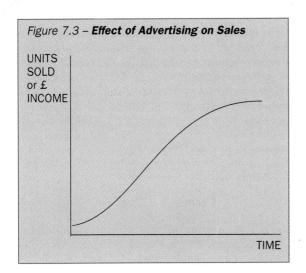

Figure 7.3 – **Effect of Advertising on Sales**

UNITS SOLD or £ INCOME

TIME

considered to have great discretionary purchasing power – that is, they are able to spend as they choose the money they have left after essentials have been bought.

• Social group C1 – lower middle class
In this group are the middle and junior managers, technicians and caring services people. They tend to be home-proud and buy conventional home furnishings, practise DIY, and buy clothes in the popular multiples like Marks & Spencer. They represent about 22 per cent of the population and have limited discretionary purchasing power.

• Social group C2 – skilled working class
These are the people who do skilled manual work and have craft or trade qualifications. They probably live in smaller houses and spend a high percentage of their money on essentials like food, drink, heating and clothing. They tend to buy the same brands, with occasional impulse purchases, and have limited opportunity for social or cultural activities. They represent about 28 per cent of the population.

• Social group D – working class
These people are semi or unskilled and have only a basic education. They tend to live in lower quality accommodation, spend their limited income on essentials and buy impulsively. Some can be caught in a poverty trap and attempts to escape from it are likely to fail. They are often poor judges of quality and sometimes rely on second-hand goods. They make up about 18 per cent of the population.

• Social group E – lowest level of subsistence
These people struggle to make ends meet. Most are on fixed incomes like state pensions, unemployment benefit or social security. They have barely enough money for essentials. About 15 per cent of the population falls into this group.

Media owners describe their readers, viewers or listeners using these classifications. A marketer whose target market may be described as 'B, C1' can find appropriate media using the same classification. This data can also be found in *BRAD*.

Despite its weaknesses as an analytical tool, and the emotive response it sometimes causes, social grading is popular because it is easy to use and helps to divide markets into target segments.

ACTIVITY 7.6

Which of the above classifications of people do you think would make up the majority of people who watch *Coronation Street* on ITV?

List some products and services that you believe those people may buy if they are subjected to effective advertising during the programme. Next time *Coronation Street* is on, watch the advertisements that are shown before, during and after, and check your judgement.

Other classification sytems
The office of Population, Census and Surveys (a government body) has produced other classifications, but they use the same basis as JICNAR – social class or occupation of the 'head of household'. However, in recent years there has been a move towards broader indicators of consumer behaviour.

ACORN (A Classification of Residential Neighbourhoods) uses the type of housing, its location and the number of people living there as the basis for its classification. Another similar system is PiN (Pinpoint identified Neighbourhoods) and both can be linked to the postcode in our address. For example, in the postcode NR31 9ER, the sector is identified by NR31 9. The types of housing in that sector are easily targeted by firms sending out direct mailshots. Lastly, SAGACITY is a classification that links class with income and family circumstances to give 'lifestyle' indications.

Target markets – producers
Similar classification systems exist for businesses. However, there is one sytem that is both popular and accurate.

SIC
The Standard Industrial Classification (SIC) classifies a firm by its main activity. It does this in four steps:

• Division
• Class
• Group
• Activity

For example, if you invented a brilliant product that stopped caravans jack-knifing and you wanted to send a message to all manufacturers of caravans telling them about it, you could look up the code for 'caravan manufacturers'. You would find that it is 3523 and that it is made up like this:

Division	Class	Group	Activity
3. Metal goods Engineering & Vehicles Inds.	35. Manufacture of motor vehicles & parts	352 M.V. bodies, trailers & caravans	3523 Caravans

Using a good industrial directory, you would then select all firms with the code 3523 knowing that they are your target market.

ACTIVITY 7.7

Look up the word 'ethics' in the dictionary. Ask your teacher to discuss its meaning with you so that you are clear about applying the concept of 'moral value' to business generally, but to marketing in particular. (This issue is considered in detail in another title in this series, *The Business Environment*.)

Consider the ethics of using 'social class' as a means of targeting persuasive advertising. Is its use justified in your judgement? Support your judgement with a balanced argument.

PERSONAL SELLING

The second way of communicating value to customers is by personal selling. You have probably had the experience of a salesperson calling at your house to sell double glazing or insurance, or similar products or services.

Some shops and stores still have expert salespeople to advise and help customers with their choices. Laura Ashley is one example of a store where the highest quality of assistance with purchases still exists.

Technical salespeople may be needed by manufacturers and service companies whose products are complicated or have to be specially designed for the customer. The salesperson is an expert who will discuss the client's needs and advise on the best product or service for that particular customer: mainframe computer manufacturers, production machinery manufacturers, major capital financing companies and pension scheme companies are examples.

In all these cases, face-to-face communication is used to inform and persuade customers to buy. Most personal selling is highly respected because the salesperson is very expert and adds value to the product with advice and guidance. The intention is that this expert service will persuade the customer to buy, but it is none the less sincere and ethical.

Sadly, a few abuse the power of persuasion in the one-to-one situation to convince people to buy things they do not need or cannot afford. How do you feel about this practice? Happily, it is only a very few salespeople who act in this way. Some time-share homes in Spain, for example, have been sold by dubious sales methods.

You will recall that advertising reached a large audience for a relatively low cost per person. Personal selling is targeted on individuals or firms and carries a high cost per person or company. However, more precise targeting is possible, the results are easily monitored and costed, and greater control can be exercised.

SALES PROMOTION

A powerful way of communicating value in a way that produces immediate sales is by sales promotion.

You have probably been offered a free taste of a product in a supermarket, or received a free sample of a new product delivered through your letter box. These are examples of sales promotion. So, too, are coupons that offer money off your next purchase or contests where you can win prizes. Demonstrations of products in exhibitions or stores is another example.

Sales promotion does not rely upon a media owner or a salesperson. It is a way in which a company offers an incentive that encourages customers to buy a product *now*. The incentive might be a saving, a prize or a free gift, but it appears to add value to the product for a limited time.

Its purpose is to create an immediate, short-term increase in sales. Many firms spend more on this than they do on advertising. The results are more immediate and measurable, and the company has more control over the targeting and duration of the campaign.

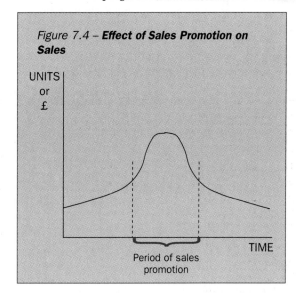

Figure 7.4 – **Effect of Sales Promotion on Sales**

Sales promotion can be directed at the consumer or at the trader. A trader may be offered prizes for promoting a particular product so as to increase its sales. Free display stands, in-store posters and shelf 'talkers' may be supplied to the trader to boost sales and profit (see Figure 7.5, next page).

PUBLICITY

Lastly, a less obvious but effective way of communicating value is by publicity.

Whenever you pick up a newspaper or watch a news programme on television you will be able to read or see news items about businesses. Some

Figure 7.5 – *Promotion material*

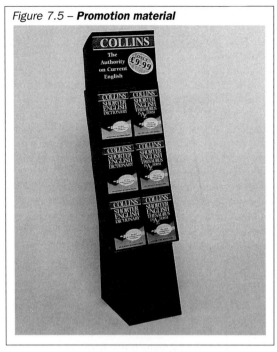

people may say that all publicity is good, but that cannot be true; bad publicity can damage a firm's reputation and can take a long time to overcome.

The contamination of Perrier Water in 1989–90 is an example of publicity that had a very damaging effect on the firm's sales (see Case Study opposite). Perrier was able to afford exceptional action to correct the matter, reassure its customers and so on. But their competitors benefited whilst they were doing it.

A firm can set out to use publicity positively. It can bring to the attention of the mass media events that can be written as news items. The opening of a new factory that creates new jobs is an example. It is not just businesses that use the media to gain positive publicity. Politicians, churches, clubs and so on use it.

There is no cost for carrying the piece of publicity in the media. But there are hidden costs in the preparation of the information in a form suitable for the media. This is usually called a press release. It is the story written in a journalistic fashion in the form of a news item, but so as to create the impression desired by the organization concerned. Often there is a lunch, or a famous person is paid to make a speech or presentation, to launch a new product or service. These hidden costs can be quite high as considerable skill and experience is needed to organize such events and to write good newsworthy press releases. Many firms engage public relations agencies to do these jobs for them.

Figure 7.6 – *Good Publicity for Branson is Bad for BA*

Branson attacks BA over Concorde

CONCORDE is the next target for Richard Branson in his battle with British Airways over unfair competition. At a meeting tomorrow, he will tell John MacGregor, the transport secretary, that BA should be stopped from using the supersonic plane as a loss-leader to attract passengers on the lucrative London–New York route away from Virgin.

For years Branson has chafed as BA has "poached" his first-class passengers by offering to upgrade them at no extra charge to seats on its fleet of seven Concordes, which were handed over free to the airline when it was privatised in 1986.

Last week Branson received £610,000 from BA after alleging that its employees hacked into Virgin's computers and poached its passengers. Now he is determined to drive home his triumph by accusing Lord King's airline of unfairly benefiting from a state hand-out.

The Virgin Atlantic chairman will urge MacGregor to strip BA of many assets originally funded by the taxpayer. These include Concorde, which cannot be rivalled by other airlines.

Branson wants MacGregor to introduce "positive discrimination" against BA so that smaller rivals such as Virgin, British Midland and Air UK will be granted any new flying rights that become available, unless there is an overwhelming reason to give them to BA.

In a further bold move guaranteed to rekindle fury at BA, he is also formally asking MacGregor to hand over 3% of all BA's landing and take-off rights at Heathrow to Virgin. This would amount to thousands of "slots", enabling Virgin to set itself up as a global network by 1995 in direct competition to BA, as well as establishing its Virgin European subsidiary airline.

MacGregor is said to be "amazed and disappointed" by the revelations about BA, especially as he was assured by the airline's officials there was no truth in the Virgin allegations.

Meanwhile, at Speedbird House, BA's Heathrow headquarters, managers are in deep shock following the High Court capitulation. "There is a dreadful atmosphere, with nobody certain about what Branson is going to do to us next, and a lot of scapegoat-hunting," said one insider.

Sources close to Lord King, the 76-year-old chairman who is due to become life president in July, said he was "devastated and depressed" by subsequent attacks in the press.

Source: Sunday Times, 17 January 1993, John Harlow.
© Times Newspapers Ltd. 1993

CASE STUDY

Poisoned Perrier

Perrier was first marketed at the turn of the century as 'the Champagne of Table Waters', and its success ever since has been associated with an image of sparkling purity. But yesterday, as tens of millions of bottles were being pulled off shop shelves throughout the world because of a scare over benzene contamination, doubts were cast on whether it would ever again be possible to present it as the last name in quality.

Source Perrier, the parent company, has made itself the most successful of mineral water firms by marketing what is essentially an idea. The fizzy water it draws from a spring at Vergèze, near Nîmes, costs only pence to bottle – but commands £2.35 at the Ritz.

During the past 10 years Perrier has led a boom in the sales of mineral water, exploiting a public mood for healthy living and becoming a status symbol along with the Porsche and the Filofax. Keen to associate itself with healthy living, Source Perrier has sponsored sporting events throughout the world, including the New York marathon. And backed by shrewd promotion, Perrier water has come to symbolize a lifestyle.

In Britain, through its advertising agency Leo Burnett, it has been responsible for one of the most successful television advertising campaigns. Based on the 'Eau' theme, it has led the way in food and drink marketing. 'H2Eau' and 'Picasseau' adverts have encouraged consumers to buy, while at the same time displaying a pleasing wit.

For consumers, the mention of Perrier evokes an image of water gushing from mountains.

If ever there was a company town Veryèze is it. Source Perrier provides work for about 3,300 people, and on the evidence of yesterday's mini-invasion by journalists, they are both proud and happy to be working for the company. According to Jean-Pierre Roux, the plant's genial director of human resources, they are positively bursting to get production back up to normal. The company has been run for the past 40 years and more by the patrician Gustave Leven, aged 75, whose family owns a substantial block of shares in the business.

On Wednesday, it was Leven's misfortune to collide with the Parisian Press out for blood at what some believe to have been the first formal news conference the company has ever organized. A pleasant-looking apple cheeked man, he seemed disconcerned by the ferocity of the attentions of the large and unruly press corps assembled at Perrier headquarters on the Rue de Courcelles.

Back in Vergèze, locals were expressing total confidence in Perrier's ability to bounce back. But advertising agencies were divided as to whether it would be able to reclaim its leading position in the mineral water market – one of the most competitive in food and drink retailing.

Several food and drink companies which have suffered health scares in the past have found that a comeback is not easy. One company selling tinned salmon took 11 years to regain its market position after a contamination problem which led to the withdrawal of all of its supplies from shops for two weeks.

Senior managers at Source Perrier were already planning a new marketing strategy as Leven announced in Paris the decision to withdraw the entire world stock. They had been preparing for the worst the moment the first hint of a contamination problem appeared last weekend, when traces of benzene were discovered in supplies in the American state of North Carolina. Within hours, Source Perrier had instructed subsidiaries in Europe to monitor customer reaction to the scare on a daily basis through market research surveys.

Like any other successful enterprise in a competitive market, Perrier has always been quick to recognize changing consumer tastes and aspirations. From the moment of the commercial launch in 1903, it has believed that selling its product is a matter of marketing an image, a concept.

In America, *The New York Times* praised Perrier's approach to the crisis. 'A company that respects the public's growing concerns for human health and the environment serves society and itself', the newspaper said. 'A company that appears to treat them casually risks a heavy loss in public trust. Perrier seems to have grasped this point.'

Source: Times, 16 February 1990, Jamie Dettmer and Philip Jacobson. © Times Newspapers Ltd. 1990

QUESTIONS

1 From the data in the Case Study, identify Perrier's promotional strategy. Discuss the extent to which this strategy was responsible for the company's worldwide success.

2 Consider how the adverse publicity might affect each of the following:
   (a) Gustave Leven, the Perrier boss
   (b) Perrier staff at Vergèze
   (c) Other manufacturers of mineral water
   (d) Major retailers, such as Tesco and Asda
   (e) Consumers of Perrier mineral water
   (f) Consumers of other brands of mineral water

3 Visit two or more supermarkets in your area. How much shelf-space is allocated to mineral water? What proportion of this space do Perrier products occupy? Does this suggest that Perrier has regained its position as market leader?

One disadvantage of this method of communicating a message to the market is that there is a loss of control. A press reporter may take the press release and rewrite it to emphasize one particular aspect of the message. Similarly, if a famous person is asked to make a speech, it will be necessary to brief her or him so that only the message that the company wants to give is presented. Any controversial issue could be exploited by the press and act against the firm's intended interest. None the less, in the hands of experts, publicity can be a very effective way to communicate with a target market.

Richard Branson, head of the Virgin Group, is a master at communicating his message through the clever use of events that have a news value – like ballooning across the Atlantic.

DIRECT MARKETING

Marketing specialists are constantly looking for new and better ways of creating satisfied customers. As society changes, the traditional ways of shopping may become inappropriate for some people. For example, as more and more women develop their own careers, shopping can be difficult for them. Car parking in town centres is becoming more difficult and more expensive. Queueing at checkouts is becoming less acceptable for busy people. Leisure time is becoming more important, and the use of leisure time for various pursuits is itself becoming big business.

Economies of scale are achieved by the big retail companies by reducing their product range to those items in greatest demand. That means that producers of exclusive or exotic products have to find other channels to distribute their products.

At the same time as these changes are taking place, new communication technology is becoming available which can be exploited by the marketing specialist to create new ways of satisfying customers.

Some of these new ways include telesales, electronic shopping, television marketing, video marketing, and updated versions of direct mail and mail order shopping.

a Telesales

This is the result of computer held lists of people in socio-economic groups, by district or postcode. The computer can actually dial the number, and when the telephone is answered, a highly trained telesales person will try to persuade the householder to agree to a visit by a salesperson. This is big business in America, where over $15 billion was spent on telesales phone calls in 1987. It is gathering pace in the UK and is expected to grow greatly by the year 2000.

b Electronic shopping

Electronic shopping uses a small keyboard linked to a BT telephone line, and sometimes also to a television. It is possible to order an item at anytime of the day or night from home, and pay by credit card. Bank of Scotland account holders can carry out many transactions in this way.

c Televison marketing

Some holiday firms and mail order catalogue firms (like Littlewoods) have bargain offers on occasions that are offered through advertisements on Oracle on ITV. (If you have Oracle on your television set, call up the index, page 199, and then Teleshopping. That will tell you the page number for Littlewoods.)

d Video marketing

Video cassettes of highly sophisticated home sound systems, exotic holidays or even training courses are relatively cheap to produce, and are increasingly beng used as persuaders in the home.

e Direct mail

This is becoming very much easier to use through the automation of several time consuming jobs. Very sophisticated and expensive equipment is now available which prints leaflets and brochures, folds them, inserts them into envelopes with samples, addresses them from computerized mailing lists, franks them and bags them for Royal Mail.

f Mail order catalogues

These can be over 1000 pages long, which can be printed, bound, packed and despatched by one automated process. These catalogues are high quality, multicoloured books showing a very wide range or goods. The fashion sections employ top models and top photographers to give the best quality image.

All these technological innovations are providing marketing specialists with opportunities of developing new ways of dealing direct with the customer and by-passing the traditional channels. Direct marketing is a growth business and will becoming a major communication tool in marketing.

Promotion Mix

The producer will promote its goods or services by one or more of these five communication methods: advertising, selling, sales promotion, publicity and direct marketing.

The decision will depend upon the type of product or service, the nature of the target market and how much money is available for promotion. How much of the promotion budget is spent on each method is a matter of judgement for the marketing manager. The policy as to which to

KEY POINTS 7.2

- **The marketing department plans, organizes and monitors communication with its target market**

- **Advertising is a process of paying media owners to carry a firm's message to their readers**

- **Target markets can be described according to social groupings or industrial classifications**

- **Personal selling is a one-to-one encounter between a potential customer and a salesperson that adds value through expert advice and guidance**

- **Sales promotion adds value to a product temporarily by offering savings or gifts to boost sales in the short term**

- **Publicity is creating newsworthy events that will appear in the media as news items**

- **Direct marketing refers to the innovative use of technology to by-pass traditional channels and deal directly with the customer**

use, and how much of the budget to spend on each, is called the promotion mix.

Promotion is a very specialized subject, and we will return to it in Chapter Nine.

ACTIVITY 7.8

The concept of promotion mix is very important. Assume that you are a marketing manager with a promotion budget of 100 per cent (it does not matter how big or small the figure is – do not be constrained in this exercise by money!). For each of the following products and services, decide how much of your 100 per cent you will spend on each of the five communication methods:

- A new, delicious, creamy instant custard
- A well established brand of coffee
- The latest innovation in multi-colour photocopiers
- A bank loan service for students in higher education
- A designer and producer of power stations
- A national supermarket chain
- Your school or college

Information Gathering

Take a moment to look at Figure 7.2 (on page 118) again. It shows that the organization must see value in offering the product or service if it is to be motivated to continue offering it. The perception of value will vary from organization to organization depending upon its objectives. A hospital may have as its objective 'restoring people to good health'. Its perception of value will be different from a company whose objective is to earn X per cent return on capital employed, or to become market leaders in its field.

However, in order for any organization to measure value, they will need information. Information is the key ingredient of decision-making; organizations cannot be efficient without good, up-to-date information. They cannot expect customers to volunteer information – they have to gather it themselves. Two ways in which organizations gather this information are:

- Marketing research
- Marketing information system

Marketing Research

Marketing research is used to gather information that is not otherwise available to the managers making decisions.

Each piece of marketing research is designed to study a defined area of information need. Its purpose is to assist in reducing the risk of making wrong decisions because there is always uncertainty about the outcome of future events. It does no more than that. In each case, the quality of decisions rests mainly upon the experience, knowledge and competence of the managers taking the decisions. The statistical methods used for marketing research are considered in another title in this series, *Finance, Information and Business*.

Marketing research is defined by the American Marketing Association as:

The objective gathering, recording and analysing of all facts about problems relating to the transfer and sale of goods and services from producer to consumer or user.

THE SCOPE OF MARKETING RESEARCH

Marketing research can be divided into three main groups:

- Market research
- Product research
- Promotion research

a   Market research

Market research gathers information about:

- Size of market
- Nature of market by social class, age and sex
- Location of customers
- Competitors, and the share of the market each holds
- Distribution channels
- Sales analysed by geographical region

b   Product research

Product (or service) research can help organizations with the following:

- Product concept testing – is the idea for a new product or service what the customers want?
- Product testing – what do customers think of the actual product?
- Product analysis – how does the product compare with competitors's products?
- Packaging research – does it protect the product? Does it look attractive on the shelf?

c   Promotion research

Promotion research is useful for monitoring effectiveness of all forms of promotion:

- Copy research – does the message create the impact intended?
- Media research – is the message getting to the target market?
- Sales research – is the message achieving its sales objectives?

THE MARKETING RESEARCH PROCESS

All marketing research is costly. The more information is gathered, the higher the cost. Its value lies in the quality of decisions that will result from effective research and the efficiency that it brings to the organization.

However, like all things, there are right and wrong ways of going about it, and the following is a five-step process suggested by marketing expert Philip Kotler in his book *Marketing Management* (Prentice Hall, 1988):

- Define the problem that is to be researched
- Design research that will focus on the problem
- Carry out the research and gather data
- Analyse the data to make it understandable
- Prepare a report that explains the findings to whoever needs to know

a   Defining the problem

If the problem definition is not accurate or clear, all that follows will not be right. Hence it is very important to spend time describing what needs to be known as a result of the research. 'What do people think of British Rail?' is vague. 'What do industrial freight users put as their top three requirements from a bulk haulier?' is much more manageable. It is possible to gather very general information as to 'what people think about ...', but it is difficult to use in decision-making. On the other hand, if British Rail learns that customers require punctuality, safe handling and economy, in that order, then it can make some relevant policy decisions.

b   Designing research

The next step is to consider different ways of finding out. In order to answer the key question above, what data must be gathered? From whom or where can it be gathered? How might it be gathered? And how much data is needed to give an accurate result?

When it is clear what data is needed, the question 'Does it already exist?' must be considered. If the answer is 'yes', then where can it be found? This sort of data is called secondary data – that is, it can be found in published sources of information and need not be gathered specially for this purpose. It is sometimes referred to as 'desk research' because it can be collected sitting alone at a desk without any contact with the outside world.

ACTIVITY 7.9

Knowing where to find data is an important business skill. Go to your school, college or local reference library and ask to see any official statistics published by HMSO, the IMF or the UN. An example is *Annual Abstract of Statistics*. Ask also for any trade directories, marketing research reports, censuses of population, production or distribution. Reference librarians are experts on sources of data. Ask them for advice. When you have done this, make a list of ten sources of secondary data that would be useful in marketing research.

If the data does not already exist, then it will have to be gathered for the first time – that is called primary data.

This is sometimes called 'field research' because it needs people to go out and contact people 'in the field' of whatever they are researching, or to contact them by phone or mail 'in the field'.

There are three main ways of collecting primary data:

- Observation
Sometimes, official-looking people with clipboards

can be seen standing in busy shopping centres. They may not speak to anyone, just click a counter as people go into certain shops or cross a busy road at a given point, or some such thing. Video cameras or tape recorders are sometimes used to do this instead of people. Almost certainly these people are 'observing' certain behaviours for marketing research.

• Experimentation
Your science teacher will describe to you the rigours of experimentation. It is a carefully designed situation that allows variables to be controlled so that evidence can be gathered in a systematic way to prove or disprove an hypothesis. It is used extensively in product development and packaging, but can also be used for behavioural matters where variables can be controlled.

• Surveys
The group of people that is being surveyed, whether it is large or small, is called the 'population'. Perhaps the population is too large to allow every member of it to be included in the survey, or it is too expensive, or there is not enough time. Then a sample is taken of the population for the purpose of the survey. It is important that surveys are conducted on samples of the population that are truly representative. For further explanation of sampling and calculations of sample sizes, refer to the companion book, *Finance, Information and Business*.

All these methods are costly, and require time and expertise.

c   Gathering data
Once the sample has been chosen, the method of collecting the data can be questionnaires, telephone interviews or personal interviews.

Questionnaires are used widely in marketing research. In preparing a questionnaire it is important to keep focus continuously on the research objective. The answer to each question should contribute to the objective or it should not be asked. Phrasing the questions is equally important. They should be clear and unambiguous, and couched in the language that individuals in the sample will understand. The choice of style of questions is rather similar to exam papers. There can be the 'yes/no' type, or the multiple choice type, or the rating scale type (for example, '1 = not at all satisfied' up to '5 = completely satisfied'). Open ended questions are often asked, but are difficult to interpret and analyse. A questionnaire ought to be 'tested' with a small sample to see if it means to the reader what it was intended to mean. Often it will need to be amended and some questions reworded. Getting it right is fundamental to the success of the research.

ACTIVITY 7.10

Examine the Peugeot Handover Questionnaire in Figure 7.7 (next page). Who would be the population? What size sample would be realistic? What style of questions is used? Critically evaluate the wording and sequence of the questions. Are they appropriate for the population? Justify your answers. What percentage return of completed questionnaires would be necessary to provide useful data to Peugeot?

Telephone interviews are becoming very popular in marketing research because they are relatively cheap and quick to conduct. However, many people consider them an invasion of privacy, and will either hang-up or provide answers that may not be reliable.

Modern technology is giving rise to new ways of gathering data. People who are willing to co-operate with the researchers allow 'black boxes' to be attached to their televisions so their viewing patterns can be monitored. The same people use special plastic cards (like credit cards) to identify the items they buy in supermarkets. Then the researchers work out relationships between the advertisements they viewed and their buying patterns, and deductions about the effectiveness of advertising are made.

Personal interviews are valuable because they allow for variations and individual reactions. A good interviewer will be able to 'read' body language and other non-verbal behaviour, and gather more information than the other methods. However, they need careful preparation; appointments are usually required and some follow-up is needed to ensure that the interview was valid. In addition, there can be problems caused by bias on the part of the interviewer or the interviewee.

d   Analysing the data
Computers have made the analysis of data gathered in these ways very fast and accurate. However, the program for analysing the data must be prepared in parallel with the preparation of the questionnaire. A series of steps, called an 'algorithm', that the questionnaire or the interview will follow is drafted, and the computer analysis is based on it. Many questionnaires are 'scored' so that the data collected can be fed straight into the computer. Once again, basic techniques are described in *Finance, Information and Business*.

e   Preparing the report
Nothing will be gained from all this work if the findings are not communicated in a clear, understandable and useable fashion to the managers

*Figure 7.7 – **Peugeot Vehicle Handover Questionnaire***

To complete the questionnaire, simply tick one circle for each of the questions.
The numbers correspond to the levels of satisfaction listed below.

①	②	③	④	⑤
Not at all satisfied	Hardly satisfied	Fairly satisfied	Very satisfied	Completely satisfied

HOW SATISFIED WERE YOU WITH:

	①	②	③	④	⑤
1 The ease with which you were able to arrange a convenient time to collect your car.	○	○	○	○	○
2 The promptness with which the person, with whom you had an appointment, attended when you arrived to collect your vehicle.	○	○	○	○	○
3 The helpfulness and consideration shown by the persons responsible for handing over your vehicle.	○	○	○	○	○
4 The completeness and availability of the necessary paperwork when you arrived.	○	○	○	○	○
5 The surroundings set aside for the handover of your vehicle.	○	○	○	○	○
6 The way in which the instruments and control layout were explained to you.	○	○	○	○	○
7 The way in which the vehicle servicing requirements were explained to you.	○	○	○	○	○
8 The way in which the Peugeot Talbot Service Charter was explained to you.	○	○	○	○	○
9 The way in which the Peugeot Talbot Warranty was explained to you (including details of any purchased extended warranty).	○	○	○	○	○
10 The way in which the Peugeot Talbot Lioncare AA Programme was explained to you.	○	○	○	○	○
11 The cleanliness and appearance of both the interior and exterior of your vehicle.	○	○	○	○	○
12 The offer made for a final test drive of your vehicle just prior to taking delivery.	○	○	○	○	○
13 The manner in which you were introduced to 'key' dealership personnel (e.g. Sales Manager and Service Receptionist).	○	○	○	○	○
14 The overall manner in which the vehicle was handed over.	○	○	○	○	○
15 Whether or not the dealer contacted you, by phone or post, to check that everything was in order with your new car.	○	○	○	○	○

Thank you again for your assistance.

Finally, we would welcome your comments on any aspect of the
vehicle handover not already covered by the above questions.

_____	Do you mind if we divulge your comments to your dealer? (Please tick)	
_____		
_____	Yes	No
_____		

Source: Peugeot Talbot

who will be taking decisions. Simplicity is a great virtue. The report should be business-like and to the point. Graphics will help to make large-scale data meaningful. It should highlight the main findings and point out any weaknesses of the research (such as possible sampling error). The decisions made as a result should be better than if the research had not taken place.

Managers may not undertake the research themselves – it is a very specialized job. But they must be trained in the interpretation of the outcomes so that they understand the implications of the findings. Numeracy is an essential skill in business.

ACTIVITY 7.11

This activity requires you to carry out a complete piece of marketing research, so it would be best to work in groups of three or four. It would help if you had a mix of people. You will need someone who can get things organized and controlled and keep things moving; someone who has 'good ideas'; someone who can think logically and be methodical; someone who is a good negotiator and diplomat. So select your team carefully.

Choose a topic to research. Here are a few examples:

- What are the top three facilities that post-sixteen students look for in your school or college?
- What are the top three sources used by local employers for the recruitment of new administration staff?
- Who does the community think should pay for clearing 'take away' litter from the streets and public places?
- What newspapers are read by the teaching staff in your school or college?

Use the five steps in conducting marketing research set out above. In your report, highlight the marketing implications of your findings. Who could you sell your report to?

Combine this Activity with the following Activity from *Finance, Information and Business* (another title in the series):

Conduct a survey to determine what percentage of students would favour a four-term academic year with each term lasting about ten weeks. Restrict your survey to a randomly selected group of at least one hundred fellow students. You could share this survey with others and pool your results.

The answer to your survey question must be a straight 'Yes' or 'No'. From the results of your survey, estimate the population response.

What are the limitations and sources of inaccuracy in your survey?

How could you make the results of your survey more accurate to reflect all students? How much do you think that an accurate survey would cost?

Do you think there is a connection between the costs of a survey and the accuracy of it?

Marketing Information System

We have already mentioned Management Information Systems (MIS) in Chapter Three. The marketing information system is a part of MIS which is designed to provide regular marketing information to management.

Data may be collected in the course of normal business transactions, for example from a sales order/invoicing system.

Orders from customers are received. The company responds by despatching the goods and sending an invoice for the price of the goods. (This is an excellent example of a formal communication system.)

By analysing the information that appears on the orders and invoices the company can monitor its performance in the following way:

- Knowing precisely who its customers are and where they are located
- Knowing which of its products each customer is ordering, the quantity they are buying and the frequency of their purchases
- Knowing how much each customer is spending with the company
- Knowing if goods are being returned and credit given
- Knowing the total sales value and volume of

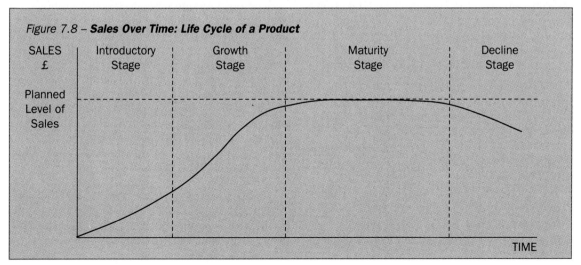

*Figure 7.8 – **Sales Over Time: Life Cycle of a Product***

| SALES £ | Introductory Stage | Growth Stage | Maturity Stage | Decline Stage |

Planned Level of Sales

TIME

each of its products, and whether these are rising, steady or declining

The use of computers has made this sort of analysis relatively easy. Once this basic data from the customer's order has been put into the system, management reports can be produced, showing, for example, the value of sales of each product, in total, by customer or by region.

PRODUCT LIFE CYCLE

The graph in Figure 7.8 (previous page) shows some distinct stages in the sales of the product over a period of time. In the early stages, sales were low then slowly began to grow. Growth then became quite rapid until it levelled out and stayed flat for a period before beginning to decline. This is true of all products, although the curve will be significantly different for different kinds of goods – for example, the curve for the Rubik Cube (a mind-bending puzzle popular in the 1980s) would be quite different from Marmite.

It is called the product life cycle and can be produced from data contained on the marketing information system. It is not unlike the human life cycle – conceived, born, grows, matures and dies. We can identify four stages in the product life cycle:

- Introductory stage
- Growth stage
- Maturity stage
- Decline stage

a Introductory stage

By examining the graph, we can see that at the beginning of the product's life, sales took off slowly. This was probably because the product was new and needed to be 'introduced' to its target market. The marketing manager would develop a promotion strategy to make it known to its target market as quickly as possible. Up to this point, it has incurred all the costs of research and development, and the costs of launching it onto the market. The firm will want to get the money it invested back as soon as possible so that it can start to show a profit. Satellite television is an example of a product in its introductory stage.

b Growth stage

The marketing manager's objective will be to get sales up to the planned level as soon as possible. The more rapid the growth, the sooner the profit. The pricing and promotion strategy adopted will set out to ensure that growth is as rapid as the company can cope with. FST (flat square tube) and NICAM digital stereo television are examples of products in their growth stage.

c Maturity stage

On the graph we see that sales have reached the planned level and growth ceases. This is the time when the company reaps all the rewards of good research and development, good product launch strategies, and good pricing and promotion. At this level of sales, the fixed costs are being shared by the maximum number of units and the highest level of profit is being made. The marketing manager's objective will be to make the most of this period by controlling costs and reducing them where possible: streamlining sales and distribution; making administrative procedures as efficient as possible and keeping customers informed and happy. Colour television is an example of a product in its maturity stage.

It makes good sense to keep the product at this level for as long as possible. For an item of fashion, a period of six months would be reasonable; for a motor car, six years; and for something like baked beans, sixty years. The marketing manager would use 'extension strategies' to extend the maturity stage for as long as possible. Advertising and sales promotion will be used to keep demand up to the desired level, but more than that will be needed from time to time.

Modifications and updates to the product will boost or maintain sales – 'Now with the new blue whitener', or 'Now with the more powerful 1800cc engine'. Sometimes a new use for the product will be promoted. For example, baby lotion is now promoted as equally good for mothers. Breakfast cereals are promoted as supper snacks.

New markets will be sought both at home and overseas. The Rover Mini is an example of a product that enjoyed a revival when it was targeted at the Japanese and French markets.

Eventually, however, newer products, competitors's actions, new technology or just changing taste and fashion will cause all products to reach the end of their lives.

d Decline stage

Decline is the stage where sales, and profits, start to drop. The decision has to be taken by management to let the product die, either by taking it off the market completely or letting it slowly fade away. Many companies are reluctant to take the axe to declining products. Whatever happens, the marketing strategy at this stage should be to minimize loss and to replace it with a new product that has been researched and designed to be at the start of its life cycle as the old one dies. Then the whole cycle starts again. Black and white television is an example of a product in its decline stage.

You can see the disadvantage of being a single product company. What will happen when the product reaches its decline stage? You can also see what might befall a company which does not constantly update its products, and seek to introduce new and better products. It is as relevant to services as it is to products. Your school or college will probably offer GCSEs, A levels, BTEC courses, GNVQs and many more.

The ideal situation is for a business to have a range of products – sometimes called the product portfolio – that spans all stages of the life cycle: some are new, some are growing, some are mature, and some are in decline. In that way, new products can be financed from the cash flow produced from growing and mature products.

PRODUCT PORTFOLIO EVALUATION

The information from the MIS described above, plus marketing research information about the size of the market, competitors and their volume share of that market, gives management the opportunity to check how their products are faring in the market. One way of doing this is by using the Boston Consulting Group's Growth–Share Matrix.

The two dimensions in the Boston Matrix are:

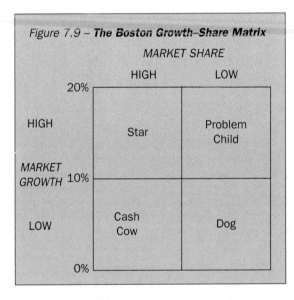

Figure 7.9 – **The Boston Growth–Share Matrix**

- What is the growth rate of each product in the portfolio?
- How does the volume sales compare with that of the market leader?

Each product is plotted on the matrix and takes the title of the segment it falls in:

- A Problem Child is a product with potential. It has a low share of a growing market. Should the company spend money developing and promoting it and making it a Star, or should it abandon the product?
- Stars are growing fast and have a large market share. It will cost a lot of money to keep them in the race to become a market leader and a Cash Cow.
- Cash Cows have made it! Market growth has almost ceased and the product is well established in its market. It requires little money to be spent on it, and is bringing in a lot of cash and is profitable
- Dogs have a low share of a low-growth market. It is possible that Dogs are products in decline and will possibly be making a loss. Alternatively, it may be an innovative product in a market that is as yet undeveloped (for example, video discs).

The product life cycle is a very useful tool to help marketing managers to help decide upon strategies to be followed at each stage. The next two chapters look at appropriate ways of developing products, distributing them to customers, promoting them and pricing them.

ACTIVITY 7.12

Reproduce the grid below on a piece of A4 paper. List at least five products or services under each type against each of the four stages of the life cycle. For example, in 1992 the Lotus Elan sports car reached its decline stage, while new, diesel-powered cars were in their introductory or growth stages.

Stage in Product Life Cycle	Food and drink	Electrical and electronic goods	Furnishings and fabrics	Leisure wear	Banking services	Motor vehicles
Introductory stage						
Growth stage						
Maturity stage						
Decline stage						

An excellent source of data in this regard is *A to Z of UK Marketing Data*, published by Euromonitor, 88 Turnmill Street, London, EC1M 5QU. It might be too expensive for a school or college library to keep, but a good central reference library should have a copy or be able to get one for you.

The product life cycle graph produces a great deal of stimulus for management action. Similar graphs and reports can be generated for most aspects of marketing activities to aid managers in their decision-making. For example, reports on stock levels, production schedules, delivery schedules, advertising expenditure, sales levels and so on can be produced in a fashion that is most beneficial to the decision-makers concerned. Other information gathered from sources outside the organization can be handled in the same way. Figures 7.10 and 7.11 illustrate how such a marketing information system might work.

The Value of Information

Marketing, like many other functions in a business, depends very much upon good communication systems. The responsibility for designing, implementing, running and updating the systems just discussed lies with the marketing manager. She or he is accountable to the chief executive for their effectiveness.

The company's overall aims and objectives will be the starting point for formulating a marketing policy, and its strategies for carrying out that policy will be the result of decisions based on the data provided by these communication systems.

The company will have learned about its customers and their needs from marketing research and the MIS, and then set out to satisify them better than anyone else. Customers will have learned of the company's product offering through advertising, personal selling, sales promotion, publicity and direct marketing.

Changes in the business environment will be monitored. Changes in the market or in customer tastes take place all the time – it is a continuous process and information about what is going on is essential if the marketing manager is to keep the organization up to date and abreast or ahead of its competitors.

Knowing its customers, learning what their needs are, developing products or services to satisfy them, and setting out to create and keep satisfied customers is the essence of good marketing.

Non-Controllable Variables

In *The Business Environment*, another book in this series, some of the external pressures on organizations that are outside its control are examined. These forces are:

- Legal
- Economic
- Competitive
- Technical
- Social

The environment in which all businesses operate is affected by each of these forces. Things are changing constantly and it is necessary to respond to these changes in order to survive. The article in Figure 7.12 (on page 134) tells the story of one product that did not survive a change in social taste and fashion.

KEY POINTS 7.3

- A company will only continue to provide a product or service if there is 'value' in doing so

- Value will be determined by gathering information by marketing research and management information systems

- Marketing research generates information that is not otherwise available to decision-makers about their market, products and promotions

- Marketing information systems provide regular data to managers about the performance of their products in the market, such as the position of a product in its life cycle

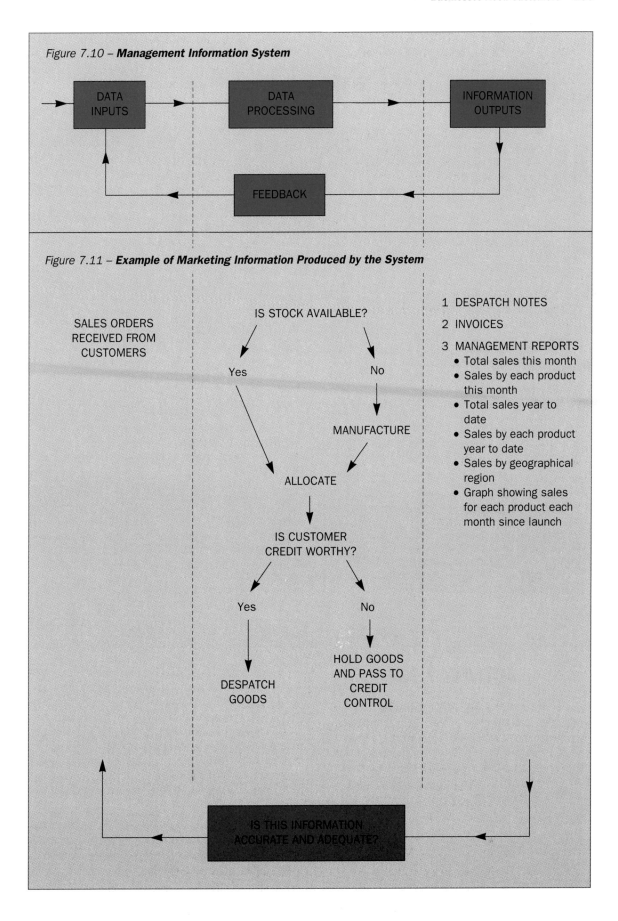

Figure 7.10 – **Management Information System**

Figure 7.11 – **Example of Marketing Information Produced by the System**

Figure 7.12 – Social Trends and Fashions

Bitter ending for 700 jobs as brewery shuts

DRINKERS switching to lager have forced Britain's biggest regional brewer to stop making beer.

Greenall Whitley said that soaring demand for nationally-known lagers had hit sales of its own bitters, making it no longer profitable to stay in the business.

Two breweries at Warrington in Cheshire and Shipstones in Nottingham will close with the loss of 700 jobs.

Original

Last night there were fears that other large local brewers might also decide to call time on making beer.

Greenall, whose advertising slogan is 'another great bitter ending' will now concentrate on running the 1,500 pubs, hotels and restaurants it owns in the North and Midlands.

Its beers, Greenall's Bitter and Mild, Thomas Greenall's Original, Shipstones Bitter and Mild, and Davenports Bitter, will still be produced but by former rival Allied at its Tetley Walker Brewery in Warrington and Ind Coope Burton Brewery, Burton on Trent.

Greenall managing director Andrew Thomas justified the closures saying: 'The average price of acquiring beer from other companies is less than our current production cost.'

Its breweries had been running at a loss for some time because of the trend towards lager, which is now Britain's top-selling drink.

Wilderspool Brewery in Warrington has a capacity of 1,300,000 barrels a year but was producing only 785,000 barrels. Shipstones in Nottingham, with a capacity of 200,000 barrels, was producing only 126,000 barrels.

But the Campaign for Real Ale, Camra, attacked the decision.

Official Stephen Cox said: 'They may say the beers will continue but drinkers will find they will not have the same taste. There is no guarantee that these beers will not eventually disappear.'

Greenall said they will now be able to offer a larger choice of beers in their pubs by selling Tetley and Stones bitter as well as Castlemaine lager.

The move to quit brewing after 220 years is causing concern that the production of beer in this country will be left in the hands of just a few major brewers.

Paul Soden of the Small Independent Brewers Association said: 'This is what we feared would happen. Big brewers will do deals with these large regional groups to squeeze out the little people.

'Drinkers will eventually have less choice, not more.'

Price

He said the Government must review the recent Monopolies Commission report into pub ownership which was meant to bring more competition into the business.

Beer drinkers in the Midlands have also been hit by a 6 per cent price rise by Mitchell and Butler.

It will mean an average 6p rise on draught bitters and 8p on draught lagers.

This pushes the average cost of a pint of Bass up to £1, Brew XI to 94p and Carling Black Label lager to £1.06.

Manchester-based Boddingtons pulled out of brewing earlier this year, selling to Whitbread.

Source: Daily Express, 1 September 1990

ACTIVITY 7.13

Choose two of the following scenarios. Consider what action you might take if you were the marketing manager in those circumstances. Prepare a brief presentation of your decisions to your group. Ask other members of your group to do the same exercise for the remaining scenarios.

1 A new law will ban the use of 'stick-on-eyes' on toys. You use thousands of these at the moment because they are cheap, easy to fix, and help to keep you competitive with cheaper Third World imports.

2 The Health and Safety Executive has issued a circular warning that fumes from some adhesives can cause cancer and that all users must have adequate ventilation systems to remove all fumes from the workplace, filter the fumes, and discharge only clean air into the atmosphere. At the moment you use some of these adhesives, and your ventilation is not up to the required standard. The additional costs of complying could force you to increase prices, and that may cause you to lose some of your market share.

3 Consumers are becoming more and more fussy about what they eat. Your marketing research is showing a trend away from traditional margarines towards low fat, low cholesterol spreads. At present you do not have a product of this nature in your product range.

4 In order to expand and take advantage of a new marketing opportunity, you will have to invest in new plant and equipment. This will mean borrowing heavily, and with present interest rates at 9 per cent, it is quite a viable proposition. You estimate that the new product will take two years to break-even at present costs and interest charges.

5 Your management information system is showing that a major competitor is employing more sales staff, altering its product design, packaging and advertising, and putting pressure on raw material suppliers that you both rely upon.

6 The addition of a microchip to your personal organizers – your main product – would give you a distinct advantage over your competitors. If you do not do this, however, there is no doubt that they will. It is a matter of getting in first. The technological problems are worrying because you do not have experience or expertise in this field.

Controllable Variables

A marketing manager is dealing with non-controllable influences all the time, trying to make allowances for the effect they may have on the business, or by turning them into opportunities. One consolation is that all or most competing UK and EC firms will be affected by the same or similar pressures. However, it is possible that overseas competitors may not be, and may have an advantage as a result.

There are variables within the business over which the manager has full control and these can be manipulated to give the company its individuality – that is, make it different from all its competitors.

A simple description of these controllable variables is the four Ps:

- *Product:* a company can make its own decisions about what *products* (or services) it will provide
- *Place (Distribution):* a company can choose its channels of distribution – the *place* where the product or service will be sold
- *Promotion:* a company can *promote* its goods by whatever means it feels is most appropriate
- *Price:* a company can decide upon the price to be charged

Each one of these will be examined in detail in Chapters Eight and Nine, with an emphasis on the sorts of strategies that the marketing manager might follow at each stage in the product life cycle.

The Marketing Mix

Another company in the same market with similar products or services may make a completely different set of decisions when confronted with the same issues. It can *mix* these four variables as it thinks fit. Consider how differently Times Newspapers mixes its four controllable variables – the four Ps – compared with your local Free Advertiser news sheet.

Figure 7.13 – SWOT Analysis

INTERNAL	EXTERNAL
Strengths	**Opportunities**
Two new products	New markets
Two growth products	Technological advance
Four mature products	Acquisitions in EC
Stable, experienced staff	Product development
Well motivated	
Finance available	
Profitable	
Sound management	
Quality assurance	
Weaknesses	**Threats**
Three declining products	Interest rates
Ageing workforce	Economy
Poor premises	Competition from EC
Four sites	Environmental issues
ROC lower than target	Demographic issues
	Consumer protection via EC

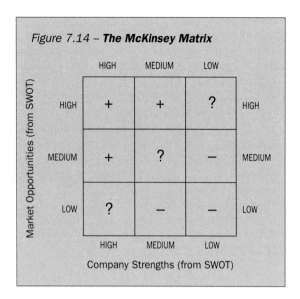

Figure 7.14 – **The McKinsey Matrix**

The knowledge, experience, ability, values and beliefs of the managers in different organizations will have a major influence on the decisions that are taken and the success (or otherwise) they enjoy. The way a company mixes the four Ps for its products or services gives it individuality and is generally called its *marketing mix.*

Marketing is mainly concerned with generating a company's income. The techniques it uses to do this are costly; so it incurs considerable expenditure. The relationship between marketing expenditure and marketing mix is called its marketing strategy.

Marketing Plans

A marketing plan is a design for achieving the business's marketing objectives. It includes information about the effects that the non-controllable variables may have on the business – the opportunities it presents and the threats it poses. It also includes an analysis of the organization's fitness to face these opportunities and threats – its strengths and its weaknesses.

A simple, subjective tool for gathering this information is SWOT analysis. SWOT stands for Strengths, Weaknesses, Opportunities and Threats. You can perhaps see that the first two are internal to the business and the second two are external factors. Figure 7.13 (previous page) contains a SWOT analysis of a particular organization.

Completing a SWOT analysis is a team effort. It requires a lot of input from every function within

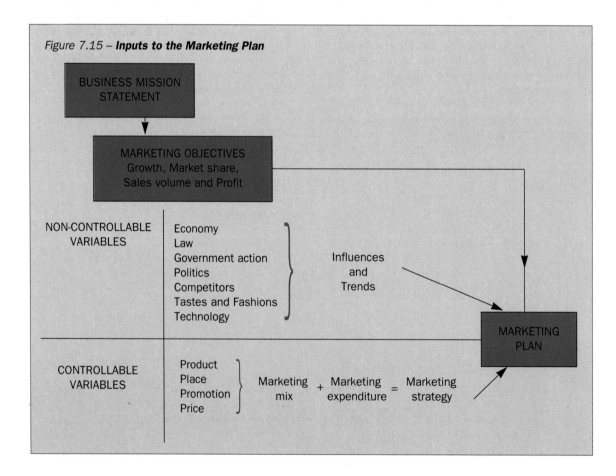

Figure 7.15 – **Inputs to the Marketing Plan**

the organization, and it requires an openness and honesty about 'the way things are'. There is no point in doing a SWOT analysis if people find it necessary to be defensive or to conceal the reality of the situation. The overriding cultural issue is the wish to become better at everything the business does, and never being complacent by believing that past performance standards will be good enough for the future. Even very good performance can be improved!

From the SWOT analysis, the information can be further refined by use of another subjective tool, The McKinsey Matrix (see Figure 7.14).

The market opportunities for each product (or service) in the portfolio are plotted against the company's strength with that product in the market. The three groups suggest:

+ Potentially attractive – the investment of additional resources to develop within this area seems sound; it is worth further analysis
? Unclear potential – before any decisions are taken, a detailed analysis would be wise
– Low or doubtful potential – resources devoted to this area could probably produce a greater return elsewhere

All these factors are brought together into a detailed marketing plan supported with financial and statistical data. Figure 7.15 contains a summary diagram that links them all together.

KEY POINTS 7.4

- Marketing is a communication system. A firm will gather information from its market and communicate its product message to the market

- External pressures are beyond the control of the firm. The marketing manager will monitor these non-controllable variables and attempt to predict how they might affect the performance of the firm

- Internal variables that the firm can control are product, place, promotion and price: these are known as the four Ps

- The firm's choice of products, prices, distribution channels and methods of promotion is called its marketing mix

- A firm may have many target markets, and may have a different marketing mix for each segment

---

EXAM PREPARATION

SHORT QUESTIONS

1 State the stages of a product's life cycle.

2 Name three elements of a firm's marketing mix. (AEB June 1988)

3 Suggest two points that must be considered for advertising to be effective. (AEB June 1989)

4 Give two reasons why a company may sell, for a limited period, part of its product range at a loss. (AEB November 1990)

DATA RESPONSE QUESTION

1 The Aquatic Leisure Centre is situated in an east coast seaside resort and is owned by Pringles plc, a national conglomerate. The Leisure Centre has a swimming pool, a large sports hall, squash courts, indoor bowling centre and various meeting rooms.

The Marketing Manager for the Leisure Centre has been asked by the Managing Director for Pringles plc to produce a report to explain the following clearly:

a current pricing policy

b the monthly usage for 1988

c the breakdown of members by age for 1988

a   Current pricing policy

The Leisure Centre has a wide variety of charges. These can be categorized into:

1   **Full membership**. £25.00 per adult. Benefits include free admission, free use of the swimming pool and 20% discount for other facilities.

2   **Local Resident's Pass**. Any person who lives in the borough is able to obtain this free pass. Free entry, but all facilities have to be paid for.

3   **Other**. Payment for entry (adults £1.00, children and senior citizens 50p) plus payment for facilities.

Swimming	Adults 90p	Children and Senior Citizens 45p
Squash	£2.50 per half hour session	
Hire of hall	£10.00 per hour	
Bowling Green	£2.50 per hour	

The admission price allows the use of a number of facilities, such as a children's entertainment area, and in the summer season entry to the ongoing show they have in the largest meeting room. There are also two bars and a cafeteria in the Leisure Centre.

b   The monthly usage for 1988

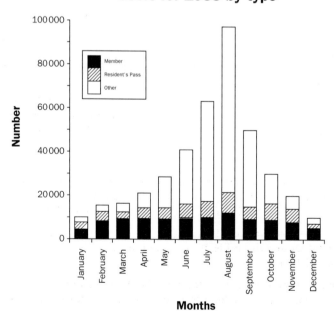

Users for 1988 by type

c   The breakdown of members by age for 1988

1988 Members by age

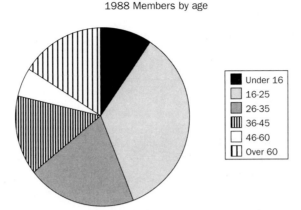

Legend:
- Under 16
- 16-25
- 26-35
- 36-45
- 46-60
- Over 60

Questions

1   **(a)** What is meant by market segmentation?

   (b) Discuss the significance of the figures in Diagram C for the Marketing Manager of the Leisure Centre

   (c) Explain another way in which the market may segment and why this might justify further market research.

2   The Marketing Manager is concerned about relatively low demand for the Leisure Centre during the winter months. Outline a suitable marketing strategy for the Leisure Centre to improve its use of facilities during the winter months explaining each of the following. Recommendations for the most suitable proposal should be outlined in each case:

   (a) analysis through market research

   (b) alternative methods of pricing

   (c) suitable methods of promotion

   (d) changes to the product

3   **(a)** The Marketing Manager for the Leisure Centre has been asked to detail a sales budget for the Managing Director. Explain what is meant by a sales budget and evaluate its usefulness to the Managing Director of Pringles plc.

   (b) It is expected that real incomes will increase in the immediate locality. Would this necessarily lead to an increase in the demand for the Leisure Centre's services?   (UCLES November 1989)

ESSAYS

1   'A high quality product does not need marketing. It will sell itself. Marketing is only necessary to overcome consumer resistance to poor quality.' Do you agree? Explain your answer. (AEB June 1986)

2   Explain and illustrate what is meant by 'the product life cycle'. Use appropriate examples and explore the implications for managers of this concept. (AEB June 1990)

3   A furniture manufacturer is concerned about a reduction in sales of its existing product range. What action should it take? (AEB June 1986)

Marketing – Supplying Products and Services

▷ ▷ **QUESTIONS FOR PREVIEW** ▷ ▷

1 *How can products be classified?*

2 *What is the process for developing new products?*

3 *How does the product life cycle*

influence marketing mix decisions?

4 *What are the channels of distribution, and how are choices made?*

Introduction

MANY OF the influences on the success of a business are external, and there is a need for the marketing manager to monitor the changes in its environment, so as to ensure that trends and effects can be anticipated and allowed for in marketing planning. Other influences are internal and within the control of the business. You will recall that these can be listed under four headings – the four Ps – product, place, promotion and price. The four are inter-related and interdependent, but in a crude sense we can split them for the purpose of study.

The first two Ps, product and place, are mostly internal activities and are concerned with developing products or services that are designed to satisfy customers's needs and moving them to the customer. The last two Ps, promotion and price are mainly external activities and are concerned with informing the customers of the products and getting them to buy.

In this chapter we will examine how each of the first two, product and place, can be manipulated to give a firm competitive advantage.

Product

There are tens of thousands of products and services available to be purchased. It would not be possible to study them as a whole because there are so many differences and such a wide variety. The following classification of products is adapted from the American Marketing Association's definitions, and is widely used and accepted. It will help us to examine the topic.

Products can be classified under two main headings:

• Consumer products
• Producer (industrial) products

As the words imply, consumer goods are used by individuals, either personally or in their homes. Producer goods are used by businesses in the production of other items or in the running of the business. Each of these can be sub-divided further. We will first look at consumer goods, then producer goods, then at services.

Consumer Products

Consumer goods can be sub-divided into three categories – convenience goods, shopping goods and speciality goods – based on the effort that the customer is willing to make to purchase them:

a   Convenience goods

These are the goods you will find in a supermarket or similar retail outlet. The modern supermarket has over 15 000 items on offer, mostly convenience goods, and displays them in a logical order to make choice as easy as possible, and as tempting as possible. Unless an item is being especially promoted, customers are given a variety to select from without undue pressure.

One major supermarket chain claims to make shopping a leisure activity which people will enjoy.

Examples of convenience goods are staple food items such as butter and toilet soap; luxury items like chocolates and cream cakes; and special items like greetings cards.

The retailer has to hold sufficient stock to meet constant demand, and has to invest money to buy stock – working capital – so as to keep the shelves full. However, these goods are sold very quickly; they do not stay on the shelves very long. Popular goods that have a high stock turnover allow the retailer to sell them with a relatively low mark-up (the percentage or amount added to the cost of the goods paid by the retailer to give the selling price). For example, if a retailer buys something for £1.00 and sells it for £1.10, the mark-up is 10p, or 10 per cent.

The problem with this is that if stock turnover falls as a result of external influences like a recession, the firm could suffer cashflow difficulties (as discussed in the companion book, *Finance, Information and Business*).

Firms that have applied this principle to goods that are not strictly convenience goods (for example, Queensway furniture, and to a lesser extent, MFI) can have major cashflow difficulties if there is a recession.

Convenience goods tend to be promoted heavily by the producer through advertising, sales promotion and attractive packaging. You will see regular advertisements on television for the brand leaders in these goods – that is, the top few producers whose sales dominate the market. Figure 8.1 shows the market size and market leaders for convenience goods.

b Shopping goods

These are goods which most people own, but which are durable and are purchased once in a while. When people are buying them, they tend to take time to gather information about several alternative makes and compare their features and price and consider additional services (such as delivery, installation, guarantees and so on). They are seldom bought on impulse.

Examples of these products are refrigerators, washing machines, bicycles, sports equipment and furniture.

People will 'shop around' and rely upon salespeople to give them information and expert advice. This is different from the supermarket approach to convenience goods, although supermarket techniques are often used to display and promote shopping goods.

These goods tend to be quite expensive, and people may need credit facilities in order to buy them. Most retailers of shopping goods offer credit. The retailer has to invest heavily in stock. Many producers have special financing arrangements with their retailers to ease the burden of having to finance their stock-holding.

Stock turnover will be much slower than with convenience goods and, consequently, the retailer will have a higher mark-up.

Many shopping goods are heavily advertised by both the producer and the retailer. You will have seen many advertisements on television for fridges, hi-fi equipment, furniture and so on, but your local paper will also carry advertisements by local retailers promoting the brands of goods they stock. Both the producer and retailer will also spend a large part of their promotion budget on personal selling. Retailers of shopping goods

---

Figure 8.1 – *Convenience Goods: Market Size and Market Leaders 1990*

Convenience Good	1990 Total Markets (£m)	Market Leaders	Market Share (% of Total Market)
Butter	332	Anchor Lurpak	26% 16%
Sweets	1060	Trebor Sharps Rowntree Mackintosh Bassett Mars	13% 12% 9% 8%
Toilet soap	89	Imperial Leather Palmolive	14% 10%

Source: Euromonitor, *A to Z of Marketing Data* (1990)

have trained salespeople who can advise and help customers with technical details of the products.

c   Speciality goods

These are items that people will go out of their way to buy. If they want a particular make or brand and cannot find it, they are quite likely to go without.

For example, some people will wait over a year to take delivery of a Jaguar motor car when another make could be delivered immediately. Some parents will make a special journey to a particular shop to buy their preferred brand of baby food. Some pet owners behave in the same way when buying dog and cat food. Other goods in this category include cosmetics, fashions, batteries, coffee, deodorants, sanitary protection and so on.

Some of these are very expensive goods, others are not. They are all big markets worth hundreds of millions of pounds a year. What makes them similar is that the customer knows what she or he wants, and will not accept another brand or make. Many of these products are available only through certain outlets, and the buyer will have to seek them out. Body Shop products are an example where only their own shops sell them; or some up-market cosmetics, such as AnaïsAnaïs by Cacharel of Paris. Cacharel even state on the beautifully printed carton: 'Distribution exclusive chez les dépositaires agrées par les Parfums Cacharel'.

Some speciality goods are purchased regularly, and have a relatively low mark-up. Others are more like shopping goods, and have slower stock-turn and a higher mark-up.

ACTIVITY 8.1

In your home, identify and make a list of three items that fall into each of the three categories of consumer goods. Who purchased them? Discuss how they made the choice to buy that particular item and how much time and effort went into each. From the answers you get, judge the accuracy of the three descriptions above. Are there any other categories that you could describe – for example, some items may have been bought purely on impulse? If so, what types of product were they and what created the impulse to buy spontaneously?

Producer Products

Producer products, sometimes called industrial products or goods, are used by a business either to manufacture another product or as an essential item for the running of the business.

a   Production machinery, plant and equipment

A printing press used to print this book, computers used to set the type, the fork-lift used to move the materials about the printshop are examples. These tend to be purchased from capital – capital items – and are for use in running the business over a long period of time; they are fixed assets and appear as such on the balance sheet. Decisions to purchase such items are usually taken at the highest level and are carefully evaluated by specialist staff, even project teams, before orders are placed.

b   Raw materials

The paper and ink are obvious examples, but there are many others, such as glue, fixing agents, binding material and so on. These are purchased from revenue and are used up in the production process either directly or indirectly – they are revenue items and will be represented as stock, work-in-progress and perhaps finished goods in the current assets of the firm. Current assets are things owned by the business which are regularly used up and regularly replaced. Decisions to purchase are normally taken by technical staff, who specify standards precisely, but then pass the task of selecting suppliers and placing orders to a specialist purchasing officer.

c   Components

Some manufacturers do not make all the components they put into their products. Motor manufacturers are a good example of firms involved in assembling other manufacturers's parts to make a final product. There are so many different kinds of component that go into making a motor car that sub-contracting work to other specialist firms is more economical than doing everything themselves. The motor car firm specifies everything in the finest detail and maintains tight controls over quality. Obvious examples are the tyres, headlights and windows, but there are hundreds more in the engines and furnishings. These, too, will appear as stock, work-in-progress and finished goods in the firm's accounts. Purchasing decisions are usually made after detailed negotiations have taken place between technical experts from both firms. The actual placing of the orders will be passed to the purchasing officer to administer, but the control remains a technical matter.

d   Supplies

These fall into two categories:

- Basic materials that are required in manufacture, such as lubricating oils, cleaning agents and materials, spare parts for maintenance and so on
- Everything needed to run the business, including stationery, printed forms and materials, catering items, toiletry items and so on

Most of these items will be current assets, although in many cases they are too dispersed to be counted for accounting purposes. They may be purchased by the purchasing officer, or by staff who have been authorized to do so. Some small items may be purchased from petty cash. Petty cash is a small amount of cash kept in coins and notes to pay small bills rather than going through the whole purchasing administrative process.

e   Business services

Many businesses do not have all the expertise needed to operate and they buy these services as and when needed. Legal, accounting, personnel, advertising, management consultancy and training services, for example, are available to those who need them. They are intangible and therefore do not appear in the accounts as an asset. They are an expense.

Decisions to purchase such services are usually taken at the highest level.

ACTIVITY 8.2

Examine the chair you are sitting on. List the raw materials that were needed to make it.

What sort of machinery might be used to convert that raw material into your chair? Are there any parts of the chair that were obviously bought-in instead of being made by the chair manufacturer? For example, fabric, screws, nuts and bolts?

How was the chair delivered to your school or college? What paperwork might be needed to ensure that it was delivered to the right place, and that your school or college paid for it? If your chair broke due to faulty materials, and you broke your arm falling off it, what sort of services might the manufacturer need to deal with any claim for damages you might make?

Your answers to these questions illustrate the different classes of producer goods we have discussed. It would be very useful if you could arrange to visit a local manufacturing firm and see how these goods are purchased and used.

Services

We need to distinguish services from tangible products. The American Marketing Association simply describes services as 'activities, benefits, or satisfactions which are offered for sale'. The following analysis is based upon data compiled by Pride and Ferrell for their book, *Marketing* (Houghton Mifflin, 1989).

Any service tends to be intangible – that is, it has not got a physical existence. You cannot touch it. On the other hand, products are tangible. You can see and touch them and watch them perform the function they are intended to serve. By working through the following Activity you will identify characteristics that help classify services.

ACTIVITY 8.3

At the back of the *Yellow Pages* telephone directory you will find a classification index which lists nearly 3 000 types of business. Select a couple of pages in the classification index and put next to each type of business what it provides – a product (P) or a service (S). If you think it might provide both, mark it so.

Who are the services aimed at – consumers or producers or both? Looking at the services, how are they 'delivered' and who are involved in the delivery? Does the nature of the service require great expertise on the part of the provider, some expertise, or could anybody do it? Why does the provider offer the service? What is the motive that gives value to the producer and make it worth offering the service?

What proportion of the businesses you have examined are supplying products? What proportion are supplying services? What proportion seem to be doing both?

Does this data enable you to assess the importance of services in business?

Some are obviously services – completely intangible: accountants, advertising agencies. Some are obviously products – abrasive machinery and equipment, access equipment. But what about agricultural dealers and repairs? They supply machines – a product – but they also repair them – a service.

Banks and financial institutions are different again. They provide services, but paying money over the counter or cashing a cheque is a personal interaction between the bank clerk and the customer. Whereas obtaining cash from a cash dispenser is technology based; there is no personal contact, yet it is still a service.

What happens to the service when there are no customers around? Can it be stock-piled in the same way as a product? And how does a prospective customer judge the quality of a service and compare it with others before purchasing it? It cannot be picked off the shelf and tried out.

The answers to these questions highlight the characteristics of services:

- They are intangible
- They cannot be displayed
- They cannot be stored

KEY POINTS 8.1

- Product and place are concerned with supplying goods to customers

- Products can be classified into consumer products and producer products

- Consumer products can be sub-divided into convenience, shopper and speciality goods

- Producer products can be divided into machinery, raw materials, components, supplies and business services

- Services can be classified according to their market, personal contact, qualifications and motives

- The customer has to be present for the service to be produced
- Quality is difficult to illustrate before delivery

With these in mind, we can develop a framework which will help when deciding upon a marketing strategy for a service:

- What is the target market – consumers or producers?
- Is the service dependent upon personal contact, or can technology deliver it?
- What level of qualification and skill is needed by the provider's staff to supply the service?
- What is the motive for offering the service – profit or social?

ACTIVITY 8.4

Return to the businesses you examined in the *Yellow Pages* (Activity 8.3) which supply services and classify them according to the four elements in the above framework. Now consider how they might be priced, promoted and delivered.

Product Policy

Being clear about the categories of products and services is the company's starting point when developing a product policy.

A business may begin its life as a single product company, but as it grows it may develop or take on other products. The decisions as to which products to add to the range will be based upon many considerations, not least its mission statement.

The mission statement is the business's vision of where it is going. Each function of the business contributes to its achievement:

- Marketing will research the needs of its target market and the extent to which the company has the expertise to meet those needs

- Finance will consider resources in terms of both capital and working capital implications
- Production will examine its capacity, technology, skilled personnel, and expertise
- Personnel will consider the development, training, recruitment and industrial relations implications

Unless all these functions are balanced and co-ordinated, growth may be hampered and profitability affected. We will return to these four considerations again when we look at the product development process.

Product Line

If the company decides to stick to the market it knows, but to capture a bigger share of it with a choice of similar products, it is probable that the company will develop its product line.

An example of a well developed product line that meets the needs of a wide band of consumers is detergents. Lever Brothers, a wholly owned subsidiary of the giant multinational Unilever, has a line of sixteen detergent products (see Figure 8.2).

Product Mix

If the company decides, on the other hand, to develop different products so as to have more than one product line, then it will develop its product mix. Lever Brothers also exemplifies this concept of product line and product mix beautifully. Besides its detergent line, it has a line of four fabric conditioners, a line of three washing-up liquids, a line of four dishwasher liquids, a line of three household cleaners, a line of two household soaps, a line of four toilet soaps and a line of four toilet cleaners. This gives it depth of product line and width of product mix.

There is a common thread in this product policy. All the products are chemical, all meet the need for cleanliness, and all are convenience

Figure 8.2 – *Lever Brothers: Product Line and Product Mix*

goods that use the same distribution channel. Therefore there can be a very similar marketing mix for each line, and economies of marketing can be enjoyed.

ACTIVITY 8.5

On your next visit to a supermarket, pay particular attention to the concept of product lines and product mix. The example above highlighted Lever Brothers involvement in the detergent and domestic cleaning agents market. If you examine competitive products on the same shelves, the name Procter & Gamble will be quite common. What is their depth of product line compared with Lever Brothers? And how many lines can you find in their product mix?

How many flavours are there in Heinz and Cross & Blackwell's soup product lines? Their product mix includes a wide range of product lines – baked beans to baby food. See how many you can spot.

In the cereal section, who are the main producers and what product lines and product mix do they have?

Developing Existing Products

A business can choose to grow by developing new products to add to its present product line and mix, or by developing and exploiting the market for its present products, or both. Its policy on growth has to be decided at the highest level in the business, and then implemented by the functional managers. To help it make decisions about its growth policy, a simple analytical tool has been developed by strategic management expert Igor Ansoff.

It is worth your while to actually copy Figure 8.3 into your notes so that you become familiar with the following terms:

- *Market penetration* relates to the strategy of gaining a larger share of the existing market for its present products or services

Figure 8.3 – *Ansoff's Product/Market Growth Matrix*

	PRESENT PRODUCTS	NEW PRODUCTS
PRESENT MARKETS	Market penetration opportunities	Product development opportunities
NEW MARKETS	Market development opportunities	Diversification opportunities

- *Market development* is a strategy that requires the producer to seek out and develop new market segments for present products or services, including overseas markets
- *Product development* strategy is the lengthy process of researching market needs, creating products or services to meet those identified needs, and obtaining all the resources to produce and distribute them. We will study this process in more detail in the next section
- *Diversification* strategy means going into entirely new markets with entirely new products

There are other strategies that a business can adopt to achieve growth. This book examines growth through market and product development. However, we will take a very brief look at two other growth strategies – integration and diversification.

Integration Strategy

The idea of integration is fairly common. Businesses bring together the sources of supply, the facilities for production and the distribution channels for their products so as to have complete control over their operation.

The forms of integration which companies undertake are:

- *Backward integration*: this relates to growth by acquiring a business that supplies the company's raw materials or components. Breweries often own the farms that produce the hops or grain needed for their products
- *Forward integration*: this relates to growth by acquiring distribution or retail outlets for the company's products. Breweries have 'tied' houses which, until 1992, only sold their own brands of beer. Recent legislation has curtailed this practice

(Backward and forward integration together are often referred to as *verticle integration*.)

- *Horizontal integration*: this relates to growth by acquiring competitors or other businesses in the same industry. Whitbread's policy of buying up small independent brewers is an example.

DIVERSIFICATION STRATEGY
Diversification, on the other hand, relates to a business moving into new ground. Again, there are three sorts:

- *Concentric diversification*: this is where a business uses its present technology and expertise to produce new products or services for different but similar markets. An example is Virgin Airlines which might use its passenger-moving expertise to add rail to its airways travel

- *Horizontal diversification*: this is where a business uses its present markets to introduce new products related to its present range, but through different manufacturing facilities. An example is Virgin Records and its introduction of CDs or cassette cleaners
- *Conglomerate diversification*: this is where a business goes into something entirely new that requires different manufacturing technology and expertise, and new markets. An example might be if Virgin decided to go into the food processing business.

ACTIVITY 8.6

Two conglomerates are Hanson Trust plc and BAT Industries plc. Both have offices in London. Research one of these conglomerates, or any other that you know, and see the extent of its diversification. What advantages and disadvantages might such diversification bring to the business?

Developing New Products

All new products and services begin life as ideas. Some ways of generating ideas are discussed in the companion book *The Business Environment*, and progressive companies encourage and reward innovation very positively.

Through the marketing information system, a company will gather information from and about customers that can lead to ideas for new or revised products. Salespeople and dealers feed back to the producer what they are learning about the market and what competitive action is happening in the marketplace. Scientists and academics constantly move the frontiers of our knowledge and publish their research findings for all who are interested to read. Licences to develop products resulting from this research are then taken out by firms.

Although idea generation can be purely inspirational (the 'Eureka' approach), there are formal techniques that have been developed that help companies to generate better ideas.

New Ideas

To develop an idea into a saleable product or service is a long and expensive process. Then to attract the attention of the target market, and show them the value of the new product so that they will buy it, is both expensive and demanding on the skills of management. There are many different views as to how many new ideas that are pursued by firms actually become profitable products. The figures range from 2 per cent to 40 per cent – one can assume that such a wide range indicates that the people who generate this data are using different criteria and are probably measuring from different points in the life of the idea. We can be certain, however, that there is a massive mortality rate, and very few 'great ideas' ever became profitable products.

Progressing new ideas is, however, an important marketing skill. Without ideas companies would stagnate and the consumers would be bored by unchanging goods and restricted choice.

An important aspect of the marketing function is to exercise a robust evaluation process that objectively examines ideas and their potential for business success. In the private sector, success is usually measured by return on investment or profitability. In the case of a service such as the Health Service, the criteria may be quite different. Success may be measured by the number of patients the new product might cure or the amount of suffering it might relieve – whatever the cost of development.

Six Phases of Product Development

The route taken to develop a nebulous idea into a successful product varies from producer to producer. It is rather different for an aircraft and a chocolate bar. However, Pride and Farrell have put forward the following six phase model which allows a study of the process and an understanding of the practice of product development.

STAGE ONE – SCREENING IDEAS

Companies need to avoid two sorts of error when screening ideas:

- They must not reject good ideas
- They must not develop poor ideas

Good ideas when developed meet the organization's objectives for sales volume and return on investment. Poor ideas do not. The obvious result of failed products is that they lose money, and this makes it relatively easy to deal with – abandon them.

But what if a product does not reach target expectations, even though it is making a contribution to overheads or a small profit? Many companies will allow it to continue despite the fact that it affects the overall performance of the firm, and despite the opportunity cost of doing so.

A common method used to screen ideas is to ask questions under the four functions listed on page 144.

Each producer would develop the questions that are relevant to its own situation. Managers will assess the level to which the company matches up to these questions. If they feel that it does, then the idea will go forward to the next stage; if not, it will be dropped. Over 50 per cent of ideas do not get beyond this stage.

STAGE TWO – CONCEPT TESTING

Turning the ideas that survive screening into tangible products that potential customers will perceive as value is the next stage. Before the company actually starts to make anything, some indication of the reaction of the possible market would be helpful.

For example, the idea is that 'word-processor VDUs ought to be on flexible stands'. The stands permit great variation in height and distance to allow for all shapes and sizes of user, and who have widely varying eyesight, glasses, bifocals and so on. How can this idea be turned into a product? What will it look like and what will it do?

A draughtsman or artist may sketch a simple stand that provides the flexibility envisaged. The drawings would set out to show that VDUs can be moved easily to a position that suits a range of users. Users would benefit because the product avoids neck ache, reduces eye strain, helps people who wear glasses, can be used in the office or the home, and is attractive on any desk.

By showing this drawing to people within the target market, perhaps with a questionnaire, the

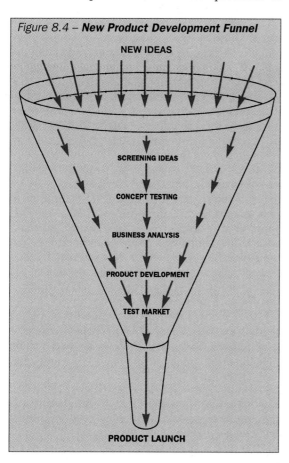

Figure 8.4 – *New Product Development Funnel*

NEW IDEAS

SCREENING IDEAS

CONCEPT TESTING

BUSINESS ANALYSIS

PRODUCT DEVELOPMENT

TEST MARKET

PRODUCT LAUNCH

company will get feedback which indicates whether a need actually exists, and whether something along the lines of the drawing would find buyers. Perhaps results might suggest that there is a need in offices but not in the home; or that only people with glasses would find the product helpful.

What valuable information! This relatively low cost piece of marketing research will allow the firm to decide whether there is sufficient potential to do more work on the concept.

STAGE THREE – BUSINESS ANALYSIS

The main reason for developing new products or services is to improve the business's performance. The next stage of the evaluation sets out to analyse the potential sales, income, profit and return on investment if the product's development continues to fruition. Will it meet the business objectives?

This is a lengthy exercise that relies a great deal on estimates and forecasts. Philip Kotler, in his book, *Marketing Management* (Prentice Hall, 1988), suggests ways of estimating sales, costs and profits which follow a logical order.

a   Estimating sales

Some products are purchased just once; some are replaced after a period; and others are purchased repeatedly. A house, a car and an ice cream are respective examples. The VDU stand would probably be a once only purchase.

Returning to our people with spectacles needing a VDU stand on their desk at work, a market segment can be defined that embraces this target market (market segmentation is discussed later on page 163).

Now the size of that segment has to be estimated, perhaps by reference to statistics about spectacle wearers, the number that are over sixteen years and under sixty-five, and the percentage of people who use VDUs at work. That would give some idea of potential customers. The number of potential customers who will buy the product will depend upon the amount of advertising, sales promotion and publicity; the sales price of the product; and the way competitors react to the new product entering the market. This data enables an estimate to be made of the rate at which sales may grow.

These two estimates – the size of the segment and the growth rate of sales – give an indication of the level of sales per period, and an estimate of sales income. By plotting the estimated sales on a graph, it might give some indication of the likely sales during the introductory and growth stages of this product's life cycle.

b   Estimating costs and profits

Variable costs for materials and labour, together with an apportionment of fixed costs to the product, will permit an estimate of gross profit to be calculated. Administrative costs and marketing costs can be estimated and apportioned to complete the calculation of probable net profit before tax and interest, and likely return on investment.

Note that they are all estimates, with some of the estimates based on estimates of other factors. The purpose is not to give definitive answers, but to give senior managers some information, to which they apply their experience and judgement, to arrive at a decision about proceeding to the next stage. They will be assisted by techniques such as break-even charts and DCF calculations (that are discussed in the companion book *Finance, Information and Business*). However, these techniques do not make decisions for managers, they simply provide information.

Forecasting and estimating are inexact techniques, but they are a lot better than pure guesswork. During the period that it takes to develop a product, both external and internal factors will be changing constantly – sometimes for better, sometimes for worse. There will always be risk in these decisions. Managers try to look at 'best' and 'worst' scenarios, or 'minimum' and 'maximum' situations, so as to understand the range of the risk they are dealing with.

One last thought about marketing costs and income. There is a relationship between the amount of money spent on promotion and the amount of sales income. To change estimates of one, will automatically change the other. It is wise to define the relationship between the two in a mathematical model. A spreadsheet used on a PC is an ideal tool for it – this will enable 'what if?' exercises to be conducted easily. For example, 'What if we increase advertising expenditure by 10 per cent?' 'What if we want to increase sales income by 20 per cent?'

Just as there can be a 'halo effect' in matters of personnel selection, there can be 'halo data' that supports a preconceived idea held by the managers. The temptation to use information to get the result they want, rather than the result which the information implies, should be resisted. In the final analysis, it is the judgement and maturity of the decision-makers that count.

If the business analysis shows that the product might meet the company's objectives, it will proceed to the next stage. If not, the product will be abandoned.

STAGE FOUR – PRODUCT DEVELOPMENT

Products that get this far in the evaluation process have cost the company relatively little, but from now on the costs escalate.

The people who turn ideas into objects are

usually the research and development engineers. They are concerned with design, materials, production processes, quality and safety. They have to take into account any consumer protection legislation and any health and safety at work regulations and ensure that no liability for negligence will rest upon the company. They will endeavour to create the most economical use of plant, materials and people, consistent with safety, quality and reliability. They will probably build a prototype, which the marketing specialists will test for the functions and characteristics that their research has shown the market wants.

They may conduct these tests themselves or use a panel of potential customers. A great deal of effort and ingenuity goes into getting the product right. There is constant liaison between marketing and production – creating satisfied customers is everyone's job. Many modifications are incorporated at this stage, because to do so later is very much more difficult and expensive.

Once the product goes into production, the company is committed to heavy expenditure and it may be some time before cash starts flowing in.

While production is getting the product right, marketing will be working on two other important elements that go into making the product attractive and accepted – packaging and branding. We will consider each of these marketing skills now before we discuss Stage Five of the product development process.

PACKAGING

Packaging serves four purposes:

- Protection
- Economy
- Convenience
- Promotion

a   Protection

An important factor in quality, and customer satisfaction, is ensuring that the product reaches the user in perfect condition. The packaging must allow for the nature of the product, the means of transport, and the ways in which it is displayed at the point of sale. In recent years, the criminal practice of tampering with products on shelves has necessitated producers making goods safe by including tamper-proof features in the packaging.

The costs of replacing goods damaged in transit – costs in both money and reputation – is an expense that marketing specialists will want to minimize.

b   Economy

The cost of packaging should be kept as low as possible so as not to add too much to the price of the product. However, in recent years, consumers have shown an increasing willingness to pay for improved packaging. Innovations in materials have improved product life and freshness, and made using some products easier. Examples of these are cling-film, aerosols, push-button cans, cook-in-bags, Tetra Paks, bubble packs of pills, batteries, nails or anything!

Supermarkets have influenced the ways in which goods are packaged. They need to reduce handling to an absolute minimum in order to reduce overhead costs. Consequently, some products are packed in such a way that whole pallets can be wheeled on to the shop floor, and stacked without unloading.

Multipacks – for example, six-packs of soft drinks – have gained favour for their ease of display, their 'pick up' attraction and the fact that they increase product sales without the promotion that would normally be associated with an equivalent increase in demand.

Bar coding has added another economy to packaging. Computerized checkout systems have enabled the job of checkout operators to be de-skilled, their training time reduced dramatically and human errors at the checkout reduced to almost zero.

c   Convenience

Packing ready-meals for one or two people is becoming very popular. Some packages allow for easy consumption – soft drinks in small cartons with a straw attached, for example. Larger packs, as with detergents, and multi-packs, as with potato crisps, are also popular. In some cases, single packs have almost disappeared. Packing for vending machines has also made distribution of some products possible through channels not available to it before. This idea is being exploited by Coca-Cola Schweppes through their new division, Vendleader (see Coca-Cola and Schweppes Case Study). Flat-packs for furniture, garden sheds and similar products have saved the cost of assembly and delivery, and increased the number and type of outlet in which these goods can be sold.

d   Promotion

Packaging is a feature of the product. In many cases the customer does not see the product, only the package. Colour, texture, shape and size can influence the purchaser. Cosmetics are good examples of products whose sales are very dependent upon the quality of their packaging. Often, the carton gives the impression that the contents are larger than they really are, and adds to the feeling of value. The aesthetics of the box sets out to convey the beauty that is inside.

The relationship between colour and the product is important. For example, green packing is seldom used for meat products, although it may be ideal for vegetables.

Advertising campaigns help people to recognize and identify the product at the point of sale. There is usually continuity between advertisements, sales promotion material and packaging.

Both UK and EC laws require the manufacturers of many goods to print the ingredients on the packaging or label, and provision has to be made for this when designing packaging.

Developing packaging that meets the four purposes is a specialized task, and a large packaging industry has grown up to help and advise companies on the subject. There is a great deal of innovation and technological improvement taking place continuously in the packaging industry.

The concern expressed by conservation and environmental groups is often directed at

---

| CASE STUDY |

Coca-Cola and Schweppes Beverages

Coca-Cola & Schweppes Beverages (CCSB) plan to develop the soft drinks market by increasing per capita consumption.

CCSB's objective is to increase dramatically the availability of cold drinks outside the home through widespread placement of chilling equipment. CCSB aims to build the 'cold habit' by providing 'within arm's reach' exposure to consumers at work, at school and at leisure.

CCSB began in 1987 with 55 000 chilling units. At the end of 1990 this had grown to 100 000 and we are planning continuing growth.

This is based on a major restructuring and investment programme. The chilling equipment is split into three basic areas:

- Dispensed postmix or draught soft drinks in pubs, restaurants etc;
- Vending, which is predominantly can vending;
- Display, which includes cooler/fridge glass fronted display cabinets.

Dispensed The dispensed engineering division of CCSB, 'Frontier', which requires a high degree of specialist technical expertise, has completed its restructuring to accommodate the growing customer requirement for quick, effective and efficient service support.

Vending A new vending division of CCSB, 'Vendleader', was launched in March 1990 to develop the enormous potential for can vending in Britain. This restructuring has enabled CCSB to accelerate its vending machine placements in 1990.

Display-Cold Drinks Division As part of CCSB's comprehensive equipment portfolio, a Cold Drinks Sales team is spearheading the placement of display units in 1991. This will be enhanced through the 90s with investment in chilling equipment and the introduction of new specialist equipment.

CUSTOMER SERVICE

CCSB has embarked on a major initiative to redefine its customers' needs, decide on the services it will provide and make the changes necessary to ensure increased customer satisfaction.

During 1990 CCSB has realised the benefit of its new factory at Wakefield, where the Company is now able to produce high quality product faster and at lower cost. Wakefield produced about 50 million cases in 1990, thereby ensuring the availability of CCSB's products and supporting the increase in business volumes over 1989. The installation of two new lines will give a potential volume of 70 million cases per annum.

Making the product available is only part of the story. CCSB has also been reviewing the way in which it delivers to its customers. During 1990 CCSB's distribution operation has made significant improvements. It is seeking to support its customers' requirements, through the adoption of new methods of working and teamwork.

Source: Cadbury Schweppes Annual Report 1991

QUESTIONS

1 Highlight evidence from the Case Study that CCSB is practising the marketing concept.
2 Explain the steps CCSB should take to 'redefine its customers' needs'.
3 Compare and contrast the promotion mix that would be appropriate to each of the three divisions.
4 Discuss the social costs incurred in CCSB's business objective. Is such an operation justifiable?

packaging. Some materials are indestructible and by their very nature have no further use and are thrown away. Some goods are 'over packed' and appear to use excessive material. An example is six or twelve or twenty-four cans of drink in heavy cardboard cartons. Another is a car roof-rack that is in moulded plastic and then inside a cardboard box.

Recycling is a way of reducing this use of scarce resources, but that depends upon people's willingness to collect rather than discard them, and upon recycling facilities being available. Of course, there are still a lot of materials that cannot be recycled. Some firms, notably BMW motor cars, use as a selling point the fact that their products can be recycled.

ACTIVITY 8.7

Prepare an argument in support of an environmental group that opposes the use of indestructible packaging materials, and then list all the consequences of that argument for the consumer. Why do firms use such materials and what might persuade them to change their ways?

BRANDING

When different herds of cattle shared grazing on common land, or could become mingled with others at market, each farmer distinguished his own cattle from all the other similar cattle with his own distinctive brand – a symbol or number or letters burnt on to the animal's hide, or on an ear tag.

This concept is used widely in marketing. A producer chooses a word, symbol or both, registers them for use only on its products, and sets out to distinguish its products from all similar products by use of this brand. It is one form of product differentiation.

Here are some examples of branding which you will probably recognize:

- Van den Bergh's margarines product line: Flora, Delight, Stork, Krona, Blue Band, Summer County, and Echo. Not only does this producer distinguish all its own individual margarines from each other, it distinguishes them from all competitors's products. This is individual product branding.
- Heinz product mix: baked beans, soups, spaghetti, beans with sausages, sponge puddings, baby foods, tomato ketchup, salad dressing and so on. Heinz has so many varieties, but this selection shows that these different products are distinguished from any others by being under the Heinz banner. This is family branding.

- Nescafé: Nescafé Instant Coffee, Nescafé Gold Blend, Nescafé Continental and so on. All these coffee blends are distinguished from any other producer's coffees by the brand name 'Nescafé'. This is line branding.
- Marks & Spencer: another example of family branding in a wider context is *St Michael's*, which appears on almost every product that M & S sells – clothes, shoes, cosmetics, foods, soft furnishings and so on. Marks & Spencer does not manufacture any of these goods. They are made to very precise specifications, under the strictest quality control for M & S and are distinguished from any other products made by the manufacturers by the brand name 'St Michael'.
- Sainsbury, Asda, Tesco: all these supermarket chains offer a wide range of products under their own brand names. Any product that sells in reasonable volume would be considered by the supermarket for own label branding. These stores have a high reputation for value and quality, and their own label goods sitting next to premier brands on the shelves offer additional choice to their customers.

Because own brands are produced in bulk for the supermarket by well-known manufacturers – who often have their own brands – fixed costs are shared over a larger output, thus making them cheaper. Add to that the facts that the own brands are not advertised, are packaged simply and do not have high distribution costs (they are moved in bulk to central distribution depots), the supermarket chain can sell them cheaper than well-known brands, and still make its full profit margins. Quality-conscious, price-conscious customers find these products good value and total sales of own brands is growing. In the United States, own brand goods represent 30 per cent of retail sales.

Small independents try to compete through group buying under brand names like Spar, Mace, Londis and Happy Shopper.

Choosing a brand name is complicated. It must be easy to say, to spell, to remember and it must be suited to the product, to the line or to the mix. Sir Adrian Cadbury said in the video, *Marketing – The Key to Prosperity* (Chartered Institute of Marketing, 1987), that his companies's greatest assets were their brands. The fact that they do not appear as an asset in the balance sheet has been the subject of great debate in accountancy circles in recent years, and the arguments in favour and against have not yet produced a consensus.

To a customer, a brand name is a shorthand for a wide range of factors. The brand name Heinz might mean: good quality, reliable, reasonably priced, readily available, safe and healthy goods. A shopper will assume all those factors for any

---

Figure 8.5 – **Advantages and Disadvantages of Branding for Producers**

ADVANTAGES	DISADVANTAGES
• A well-known brand ensures instant recognition of the goods	• Costly promotion over a long period is needed to gain brand recognition
• This makes it easy for the buyer to pick up that brand	• Constant promotion is necessary to maintain brand visibility
• This will lead to brand loyalty, public trust in the product and repeat purchases	• A single bad event may affect all the brand's products
• This will give a reasonably stable demand for the product	• Brand names have to be protected by registration worldwide
• This allows for better production planning and optimum use of resources	• Imitators are hard to stop
	• Legal actions against imitators can be time consuming and costly

---

product carrying that famous brand name. Psychologically, there is a reassurance that the buyer is feeding her or his family well by buying that product. On the other hand, loyalty to a small number of reliable brands might mean a fairly repetitive diet without the chance of discovering new and exciting goods.

To the producer, there are both advantages and disadvantages to branding, as set out in Figure 8.5.

Branding is an effective method for giving a product a differential advantage over its competitors. The marketing specialists can use it to develop a marketing mix that appeals to the target market.

At the end of this product development stage – where the product has a name, can be packaged appropriately and the basis of a marketing mix

has been decided – the producer is in a position to manufacture the product in quantity. But before proceeding, the producer has to decide whether to launch the new product at this stage or whether to undertake a test market first. Most fast-moving convenience goods will benefit from test marketing before they are launched nationwide. Producer goods, however, seldom require this sort of technique. They are usually launched through exhibitions, demonstrations and sales representation. The producer relies upon informal feedback from prospective users in an informal manner, via the sales representatives (see Figure 8.6).

The criterion for the decision to use a test market approach is:

• Do we know enough about the product and the

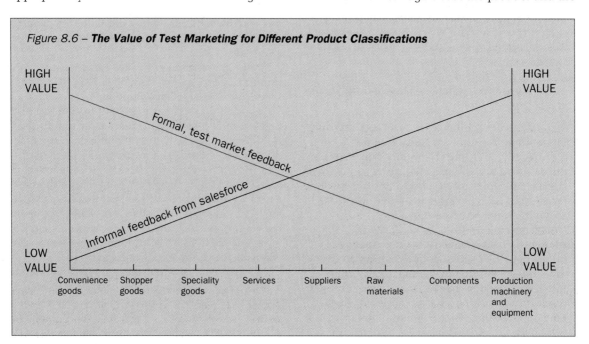

Figure 8.6 – **The Value of Test Marketing for Different Product Classifications**

target market to keep the risk to an acceptable level?

If there is any doubt, it is probably wise to go for a test market first.

STAGE FIVE – TEST MARKETING

Rather than launch a new product nationally and risk failure, it may be wise to undertake some marketing research with a test market. The aim of a test market is to see how the target market reacts to the product, the packaging, the promotion, the distribution and the price, under normal market conditions; and to see if the product performs as intended. The area for a test market should, as far as possible, be a representative sample of the whole market. Often, it is convenient to choose a television area. For example, the Tyne Tees area was used as a test market for Whispa chocolate bars.

Test marketing is costly, and only large companies will have the resources or expertise to conduct one. It is wise to be guided by a marketing agency that has experience and expertise, but care should be taken in selecting an agency with proven competence in the type of product being tested.

The producer will need guidance in the following matters:

- Selecting a test area that represents the population
- Deciding upon the data to be gathered throughout the test
- Estimating the time needed to gather sufficient data
- Designing the methods of data gathering
- Designing the system to analyse the data and make it meaningful (usually computer assisted)
- Deciding how to interpret and use the resulting information
- Making the amendments and adjustments to the product, packaging, and so on before the big launch

Some important information will be gathered from internal systems. Analysing orders received, as discussed in Chapter Seven, will help to confirm the estimated market penetration rate, sales volume and sales income. Shop audits will show how retail sales are progressing within the retail outlets. Careful analysis of sales volume and sales income through the different types of retail outlet will give data on channels of distribution.

A consumer panel can be formed out of a sample of households in the test area. This will enable the producer to obtain consumers's opinions of the product, and an indication as to whether they would continue to buy it.

Other marketing research can be undertaken to find reaction to advertising, sales promotion and packaging. This information will assist the marketing manager in modifying the first designs of the marketing mix to make it more effective.

The evidence from the test market activities will be used by management to ensure that they get things right and to speed the product to profitability. Marketing guru Philip Kotler suggests four possible outcomes:

- If the test results show a steady growth in purchases, and repeat purchases, it implies that the product is being accepted
- On the other hand, if there are first time purchases, but few repeat purchases, there is something wrong with the product that must be sorted out if a national launch is to be worthwhile
- It may show that sales growth is very slow, but those who did buy are repeating their purchases. This implies that the promotional activity might not be right
- But if there are low sales and even lower repeat sales, maybe it would be wise to cut losses and abandon the product

ACTIVITY 8.8

We have sounded warnings about the accuracy and value of research, statistical and accounting data several times in this series of books. The same caution is given about test market data. It is worth discussing the following questions in a small group:

(a) How accurately may the test market represent the whole market?
(b) How accurate are the various data gathered during the test?
(c) Is the analysis of these data telling what needs to be told?
(d) Can the analysis be extrapolated to predict behaviour in the whole market?
(e) Will things that affected the test market be the same next month or next year?
(f) Will competitors react to the national launch as they did to the test?
(g) Will the logistics for a national launch be handled as well by management as the smaller test market?
(h) Will management take notice of the evidence to make radical changes if needed?

Whatever your conclusions, is it better to have the data or not?

STAGE SIX – PRODUCT LAUNCH

The run up to the full scale launch of a product is a very busy period. There are a lot of interdependent activities going on in various departments of the organization. Planning and co-ordinating are

*Figure 8.7 – **Checklists for Product Launch***

MARKETING DEPARTMENT

- ☐ Advertising design and preparation completed
- ☐ Media scheduling finalized
- ☐ Sales promotion materials ready
- ☐ Distribution channels tested and primed
- ☐ Salesforce job descriptions prepared for recruitment and training by personnel specialists
- ☐ Dealers training programme arranged
- ☐ Terms of trade agreed with the accountant
- ☐ Pricing structures and discounts finalized
- ☐ Sales territories organized
- ☐ Sales targets set
- ☐ Launch dates fixed

PRODUCTION DEPARTMENT

- ☐ Production machinery installed and set
- ☐ Production methods and schedules prepared
- ☐ Production staff trained and briefed
- ☐ Raw materials and components ordered
- ☐ Quality standards installed
- ☐ Packaging materials ordered
- ☐ Transport arrangements made
- ☐ Industrial relations managed
- ☐ Health and safety ensured

the two most crucial management activities. In all probability, critical path analysis (which is explained in the companion book, *Finance, Information and Business*) will be used to highlight the relationships between all these activities. Project meetings will be held regularly to deal with the difficulties that will inevitably arise. Production, finance and personnel departments will be as involved as marketing specialists – getting products to customers and creating satisfied customers is a company-wide responsibility requiring commitment from everyone.

Launching a product is a very costly operation. Pay-back – the time it takes to recoup the money invested in the product – will occur in the shortest period if all the elements of the launch come together at the right time without any delays. Coordination of all activities is essential.

Once the product is launched it begins the introductory stage of its product life cycle.

There is a well known story about the launch of a dog food in the early 1970s. The product had been developed and manufactured, the advertising and sales promotion had gone out, customers were asking for it in the shops – but it had not arrived at the point of sale. People asked once, twice and maybe three times for it, but it was not available. So they abandoned their attempts – then the dog food arrived in the shops and nobody wanted it. They had completely lost any interest they had in it. The result was that the firm had to withdraw all stocks and re-launch the product under a different name some months later. It is rumoured that company lost £1 million in costs and lost revenue. And, of course, they lost face!

Pareto's Law

An interesting phenomenon is that in many businesses, 80 per cent of sales comes from 20 per cent of their product range. It has also been found that the weakest 20 per cent of products takes up 80 per cent of sales and marketing

KEY POINTS 8.2

- **Product line relates to the number of the same type of product produced by a business. Product mix relates to the range of different products produced by a business**

- **Developing existing products is safer, quicker and cheaper than developing completely new products, but it is not always possible**

- **There are six stages in the development of a new product. Very few that start Stage One reach the final launch stage**

- **Packaging serves four purposes: protection, economy, convenience and promotion**

- **Branding is a means of giving a product differential advantage over similar, competing products**

- **Creating and developing new products involves all the functions of a business. Success results from efficiency throughout the organization**

effort. The analytical tool, known as Pareto Analysis, is described in the companion book, *Finance, Information and Business*.

Acceptance of New Products

It would be unwise to expect a great rush to buy a new product immediately after it was launched. There will be a small group of people who like being first and being seen to have the latest product. Shortly after them will come a group of people who enjoy recognition; they feel looked-up-to if others comment upon or admire their possessions. These two groups will open the way for those less adventurous people who do not take great risks, but who like new things. Next will come the sceptics who require evidence from others that it is worthwhile changing. Lastly, there will be a small group who will wait until something is well tried and tested – by the time they get around to trying it, it will probably be no longer considered new.

Much human behaviour follows a normal distribution curve, and Everett M Rogers, author of *Diffusion of Innovations* (Free Press, 1962) illustrated the above groups in that form (see Figure 8.8).

ACTIVITY 8.9

Where do you think you fall on the curve in Figure 8.8? How did you make that decision?

Design a simple questionnaire which you could ask a sample of your friends and relatives to complete in order to give you an idea of their position. Does the result of your sample produce a normal distribution curve? What value would knowledge of this distribution be to the marketing manager?

Strategies and the Product Life Cycle

We examined the product life cycle concept in general in Chapter Seven and you will recall that all products and services go through four stages: Introduction, Growth, Maturity and Decline. We also looked at marketing plans and marketing strategy. Here, we will put the two together and examine the four Ps in relation to each stage of the product life cycle.

But first, there are some additional pieces of information that we can add to the product life cycle graph.

A life cycle might relate to a generic product – motor cars. Or it might relate to a particular form of motor car – sports cars. Or it might relate to a specific brand of sports car – Porsche. The life cycle is different for each of these. Figure 8.9 (next page) shows a single product life cycle seen in the context of the other two. (Figure 8.9 is for illustration purposes only and does not accurately represent a given product.)

It shows that whatever happens to a particular product, the world goes on. It is partly in the hands of the marketing specialists as to how the product's life takes shape, and it is subject to all the external variables discussed in Chapter Seven.

It is also possible to show costs on a life cycle graph (as in Figure 8.9). It helps to illustrate the

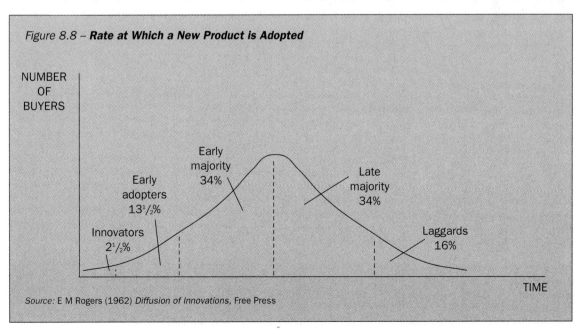

Figure 8.8 – *Rate at Which a New Product is Adopted*

NUMBER OF BUYERS

Early majority 34%

Early adopters 13½%

Late majority 34%

Innovators 2½%

Laggards 16%

TIME

Source: E M Rogers (1962) *Diffusion of Innovations*, Free Press

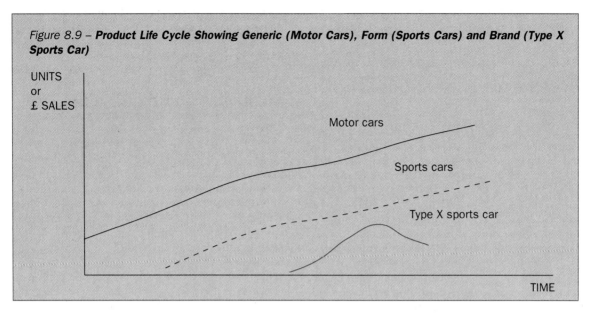

Figure 8.9 – **Product Life Cycle Showing Generic (Motor Cars), Form (Sports Cars) and Brand (Type X Sports Car)**

heavy expenses incurred during the development and introductory stages of a new product, and highlights the need to progress the product through its life cycle as certainly as possible, to reach maturity as quickly as possible, and to keep it there for as long as possible. These are challenges to the competent marketing manager. (Once again, Figure 8.10 serves to illustrate a concept, not an actual case.)

ACTIVITY 8.10

This activity is in four parts: (a), (b), (c) and (d). (a) will come after the Introduction Stage, (b) will come after the Growth Stage and so on.

Consider the marketing strategy – the four Ps – for three products at the end of each stage. The products must be:

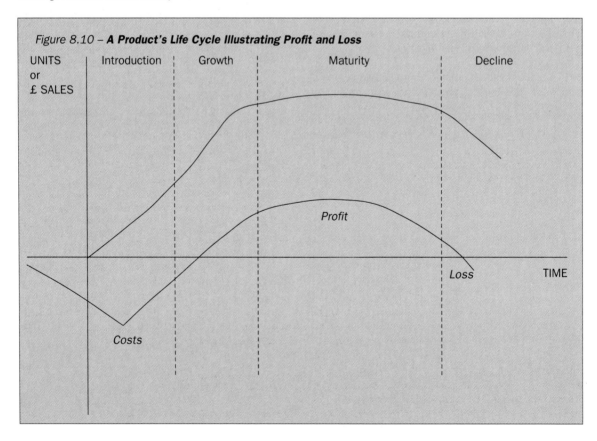

Figure 8.10 – **A Product's Life Cycle Illustrating Profit and Loss**

- One primary (for example, fresh salmon)
- One secondary (for example, training shoes)
- One tertiary (for example, activity holidays in the UK)

Bearing in mind each product's position in its life cycle, how would you make sure that it is successful in getting to the next stage? Be imaginative, but realistic. Use real-life examples to guide your decision-making.

Introduction Stage

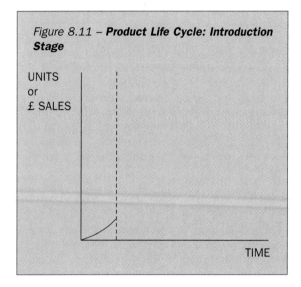

*Figure 8.11 – **Product Life Cycle: Introduction Stage***

The new product's sales growth will be slow at first as few people know of its existence. The innovators and some early adopters are beginning to purchase. It may be the only product of its kind on the market, or it may be one of only a few. The amount of public awareness is still low as promotion is in its early stages.

PRODUCT
Some of the problems tackled during the launch phase may hangover into this stage: there may be teething problems with the technology or production has not come on-stream as planned.

PLACE
An early headache for the marketing manager is the distribution (place) of a new product. Often it is not completely within her or his control, and the distributors may not react as anticipated. An appropriate distribution tactic at this stage is to offer a package of incentives for the distributors and help with the logistics of obtaining the product, stocking it and distributing it to the retailers. Often, the producer's own salespeople visit the retailers and obtain orders which are passed to the nearest middleman for supply. In this way, the producer secures both distributors and retail outlets at the same time. The earlier this

distribution network is established, the sooner the product is likely to enter the growth stage.

PRICE AND PROMOTION
The greatest difficulty at the introductory stage is persuading customers to try the new product – it might involve customers having to change loyalty from their usual purchase, which takes time.

There are four possible strategies, put forward by Kotler, that the marketing manager might choose from to tackle this difficulty, and they link price with promotion. The one chosen will depend mainly upon the nature of the product and the target market:

a   High price plus high promotion
The high price will recover the development costs and pay for the high level of promotion. The high level of promotion will help to attract the target market before competitors join in. An example of this is Compact Disc players.

b   High price plus low promotion
This strategy assumes that people know about the product and are willing to pay a high price to own it. An example might be the latest Halogen electric cooker. The segment is a small part of the market and potential customers will not be put off by the high price. It is fairly price inelastic (elasticity is discussed fully in Chapter Nine).

c   Low price plus high promotion
This option will be adopted by firms who are concerned with their market share. The new concentrated detergents are an example. The product is fairly price elastic, and it is a very competitive market. All the firms in the market are high volume producers and can take advantage of economies of scale.

d   Low price plus low promotion
If demand for a product is price elastic but is promotion inelastic, this strategy makes some sense. It is most likely to be used by a small producer with a concentrated local market.

During the introduction stage of the product life cycle, the aim is to increase awareness of the product so as to increase sales and move towards the growth stage. It is a time of market education through all means of promotion, and slow sales growth means that a return on investment will be some way off. Marketing managers need the courage of their convictions at this stage. Some products never reach the growth stage. Do you remember the Sinclair C5?

ACTIVITY 8.10 (a)

What strategies (four Ps) would you recommend for

your three products during the introduction stage? Do they differ for the different products? If so, why?

Growth Stage

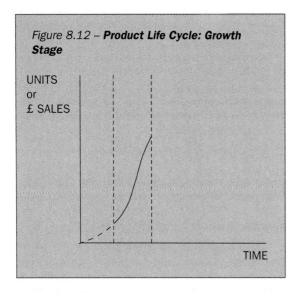

Figure 8.12 – **Product Life Cycle: Growth Stage**

UNITS
or
£ SALES

TIME

If the strategies followed during the launch and introduction stage have been successful, the growth rate will increase (as illustrated in Figure 8.12). The marketing information system would show that the number of new customers is increasing and repeat orders are building up. This pattern leads to exponential growth which is shown by the increasing steepness of the curve.

PRODUCT
In Figure 8.12, the difference in volume of sales between the beginning of the stage and the end is about three times, and this growth takes place in a relatively short space of time. Can you imagine what that means in terms of producing the product?

For example, if during the growth stage demand for baked beans increases from 330 000 tins a day to 1 000 000 tins a day, the following would be required by the producer: 1 000 000 empty tins (probably twenty-five juggernaut loads); tops, labels, 40 000 cardboard cartons, 1 000 pallets, about 400 tonnes of raw beans and all the sauces and spices; then twenty-five juggernauts to take away the finished, packaged products.

The production department will be very busy. It will receive demand forecasts from the marketing department from which it will prepare production schedules that will meet the increased demand. Production planners will have to plan and control increasing inventories, schedule production, allocate production resources, and bring new plant, machinery and people on stream to

cope with the growth. And most important of all, they must despatch the right quantity of the right quality of the right goods to the right destinations at the right time.

In the early part of this stage, the emphasis will tend to be on coping with rapid growth, but in the later stages things should be running relatively smoothly. The marketing specialists would use their knowledge of both the product and the market to review the situation. Manufacture of the product should be relatively trouble-free by the end of the growth stage, and resources could be released to consider how best to make the product more attractive in both appearance and function. Additional or supplementary products may be considered, as well as variations of the same product to give a price range – for example, bathroom showers come in plastic, chrome or gold versions, each at a different price. Quality has always been important, but at this point in time some resources may be freed to develop ways of giving greater customer satisfaction.

PLACE
Marketing will have similar challenges. The sales team will have more and more dealers and retailers to care for. More and more orders will have to be processed. Despite these pressures, the marketing manager must continue to monitor and modify the marketing strategy as the growth stage progresses.

The work done to establish distribution networks is rewarded with retailers allotting shelf space or distributors supporting and recommending the product. One of the effects that this initial success is likely to have, is that competitors will have monitored the product's progress through their MIS and seen an opportunity to enter a potentially profitable market. At this stage some competitive products may appear supported by their own promotions. Although this creates competition for the original product, it also brings benefits. Now two or more organizations are working at creating awareness and opening up channels of distribution. This may actually increase the rate of growth of the original product.

If growth is to be maintained, special attention will be needed to develop other market segments. New segments can mean access to new channels of distribution, and this, too, tends to accelerate growth.

PROMOTION
The emphasis on promotional activities should gradually change as the growth stage progresses from educating the market towards establishing brand loyalty.

PRICE

Prices remain relatively high because demand is still increasing. This should help the producer to recover development costs – from now on the product is paying its way and giving a return on the capital invested in it.

Competition, however, will begin to put pressure on prices. The producer must be ready to lower prices in order to maintain its growing market share. Lower prices may affect profits in the short term, but with more people able to afford the product, they should increase demand for the product. The added economies of large scale production should redress this in the medium term.

Growth must come to an end. All markets are finite, and competition will become intense as other firms come in with newer versions, lower prices, different promotions and so on. The fact that growth slows and eventually ceases is perhaps the biggest opportunity for the producer to consolidate its position and optimize its profits.

ACTIVITY 8.10(b)

What strategies would you follow to lead your products safely through the busy growth stage? How do they differ from the introduction stage? And how do they differ from one another? Why do these differences occur?

Maturity Stage

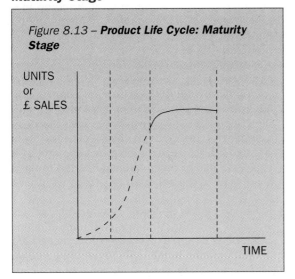

Figure 8.13 – *Product Life Cycle: Maturity Stage*

UNITS or £ SALES

TIME

This is the point in a product's life that all marketing efforts have been designed to achieve. It is a great achievement for all who have contributed to the marketing plan – production, finance, personnel and, of course, marketing.

During the maturity stage sales levels remain relatively stable. Its duration depends upon the nature of the product concerned. In Chapter Seven, we noted that fashion may have a maturity stage lasting six months, a car, six years, and baked beans, sixty years.

Maximum demand for the producer could result from market saturation – all the people who could buy the product in all segments of the market are buying the product (even the laggards have entered) – or because the producer has reached the limits of its production capacity. The ideal situation would be for maximum demand to be achieved as a result of both market saturation and production capacity occurring together.

MARKET STRUCTURE

If there is still market share to be gained, but capacity is fully utilized, the decision to expand production facilities would be treated as a major investment decision and would require detailed appraisal, as described in the companion book *Finance, Information and Business.*

The marketing manager's main concern throughout the maturity stage should be to maintain the product's position in the market and to protect its market share. The marketing manager of each competing product will be doing the same and looking for opportunities to improve at the expense of other products. Usually, the market settles down to a structure where there are a few market leaders who control most of the total sales between them. When we were discussing convenience goods earlier in this chapter, we noticed that just two companies shared 42 per cent of the butter market and four companies shared 42 per cent of the sweet market.

They are powerful enough to see off any challenge to their leadership. They dominate the mass market. Then there is another layer of large and medium-sized firms who are happy to occupy other segments and do not have the clout to climb up with the leaders. In some markets, there are a great number of medium and small firms who have found specialist segments or niches which do not interest the leaders. There may be changes in the lower levels, with firms entering and leaving the market, but the top few have fairly stable markets. This topic is considered in detail in *The Business Environment,* another title in this series.

PURSUING EFFICIENCY

At the end of the growth stage, thought was being given to enhancing the product in the customers's eyes. Now that the pressures of coping with rapid growth are over, thought should also be given to the manufacturing method and the materials used with a view to reducing costs and expenses:

- A technique called 'value analysis' can be employed to examine all the materials and components used in the product. Standardization of materials used in this and other products can lead to additional economies of scale
- Method study can help to streamline the manufacturing process by reducing operations and cutting out waste
- Opportunities to automate labour-intensive activities and introduce computerized control systems might be considered
- The reduction of costs should receive constant attention throughout the maturity stage

The sales administration procedures should come in for similar scrutiny:

- Sales invoices should be sent as soon as goods are despatched
- Order size should be monitored and uneconomic orders referred to the sales manager
- Prompt payment should be encouraged; bad payers should be referred to the sales manager
- The size of inventories should be monitored and lowered as far as possible; 'Just in Time' or similar appropriate techniques should be considered

With sales at their maximum, production and administration at their most efficient, profit should be at its optimum. The marketing specialist therefore has far more scope for responding to any actions by competitors.

To maintain the product's position, the marketing specialist may decide to modify some or all of the elements of the marketing mix. This is how a product gains its individuality from its competitors. It is where the quality of the marketing specialist can be seen.

Marketing expert Philip Kotler offers clear guidance as to how the marketing manager might modify the elements of the marketing mix to keep the product in its maturity stage for as long as possible.

PRODUCT
The product should be improved continually:

- Convenience goods are often presented as 'new improved', 'now with extra whitening power', ' the battery with the lasting power'
- New features are added to make the product more effective – for example, power tools that are rechargeable and do not need an electric cable; remote control 'zappers' for televisions
- Products are restyled to make them more attractive or more aesthetically pleasing – for example, motor cars, kitchen furniture and household equipment

Some of these changes are fairly big. Just as the market was researched and tested before the launch of a new product, it might be wise to repeat the research before major changes are made to a mature product. Since there are a lot of people buying the product already, it would be foolish to upset them.

PLACE
The market should be kept under review:

- New applications – plastic sheeting originally developed for wrapping is now used for bedding, in building, for greenhouses, for curtaining and many more major applications
- Increased usage – shampoos are 'for frequent use'; an OXO can be added to almost any savoury casserole – as well as being a delicious winter drink
- New users – seeking new market segments that have not been previously targeted. For example, older people are being targeted for higher education; undergraduates are being courted by banks who are offering loans to see them through their student days in the belief that they will stay customers once they become earners

PROMOTION AND PRICE
The promotion and price should be kept under review:

- For many price elastic goods, lowering price will tend to increase demand, by bringing in a new level of price-sensitive buyers or by attracting customers away from competitors's products
- Advertising effectiveness should be monitored and new ways of appealing to the market found. The Nescafé Gold Blend 'soap opera' advertisement proved so popular that the times they were to be shown were advertised in newspapers in advance. The Guinness 'Pure Genius' advertisements have become almost a cult – in some of them, the name of the product is not used in the belief that if you do not know, you are 'out'
- Sales promotion is used heavily during this stage. It has almost become a part of some products – a cereal packet without something to read over the breakfast table is an exception. Many food products offer '10 per cent extra', or '20p off' or 'free gift'. Others products carry offers of holidays or competitions with incredible prizes
- Trade competitions are offered to dealers to encourage them to favour one product over others. The prizes are often dressed up as business conferences in exotic places, presumably for tax purposes!

All of these strategies and more are used by innovative and creative marketing specialists to keep their particular product in its maturity stage for as long as possible. The four Ps are the controllable variables that all marketing specialists manipulate, and consequently there is a lot of imitation. It is relatively easy and quick for one producer to react to a competitor's initiative – one price cut leads to lots of price cuts. Smaller producers are at risk if they should decide to take on the market leaders through a price war – many have fallen as a result. Laker Airways went bust in a price war with the major airlines.

The large companies can react forcefully to threats from competitors, but in the competitive climate of free market economics and the Single European Market, it is much more likely that the healthiest response is being best at what you are doing. The great Henry J Heinz had a clear principle for his staff: 'To do a common thing uncommonly well brings success'.

However, it is inevitable that the majority of products, perhaps with the exception of staple foodstuffs, will reach the end of their lives and sales will decline until they are no longer viable. The marketing specialist has to deal with the funeral arrangements.

ACTIVITY 8.10(c)

What strategies would you adopt to keep your products at their maturity levels for as long as possible? Were they different from your growth strategies? And were they different for each of your three products? Have you been able to see any 'rules' for making these decisions?

Decline Stage

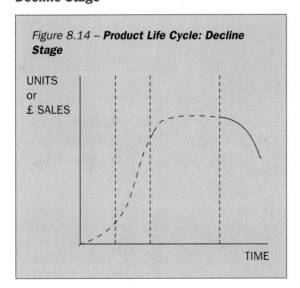

Figure 8.14 – **Product Life Cycle: Decline Stage**

Information from the MIS should sound the alarm that sales of the product are beginning to decline and profits are disappearing. During the maturity stage, many modifications to the product and the marketing mix would have been made. It is most unlikely that there is a magic 'extension strategy' that is going to return it to its former glory.

New markets may be found overseas, but in most cases they would be inadequate compensation for decline at home. Some producers will leave the market immediately, and their share may be picked up by those remaining. Initially, some of the remaining producers may mistakenly think that there is a revival and see it as an increase in demand. Most probably, the decline will continue, and it should become apparent in due course that little can be done other than to withdraw it from the market.

Withdrawing from the market is not easy. Kotler suggests three approaches:

- Withdraw the product quickly, and suffer the loss of having stocks of raw materials, packaging and even some of the product itself. The advantages of this approach are that the profit erosion is halted, and steps can be taken to use the resources to greater benefit. The disadvantages are that some dealers and customers may be upset at the loss of the product and withdraw support for other products in the producer's range.
- Plan a withdrawal over an appropriate period of time. In this way, stocks can be run down, dealers advised and reassured about the future, customers appeased and assisted in making other arrangements should that be necessary.

  Promotion can be reduced and then ceased. The product can be withdrawn from one segment at a time. The price can be reduced to keep demand going until all stocks are exhausted.

  However, all this could be expensive as the product will probably not be making profits during the run down. But it may preserve the goodwill that the producer has built up with its customers.
- Seek another producer who will take over the product and accept responsibility for it in the future. In the past, some motor cars have been discontinued in the UK, but the production machinery and all the tooling have been sold to another company in another country, which has continued production for many years. Although the producer would make very little, if anything, out of the deal, it has the advantage that there is no stock loss, and there is a ready source of spares for the future.

The unthinkable option is to allow the product to drift on and become more and more of a liability to the producer. This should not happen, but it does. Some of the excuses which producers give include:

- The product is making a contribution to fixed costs and should continue until it can be replaced
- It is a traditional part of the producer's range and people would be unhappy if it were withdrawn
- The product's demise is due to some other factor – for example the economy or the advertising – and all will be well when that is sorted out
- Or it could be that the MIS is inefficient, and nobody has registered the fact that the product is losing money

The loss in profits is compounded by the other hidden costs:

- Working capital will be tied up in slow moving stock
- Someone has to spend time making decisions about a product that is not going to do anything but die
- Salespeople will be promoting a dying product to the detriment of their reputation
- Production resources will be wasted on short runs

All these things would be much better spent on a product at an earlier stage in its life cycle.

HJ Heinz Company Limited has been operating for over a hundred years, and today markets over 1 200 products all over the world. The last words in its publication, *100 Years of Progress*, are:

'And horseradish? One of the many varieties, sadly, which have succumbed to change in public tastes. After all, Heinz has always existed to give customers what they want.'

ACTIVITY 8.10(d)

Which of Kotler's strategies would you think most appropriate for each of your three products? What steps would you take to avoid the risk of causing dissatisfaction to your customers during the withdrawal period?

Product Life Cycle – A Management Tool

A chisel has no skill of its own – it depends on the carpenter's hand. The product life cycle concept is just one tool to help managers make business decisions at different times in a product's life. It does not make decisions for them. The quality of decisions rests mainly upon their knowledge, experience and judgement.

STRENGTHS AND WEAKNESSES

The product life cycle has its weakness. We can never be certain that the future will be like the past, because so many non-controllable things will have changed in the interlude. The life cycle for a similar past product does not highlight such things as price changes during its life; the effects of competitors's activities; the effects of economic fluctuations; the state of industrial relations and so on. All or any of those things may be quite different in the lifetime of the new product, and alter its performance in the market.

The product life cycle helps the marketing specialist to prepare a long-term strategic plan for the product, knowing that certain things occur at different times in the life cycle. It might not be possible to say precisely *when* these things will occur, but it is almost certain that they will occur. The MIS will provide a continuous update, and permit short-term tactics to be implemented.

Its greatest strength is that it allows actual performance of a product in the market-place to be

---

KEY POINTS 8.3

- **The rate at which potential customers adopt new products take the form of a normal distribution curve**
- **There are different marketing strategies for each of the four stages of the product life cycle**
- **It is desirable to keep the product in its maturity stage for as long as**

possible, so that the business can gain maximum benefit from it

- **The contribution of every function in the organization, properly co-ordinated, leads to efficiency and success**
- **Marketing tools are only as good as the managers using them**

compared with planned performance. It also permits comparisons to be made with the performance of other similar products in the product line or the product mix, and may highlight differences that call for corrective action.

Place (Distribution)

The word 'place' is convenient because it starts with the letter 'P' and fits into the acronym 'four Ps'. It refers to the route by which goods or services are moved by the producer to the ultimate users or consumers. Other terms used to describe the route are 'marketing channels' or 'channels of distribution'. They all refer to the same process of making goods available to users or consumers. We will start by looking at the way businesses may segment their market. We will then examine the variety of organizations that exist to help move products from producers to users. Lastly, we will discuss the factors that influence a marketing specialist in the choice of distribution channel.

Market Segmentation

The term 'market segment' has been used several times already. Targeting the marketing effort has already been described as a key skill of the marketing specialist. It is unlikely that a producer can produce one product that is so universal in its appeal that it satisfies all the needs of all the potential users of that product. It might seem desirable for a firm like Ford or Rover to produce just one model of motor car and for all people in the world who need personal transport to buy it. But life is not like that, is it?

ACTIVITY 8.11

For what reasons is life 'not like that'? Consider a wide range of factors: economic, types of people, geographical, psychological and so on. Consider from both the producer's and the user's point of view.

One of your reasons may have been limited resources. It may just be impossible for any one organization to supply efficiently all the needs of all possible users. An organization will want to identify and describe customer groups in such a way that it can select one or several groups. In this way it will have to utilize its limited resources effectively and achieve high levels of efficiency.

Let us look at clothing as an example to illustrate the point. Young people do not like to wear the same style of clothes as businesspeople –

jeans and teeshirt versus formal suits. Clothing that is suitable to wear in Spain is probably not suitable in Scotland. Clothes that models wear are probably not suitable for busy, working people. Designer clothes are too expensive for the average person.

It might be possible to produce a different range of products specifically for each of these different groups, and market them in a way that targets each group separately. This practice is called 'market segmentation': dividing a market into separate groups each of which has something in common which would influence the buying of the product.

The marketing manager would design a marketing mix for each market segment that the firm aims at. In the clothing example we have just used, the markets were segmented by age, geographical area, lifestyle and price. These are simple segmentations.

Pride and Ferrell in their book, *Marketing*, suggest that segments can be classified under four main headings:

- Demographic segmentation – relating to population (age, sex, social class, income, family size)
- Geographic segmentation – relating to area (city, county, country, climate, culture)
- Psychographic segmentation – relating to personality (lifestyle, status, values and beliefs, culture)
- Behavioural segmentation – relating to price and usage (adopter type, loyalty, sensitivity to price or advertising, rate of use)

An example may be your local college of further education. One group – market segment – may be the sixteen to nineteen age group who want to study craft skills, or A levels or BTEC. Another may be sports people who want to keep fit and develop their skills in a given sport. Another may be the managers from local industry and commerce who need to be kept up to date with technology or management skills. As a result, the college might have a marketing mix for each of its market segments.

Häagen-Dazs realized from market research that there existed a market segment which regarded eating ice-cream 'as a sensual, private experience' (see Figure 8.15, next page). This is an example of psychographic segmentation. Häagen-Dazs then focused all its promotional activities on this segment, apparently to good effect.

ACTIVITY 8.12

Which of the above classification headings describe the market segmentation for the following products:

Figure 8.15 – *Häagen-Dazs*

ASA: Ice-cream and hot sauce stays on menu

SENSUALITY and ice-cream are an acceptable combination, according to the latest Advertising Standards Authority report, which rejects 64 complaints about sexy ice-cream ads.

Häagen-Dazs' smouldering press advertising, which uses scantily-clad models, provoked the highest number of complaints in the ASA's November report. However, it says that 'while the advertisements could be described as erotic they were not sexually explicit' and it concludes that they are not in breach of the Code of Practice.

Marketing director Simon Esberger says: 'Naturally, I am extremely happy with its decision, it justifies our approach. You have got to make your advertising stand out and we felt that we had done that while staying on the right side of good taste.' Esberger says that extra coverage generated by national press editorials at the campaign's launch provided the equivalent of £250,000 worth of free exposure (according to estimates by the ads' creator Bartle Bogle Hegarty).

The ASA acknowledged the company's rationale, which was based on consumer research which showed that Häagen-Dazs' customers regarded ice-cream eating as a sensual, private experience.

The British attitude to sexuality in advertising is far more restrictive than the prevailing European mood. France, in particular, favours the use of heaving or half-naked bodies to sell everything from live yoghurt to menswear. 'By comparison, we are a little behind the French,' says BBH board account director Andy Jackson.

Source: Marketing Week, 15 November 1991

(a) Ford Fiesta motor car
(b) Heinz Weightwatchers products
(c) Levi Jeans
(d) Brüt deodorant

When a company is making decisions about segmenting, it must consider whether it has all the resources that will be needed to meet the diverse needs of several different segments. Spreading them too thinly over many segments may be less efficient than dealing in fewer segments. Managers will have to calculate what the effect will be on sales, costs and profits. They will have to decide whether a multiple marketing mix strategy is worthwhile.

NICHE MARKET SEGMENTS

Many small and some medium-sized companies come into the market to serve a segment that is very small or is very difficult to communicate with. Big businesses, or those who use mainstream distribution channels, will not be interested in these niche segments as the returns may not justify the effort and costs. For entrepreneurs, however, discovering and exploiting niche market segments is often a very lucrative opportunity.

An organization which adopts the marketing concept, puts the customer centre stage, and sets out to create satisfied customers will develop its marketing strategy by taking into account their needs and the influences of the dynamic environment in which it operates.

Distribution Channel Members

Organizations that operate in the distribution process are wholesalers, agents, brokers and retailers. They are often referred to as channel members.

Transportation is a service to channel members and is most often provided by a sub-contractor who specializes in moving particular goods or services. For example, moving frozen foods and fresh produce require different vehicles, timescales and expertise from moving steel bars and plates.

ACTIVITY 8.13

What sort of 'vehicle' (with or without wheels!) would be most appropriate for transporting the following goods (a) throughout mainland Britain and (b) throughout the EC:

- Iron ore, coal, potatoes, crude oil, gas, electricity, water.
- Transformers for power stations, new motor cars, large panes of glass, refrigerators, clothing, frozen foods, bread
- Money, written messages, spoken messages, business people, holiday makers

Give reasons for your choice.

Decisions taken by a producer at the introduction stage of its product's life that relate to 'place', usually called 'channel decisions', are complex and important. Once these 'place' decisions have been taken and implemented, it is difficult to change them, unlike promotion and price which can be changed at short notice.

The most visible member of a channel is the retailer. We are all familiar with the range and variety of retail outlets that sell everything from A to Z – from aba (a type of cloth from Syria, made of goat or camel hair) to zucchini (another name for courgettes).

How does the aba get from the goat hair spinners in Syria to the shop in a town in the UK? How does the zucchini get from the field or greenhouse in Lincolnshire to the greengrocer in the centre of a city?

It would be impossible for the goat hair spinner or the zucchini grower to deliver to every outlet for their product – besides the costs involved, there is the selling, the storing, the transportation and the payment to be considered, and each of these requires a special expertise which the spinner and the grower are unlikely to have.

Moreover, shops in the centre of cities or anywhere else would not want to deal with one producer for zucchinis, another for garlic, another for artichokes and so on – there would be an endless queue of lorries at their door, and they would have to pay each one separately. The shops would find it much more economical and efficient to deal with one organization that could supply all their needs.

One of the features of a free market economy is that if there is a need, an entrepreneur will step in to meet it. The entrepreneur is able to spot an opportunity and turn it into a profitable venture. If the nature of the opportunity changes, or if it disappears, so does the venture. This is certainly the case in distributive trades.

Several different types of middlemen exist where they are needed to speed and facilitate the distribution of every sort of good, from the producer to industrial user, or from the producer to consumer, wherever they happen to be. Figures 8.16 and 8.17 (next page) show where each one is positioned in the distribution chain.

WHOLESALERS

Wholesalers (sometimes called merchants) buy goods in bulk from producers, pay for them immediately and then sell them on to retailers. They actually own the goods and accept the risk if they are lost, damaged or go out of fashion. By selling to the wholesaler, the producer can despatch its goods in bulk to one destination, issue one invoice, use its space for manufacturing purposes, use the cash which has flowed in to finance more production, and get on with what it is good at – making products. Information from the wholesaler about customers's reaction to the product is fed back into the producer's MIS to guide it in future marketing decisions.

The wholesaler will have bought many lines of products from many producers, and a mix of related products, so that it can meet the entire needs of a retailer. A retailer visiting the wholesaler can inspect a wide range of goods, receive advice about them, select those that are most appropriate, buy small quantities, have them delivered to the shop and pay the wholesaler for them later. What is more, the retailer knows that the wholesaler will have stocks of all the goods, most of the time, ready for immediate delivery.

Because the producer passes a lot of the work and risk to the wholesaler, it can charge less than if it was selling to hundreds of retailers or thousands of consumers. And because the wholesaler is selling such a volume of goods, a relatively

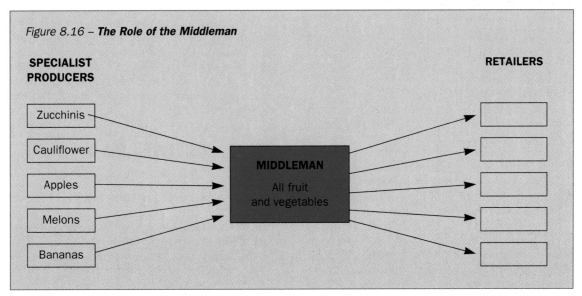

Figure 8.16 – *The Role of the Middleman*

SPECIALIST
PRODUCERS

RETAILERS

Zucchinis

Cauliflower

MIDDLEMAN

All fruit
and vegetables

Apples

Melons

Bananas

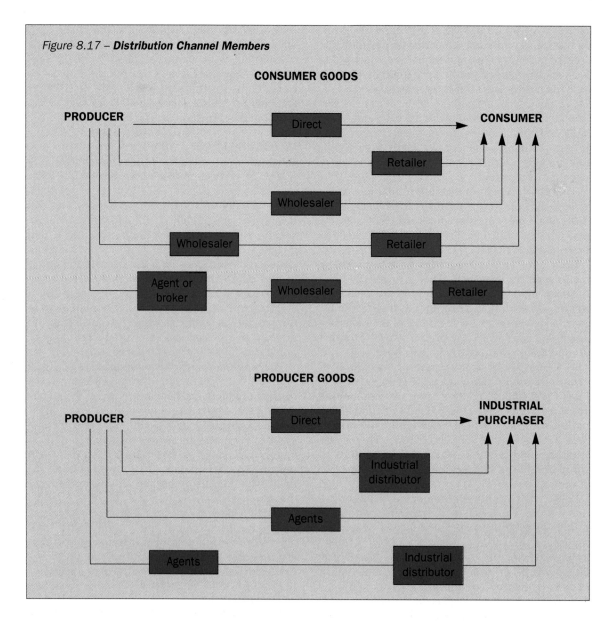

*Figure 8.17 – **Distribution Channel Members***

small mark up will be sufficient to pay the costs of the operation and provide a profit. It is argued that this is efficient and cost effective, and helps keep prices down.

The use of wholesalers benefits the producer and the consumer by bridging the gap between supply and demand, and keeping distribution costs down. The main costs of distribution are premises, storage, goods handling, transportation, financing stock, financing credit and insurance. Keeping some goods in saleable condition, often over a long period of time, relies upon storage conditions being controlled and constant.

Wholesalers who stock goods such as frozen foods, fresh meat and provisions, fruit and vegetables, electronic components, drugs and medical instruments must invest in specialized bulk storage facilities for these products, such as cold

stores, sterile stores, chilled stores with low light and increased carbon dioxide and so on.

For very small retailers, the costs can be kept lower still by cash and carry wholesalers, who provide the stock holding service, but not transport and credit facilities.

ACTIVITY 8.14

Wholesalers can be found in every trade. The *Yellow Pages* classification index lists dozens of them: Builders' Merchants, Agricultural and Horticultural Wholesalers, Seed Merchants, Baby Food Wholesalers, Children's and Baby Wear Wholesalers, Bakers and Confectioners Wholesalers and so on.

Find one in the *Yellow Pages* that is near to your

school or college and arrange a visit. During the visit, discuss the points described above, and identify the benefits that wholesalers bring to businesses. Ask what changes have taken place in wholesaling during the past ten years, and what changes they are anticipating in the next five years. (See also Activity 9.8.)

AGENTS

Agents develop specialist sales expertise in particular products and markets. They can provide a producer with a highly professional personal selling effort that it could not afford itself.

There are several types of agent. None of them takes title to the products they are selling – they never own them. For example, estate agents never own the houses they sell – they act on behalf of the vendor, and are obliged to act in the vendor's best interest.

Some agents work under strict contracts restricting them to a defined territory, and limiting other products they can handle. Usually this agent will carry a wide product mix made up of product lines from several producers. This is attractive to their customers who can satisfy all their needs through one expert salesperson. These agents keep their producers informed about reactions to their products, and keep them up to date with competitors's activities. They are the producer's eyes and ears. Because they are restricted by contract to a limited number of products to sell, they charge a high commission. However, the producer saves by not employing a sales team.

Other types of agent take over the entire selling function for a producer, or several non-competing producers in the same field. They take the goods straight from the factory and warehouse them, although they never actually take title. They may undertake the whole marketing function for the producer: organizing promotion, setting prices and segmenting the market. The producer is left to get on with production without the expense of having its own marketing function.

BROKERS

Brokers put buyers and sellers in touch with one another. What they offer the seller is specialist knowledge of a complex topic – for example, stock brokers, coffee brokers, ship brokers. Usually they are paid a commission by the seller, although some charge both the seller and buyer. Many brokers operate from premises that specialize in certain commodities.

All these institutions are worth a visit if you would like to see how transactions worth millions of pounds are concluded at the nod of a head. They include the London Metal Exchange where copper, tin, zinc and other metals are traded; the Baltic Exchange where cargo space in ships and aeroplanes is joined to people with cargo to move; the London Commodity Exchange where coffee, cocoa, vegetable oils and so on are traded in very large quantities. Most of these institutions are willing to organize visits and some are really quite entertaining. Computerization has created new methods of buying and selling some items like stocks and shares, and foreign currency. These are good examples of the entrepreneur adapting to the changing environment.

RETAILERS

Retailers buy goods from producers and wholesalers to sell to the final consumer. A consumer is a person who purchases goods and services for her or his own personal, or family, needs.

Retailers accumulate the product lines that their target market may demand. Their depth of product lines and the width of product mix – sometimes referred to as their product assortment – will depend upon their objectives. A retailer who sets out to provide every household need to an A,B,C1 target market will hold a different stock from a retailer who sets out to supply all the home needs of a C1, C2, D target market at the lowest possible prices. Following on from this, they will make decisions about the best location for the shop, the level of customer service to offer, the comfort within the shop and the general image they will project.

The types of retail outlet can be classified by ownership or by their product assortment. In the context of distribution, the product assortment classification is the more appropriate of the two. Here, there are two main classes: department stores and multiple stores.

a   Department stores

A department store carries a wide mix of products, and each in depth. When large department stores first appeared at the turn of the century, their aim was to offer everything that would be needed to feed and furnish a well-off, middle-class family. Shopping was made to be an enjoyable experience, with everything under one roof, high quality service and luxurious surroundings. One of the few surviving in that form in the UK today is Harrods of Knightsbridge.

The concept is still seen in stores like Selfridges, The John Lewis Partnership and Debenhams. Most towns have at least one independent department store, which relies for its appeal to customers on its wide range and depth of fashion goods, furniture and soft furnishings; and its wide range of other goods. It has sufficient sales staff to offer customers a high level of individual service and expert sales advice. The surroundings are pleasant and a customer is able to browse and find sufficient variety in most product lines to make comparisons and choose the most suitable item. Credit is usually provided and a free delivery service is often available.

Department stores spend a large part of their promotion budget on sales training and personal selling, but they also advertise in local publications, often in conjunction with the producers of goods they sell.

In order to maintain this width and depth, many department stores lease space to other retailers on a shop-in-shop basis. In your local department store you may find a travel agent from a well-known national chain, cosmetic firms and some high-quality fashion houses with their own space and staff.

ACTIVITY 8.15

Identify a local department store and visit it as a shopper. Analyse the range of product lines and the depth of each line. What is the level of advice available? Repeat the exercise at Currys or MFI and compare the two.

b Multiple stores

These can be sub-divided into three groups:

- *Speciality chain stores* – these differ from department stores in that their objective is to provide a limited width but great depth in a particular type of good. For example, Halfords which provides cycle and motor accessories, Mothercare and baby goods, Etam and women's wear, Austin Reed and men's wear, Freeman Hardy & Willis and shoes, WH Smith and books and newspapers; Superdrug and toiletries and patent medicines. Many more exist – there is probably at least one for every type of good
- *Variety chain stores* – some businesses that set out as speciality chain stores have broadened their product assortment and have moved towards department stores. They include Boots who started out as chemists, Marks & Spencer who sold clothes, BHS who, as British Home Stores and FW Woolworth, were the original variety chain stores
- *Supermarkets* – these started out as large stores which sold little else other than food. Over 200 square metres of floor space qualified them as supermarkets, and over 2 500 square metres qualified them as superstores (sometimes called hypermarkets). Besides a very wide range of packaged food, most supermarkets are now licensed to sell alcohol, and many have their own bakery, delicatessen, fresh meat, greengrocery, toiletry and patent medicine sections

Superstores such as those of Sainsbury, Tesco, Asda and Safeway are usually located on the outskirts of towns, near junctions of major roads, and often share enormous car parks with other non-competing stores. In addition to their wide range of foodstuffs, they stock a wide variety of non-food products, though probably not in great depth. The main store is often surrounded by small, independent speciality stores. It is a shopping complex under one roof that allows variety and competition.

Most of the main supermarket chains in the UK are developing superstores. Some continental firms are beginning to open up in competition with them in response to the Single European Market. If you have visited France or Germany you may have visited their out of town shopping complexes. They are expected to offer serious competition to UK firms in the near future.

> *Figure 8.18 – **Characteristics of a Multiple Store***
>
> - Its trade name is well-known – for example, Sainsbury's, Woolworths, Comet
> - All its shops look the same, interior design and layout are similar, and all branches carry the same range of stock
> - Most are controlled from head office – branch manager has limited authority
> - Economies from bulk purchasing and central warehousing keep costs down and allow lower prices
> - Most stock only fast-moving popular brands and own brands
> - The number of staff is kept relatively low by using self-service shopping except where goods have a high value (for example, jewellery) or where personal service is a feature (for example, delicatessens and meats)
> - There is little assistance or advice available
> - Automated stock control and centrally controlled stock replacement reduce administration costs
> - The latest automation is used – for example, barcode readers, switch cards and, in some stores, automated bag packing
> - The emphasis is on high stock turn and low gross margins
> - It spends the greatest part of its promotion budget on national advertising and sales promotion

ACTIVITY 8.16

In 1992 the four leading UK supermarkets were heavily criticized for making excessive profits in a recession. Read the article in Figure 8.19 and, based on the characteristics listed in Figure 8.18, evaluate the reasoning offered by the four companies for their pricing and profits.

Within these classifications, there are small, medium and large firms operating. Degrees of specialization vary greatly. Some attract mass markets, others have small niches that larger firms are unwilling to supply. Changes in consumer taste and fashion create some new opportunities, while they cause others to die. The ability to keep up with changes in the market and adapt accordingly is essential to survival. Small firms are more vulnerable to change than others, and the number of small retailers has declined greatly in the last decade.

On the other hand, the volume of goods sold by vending machines has increased. For example, Coca-Cola & Schweppes Beverages (CCSB) has set up a new division, 'Vendleader', to develop the enormous potential for can vending in Britain (see page 150).

Mail order companies have introduced telephone shopping to add to their free delivery, free home approval, free returns, and no deposit interest free credit. Their catalogues carry a more comprehensive range of goods than the average department store and are displayed in a most attractive way. Fireside shopping through Oracle and banking by telephone suggest ways in which 'place' is developing in response to consumer demand and technological innovation.

Distribution Decisions

A marketing specialist would understand how each of these four channel members (whole-

---

*Figure 8.19 – **Supermarkets Under Pressure on High Profit Margins***

'Top value' Tesco raises prices fastest

TESCO, which claims to offer the best value for money of any British supermarket, is increasing food prices faster than any of its main rivals.

The store, at present promoting discounts in a national advertising campaign, has added more than 5% to the cost of basic foods since the beginning of the year. The increase significantly outstrips overall food prices, which according to Central Statistical Office figures have risen by less than 1% over the same period.

An investigation by the *Sunday Times* has shown that Tesco's three leading rivals – Asda, Safeway and Sainsbury – are also increasing their prices sharply.

The study will further fuel criticism of the high level of supermarket profit margins. The Safeway supermarket group announced on Wednesday that it had increased its margins from 6.3% to 7%. Safeway's annual pre-tax profits rose to £275m, a six-fold rise in five years on sales that are up three-fold. Sainsbury has become Britain's most profitable retailer, although a *Sunday Times* investigation last weekend showed how shoppers were paying a price for its success.

The latest survey compared the cost of 34 popular foods and household goods with prices in January, when researchers conducted a similar study. The basket, selected by the Consumers' Association, included leading brands, fresh meat and vegetables.

Tesco, which last month announced a rise of nearly one third in annual pre-tax profits to £545m, has put up the price of the basket by more than 1% each month this year, the fastest among the big chains. It came to £30.14 compared with £28.67 in the previous study, a rise of 5.1%, with a loaf of Hovis bread increasing by 19%.

The basket cost £30.19 at Safeway, Britain's third biggest food retailer. This represents a 3.2% increase, with tomatoes at 62p per pound, up 27%, and a pack of ten Birds Eye fish fingers costing £1.17, up 18%.

Sainsbury claims its prices are on average 2% lower than those of its rivals but it charged the most at £30.23, a rise of 4% on the cost of the previous basket. Even Asda, attempting to promote itself as a cost-conscious retailer, put up the price of the goods by 2% to £29.75.

Experts said yesterday that supermarkets were disguising price increases behind a barrage of discount promotions while extending their profit margins. John Winkler, who advises firms on ways to improve profits, said one tactic was to drop prices only to put them back up to a higher level. "The aim is to break down the consumer's memory for prices," he said.

Supermarket shares were hit last week as politicians complained about their profits achieved during the recession, strengthening the possibility of an inquiry by the Office of Fair Trading (OFT) into food prices.

Source: Sunday Times, 24 May 1992. Times Newspapers Ltd, 1992

salers, brokers, agents and retailers) could benefit the efficient distribution of a particular product. The decisions about constructing a distribution network would be based upon an analysis of the characteristics of the company, the product, the target customers, the product's competitors, the middlemen and the environment.

a　The company

The starting point of most decision-making is to answer the question: 'What are we trying to achieve?'

The impact of the answer on channel decisions has to be determined. If the answer was 'To increase market share from 16 per cent to 20 per cent in the next two years', a mass distribution channel may be appropriate. On the other hand, if the answer was 'To create an exclusive image for the product', it may suggest a narrow, selective distribution channel of high quality retailers.

The next question should relate to the resources the producer can devote to achieving the objective. Large companies can have the expertise, staff and finances to pursue mass markets, even taking over the whole distribution responsibility themselves. Smaller companies invariably do not have such resources and may have no alternative but to use all the expertise they can find within the channel members.

b　The product

Is the product a consumer good or a producer good? Is it a convenience good, a speciality good, a component or something else? Is it perishable, heavy, bulky, expensive and so on? What is the producer's product policy? Is it like that of Lever Brothers which has a policy of deep product lines and wide product mix? Or is it a single product?

Perishable goods need speed and possibly special conditions. Technical goods may need expert sales advice. Bulky, heavy goods, particularly if they are low-cost, will need different consideration from high-cost electronic components the size of your finger nail.

c　The target customers

Are there a lot of them or only a few? Where are they? Are they scattered or concentrated in one area? Do they buy large or small quantities? If they buy large quantities, supplying direct may be feasible. If there are a lot of them all over the EC buying very small quantities, perhaps it will be necessary to use a large number of middlemen and a lot of retail outlets.

d　Competitors

Convenience goods in supermarkets stand on the shelf next to their competitors. On the other hand, some producers will see advantage in looking for distribution channels not used by competitors. If competitors hold a large share of the market and are aggressive in their promotions, it may be that the producer would seek a niche market where the leaders will leave it alone.

e　Middlemen

What functions are required from the middleman? If there are appropriate middlemen available, are they competent to handle the product? What are their charges? Does it leave the product competitively priced? Are they capable of carrying out other elements of the marketing mix if required?

f　The environment

Legal, ecological and social considerations are ignored at the producer's peril. In a recession, some middlemen may find it hard to give credit to retailers, and retailers may be seeking extended credit because of the recession. In a boom, will the middlemen be able to handle increased throughput without running out of storage space or into cash flow problems?

The analysis of all these matters is difficult, but it is important enough to demand careful attention. The amount of data that it throws up may be hard to assimilate and interpret, but charts, grids and diagrams should be devised to make it easier. The decision about distribution channels is difficult to alter once it is taken and implemented, so it is worth investing time and expertise in it.

KEY POINTS 8.3

- **Market segmentation is a technique of dividing a market into groups of potential purchasers who have some common characteristics that would influence them to buy**

- **Distribution channel members include wholesalers, agents, brokers and retailers**

- **Channel decisions are influenced by the company's objectives, the nature of the product, the target customers, the strength of competitors, and the availability of appropriate channels**

EXAM PREPARATION

SHORT QUESTIONS

1 Give two ways in which decisions made within the marketing department might affect activities in the personnel department. (AEB June 1991)

2 State two pricing strategies available to a firm about to launch a new product on the market. (AEB June 1991)

3 Suggest three features of product design which might be considered important by a firm producing hi-fi equipment. (AEB June 1989)

4 What are 'extension strategies' as related to a product's life cycle? Give an example.

5 Distinguish between a 'consumer good' and a 'producer good'. Give one example of each.

DATA RESPONSE QUESTIONS

1 Grenshams Ltd are a small company based in the North West of England, specializing in the manufacture of boxed chocolates. Their main products are fondant filled chocolates and liqueur chocolates. Within these segments of the market, Grenshams have a very small share.

An initial survey on the UK market for boxed chocolates was carried out by a market research organization. The main conclusions are outlined below.

- The market is highly seasonal, with the bulk of the sales at Christmas.

- As a gift for women, chocolates are not as fashionable now as they were six years ago. Having a fattening image, they are regarded as unimaginative and the alternatives today are perfume, flowers, and meals out.

- The less expensive twist-wrapped chocolate assortments, for example Quality Street, have held up well, as have brands promoted as a general 'thank you'. 'Romantic' counterparts have performed badly.

- There appears to be growth potential in three main segments:
   (a) Chocolate liqueurs – but they are only 5 per cent by value of the chocolate market, and in 1987 70 per cent of liqueur sales were imports.
   (b) Health foods – Although the market for Health foods is less buoyant, there is still considerable enthusiasm for this kind of product.
   (c) Chocolate Truffles – 2 per cent by value of the total market but potential for growth as disposable incomes rise. Imports represent 65 per cent of sales.

- Other findings are summarized by the graphs below.

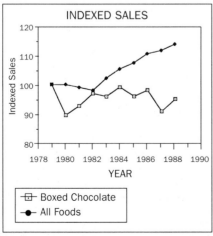

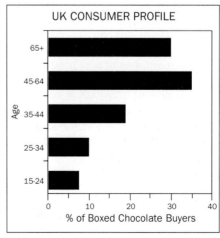

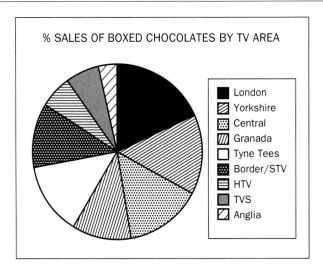

% SALES OF BOXED CHOCOLATES BY TV AREA

- London
- Yorkshire
- Central
- Granada
- Tyne Tees
- Border/STV
- HTV
- TVS
- Anglia

Questions

(a) Grenshams have decided to ask the market research organization to test a new range of chocolate truffles. A sample of 1 000 people are going to be interviewed in the street.

(i) What problems are there for market research by interview? Suggest an alternative method to market research by interview and evaluate its effectiveness. *(16 marks)*

(ii) What do you consider to be the target segment for truffle chocolates in terms of age, sex, socio-economic grouping and geographical location? *(16 marks)*

(iii) How might your conclusions on the target segment affect the marketing strategy for truffle chocolates? *(28 marks)*

(b) In 1989 there was a significant increase in United Kingdom interest rates.

(i) Explain clearly how this might lead to a fall in demand for Grenshams' liqueur chocolates. *(8 marks)*

(ii) Would such a fall in demand mean that Grenshams would delete this product from its product range? Explain your answer. *(12 marks)*

(UCLES May 1990)

2 The Product Manager of a large manufacturing firm supplied the following information on 32 new product ideas examined over a period of two years. These ideas led to the full development and successful launch of only one new product.

He commented on the fact that new product development is becoming increasingly difficult to achieve because of:
   1 growing social and governmental constraints
   2 costliness of new product development
   3 capital shortage
   4 shorter life spans of successful products.

Estimated cost of finding one successful new product
(starting with 32 new ideas)

	Stage	Number of ideas	Pass rate	Cost per product idea (£)	Cost of each stage (£)
1	Idea screening	32	1 in 4	500	16 000
2	Concept test	8	1 in 2	10 000	80 000
3	Product development	4	1 in 2	100 000	400 000
4	Test marketing	2	1 in 2	250 000	500 000
5	National launch	1	1 in 1	2 500 000	2 500 000

(a) 32 ideas were considered. How many passed the concept testing stage?

(1 mark)

(b) What was the total cost of developing and launching one successful product? *(2 marks)*

(c) Discuss two sources of new product ideas. *(6 marks)*

(d) Comment on each of the reasons put forward to explain why new product development is becoming increasingly difficult. *(12 marks)*

(e) Explain **three** reasons why new products often fail to win acceptance in the market. *(6 marks)*

(AEB June 1990)

ASSIGNMENT

1   Selecting a named good or service, examine and assess the marketing strategies employed in its launch.

(SEC June 1992)

ESSAYS

1   **(a)** Differentiate between 'brand substitution' and 'product substitution'.

(b) Using appropriate examples, explain how the marketing strategies aimed at achieving each of the above might differ.

(UCLES June 1990)

2   Filocopy Ltd believes it has identified a market opportunity in a field dominated by one firm, the originator of a novel product. Filocopy has asked you as a marketing consultant to advise it of the actions it should take.

(AEB June 1989)

CHAPTER 9

Marketing – Creating Demand

▷ ▷ **QUESTIONS FOR PREVIEW** ▷ ▷

1   How does communication change behaviour?

2   How should promotion methods be used, and how are promotion mix decisions made?

3   What pricing methods are available to businesses?

4   How do supply, demand and elasticity affect pricing?

5   How should businesses protect consumers?

I N THE last chapter we looked at the lengthy and expensive process of developing new products and steering them through their life cycle. We also looked at the distribution options open to firms. Designing channels that ensure the product is conveniently available to those who want to buy it is an important aspect of marketing. These decisions about product and place are difficult and costly to alter once they have been implemented. Getting them right first time is the job of the marketing specialist.

In this chapter, we will consider some ways in which products and services can be *promoted* and *priced* so as to create sufficient demand to satisfy the business objectives.

Promotion

We have said that marketing is a communication process. We have stressed the need for marketing specialists to gather information about their target market so that they know their potential customers better than anyone else. Once this is done, they must set out to satisfy their potential customers better than anyone else. To adopt the product or service offered, potential customers would need to be told of its existence, and how it will satisfy their needs. This can be achieved by using a mix of five different promotion methods:

• Advertising
• Personal selling
• Sales promotion
• Publicity
• Direct marketing

Each of these five methods is valuable in communicating the message, but each has different characteristics and is more useful in some situations than in others. Direct marketing is a term used to categorize a number of specialist methods, which are new developments and were discussed on page 124. They will not be developed further in this section – we will concentrate on the four most commonly used methods. The issues that the marketing specialist must consider in deciding which to use and how much of each to use – the promotion mix – will be examined in this section.

The Communication Process

ACTIVITY 9.1

What does the message 'They were eating apples' mean to you? Stop and think about it. We will return to it in a moment.

The simplest model of the communication process illustrates the basic idea quite clearly (see Figure 9.1). *'Who, says what, through which media, to whom, and did they understand it?'*

Communication is about understanding. The audience should know and comprehend the meaning the communicator intended. In the

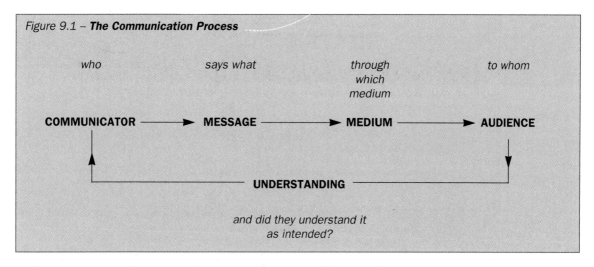

Figure 9.1 – *The Communication Process*

who   says what   through which medium   to whom

COMMUNICATOR → MESSAGE → MEDIUM → AUDIENCE

UNDERSTANDING

and did they understand it as intended?

'eating apples' example above, the communicator meant that they were not cooking apples. How did you interpret the message? If you understood that *some people were eating some apples*, did the piece of communication achieve its purpose? Is there anything wrong with this interpretation? If you had understood something that the communicator did not mean, whose fault was it?

In planning any piece of promotional communication, the marketing specialist should first answer the question: 'Who is the message aimed at – who are the target audience?' Until this is clear, it is not possible to decide:

- The meaning that has to be communicated
- The level of language, signs or symbols to be used
- How the message might be delivered to the target audience
- When the audience will be available to receive the message
- Who should deliver the particular message to that audience

Changing People's Behaviour

'How the message might be delivered' prompts a supplementary question: 'How quickly is a response expected?'

People do not react immediately to communication. From communication they learn new knowledge and ideas which may result in them changing their behaviour. The marketing specialist attempts to change buying behaviour. Each of the four ways of communicating the message will have a different timescale for results. Publicity and advertising usually takes longer than sales promotion and personal selling, but they have other benefits – reaching a wider audience at one time for a lower cost per head, for example.

Most people go through three stages in changing their behaviour as a result of new learning:

- The cognitive stage
- The affective stage
- The behavioural stage

The rate at which they pass through each stage will vary from person to person. You will recall that there are people who respond quickly to messages about innovation, and there are people who adopt new products earlier than others. Laggards are a communicator's nightmare!

There are several models to help marketing specialists steer people through the three stages. In essence they are all the same, so we will use one of the best known – AIDA (attention, interest, desire, action).

AIDA

Stage 1: The cognitive stage

This relates to the audience receiving information, knowing about the product, and perceiving its use. The problem that the communicator has at this stage is getting the *attention* (A) of the audience so as to give them the information – no attention, no communication!

Stage 2: The affective stage

This relates to the attitude of the audience to the product. Assuming that the message is getting through, the individuals in the audience will begin to learn what the product will do for them. As they learn about it, they may become more *interested* (I) in it. The communicator at this stage must know the target audience and focus the message on the product features that relate to their needs. If that is successfully achieved, it is possible that the attitude will change from passive to a positive *desire* (D) to try the product.

Stage 3: The behavioural stage

Up to now, everything has gone on in the minds of the audience. They know about the product

KEY POINTS 9.1

- **Communication is about getting the audience to understand the meaning of the message as intended by the communicator**

- **Communication must be planned to create the required change in behaviour**

- **There are three stages in changing behaviour – cognitive, affective and behavioural**

- **Knowing and understanding the target audience is essential to effective communication**

and what it will do for them; they are interested in it and desire to try it. This stage relates to them actually doing something. They have to be motivated enough to take *action* (A) – to use their energy, to obtain the product. The issue here relates to making the product available to individuals in the target audience, so that they can obtain it within the energy they are willing to expend to get it (that is, 'place' in the marketing mix).

AIDA is a great help when thinking through the problems of communicating with potential customers. But knowing and understanding the target audience is the essential first step which comes from good marketing research. The communicator should have empathy with the audience – that is, the power of understanding and imaginatively entering into the target audience's feelings about the product.

Preparing the Message

Preparing the message is a task that calls for very special skills. The message should be in the language and use the symbols and signs that the target audience is familiar with and understands.

Two opposing schools of thought argue that pleasantness is more effective than unpleasantness and vice versa. If people are told that they will be more attractive if they have sweet smelling breath, they will be more ready to purchase a mouth wash than if they are told that their breath stinks and they are awful to be with. Which would cause you to go out and buy the product?

There are examples of messages that have actually put people off from buying a product, so mistaken has been the marketing specialist. 'You're never alone with a Strand' was the copy platform – slogan – used to promote a new brand

of cigarettes in the early 1970s. It failed to produce the levels of sales expected, and analysis of the reasons for the failure seemed to show that the message understood by the target audience was that people who bought Strand were loners. So those who did not want to be thought of as loners bought something else.

Advertising agencies are experts at communicating messages through advertising, sales promotion and publicity. Most companies who spend significant amounts of money on promotion employ the expert services of an advertising agency.

However excellent the message, adoption takes time, as we discussed earlier when considering the life cycle. The implications of such a time delay are that a lot of the money invested in promotion will not have an immediate return. Some senior managers may have expectations of immediate returns on promotional expenditure. If the marketing specialist does not make the characteristics of each method clear, particularly in relation to time scale for returns, promotion budgets might be cut.

Figure 9.2 contains the characteristics of the four methods of promotion. By looking at this, we can make some judgements as to the use to which each method can be put.

Advertising

Any organization wishing to publicize a message about its product or service can pay the owners of appropriate media to carry its message to its audience – readers, listeners or viewers. Advertising can be used for:

a Introducing a new product, service or concept to the market
This is called creating 'primary demand'. Primary demand relates to a product generally, rather

*Figure 9.2 – **Characteristics and Uses of Promotional Methods**.* The following analysis and comparison of the four methods is useful in choosing appropriate and effective methods to meet different objectives.

ADVERTISING	PERSONAL SELLING
The message • Public • Same for everybody receiving it • Easily repeated • Easily dramatized • Covers large/wide audience • Is inexpensive per person receiving it **But** • Impersonal – people need not pay attention • Once published, advertising has no further control • Total expenditure is high • Long time scale for returns	**The message** • Private • Can be tailored to each person receiving it • Personal and individual • Creates relationships which affect results • Assists positive decision to buy • Is controllable, being delivered only to likely buyers • Short time scale for results **But** • Open to abuse • Is expensive per person • Good salespeople are relatively hard to find
SALES PROMOTION	**PUBLICITY**
The message • Targeted precisely • Exciting, with prizes or savings • Creates 'buy now' action • Attracts next level of price-sensitive buyers • Costs are more directly related to results • Short time scale for returns **But** • Can be seen as environmentally unfriendly • Often unfair to people who have recently bought • Can be used to disguise price rises • Too much can devalue the product in consumers's eyes	**The message** • Is easily believed if it is news • Contains much more information than an advertisement • Not associated with promotion or persuasion • Has access to people who resist persuasive promotions **But** • Single exposure • Not targeted • Not controlled by producer • Vulnerable to controversy and mis-reporting • No measure of returns

than to a specific brand of the product. The Meat and Livestock Commission advertises 'lean meat' without any particular brand being mentioned, and offers a free information pack to educate the market in the health issues associated with eating meat.

At the introductory stage, marketing specialists may try to educate people to the existence of a new, innovative product (for example, microwave ovens) and develop an understanding of its functions. A new product, perhaps using new technology or materials, will need to establish its credibility and reliability, irrespective of brand, before the majority of the target market will risk buying it.

b   Creating brand preference.
By highlighting the exclusive features of a firm's product and stressing how it benefits the customer, the marketing specialist hopes to create a preference over other makes for its brand. This is valuable during the growth stage.

c   Increasing market share
The features of a firm's product are compared with the features of competing brands to show its advantages and draw demand from competitors. Later in the growth stage, this strategy prepares the product for maturity.

d   Maintaining market share
As a defence against attacks by competitors on the firm's market share, the advertiser highlights the risk of changing to another brand. This is a counter-move and will most likely occur as the product is levelling out and entering the maturity stage.

e   Increasing product usage
Introducing the product into new market segments, or new geographical areas, will require

market education. However, if saturation has been reached, additional uses for the product may be found and the market informed about them through advertising.

f   Reinforcing demand

During the maturity stage, advertising, sometimes called 'tickle advertising', can keep the product's name in the mind of the customers.

ACTIVITY 9.2

There are six uses for advertising listed above. Find at least one advertisement in newpapers, magazines or journals to illustrate each use.

Personal Selling

Any face-to-face communication that sets out to inform or persuade a potential customer to buy a product or service, however formal or informal it may appear, is personal selling. In this section, retail selling is excluded although there is much common ground between the two. Personal selling can be used for:

a   Gaining new customers

The salesperson can focus on potential customers who are nearing a decision about purchasing, and persuade them to buy.

b   Increasing sales

Providing good customer care, and ensuring that the producer is sensitive to the needs of the customer, may lead to repeat orders and increased usage of the product.

c   Dealing with customer dissatisfaction

Disagreements and misunderstandings can be resolved to the satisfaction of both parties by personal contact, which often results in better relationships.

d   Opening up new market segments

A sales blitz on new territories can speed the adoption of products.

e   Giving technical help

Technical salespeople can assist customers with developments which incorporate the firm's product, and add great value to the product in so doing.

Many firms with a technical or complex product or service spend a greater part of their promotional budget on personal selling than the other elements of the marketing mix. Salespeople are expensive. In many cases they will be graduates or have other technical qualifications, and will have had extensive sales training. Their basic salary will be supplemented by commission on sales, or bonuses, and possibly profit sharing. Add to that a company car, expenses for travelling and accommodation, entertaining customers and potential customers, plus administrative support and sales management. The only way this expenditure can be justified is by the income they generate.

A competent salesperson is a valuable asset to the firm. The recruitment and selection of the right sort of person for a job is the subject of Chapter Three.

ACTIVITY 9.3

Refer back to Chapter Three and prepare a person specification for the sort of person you think would be right for selling a computer company's products.

Publicity

Any event that can be turned into an interesting piece of news for a newspaper, magazine, television channel or radio station can produce publicity for a business. The publishing of the news item is free, but the costs of creating the event or preparing the press release (the written news item) can be high. Publicity can be used for:

a   Creating an image

Good publicity can enhance the status of a firm in its community.

b   Informing the community

It can make people aware of the firm's products and events.

c   Publicizing progress

News items relating to innovation, technology and so on create confidence and aid recruitment of good staff.

d   Raising morale

News items that highlight achievements of the firm or individual members of staff can boost morale.

Many firms use publicity objectively. They set a public relations policy, provide resources for its operation, and use it to develop their image in the community. As a result, they achieve a good reputation as employers, and benefit from better recruitment.

ACTIVITY 9.4

Examine your local newspaper – not the free advertiser – and identify articles that come into this category of publicity. How do they differ from other news items?

Sales Promotion

Sales promotion is any incentive that causes a customer to buy *now* rather than postpone the purchase or not make it at all. Sales promotion can also be directed at dealers and salespeople to give them extra incentive to buy and sell. Sales promotion can be used for:

a Launching new products
To offset the lack of customer awareness of the product, incentives to entice customers to try it are used to assist the product through its introductory stage.

b Offsetting inflation
During periods of inflation, any price reduction, real or imaginary, is an effective incentive.

c Increasing demand
Usually short-term increases in demand are achieved.

d Maintaining market share
During the maturity stage, it is used to offset competitive activities, and keep interest in the product.

e Bringing more people into a shop
People will visit stores that have a 'sale' on or special offers on certain popular items.

f Getting more shelf space
Retailers usually allocate shelf-space on the basis of income and profit per metre. If demand is increased by sales promotion, more space may be allocated.

g Encouraging wholesalers
Offering special deals to middlemen will encourage them to buy now. This will enable the producer to transfer stock from its warehouse to the wholesalers's showrooms.

Sales promotion methods are many and varied. Marketing specialists are always looking for new, novel and compelling ways of encouraging people to buy *now*. You may have received letters offering free gifts, with 'stamps' to indicate whether you say 'yes' or 'no' to receiving the gift. It is sometimes difficult to find the real message; it might be that you have to read quite a lot of small print to get to the real product that is being sold and then it is embellished with the free gift.

ACTIVITY 9.5

Is anything really free? Is using the notion of something free as a type of persuasion morally acceptable? Prepare an argument that supports the use of free gifts as an incentive to buy. Your argument should include production, financial, personnel and marketing issues.

Promotion Mix Decisions

These analyses of the different methods provides the marketing specialist with the basic knowledge needed for making decisions about the promotion mix – including the *objective* of the promotion, how much money should be allocated to achieving the objective (*budget*), the *type* of product being promoted, the market *size*, and the *position* of the product in its life cycle.

*Figure 9.3 – **Promotion Objectives***

Jaguar starts TV ad drive

JAGUAR, the luxury-car maker, is launching a £6m advertising and marketing campaign next week in a bid to revive sales that have halved since 1988. The sales push coincides with the introduction of improved models for 1993.

At the centre of the campaign is a television commercial – its first for 12 years – that attemps to tap into the emotional values of the marque, with the story of a boy who falls in love with a Jaguar. Created by J Walter Thompson (JWT), its slogan is: "What are dreams for, if not to come true?"

Chris Donkin, director at JWT, said: "The advertising is not designed simply to shift metal off the production line. It is a long-term branding job."

Roger Putnam, sales and marketing director of Jaguar, hopes the campaign will encourage people to test-drive the new models. "We want to stir them emotionally to put Jaguar back on the shopping list and let the product do the rest."

Since Ford bought Jaguar for £1.6 billion in 1990, it has been wringing costs out of the British car company, improving quality and productivity. A £750m investment is being made in new models, and almost 5,000 jobs have been cut.

Jaguar, however, continues to bleed the American car giant of cash. It has lost £176m so far this year. Sales of the luxury cars have crashed from the peak of more than 51,000 in 1988 to just 25,000.

Putnam will not predict when Jaguar will return to profit, but aims to quadruple sales to 100,000 by the end of the decade. "Volume is the key," he said. "We have taken out as much cost as we can and we are now very lean."

Source: Sunday Times, 29 November 1992. Times Newspapers Ltd, 1992

PROMOTIONAL OBJECTIVES

The first step in preparing a mix is to set clear promotional objectives: what is the promotional campaign intended to achieve? The objectives should be stated in a way that allows progress to be measurable, and provide feedback throughout the period of the promotion about its effectiveness.

For example, the objectives might be to capture a market share of (say) 15 per cent for the product. Or it might be to increase sales volume by 10 per cent. Or it might be to increase sales revenue by 25 per cent. Or it might be to break into a new, defined, market segment.

Statements of return on investment or profitability tend to be more corporate as there are issues remote from promotion that can have a great impact – for example, the state of the economy.

From that starting point, the marketing specialist will determine the quantity and types of promotion that will be needed, over what period, to achieve the objectives. Too much would be wasteful; too little would result in losing the opportunity to gain potential sales income.

Money spent on promotion cannot be spent on anything else; the opportunity cost should be taken into account. Perhaps if some of the money was spent on marketing research, or in lowering prices, the overall impact on sales would be greater. But the decision, as to what mix of the four methods would most probably help the organization to achieve its objectives for this product, would still remain.

The four methods of promotion – advertising, personal selling, publicity and sales promotion – are available to every marketing specialist to use in whatever ratio is considered best for the particular product. But there are constraints. Promotion costs a great deal of money, and the size of the budget should be the first consideration.

Figure 9.4 – *Advertising/Sales Ratios 1990*

ADVERTISING/SALES RATIOS 1990

Product category	Consumer expenditure £m	MEAL expenditure £000	Advertising/ sales ratio %
Mouth washes/fresheners	13	12 709	97.76
Cleaners, household, scourers, detergents	52	20 912	40.22
Accident/insurance payments	131	40 152	30.65
Deodorants	157	19 435	12.38
Processed cheese	101	11 695	11.58
Cold, ready to eat breakfast cereals	672	71 728	10.67
Cinema	350	36 647	10.47
Men's electric shavers	48	4 051	8.44
Trade & technical magazines	516	37 038	7.18
Electric cookers	150	8 719	5.81
Ice cream – impulse buying	221	9 303	4.21
Chocolate confectionery	2 505	83 327	3.33
Dog food	630	19 193	3.05
Postal communications	666	16 388	2.46
New motor cars	18 132	331 904	1.83
Butter	337	5 037	1.49
Books	1 240	14 148	1.14
Bedding plants, seeds & nursery stock	630	6 120	0.97
New motor bikes, mopeds & scooters	236	1 965	0.83
Colas	1 582	12 017	0.76
Rail travel	2 365	15 483	0.65
Petrol	9 844	16 427	0.17
Carpets, rugs, underlay	1 128	535	0.05
Slips, pants, vests (women's)	556	189	0.03
Men's shirts	1 451	143	0.01
Total knitwear	2 166	89	–

Source: *Advertising Statistics Yearbook 1992*, Advertising Association

BUDGETS

Some promotion budgets are set arbitrarily – that is, the marketing specialist picks a figure that seems about right, but then cannot justify it in terms of planned results.

A better approach is a percentage of the forecasted sales income. Many businesses choose a percentage figure that is considered to be an average for their industry and spend that amount on promotion. Figures for particular products can be obtained from various sources, such as the Government Business Statistic's Office, the Advertising Association, A C Nielson & Co Ltd. Figure 9.4 shows examples of advertising/sales ratios for different categories. (You might be able to argue why such expenditure is justified, or perhaps why it cannot be justified.)

A problem that might occur, however, is that a fall in sales will have the effect of reducing the amount of money spent on promotion, when an increase might be the better option.

Many large businesses, particularly those producing convenience goods, try to maintain the same level of promotional activity as their main competitors. Advertising campaign is matched with advertising campaign, and sales promotion is matched with sales promotion. This policy may be effective in building differential advantage, but if products are obviously different or serving different market segments, the policy is likely to be inefficient.

Some smaller firms use an 'as and when' approach. They will promote new products in a short burst of activity, and spend money on promotion as they can afford it.

ACTIVITY 9.6

Which of the four methods of promotion would you choose for a small, local firm if its objective was to launch a new, low-price shopping product in a limited area? You can decide what that product might be. Choose one method only.

Why have you chosen this method? What advantages does it have for your particular product over the other options the small firm may have considered? Justify your decision.

Budgets should be set to achieve specific promotional objectives. If a firm's objective is to increase its market share by 2 per cent, the number of additional sales should be calculated, and ways of making these additional sales should be examined. One option would be to increase the amount of promotional activity to attract the additional number of customers required. The cost of this promotional activity would become the promotion budget for achieving the objective of a 2 per cent increase in market share. A management decision to cut the budget would require an associated cut in the 2 per cent objective. Any additional resources that would be needed – for example, another salesperson or additional production plant – would also have to be taken into consideration.

TYPE OF PRODUCT

In making decisions about the mix of promotion methods to be used by a producer, the marketing specialist would consider the type of product and its channels of distribution.

A convenience product may be heavily advertised to create awareness, and demand at the retail end of the channel would cause wholesalers and retailers to respond by stocking it. On the other hand, some shopping goods may require personal selling to the wholesalers and retailers, with a little backing from sales promotion and advertising.

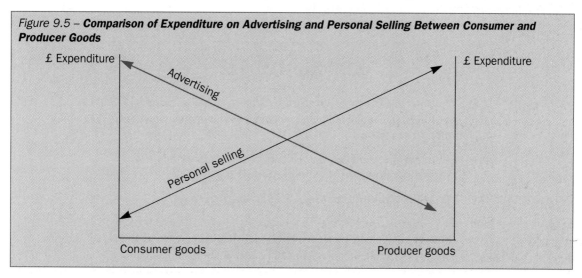

Figure 9.5 – *Comparison of Expenditure on Advertising and Personal Selling Between Consumer and Producer Goods*

£ Expenditure

£ Expenditure

Advertising

Personal selling

Consumer goods

Producer goods

Producer goods, as we have said before, often require expert advice and guidance provided by technical salespeople direct to the potential user. This does not preclude the use of advertising and publicity in appropriate technical journals. Figure 9.5 (previous page) illustrates the point.

MARKET SIZE

Another consideration would be the size of the market. A small, concentrated market would require a different promotion mix from a very large market dispersed over a wide geographical area. In the first case, advertising may be too general and wasteful, and therefore sales promotion or personal selling, which can be targeted, might be more effective. In the second case, national advertising may be the most effective and economical communication method, whilst personal selling would be very expensive.

POSITION IN LIFE CYCLE

Of course, besides the type of product, the position of the product in its life cycle is a consideration. As we have already discussed, the introductory stage needs product awareness; the early growth stage needs incentive to try the product; the late growth stage needs consolidation of the product's position in the market and brand loyalty; the maturity stage needs constant reassurance and defence against poachers; and the decline stage needs dignified withdrawal. Each of these stages requires a different promotion mix.

If the same promotion mix problem was posed to several different marketing specialists it is likely that each would come up with a different solution. It is all a matter of experience, knowledge and judgement – and often flair, imagination and the ability to handle risk. It would be quite possible for an emphasis on advertising in one firm to generate the same level of sales as an emphasis on personal selling under a different marketing specialist in a similar firm. An example of this is Max Factor which uses sophisticated advertising and sales promotion compared with Avon, which uses a novel form of personal selling.

Although the promotion mix decisions taken by a firm are intended to be fairly long term, and have the status of 'policy', they can be changed without great expense and in a relatively short time.

Price

The price of a product is a key influence on demand for that product. Demand and price make up revenue. Revenue less costs leaves profit.

Price also influences the willingness of producers to continue supplying the product. If it is not generating enough profit to justify the investment, there will be no motive to continue, and resources will be diverted to another means of creating new wealth.

Setting prices at the right level is not just the job of the marketing specialist. Keeping production costs as low as possible, and keeping sales and administration overheads under control, are a part of the process of keeping prices competitive. Even if costs are kept as low as possible, actions of suppliers can affect prices. Similarly, the actions of government (through VAT increases and decreases, for example) and the actions of competitors can affect prices.

Price can differentiate one product from another similar product. It can be varied more easily and quickly than the other marketing mix elements to gain advantage or to respond to competitors's actions. Price is more directly related to a firm's success than the other elements of the marketing mix.

KEY POINTS 9.2

- **The four methods of communicating with the target audience are advertising, personal selling, publicity and sales promotion**

- **Each has distinctive characteristics, which assists the marketing manager in the choice of method**

- **Promotion mix decisions differ from producer to producer**

- **Budgets are set to achieve promotion objectives; if the budget is changed, the objective must also be changed**

ACTIVITY 9.7

List three convenience goods, three shopping goods and three speciality goods that use price as a means of product differentiation.

Pricing Objectives

In setting the price for a product, a firm would consider both its short and long-term objectives for each of its products. There are a great many pricing objectives. The following selection is not exhaustive, but covers most pricing objectives found in popular texts. In reality, many businesses do not have clear pricing objectives.

a   It may price to survive
If the economy is in recession, it may set out to maintain its position in the market until there is an upturn. Some large firms can withstand loss for a time in order to survive in the long term. Smaller firms may go bankrupt in such situations.

b   It may price to gain market share
By setting low prices, the firm would hope for fast growth to its desired market share. As we discussed earlier, the firm's intention may be to create profits through economies of scale at high volumes of output. This is sometimes referred to as *penetration pricing*.

c   It may price to make high profits
The innovators and early adopters are usually willing to pay a high price for exclusive goods. High quality and uniqueness may allow a firm to charge high prices, particularly if demand for a product is price inelastic, and if there is no immediate threat from competitors. This is sometimes called *price skimming*.

d   It may price to recover investment
Many firms develop new products only if they will earn enough to pay back the development costs and investment in a specified period – often two or less years. Prices are set to achieve this without regard to demand or the fact that a higher or lower price may have been more profitable.

e   It may price to give a specific return on investment
The ROI ratio is discussed in the companion book, *Finance, Information and Business*. This has similar weaknesses to the above.

f   It may price in relation to a product line
As with Lever Brothers detergents, a wide range of customers's needs are covered through the depth of the product line, including a price range from low to high.

g   It may price to avoid a price war
Depending upon the market structure for a product, including its near substitutes, most firms will follow the price leader and avoid a price war with stronger competitors. This leads to fairly common prices throughout a market, the members of which compete on a non-price basis. Petrol retailers tend to compete through sales promotion.

Pricing objectives often indicate whether a company is production-led, marketing-led or accounting-led. A production-led company might be more concerned about cost recovery and long production runs. A marketing-led company may be concerned with market share. An accounting-led company may be concerned with short-term profitability and cash flow. Resolution of such conflicting objectives would rest with the senior managers who should evaluate the options and choose the best for the business.

Pricing Methods – To the Consumer

Depending upon its objectives, the firm would formulate a pricing method which it believes will achieve its objectives.

There are many pricing methods used throughout business as a whole. Retailing lends itself to different methods from the manufacturing industry or the construction industry and so on. However, marketing expert Philip Kotler slots them into three categories, each of which reflects the basis of the method:

- Concern with costs
- Concern with demand
- Concern with competition

CONCERN WITH COSTS

a   Mark-up pricing
Where a product is bought-in at a known cost to be resold, it is usual to add a percentage mark-up to its cost in order to calculate the selling price. The amount of the mark-up will depend upon the nature of the product. Fast-moving, convenience goods will be marked up less than slower moving goods. For example, the mark-up for a staple food item might be 25 per cent, a fashion item 100 per cent, and an exclusive gold necklace 200 per cent. The total price is intended to produce enough income to recover its direct costs and make a contribution to overheads and profit.

Within this category there are many variations, some of which are traditional rather than credible:

- *Psychological pricing* – there are imaginary boundaries which are supposed to affect people's willingness to buy. For example, people will consider £4.99 but not £5.00, £9.99 but not £10.00

- *Odd pricing* – in the same vein, particularly in food retailing, 29p is thought to be more acceptable than 28p or 30p; £1.55 rather than £1.50 or £1.60. Outside food retailing, however, VAT has an influence on the final price that does not always allow for this practice
- *Customary pricing* – some goods are expected to be a certain price and to make them dearer or cheaper may affect sales. For example, a chocolate bar seemed to be 20p for many years, though recently many ploys have been used by the producers to raise this to around 25p and to break the expectation of a customary price
- *Prestige pricing* – in order to give some goods an exclusive aura, like some perfumes and chocolates, they are priced very much higher than competitive brands

b   Cost plus pricing

As the name implies, the total cost of a product is calculated and a set profit margin is added to it. It is important to think about the link between price and demand that we mentioned earlier. Fixed costs are apportioned to unit costs on the basis of the forecast volume of production. Price is derived from that. If, in fact, the price attracts more or less demand than used in the cost calculation, then the calculation is valueless. The firm will make more or less profit than it anticipated. The marketing specialist adjusts price to influence demand during different stages of the product's life cycle; an inflexible approach to pricing would lose this opportunity.

c   Target pricing

(Sometimes called break-even pricing or contribution pricing.) A break-even chart, with all its limitations, can be useful in developing a crude model of profit at various prices and at various volumes of sales (see Figure 9.6).

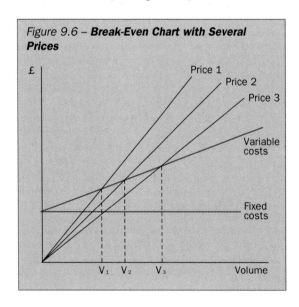

Figure 9.6 – **Break-Even Chart with Several Prices**

A full coverage of break-even theory appears in the companion book, *Finance, Information and Business*. We will not take it further here, but further study is recommended.

Once again, this method relies on assumptions of demand to reach decisions about prices without considering the converse.

In all these decisions, some thought should be given to the degrees of price elasticity that might exist at different price levels, in different economic climates, in different segments and at different times in a product's life.

CONCERN WITH DEMAND

a   Life-cycle pricing

The level of price will be decided in relation to the amount of demand existing or anticipated. As we discussed earlier, at each of the four stages of a product's life, different prices will have different impacts upon the rate of growth and level of sales. When demand is strong, prices will tend to be higher; when demand is steady, prices will tend to be stable; when demand is weak, prices will tend to be lower.

b   Discrimination pricing

Examples of price discrimination can be seen in British Telecom's, British Rail's and the electricity supply industry's pricing structures.

If you make a telephone call on a weekday morning, it will be expensive because demand is at its highest and all BT's switching resources are being utilized. The same call in the afternoon will be cheaper than in the morning when demand on resources is less, and cheaper still if you leave it until after 1800 hours when BT has spare capacity. Exactly the same pattern is followed by the other two examples, and any other producer of a product or service that has fluctuating demand upon resources in this way, most particularly where the product (like electricity) or service (like transport) 'cannot be stored'.

CONCERN WITH COMPETITION

a   Competition pricing

Many price followers watch their main competitors's prices and follow their lead; they will choose to be either just above, the same as, or just below them. So long as they do not try to compete on price, they will not get involved in a price war they cannot win. This practice is common and seems to imply that there is a price norm for a product that meets most firms's needs.

There is also some indication that there is a price expectation held by customers, which is vague, but 'they know what is reasonable' and will only pay above or below with good reason. Something that appears too cheap may experience the same resistance as something that appears too dear.

b Promotion pricing

Particularly during the maturity stage of a product's life, price is used to maintain market share by both short-term reductions and by giving more product for the same price. Competitors do not consider this as the start of a price war and respond to it by using similar tactics. It becomes a bit of a merry-go-round, with each of the large members of the market trying to be more imaginative than the others.

Most businesses are concerned with costs, with demand and competition, but probably one will predominate and influence pricing decisions more than the others.

ACTIVITY 9.8

This activity asks you to be observant. All the pricing methods that we have discussed are happening around you all the time – every time you go into a shop of any type, you are being subjected to some firm's pricing method. Notice the competing products that seem to be the same price. Why might that be? Notice the prices that vary for the same product at different times. Why might that be? And so on for all the methods we have discussed. Be inquisitive. If you have a chance to see, for example, how a builder prices a job around your school or home, ask how the price is arrived at. Ask sensible, interesting questions and businesspeople will be pleased to respond!

Pricing Methods – To the Trade

Other pricing methods are used by manufacturers who are selling to middlemen, and by industry selling capital items to government and businesses. They include the following:

a Trade discounts

Where the retail price is recommended by the producer (RRP), it is normal to have a price list for a range of products. The retailer does not have to use the RRP, it is only a guide. It is illegal for a manufacturer to fix retail prices, except in the case of books, and even that is under challenge at the moment. The producer gives discounts to the middlemen in the distribution chain against the list price. The size of the discount is based upon the nature of the good, the quantity ordered or the value of the total order. A middleman who gets involved in selling or promoting the product will receive a higher percentage than someone who does not.

b Cash/early payment discounts

In addition to trade discounts, some producers allow between 1 per cent and 2.5 per cent for payment on delivery or payment within seven days. The cost to the producer of this additional discount is offset by the savings made through improved cash flow. The middleman gains by having a bigger margin to use as a contribution to profits, or to reduce the selling price of the good to the retailer in the hope of increasing demand. Many middlemen and producers who sell direct to retailers offer cash/early settlement discounts to retailers, and retailers in turn offer them to customers.

c Quantity discounts

Various economies can be gained by the producer if its customers buy its products in bulk. Some of the savings are passed on to the buyer in the form of further discounts.

ACTIVITY 9.9

In Activity 8.13 you were encouraged to try to visit a local wholesaler. Include in your discussion the following pricing policy matters:
(a) the way the wholesaler purchases products from producers
(b) the way the wholesaler prices the same products to the retailer.

d Tenders

Where the value of an order or contract is very high, such as the building of a ship or an office block or military hardware, the contractor invites tenders from selected companies. Detailed specifications of the work to be done are issued to firms or consortia of firms that are big enough to meet the contract terms. Each will calculate how they will undertake the work and what their charges will be, and submit their tender in a sealed envelope on a certain day. All tenders are opened at a prescribed time and consideration is given to the price offered and the operating methods proposed. A decision upon known criteria is made and the contract placed.

e Fees and charges

Professional people call their price 'fees'. They are often charged at an hourly rate, a client paying for every quarter of an hour of the practitioner's time. Other services have 'charges' such as bank charges for transactions undertaken by the bank on behalf of the customer.

In all matters of fixing prices, it is illegal for firms to get together and secretly agree to charge the same prices. If firms are thought to be operating a cartel – an association of independent enterprises formed to monopolize production and distribution of a product or service – it can be investigated by the Monopolies and Mergers Commission, and if found to be so, legal action can result.

Markets and price

It is important to remember that this series of books relates to business studies. Business studies is not a single subject but a stewpot of many – finance, law, mathematics, psychology, sociology, communication and so on. However, the most influential subject, and some people think of it as the 'mother' of business studies, is *economics*.

The economist can add a great deal to our understanding of pricing decisions, and the next section sets out some important theories that are important to the student of business studies.

The Effect of Price Changes

We have seen that both demand and supply are dependent to some degree upon price. However, although they respond to price changes, they do so to differing extents. This degree of responsiveness to price changes is termed elasticity and has considerable implications for business. Elasticity exists in a number of forms.

Price Elasticity of Demand

This measures the responsiveness of demand for a good or service to the change in price that brought it about. Demand for some goods and services is not responsive to price changes – alcohol falls into this category. This means that if the price of these goods rises then demand changes by a relatively small amount. Goods and services of this type are termed inelastic goods. The Demand Curve A in Figure 9.7 illustrates this type of demand for an imaginary good. You can see that the price fall from £8.00 per unit to £6.00 per unit provokes a relatively small increase in the quantity that is demanded.

By comparison some goods and services are highly sensitive to price changes. For example, if retailers of a particular brand of petrol increase

their prices and others do not, then they can expect to lose a substantial number of sales. Similarly, a reduction in price might lead to a significant increase in demand for the fuel. The demand for this type of product is highly sensitive or responsive to changes in price. Goods and services of this type are termed elastic goods and are illustrated by Demand Curve B in Figure 9.7. We can see that the same price reduction as for our inelastic product now provokes a much larger rise in quantity demanded.

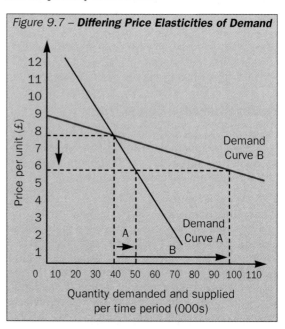

Figure 9.7 – **Differing Price Elasticities of Demand**

FACTORS THAT AFFECT PRICE ELASTICITY

A number of factors affect the price elasticity of demand to which goods and services are subject:

a Availability of substitutes at a similar price

As the price of a good or service falls it becomes cheaper relative to substitutes. Consumers are induced to buy the now cheaper alternative. The extent to which this substitution occurs depends upon whether the good or service in question has many close substitutes. Goods with few or no close substitutes, such as water, have inelastic demand – that is, they are not particularly responsive to price changes. Firms with many competitors (and many substitutes for their products) face elastic demand.

b   The proportion of income spent on the good or service

When only a small proportion of a consumer's income is spent on a product (for example matches or salt) no great effort is made to seek a substitute when the price rises. Equally, it is unlikely that a price reduction will attract many extra sales. Demand for such goods is inelastic.

c   Whether the good is a necessity or a luxury

Essential items such as food or clothing tend to have inelastic demand because consumers have to purchase them to survive. Other less essential items, such as video recorders or compact disc players, may not be purchased by many potential consumers if prices rise. A price fall might bring them within the reach of a large number of purchasers. Thus, such goods have elastic demand. However, over time what were once thought of as luxuries become to be regarded as necessities. Refrigerators and cars may fall into this category.

d   The period of time

Since it takes time to find substitutes or change spending habits, demand for goods and services tends to become more elastic as time passes.

ACTIVITY 9.10

(a) Look at the advertisements for ten goods or services on television, in newspapers or magazines. Decide which have elastic demand and those which are subject to inelastic demand. Which category of good emphasizes price heavily as a part of its promotion?

(b) Why do you think that the Chancellor of the Exchequer imposes taxes upon petrol, alcohol and tobacco?

(c) What do you think is the difference in terms of price elasticity of demand between alcohol as a group of products and a single brand of lager? Why does this difference exist?

(d) What does price inelastic demand mean to a business when it comes to set its price?

Price Elasticity of Demand and Total Revenue

It is a great advantage if the managers of a business have some knowledge of the price elasticity of demand for the goods or services that it sells. Price elasticity of demand tells them what will happen to sales, and hence the total revenue generated from those sales, following a change in price. A rise in total revenue (TR) does not necessarily mean a rise in profits since we do not know what effect increasing output will have upon costs. A rise in price will increase total revenue if demand is inelastic. To increase total revenue when demand is elastic, a price fall will be required.

Figure 9.8 – **Price, Elasticity and Total Revenue**		
	Price rise	**Price fall**
Elastic demand	TR falls	TR rises
Inelastic demand	TR rises	TR falls

Calculating Price Elasticity of Demand

Price elasticity of demand is calculated by dividing the percentage change in the quantity demanded by the percentage change in price. Thus:

$$\text{Price elasticity of demand} = \frac{\text{percentage change in quantity demanded}}{\text{percentage change in price}}$$

This formula becomes more manageable if it is rearranged as follows:

$$\frac{\text{change in quantity demanded/original quantity demanded}}{\text{change in price/original price}}$$

An example should make this easier to follow. If an engineering firm raises the price of its 2cm-diameter steel rod from £1.50 a metre to £1.65 a metre and this results in a fall in weekly demand from 10 000 metres to 8 000 metres, then the calculation will be as follows:

$$\frac{2\,000/10\,000}{15/150} = \frac{1/5}{1/10}$$

$$= 2$$

The figure which results from calculations such as this is known as the coefficient of elasticity. A figure in excess of one denotes the good as having elastic demand. The higher the figure the more elastic – or responsive – is demand. On the other hand a coefficient with a value of less than one indicates that demand is inelastic. A figure of zero shows that the quantity of a good or service that is demanded is completely unresponsive to price changes.

To illustrate further the impact of how price elasticity of demand affects total revenue following a price change consider the following case.

Maple & Son Ltd sells a certain product at a price of £10.00 per unit. It currently sells 1 000 units. Hence its current total revenue from selling this product is £10 000. It knows that the price elasticity of demand for this product is 0.5 and is therefore price inelastic. If it now raises its selling price by 10 per cent to £11.00, then we know that the change (in this case a fall since price is increasing) in quantity will be half as much because elasticity is 0.5 or ½. Thus, the new quantity demanded will be 5 per cent lower (half of the 10 per cent price change) which is 920 units. Hence the new total revenue will be 920 × £11.00 = £10 120. We should expect this to be higher since we raised the price of a product which had inelastic demand.

ACTIVITY 9.11

(a) With reference to Figure 9.7 above, calculate the coefficient of price elasticity of demand for the price fall from £8.00 to £6.00 for the products whose demand is shown by Demand Curves A and B.
(b) By multiplying the price and quantity demanded for each of the two products at each of the two prices, show which benefits from a rise in total revenue as a result of the price cut.
(c) With reference to the example of Maple & Son Ltd above, calculate what would happen to their total sales revenue if they decided to lower the original price for 1 000 units by 10 per cent.

The theory of price elasticity of demand is valuable in that it helps businesses to predict the likely financial consequences of altering the prices of their goods and services. In practice, however, firms often lack enough data to make use of the theory. They rarely have sufficient knowledge of their markets to allow them to construct demand curves. This means that it is nearly impossible to calculate accurately price elasticity of demand in any market. In any case price elasticity may vary over time or between market segments. An *essential* item to one group of consumers may be a *luxury* to another, *different* group.

Other Types of Elasticity

Three other types of elasticity have relevance to businesses:

- Price elasticity of supply
- Advertising elasticity
- Income elasticity of demand

PRICE ELASTICITY OF SUPPLY
Price elasticity of supply measures the responsiveness of supply to changes in price. As with price elasticity of demand, goods and services are categorized as having elastic supply or inelastic supply.

Price inelastic supply exists when the output of goods or services is not responsive to price changes. Thus an increase in the price of natural rubber may not provoke an increase in supply as it takes a considerable time to grow extra rubber trees. This example highlights the fact that over time a product may become more responsive to price changes. In general the greater the time period in question the more elastic becomes supply. Stocks of unsold goods also help to make supply more elastic.

Goods and services which have elastic supply are those which can respond significantly and quickly to price changes. Thus a rise in price of a product may lead to a substantial and rapid increase in supply. Manufactured products which do not require a long process are often regarded as price elastic in supply. For example, if the demand for, and price of, an item of fashion clothing rises, then supplies can react to supply the market and earn profits.

Price elasticity of supply is calculated in a similar manner to price elasticity of demand using the following formula:

$$\text{Price elasticity of supply} = \frac{\text{percentage change in quantity supplied}}{\text{percentage change in price}}$$

ADVERTISING ELASTICITY
Through the use of this concept marketing managers can assess the impact on sales of an increase in expenditure on advertising or other sales promotion. The formula necessary to calculate this is:

$$\text{Advertising elasticity} = \frac{\text{percentage change in quantity demanded}}{\text{percentage change in expenditure on advertising/promotion}}$$

The higher the coefficient which results from this calculation the more effective (in terms of increasing sales) is the expenditure on advertising or sales promotion.

INCOME ELASTICITY OF DEMAND
Income elasticity of demand measures the responsiveness of demand to changes in income. Changes in the incomes of consumers will lead to changes in demand for most goods and services.

However, the change in demand from any given alteration in income is likely to vary according to the nature of the good or service. Thus we might expect that the demand for food would remain relatively unchanged when incomes alter, whereas the demand for foreign holidays or leisure activities are more sensitive to changes in incomes.

The following formula is used to measure income elasticity of demand:

$$\text{Income elasticity of demand} = \frac{\text{percentage changes in quantity demand}}{\text{percentage change in income}}$$

For example, if incomes rose by 10 per cent and as a consequence the demand for cars increased by 20 per cent, then income elasticity coefficient would be:

$$\frac{20}{10} = 2$$

The higher the coefficient of income elasticity the more sensitive demand for the good or service is to changes in income. Income elasticity of demand for most goods and services is positive as we demand more of them as we become richer.

However, demand for some goods and services may fall as incomes rise. Public transport and black and white televisions come into this category of inferior goods and they have a negative income elasticity figure.

Markets and Price

A market is simply a place or an area where buyers and sellers of products contact one another and set prices. These may be international (for example the oil market), national or local (your local street market, for example). Famous examples of markets include the Stock Exchange in London, where stocks and shares are sold or Hatton Garden, also in London, which is the market for precious stones.

If a product is perishable or bulky, and therefore costly to transport, the market is likely to be a local one. Many markets, however, have no single location and much business is conducted worldwide, twenty-fours hours a day, through telephone, fax and computers.

All sorts of goods and services are exchanged in these markets, where the forces of supply and demand interact to establish their prices. We shall look at each of these factors in turn and shall develop the classical demand and supply model to explain pricing.

Demand for Goods and Services

The demand for a product is the amount that people are able and willing to buy in the market over a certain time period at the prevailing price. Any assessment of the demand for a good or service must:

- Refer to the effective demand – that is, the quantity which consumers can actually afford, not the quantity they would like to buy given the money
- Relate to a certain time period – a week, month or year are typical examples
- Relate to a certain price level per unit

A number of factors influence the quantity of a good or service which is demanded, the most

---

KEY POINTS 9.4

- **Price elasticity of demand measures the responsiveness of quantity demanded to a change in price**

- **Availability of substitutes and the proportion of income spent upon the good are important determinants of price elasticity of demand**

- **Price elasticity of demand determines the effect upon quantity demanded and total revenue when price is changed**

- **In reality, a lack of data means that few firms are able to calculate**

- **accurately price elasticity of demand for their products**

- **Price elasticity of supply measures the responsiveness of supply to changes in price**

- **Advertising elasticity measures the effect on sales of a change in expenditure on advertising and promotion.**

- **Income elasticity can be negative or positive depending upon whether more or less of the product is demanded as incomes rise**

notable of which is the price of the good or service in question. As the price of most goods and services rise then the quantity of that good or service demanded in each time period will fall (assuming nothing else changes). You should be able to relate this to your own circumstances. How will your purchases of a certain brand of clothes alter as their price rises? Industry faces the same situation: a rise in wages makes labour more expensive within the organization and may result in less labour being employed. Perhaps firms may use more machinery in place of labour.

The Relationship Between Price and Quantity Demanded

An inverse relationship exists between the price of a good or service and the quantity of which it is demanded. This relationship can be set out as a demand curve similar to the one shown in Figure 9.9 for toasters.

The demand curve will show that as the price of a product or service falls, then the demand for it will rise. This is represented by a movement down the demand curve. However, if the price rises, then demand will fall and is represented by a movement up the curve. Thus, if price changes so will the quantity demanded in that time period. This relationship is of fundamental importance for business and is one to which we shall return a little later.

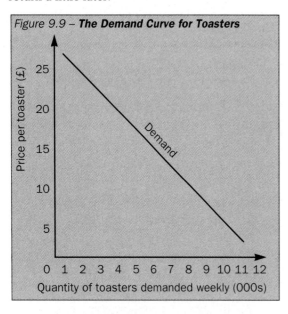

Figure 9.9 – **The Demand Curve for Toasters**

ACTIVITY 9.12

Using Figure 9.9 as a guide to labelling the axes, plot the following data to create a demand curve. You should put price on the vertical (or y) axis and

the quantity demanded on the horizontal (or x) axis. The data refers to the demand for transistor radios in a certain town.

Price per radio (£)	Quantity of radios demanded weekly
60	130
50	375
40	565
30	890
20	1 620
10	2 500

You should produce a demand curve similar to the one in Figure 9.9. Now calculate the revenue that the electrical shop can earn from selling the radios at each of the six prices. Which is highest? Would it be sound advice to recommend that this is the correct price at which to sell? You need to explain your answer to the final part of this question.

The Conditions of Demand

There are a number of other factors that can also influence the demand for a product. Collectively these are known as the conditions of demand. These conditions include the following:

a   Tastes and fashions
Choice is important in a free-market society. Taste will determine the choice of a consumer and this will, in turn, affect demand. However, our tastes tend to change over time as fashions begin to play a role. This is particularly true of certain products (for example, clothes and popular music). Our tastes are also influenced by advertising and the introduction of new products.

b   Complementary goods
The amount of a good or service that is demanded depends upon the state of other goods and services. For instance, the increasing popularity of foreign holidays in recent years has led to rising demand for products associated with such holidays, for example, maps of other nations, suntan lotion and foreign language tapes and phrase books. Goods and services which are purchased jointly in this way are called complementary goods.

ACTIVITY 9.13

In Activity 9.12, you constructed a demand curve for radios in a certain town. Now imagine that a new local radio station has commenced broadcasting in the area, which has led to a 10 per cent rise in demand for radios at all prices. Calculate the new levels of demand at each price and plot the new demand curve on the original diagram. Your new curve should be to the right of the original curve. Can you think of any factors that might cause the demand curve to move to the left?

However, another group of goods and services exist. These are in competitive demand – that is, one or another type of good is in demand, but not both. Over recent years, the UK government has cut the subsidy it pays to British Rail, resulting in higher rail fares. Travellers have consequently switched to road and air transport. Thus, rail, road and air transport can be said to be substitutes for one another.

c Real incomes

Real income is income adjusted for inflation. The level of real income can also affect demand for goods and services – though some goods are more sensitive than others to changes in income. We mentioned above the rising popularity of overseas holidays. This partly reflects changing tastes and fashions. It is also a result of rising real incomes over time. When people's incomes rise in real terms, they do not tend to spend their extra income on essential products. Instead they look for new, and often more luxurious goods and services to purchase. Many UK citizens have chosen to spend this 'extra' income on overseas holidays. This change has led to the demand curve for foreign holidays to shift to the right over time. At the same time, the demand curve for UK holidays has shifted to the left as they have declined in popularity.

d Government policies

The government can have a huge impact upon business. Certainly it can significantly influence the demand for goods and services. The government purchases huge amounts of goods and services. It equips schools and hospitals, provides social services and defence. A government decision to cut expenditure will cause a fall in demand for a wide range of goods and services. Further, the government can influence households's demand by altering taxation, interest rates, pensions and unemployment benefit.

e Cultural and Sociological factors

Sociologists would add other factors to this list. They would say that consumer purchases are determined to some extent by social changes and their cultural background. Education and upbringing will help decide what it is that we consider important to purchase. The Conservative governments of the 1980s and early 1990s encouraged a more self-reliant society. This change manifested itself in terms of more self-employed people and a dramatic increase in home ownership amongst other factors. The implications of such changes for producers have been very significant.

*Figure 9.10 – **Business and Changes in Demand***

Flexibility falls foul of fortress mentality

EUROPEAN manufacturers are in serious danger of being driven out of business by the Japanese, according to a survey from Insead, the international business school at Fontainebleau in France.

European factories are run like fortresses, taking no account of the customer, says Arnoud de Meyer, Insead's professor of technology management. It says that managers are to blame: "They want the easy life, set rules and a stable product."

Yet in the long run they cannot hope to compete that way. Customers demand new products, models, colours – and they want them yesterday.

The Japanese are responding to customer demand by using computers to give them manufacturing flexibility. Having spent six months in Japan studying manufacturing methods, Professor de Meyer is aware of how far ahead the Japanese are.

By comparison, European management's aims for the next two years, shown in Insead's survey of 224 large manufacturers, seem wildly off target. Their priorities are: quality, delivery and price. Flexibility comes last on the list.

Professor de Meyer and Professor Kasra Ferdows, the survey's co-author, reckon that only one in four European companies have any kind of integrated computer-aided design (CAD) and computer-aided manufacturing (CAM) equipment.

But they find that those European manufacturing companies which have invested in flexibility have been rewarded.

Among them is Benetton, the Italian clothing chain, noted for having upgraded its production plants at Veneto, near Venice, so it can change the colours and designs of its clothes in 10 days to respond to fashion demands.

ICI is another. Its speciality chemicals business in Manchester discovered a huge demand for small batches of particular chemicals. Using a new process, it can now switch rapidly from one to another.

The professors emphasise that in order to succeed, European companies must adopt a new attitude towards manufacturing if they are to sweep away barriers that insulate their factories from the market. This includes integrating functions which currently operate separately from production, such as inventories, forecasting systems, distribution, purchasing and marketing. "Most of them protect manufacturing, to make it easier to manage . . . but now we need a different model," the professors argue.

Source: Independent on Sunday, 3 February 1991

CASE STUDY

Smarties

This case study sets out to examine how the people that make Smarties reacted to the arrival of M&M's in the 'bite size' sector of the confectionery market. Today, there are a number of sectors to the confectionery market, including chocolate bars, assortments, individual chocolate covered confections (such as Mars Bar, Kit-Kat or Marathon) and bite sized sweet products. The bite sized sector consists of those chocolates that are small enough to be eaten in one bite, such as Minstrels, Maltesers, Buttons and Smarties.

Since Smarties's launch in 1937, demand has increased and Smarties has become a strong brand in an established part of the confectionery market. Rowntree is a market led company. The major objective of a market led company is to satisfy the desires of consumers by identifying and anticipating their wishes and matching these in the production of goods and services.

Competition emerges
Competitors
Every business must be aware of its competitors. Direct competition exists when businesses produce similar products and appeal to the same group of people, eg two 'popular' tabloid newspapers.

Even when a business produces a unique product with no direct competition, it must still consider indirect competition. Consumers can still choose to spend their money on one product rather than another quite different product – for instance, if it is too expensive to buy a branded perfume you might buy scented soap instead.

In reality, the most critical competitive factors any company has to cope with are the knowledge, intelligence, experience, doubts, and sometimes reluctance to buy, of the prospective customer. No company that wants to stay successful ever takes the customer for granted. We are now living in a 'consumer' society, with a market that is educated, aware and prepared to give and withdraw its custom as it decides.

The background
For most of its life Smarties had been considered a relatively safe brand, because it is a unique product quite distinct in taste, colour and image. Over the years there has been little direct competition, though it still has to compete generally with all other sweets. For this reason it has always had advertising support, to ensure it kept its position as the most popular children's line.

In the late 1970s and early 1980s the volume sales of Smarties fell back from previous heights. This trend was typical of that for many products in the UK where many were feeling the effects of a world recession in demand for goods and also of a declining birth rate.

Index of Smarties Sales

Year	Index of Sales Volume
1977	100
1978	95
1979	90
1980	84
1981	75
1982	83
1983	79
1984	80
1985	83
1986	101
1987	103
1988	108
1989	100 (estimate)

Despite the decline in sales volume in the late 1970s and early 1980s, Smarties continued to make healthy profits for the Rowntree group. It maintained a high profile and stayed the leading children's brand in the 'bite-sized' market.

The competition tests the market
Mars is another of the major chocolate and sweet manufacturing groups in the UK. In July 1985, Mars prepared to launch M&M's in the UK. The product was already a major seller in the US and other countries. M&M's are brightly coloured, chocolate centred buttons and the closest thing to Smarties available.

M&M's was originally test marketed in the Tyne Tees television area. Manufacturers of consumer products such as chocolate often used Tyne Tees for test marketing products, as consumer profile is very close to national profile and Tyne Tees TV area does not have large areas of overlap with other TV stations. The packaging material used was different to that of Smarties and prices were set at competitive levels.

Mars followed up the test market launch with a full scale national advertising campaign targeted at the eight to teenager age group. This is a slightly older range than the main target group for Smarties.

Shortly before the introduction of M&M's in the Tyne Tees region Smarties share of the 'bite-sized' confectionery market was 29 per cent of sales value. The remaining 71 per cent of sales value was shared between a number of other brands including Chocolate Buttons (Cadbury's), Maltesers (Mars) and Minstrels (Mars). The launch and subsequent promotion of M&M's quickly saw this brand gather a 43 per cent share of sales value of the Tyne Tees market.

However, because of increased promotion and an increase in interest in the 'bite-sized' market, total sales of all 'bite-sized' brands increased by a third. Although Smarties sterling sales share of the Tyne Tees market dropped by almost a third, sterling sales shares of most other 'bite-sized' products dropped by half.

How Smarties managed to weather the storm
Successful marketing is often said to depend on combining four ingredients (known as the marketing mix) in an effective way. They are often called the 4 Ps: product, price, place and promotion. Getting the right mix involves making sure that the product has the right features, that the right price is being charged, that the goods get to the right place through the distribution network and that its existence and features are known through its promotion.

In anticipation of the arrival of M&M's in the Tyne Tees area market, Smarties used and developed their marketing mix to meet the challenge. In 1984 Smarties brought out a new advertising campaign using computer graphics. They decided to try to move away from the toddler and primary school image in order to appeal to older children and so increase the number of potential eaters. By doing so, they moved into the same target group as M&M's.

Sales incentives were provided for retailers and advertising time and expenditure were increased in the Tyne Tees region. In addition, general promotional activity was increased and included '10% extra' across all packs, and this was made available by improved productivity and lower costs. Rowntree also emphasised the unique qualities of the tube. Promotional activity was geared at 'good value for money'.

Between May/June 1985 and October/ November 1987 sales of all brands in Tyne Tees 'bite-sized' market increased from £540,000 to £718,000. In the first of these periods Smarties had accounted for 29 per cent of all sales in sales value, and in the second for 26 per cent. The overall effect was that far more Smarties were being sold.

M&M's enter the national market
M&M's was introduced to the nation from July 1987. During the first four months of 1988 Smarties sales fell slightly.

The Blue Smartie
It was time for Rowntree to play another card. A unique and unusual step was taken. It involved a major product change as a form of promotion. It came in the form of the blue Smartie.

From mid-May 1988 for three months all packs contained blue Smarties and were flashed with the words 'special edition' for a temporary period. The blue Smartie was mentioned on national television and radio news, and in all the major daily newspapers.

Smarties take an increased share of the growing market
In March/April of 1987 Smarties held 26 per cent sales value of the 'bite-sized' market nationally. With the launch of M&M's this had fallen to 20 per cent of a bigger market by March/April 1988. The impact of blue Smarties increased the market size further and provided Smarties with a 27 per cent share of sales value by July/August 1988. During the three month period of the blue Smarties promotion, sales volume had increased to 31 per cent. Smarties had not only broadened its market to add an increased number of older children to its existing regular customers but had increased purchases too. A craze for blue Smarties started amongst teenagers and older children. It became fashionable for them to eat blue Smarties. Not only was the target market protected, its base was also broadened.

Source: Nestlé UK Limited

QUESTIONS

1   What is the structure of the market in which Rowntree operates?

2   Draw a demand and supply diagram to illustrate what happened to the demand for and supply of Smarties in the late 1970s and early 1980s.

3   Does the Case Study suggest that advertising elasticity for Smarties is elastic or inelastic? Explain your answer.

4   In what ways could it be argued that Smarties has (a) benefited and (b) lost out as a result of the introduction of M&M's?

5   For many years Smarties had never had a direct competitor and had never had to respond directly to competition. To what extent do you think this is a good thing? In what ways did the company have to change its promotion of Smarties once competition appeared?

6   What target market did M&M's aim for? In what ways was this different from Smarties's target market at the time? Why do you think that M&M's chose this target market?

KEY POINTS 9.5

- A market is a meeting place for buyers and sellers, though it may not be a single location

- An inverse relationship exists between price and quantity demanded

- Only a price change can cause a movement along a demand curve

- Other factors such as fashions and real income can change and cause the demand curve to shift

- Cultural and sociological factors also influence our choice of goods and services

Figure 9.10 (previous page) highlights how important it is for firms to respond to changes in demand. It also illustrates how being responsive to changes in demand has implications for the organization and structure of the entire business.

So far we have seen that a change in price causes a rise or fall in demand and that this is represented *only* by a movement up or down the existing demand curve. As we saw, however, there are a number of other influences on the level of demand (known collectively as the conditions of demand) which can increase or decrease demand, but these cause the demand curve to shift to the right or left. Changes in price alone cannot do this. This is an important distinction.

Supply of Goods and Services

Supply is derived from the word 'sellers' and is the quantity that sellers make available for purchase in the market over a given period at any prevailing price. A direct relationship exists between supply and price: if price rises so will supply; if it falls then supply does also.

Supply increases along with price because the greater return is sufficient to attract additional producers into the market who believe that they can earn a profit. Equally, a fall in price may dissuade some existing suppliers from continuing to produce and the quantity reaching the market will decline.

The supply curve shown in Figure 9.11 is typical in its shape. The upward slope from left to right illustrates the direct relationship between supply and price.

The Conditions of Supply

As with demand, supply is subject to other factors apart from price. These factors are termed the conditions of supply and cause the supply curve to shift to left or right depending upon the circumstances. Decisions on whether or not to supply goods or services depend upon the judgement of entrepreneurs or groups of entrepreneurs. Clearly what are considered to be appropriate conditions to increase output by one group may be deemed unsuitable by another. The conditions of supply include:

a The cost of inputs

Changes in the cost of labour, raw materials and so on will alter production costs. This will cause

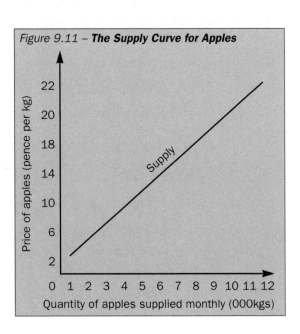

Figure 9.11 – *The Supply Curve for Apples*

the supply curve to shift to a new position. For example, rises in the rate of interest will increase the cost to businesses of capital. This might mean that some firms would not be able to continue to produce and will cease trading. As a result the supply curve will shift to the left.

b   Natural influences

Industries such as building and agriculture are particularly susceptible to changes in weather conditions. For example, the death of many bees in the summer of 1991 shifted the supply curve for honey to the left. Alternatively, if a late frost destroyed much apple blossom then the supply curve for apples drawn in Figure 9.11 may shift to the left.

c   Techniques of production

New inventions tend to lower costs of production and shift the supply curve for goods and services to the right. Many new newspapers have appeared since the introduction of new technology into the industry.

d   Joint supply

Some goods are in joint supply. For instance a decision to slaughter cattle to supply beef will inevitably create a supply of hides to the leather industry. Similarly, growing barley for, say the beer industry, entails the supply of large quantities of straw. Indeed, in recent years disposing of surplus quantities of straw has posed problems for many farmers.

Supply and Demand Together

Neither supply nor demand operate in isolation. Both respond to the level and changes in the other which are signalled by price changes.

In Figure 9.12 we can see that the market price is determined at the price and quantity at which supply of, and demand for, chocolate bars are equal. The equilibrium price is 17½ pence per bar and the quantity that will be bought and sold each week at that price is 6 000 bars.

A higher price would mean that more of the product would be supplied than consumers were willing to purchase at that price. If, for example, the price was set at 25 pence per bar then a surplus of chocolate bars would accumulate. Suppliers would be bound to lower their price to clear this surplus. Equally, at a price below the equilibrium demand would exceed supply and consumers would be seeking supplies of chocolate bars which are not available.

The market for chocolate bars as shown in Figure 9.12 is in equilibrium since the price has settled at a level which equates supply and demand. Indeed, one of the strengths of this market

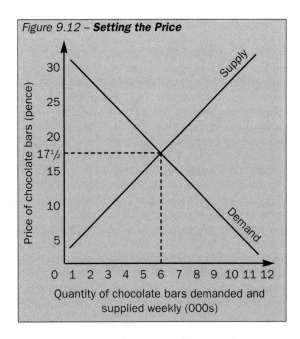

Figure 9.12 – **Setting the Price**

system is that this level is found automatically. No government intervention is required.

SHIFT IN THE DEMAND CURVE

Changes in a number of factors can upset this equilibrium. A change in any of the conditions of demand can cause the demand curve to shift creating a new equilibrium in terms of price and quantity. In Figure 9.13 the demand curve for chocolate bars has shifted to the right. This may have been caused by the fact that eating chocolate bars has become more affordable following a rise in consumer income.

You can see in Figure 9.13 that the demand curve for chocolate bars has shifted to the right

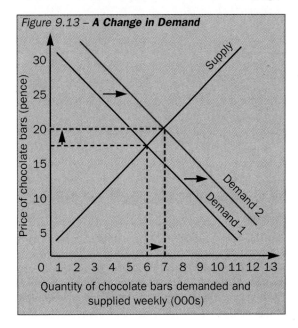

Figure 9.13 – **A Change in Demand**

(Demand 2) causing a rise in price to 20 pence per bar. This in turn has led to suppliers being willing to increase their supply, sensing higher profits. The new equilibrium is therefore represented by a higher price and a greater quantity traded on the market. You should be able to think of changes in demand factors that would cause the demand curve to shift to the left, lowering price and supply.

SHIFT IN THE SUPPLY CURVE

Figure 9.14 shows a change in supply and the changes which follow this. If a new, more efficient method of producing chocolate bars were introduced then, assuming no other changes, the result would be a rise in the supply of chocolate bars on to the market. This is shown by the shift of the supply curve to Supply 2. The result is a lower selling price that creates additional demand. A new equilibrium is therefore established at a lower price (15 pence) and a larger quantity (7000). Changes in other conditions of supply (for example, bad weather and a poor harvest of cocoa beans) can cause the supply curve to shift in the opposite direction.

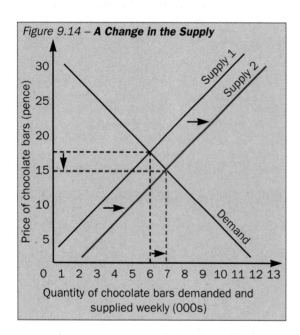

Figure 9.14 – *A Change in the Supply*

Price of chocolate bars (pence)

Quantity of chocolate bars demanded and supplied weekly (000s)

An Assessment of the Supply and Demand Model

The classical model of price determination that we have discussed here is *highly theoretical* and the real world doesn't always operate in this manner. There are a number of factors which have to be considered as a part of any assessment of the model.

Firstly, the model of supply and demand attributes a central role to price in the marketing mix and gives scant attention to the other elements of the mix. Although the demand aspect of the model reflects factors such as tastes and fashions, it fails to allow for the firm's promotional activities. Advertising and other promotional work has a major influence on both demand and the pricing strategy that the firm may elect to follow.

The theory fails to acknowledge that other non-price elements play a critical role in determining demand. Certainly, a marketing manager would stress the importance of factors such as design, product range, delivery dates, after-sales services and, crucially, quality. Many firms emphasize quality rather than price when advertising; clearly they believe that consumers consider this to be important.

The theory assumes that consumers have a perfect knowledge of the current market price for a good or service and hence will not purchase more expensive items. This is unlikely in spite of the efforts of various consumer magazines to increase consumers' knowledge in this area. Furthermore, the model assumes a single product – or at least little or no variation in quality – and so a unique price for each good or service. In reality a range of prices exists for each good or service according to its attributes and qualities.

In spite of these criticisms, the model has an important role in the theory of pricing. It provides a broad framework within which managers can assess the likely implications of a variety of changes. For example, it is likely that increasing supply will depress prices.

ACTIVITY 9.14

Using the supply and demand model we have so far developed, sketch a diagram to analyse what will happen to price and the quantity traded in the market in the following circumstances:

(a) The market for luxury cars after a rise in real incomes.
(b) The oil market, after a minor civil war breaks out in one of the supplying nations.
(c) The market for season tickets at a certain football club, following its relegation to a lower division.
(d) The market for salmon, as salmon farming becomes a more practical proposition and more common.
(e) The market for running shoes, as the health and fitness craze catches on.

KEY POINTS 9.6

- **Supply is the quantity that sellers make available onto the market over a given time and at a certain price**

- **Factors such as the cost of inputs and natural influences cause the supply curve to shift when they change**

- **Market price is established at the price at which the demand for the product is just equal to the supply of it**

- **This classical model of price determination gives little or no role to factors such as advertising and quality**

Consumer Protection

Throughout this book, we have mentioned various legal responsibilities of businesses. There are common law duties, legislation, regulations and EC directives that affect just about every function of every business. This applies equally to all the products and services a producer, middleman or retailer sells to a customer. The companion book, *The Business Environment*, provides a fuller overview of business and the law.

In this section we will focus on the business and what it must do to ensure that it is meeting the requirements of the law so far as consumer protection is concerned. The actions of the production department and administrative services have an impact on consumers, though it is usually the role of marketing to assure consumer rights. The positive approach is to consider consumer protection as an opportunity; it is only if firms ignore or reject it that it becomes a threat.

Consumers's Legal Rights

PRODUCT

Every consumer has a right under The Sale of Goods Act 1979 to goods that are of merchantable quality, are fit for the purpose, and are as described on the package when unpacked. Similarly, every user of a service has a right under the Supply of Goods and Services Act 1982 to a service that is delivered with reasonable care and skill, within a reasonable time, and for a reasonable charge. In addition, the consumer has the same rights regarding any goods supplied as a part of the service – for example, a new exhaust fitted to your car by a garage – as described under the Sale of Goods Act 1979.

PLACE

No person is required to pay for goods that she or he has not ordered. The Unsolicited Goods and Services Act 1971 protects people from the practice called 'inertia selling'. A person who has been sent goods that she or he has not ordered has a right to demand that they are taken away by the sender. If they are not collected within thirty days, they become the property of the recipient who can dispose of them as she or he wishes. Should the recipient not wish to contact the sender, the goods will become the recipients property after six months if not collected. It is illegal to demand payment for such goods.

PROMOTION

Goods and services must be described accurately on packaging, by salespeople and in promotional materials. The Trade Descriptions Act 1968 protects consumers from misleading claims about a product's contents or performance.

PRICE

It is an offence under the Consumer Protection Act 1987 to give misleading information about a product's price. (This Act also brings into UK law some EC directives relating to product liability and consumer safety.) Many shopping goods are bought on credit. The price of the good can increase markedly once interest is added to the repayments. The Consumer Credit Act 1974 ensures that people buying on credit know the extent of their commitment before they sign a contract.

Management Action

The law requires every producer to take whatever action is necessary to protect consumers. It does not tell them what to do, it simply states the consequences of failing to comply.

Firms which do not plan consumer protection into all their procedures and processes often claim that it is adding to their costs. But efficient producers will take it into account at every step of the planning process, so that it is built in to all its activities. Customers who feel assured that

*Figure 9.15 – **Letter Sent to Customer from Birds Eye Wall's***

Dear Mr Gunn,

I have received your letter of 14th April, and I was concerned to learn of your unsatisfactory purchase of a pack of our Steakhouse Grill Steaks. I was sorry to hear of the very upsetting experience you suffered while enjoying these burgers, I do realise that it must have been most painful and unexpected to bite down on a piece of meat bone. I was concerned to learn of the damage you did to your tooth, and subsequent dental treatment you required. I am sorry for this unpleasant experience. Please accept my sincere apologies on behalf of the company for any distress or discomfort you were caused.

This product is produced at our Lowestoft factory, and I would assure you that a great deal of care is taken with the preparation of the meat to ensure that every fragment of bone and gristle is eliminated. The staff in the unit are thoroughly trained and continuous checks are carried out on the meat product.

However, despite all our precautions it would appear that this piece of bone was overlooked, we very much regret this departure from our normal high standard. The details were immediately passed to the Quality Assurance and Production Management concerned. The Quality Assurance Manager has been made fully aware of the pain and inconvenience you were caused.

I note the costs that you have incurred, and we will be pleased to reimburse you. However, our insurers and auditors require me to have your actual dental receipt. I would appreciate it if you would send this to me please and I am enclosing a stamped addressed envelope to assist you.

I would once more offer my sincere apologies on behalf of the company for this regrettable incident, and I look forward to hearing from you soon.

Yours sincerely,

Mrs M M McQueen
Customer Service Supervisor
Birds Eye Wall's Limited.

their rights are important to a firm will be confident in buying its products. The firm's reputation will be enhanced as a result.

PRODUCT

The starting point for ensuring that the product is of merchantable quality and fit for its purpose is good design.

The British Standards Institute (BSI) produce very detailed standards for most products. Many standards are written to meet legal requirements, though some do not have that purpose. These BSI standards are being taken into the EC directives about product testing and performance. Instead of the BSI mark, the CE mark will become the norm. This point is discussed in more detail in the companion book, *The Business Environment.*

The firm should investigate which standards must be complied with for each product manufactured. The Single European Market has brought many changes in standards and rules, so past practice may not be good enough in the future.

Once all the standards and rules are known, plans should be made to implement them. It would be necessary to set up tests that prove that the product complies with the standard and for certificates of 'attestation' to be issued. The

Department of Trade and Industry (DTI) defines testing as:

'A technical process which uses a specified procedure to measure one or more characteristics of a product. It is a major activity, undertaken mainly by manufacturers for their own purposes during design, product development, manufacture and product use'.

Firms whose products meet these standards can put the BSI 'Kitemark' on them, or the new European Community CE mark, for all customers to see that the product is of the required legal standard.

The firm benefits because these marks give customers confidence to buy goods that are technically complex, or goods that cannot be examined because of the way they are packaged. Additionally, it would be unlikely that a firm that has set up and implemented procedures to ensure that standards have been met, would be found guilty of negligence if something did go wrong.

It is all very well setting up a system of standards, but it is also necessary to ensure that those standards are being met for every item produced. The firm would also need a quality assurance

Figure 9.16 – *Second Letter Sent to Customer from Birds Eye Wall's*

Dear Mr Gunn,

Thank you for your letter of 12th May. I was pleased to learn that your dental treatment had now been completed. I hope it did not prove to be too painful. Please accept my renewed apologies on behalf of the company for any upset caused.

I trust that in my previous letter to you I was able to provide some reassurance about the very great care taken in our factories to ensure that an incident of this nature is totally isolated.

I am enclosing a cheque to cover the cost of your dental treatment. I am in agreement with the balance you asked for to cover the cost of the inconvenience and pain and distress you were caused. Please accept this with, again, our apologies and best wishes.

Yours sincerely,

Mrs M M McQueen
Customer Service Supervisor
Birds Eye Wall's Limited.

system as discussed in the companion book, *Finance, Information and Business*, such as BS 5750. This complies with both European EN 29000 standards series, and international ISO 9000 standards. The firm that is truly European or international will benefit from its goods being acceptable in many countries without modification or re-testing.

The firm might also give a guarantee with its products that extend a customer's common law and statutory rights.

Where appropriate, it should set up a customer service department, with carefully trained staff, to deal with customer complaints and worries. There might be a policy of replacement or compensation in genuine cases. Its aim would be to protect the firm's reputation and create good public relations. The customer's right is for a refund of the price of the good. It is not legal for a firm to insist on repair or replacement.

Where a product, like a washing machine, may need spare parts and servicing, the firm should set up a network of 'approved service dealers' who would hold stock and deal promptly and efficiently with customer needs. Special training should be organized for dealer's engineers, and quality standards should be set for them along the same lines as those operated within the firm.

The firm might adopt a code of practice. Many trades and professions have voluntary codes of practice controlled by a trade association or some such body; some firms develop their own. These set down the minimum standards of service and behaviour that customers can expect from the firm. Failure to achieve the standards gives the customer the right to redress.

PLACE

A firm should avoid the risk of its products being distributed in a way that might be illegal or disreputable. Careful selection of distributors and clear contractual duties are important. If the firm has its own salesforce, particularly if door-to-door selling is involved, a high ethical standard should be enforced without exception. Any breach should be dealt with firmly through the firm's disciplinary procedure.

Figure 9.17 – *ASA Advertisement*

Are You....

LEGAL..DECENT..
HONEST..TRUTHFUL?

Advertisers have to be.

The Advertising Standards Authority controls the content of print and cinema advertisements.

The Advertising Standards Authority. Brook House, 2-16 Torrington Place, London, WC1E 7HN.

THIS SPACE HAS BEEN DONATED BY THE PUBLISHER

Source: Advertising Standards Authority

PROMOTION

The Advertising Standards Authority (ASA) and The Independent Television Commission (ITC) have codes of practice with which they require all advertisers to comply. All advertisements and other promotions material must be 'legal, decent, honest and true' (see figure 9.17, previous page). Besides this, the marketing specialist must be responsible for the truthfulness and accuracy of information that appears on any product or piece of publicity. A firm's reputation can be seriously damaged by exaggerated claims and misleading information, particularly if it results in prosecution.

PRICE

There is a statutory code of practice relating to pricing which sets down rules that, if followed, avoids a firm giving false or misleading price information. By following this code, the firm will keep within the law .

Business ethics are discussed more fully in the companion book, *Business Environment*. It is clear that powerful firms could take advantage of the weakness of an individual customer. The fact that it has been necessary to bring in so much legislation in the last twenty years to protect consumers suggests that the balance of power needed correcting.

However, any company that puts the customer centre stage, and sets out to satisfy that customer better than anyone else, is unlikely to fall foul of the law. It views good customer relations as a strength that gives it a distinctive advantage over its competitors. Good marketing encompasses all that is required by the law.

KEY POINTS 9.7

- Consumer rights are protected by law – businesses which take a positive approach to consumer protection enhance their reputation

- Consumer rights have to be considered in every part of marketing strategy – product, price, promotion and place

- Positive management action is needed to comply with consumer protection law

- Setting, monitoring and controlling standards is assisted by publications from the BSI. All BSI standards meet the EC requirements and will be subsumed into European standards

- All products carrying the CE badge can be sold in any EC member state without further testing

---

EXAM PRACTICE

SHORT QUESTIONS

1   Give two examples of sales promotion. (AEB November 1989)

2   Explain the term 'loss leaders'. Why are they used? (AEB June 1990)

3   Suggest two points that must be considered for advertising to be effective.(AEB June 1989)

4   Demand for a particular product is price inelastic. What is the significance of this for a firm when considering a change in price for this product? (AEB June 1989)

5   Name three Acts of Parliament passed for the protection of consumers.

DATA RESPONSE QUESTIONS

1   The following information is taken from the Chairman's statement in *W H Smith Annual Report 1986*. Study the information and answer the questions below.

Customer Service

I have written before about the importance of service to customers and this includes not only the approach of our staff but the selection of products and the environment provided by the shop itself. For years we have had many own brand and exclusive goods in W H Smith shops, and these ranges are being increased and improved, particularly in the selection of our own books. Do It All introduced own brand goods last year and this is just the beginning of an extensive programme. In all this, good product and packaging design is a key factor. The design of our shops is equally important and we have commissioned new concepts for W H Smith, Do It All and the specialist book chain. The first of each of these will be opened this autumn and I believe will prove to be popular and commercially sound and therefore the blueprint for each chain over the next few years.

Training

Good training for all our staff is a fundamental ingredient of success and our commitment to it continues and grows. A well-trained staff is our strongest resource.

The Future

Each business in W H Smith – whether retail, wholesale or distribution – caters ultimately to the constructive use of spare time and so the Company is especially well positioned for growth.

Analysis of staff

The average number of persons employed by the Group during the 52 weeks ended 31st May 1986 analysed by activity and by hours worked:

	Total	*Male*	*Female*
Retailing	18 522	4 871	13 651
(Books stationery, news, recorded music etc.)			
Do it yourself	2 295	1 119	1 176
Wholesaling	4 000	2 868	1 132
Others	893	454	439
	(Europe, Canada, USA and UK)		
Full time	13 294	6 714	6 580
8–29 hrs per week	6 824	1 080	5 744
Less than 8 hrs per week	1 882	561	1 321
			(UK only)

Questions

(a) Make **three** general observations that can be drawn from the data in the table.   (*3 marks*)

(b) Explain the term 'own brand' goods and give a reason for their use.   (*3 marks*)

(c) State and explain **three** areas in which W H Smith considers design to be important.   (*6 marks*)

(d) 'A well-trained staff is our strongest resource.'

  (i) Explain why this statement is true for an organisation like W H Smith   (*4 marks*)

  (ii) Comment on the knowledge and skills which might be required by a sales assistant in a firm like W H Smith   (*4 marks*)

(AEB November 1988)

2   Weblite plc manufacture textiles. They have concentrated on producing high quality fabrics for specialist uses. They maintain an R & D department which attempts to investigate products with an identifiable demand. A major result of this policy was the production of Fabbro in 1985. This was a unique waterproof but breathable stretch fabric. Weblite sell all their products 'down the line' to manufacturers and Fabbro was no exception. They began supplying several makers of specialist sports clothing.

The firm adopted a skimming price policy and promoted the fabric as 'high quality, high performance'. They sold only to firms producing articles meeting this description and engaged in no wider promotional activities beyond a direct approach to identified customers.

DISTRIBUTION CHANNELS

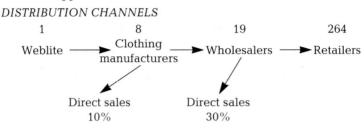

Direct sales are from the factory/warehouse and catalogue/mail order.

Initial reaction was very favourable and the expanding leisure wear industry quickly showed an interest. In 1987 rival companies began producing competitive fabrics. For a short time Weblite was able to maintain a high market share through brand name goodwill, and consequently it recovered its research and development costs.

However, as the market grew, competitors were able to lower prices and challenge Weblite's dominance. Clothing manufacturers' buyers proved very price conscious. As a result Weblite changed its method of pricing to make it more cost-based and related to competitors' charges.

The rapid market growth was partly due to rising disposable incomes, partly to fashion trends and partly to the increasing role of leisure activities. By 1990 Fabbro was still being sold mainly for sports-related clothing products and there was evidence that rising sales would be unlikely to continue in this area.

A report commissioned by the marketing manager forecast that overall market growth was slowing and would reach only 102,000m^2 in 1991. Weblite would hold a 40% share if relative prices were maintained. She therefore recommended that Weblite change from cost-price competitive pricing to marginal pricing in an attempt to keep up sales and market share. She also felt it would be worthwhile considering other possible uses for Fabbro, a different structure of distribution and the possibility of becoming a manufacturer of products made from Fabbro. The company badly needed alternatives to letting current practice continue.

Fabbro's Market

Year	Price of Fabbro £/m^2	Fabbro's Market Share %	Mean Price of Competitors	Total Market Sales 000s m^2
1985	12	100	—	10
1986	12	100	—	15
1987	12	95	12	30
1988	10	85	9	50
1989	7	70	7	80
1990	5	50	5	95

Questions

(a) When Weblite introduced Fabbro they adopted a *skimming price policy*. Give possible reasons why they did this. *(15 marks)*

(b) *Brand goodwill* enabled Weblite to maintain a high market share for a short period.
(i) Explain how they might have gained brand goodwill. *(12 marks)*
(ii) Suggest why its effect did not last longer. *(15 marks)*

(c) The marketing manager's report recommended a change of pricing policy in the light of the market situation.
Discuss
(i) the difference between cost-price competitive pricing and marginal pricing and the implications of the change for Fabbro's price *(10 marks)*
and
(ii) how the proposal will help achieve the company's objective. *(10 marks)*

(d) From 1989 onwards the directors became more and more concerned at the sales record of Fabbro. They did not want to lose their market leadership but were not all convinced it could continue as a 'flagship' product. Prepare a discussion document for the Board which includes the following:
(i) reasons for concern and/or optimism, *(10 marks)*
(ii) a set of proposals for the marketing of Fabbro during the next phase of its life cycle, referring to:
• alternative markets for Fabbro *(8 marks)*
• further promotional activities *(10 marks)*
• production/distribution channels. *(10 marks)*
(UCLES May 1991)

ESSAYS

1   Explain why different pricing tactics may be used in a marketing campaign when economic theory might suggest that price is determined solely by demand and supply.
(AEB November 1988)

2   The percentage retail mark-up on a bar of soap is quite different from that on a diamond ring. Explain fully why this is so.
(AEB June 1988)

Dictionary

'above-the-line' promotion a form of promotion, especially advertising, where an advertising agency is paid a commission by a media firm such as a newspaper or commercial television company for buying space or time.

absenteeism the absence of members of a workforce contracted to be at their place of work.

advertisement a written or visual presentation in the media of a brand of good or service supplied by a firm (or some other organization, for example the government), which is aimed at encouraging either prospective buyers to purchase the product, or greater usage of a facility, or to provide the population with public safety information.

advertising a means by which a seller of a brand of good or service attempts to increase its sales by communicating with buyers, informing them of the nature and attributes of its brand and persuading them to buy it in preference to competitors's brands.

advertising agency a business which specializes in providing various marketing services for firms and other organizations, particularly advertising services.

advertising campaign a planned series of advertisements aimed at increasing the sales of a particular brand of good or service.

advertising message a communication designed to influence buyer behaviour.

after-sales service back-up services and facilities provided by the suppliers of goods and services to their customers (eg, free maintenance and repairs, a telephone service for dealing with customers's queries, an express parts delivery service).

agent a person or company employed by another person or company for the purpose of arranging contracts between the principal and third parties.

AIDA acronym for 'Attention, Interest, Desire, Action'.

annual report and accounts a yearly report by the directors of a company to the shareholders. It includes a copy of the company's balance sheet and a summary profit and loss account for the current and immediately-prior year, along with other information which directors are required by law to disclose to shareholders.

appraisal see **performance appraisal**.

apprenticeship a system of training for craft skills or a profession, where young people are given on-the-job training through working alongside a skilled worker.

aptitude test a test of fundamental abilities or aptitudes, such as mental abilities, to discover that person's capacity to acquire new skills in future.

arbitration a procedure for settling industrial disputes in which a neutral third party (arbitrator) makes an award which is usually binding on all parties to the dispute.

authority the capacity to give commands which are accepted as legitimate by others.

backward integration when a firm engaged in assembly operations integrates backwards to produce it's own components or raw materials.

bankruptcy see **insolvent**.

bar chart or **histogram** a graphical presentation of data in which the absolute and relative size of each category in a total is portrayed by means of the height of the 'bar' or block representing that category.

'below-the-line' promotion a form of promotion, such as point of sale displays and demonstrations, which does not involve the payment of a commission.

blue-collar worker people who work mainly with their hands, particularly in production in a factory.

bonus payment a payments system where one method of payment is used to provide an incentive for employees to reach or exceed a production or sales target.

boom   a level of business activity in an economy characterized by full-capacity levels of output and employment, but with a tendency for the economy to 'overheat', producing inflationary pressures.

brainstorming   a technique for generating ideas in which members of a group express ideas as they think of them. The object is to compile a list of ideas which can subsequently be considered and evaluated in greater depth.

brand   a name, term, sign, symbol or design used to identify a supplier's good or service and to distinguish it from similar products offered by competitors.

branding   a means of helping consumers to identify a particular supplier's brand of good or service, and to create and maintain consumer confidence in the performance of the brand. This is achieved by ensuring consistent brand quality and reinforcing this by appropriate advertising and sales promotion in order to foster consumer goodwill.

brand loyalty   the extent to which consumers buy a particular brand of a product in preference to similar brands.

break even   the rate of output and sales at which a supplier generates just enough revenue to cover its fixed and variable costs, earning neither a profit nor a loss.

British Standards Institute (BSI)   a body that established the UK standards of safety and quality that consumer products should reach, using its kitemark as a recognition that the standard has been reached.

broker   see **agent**.

budget   a firm's predetermined plan (expressed in quantitative or financial terms) for a given future period.

bulk buying   the purchase of raw materials, components and finished products in large quantities, which enables a buyer to take advantage of discounts off suppliers's list prices.

business or **firm**   a producer or distributor of goods or services.

business objectives   the goals which a firm sets for itself in respect of profit returns, sales and assets growth, etc, which in turn determine the strategic and operational policies it adopts.

business strategy, business policy, corporate strategy or **strategic management**   the formulation of a unified body of strategic plans by a firm in order to achieve its business objectives.

buyer   a purchaser of a good or service.

buyer behaviour   the purchasing decisions of buyers as shaped by their functional and psychological motivations and needs.

capital-intensive   this describes a system of production where the production process relies heavily on capital as a resource (eg, chemical production, oil refining).

cartel   a form of collusion between a group of suppliers aimed at suppressing competition between themselves, wholly or in part.

cash and carry   a form of wholesaling which requires customers (predominantly retailers) to pay cash for products bought and to collect these products themselves from a warehouse.

cash discount   a reduction in the total amount of money owed by a customer to a supplier in return for prompt payment.

cash flow   the money coming into a business from sales and other receipts and going out of the business in the form of cash payments to suppliers, workers, etc.

catalogue showroom   a means of retailing products from premises displaying catalogues from which consumers purchase products for immediate collection and payment.

census   a survey carried out by a government department to obtain economic and social data which can be used in the formulation of social and industrial policies. In the UK a *population census* is carried out every ten years to obtain data on demographic trends.

Central Statistical Office (CSO)   the UK government department which collects and publishes statistics concerning the economy, such as the National Income 'blue book' and the Balance of Payments 'pink book'.

chain of command   the line of command flowing down from the top of an organization to the bottom.

chain store   a multibranch retail business. All types of retailer, ranging from specialist shops to supermarkets, can be organized to take advantage of the growth and competitive opportunities deriving from large-scale operations.

chief executive   the person who has overall responsibility for the management of a firm.

closed shop   a requirement that all employees in a given workplace or organization be members of a specified trade union. Now unenforceable.

code of practice a set of guidelines used to encourage desirable patterns of behaviour but which generally lack any formal sanctions to punish inappropriate behaviour. Often codes of practice are developed as an alternative to legal regulation. For instance, companies engaged in food production might develop a code of practice between them to define hygiene standards.

collective bargaining negotiation between employers or managers and representatives of the workforce to determine rates of pay, conditions of employment, etc.

commission a payment to an agent or employee for performing particular services on behalf of a buyer or seller of a product, the sale of a financial security by a stockbroker (paid by the client).

common law laws based upon the outcome of previous court cases which serve as a precedent in guiding the judgement of present court cases.

common market see **European Community**.

communication the exchange of information in an organization.

communications mix see **promotional mix**.

company bargaining see **collective bargaining**.

competition the process of active rivalry between the sellers of a particular product as they seek to win and retain buyer demand for their offerings. Competition can take a number of forms including price cutting, advertising and sales promotion, quality variations, packaging and design, and market segmentation.

competitive advantage the possession by a firm of various assets and attributes (low cost plants, innovative brands, ownership of raw material supplies, etc) which give it a competitive edge over rival suppliers.

competitor a business rival of a firm supplying a particular good or service which offers a buyer an identical or similar product.

component or **part** an item such as a gearbox, steering wheel, etc which is used in the assembly of another component or final product (such as a motorcar).

concept testing testing a new product concept with a sample of target consumers to assess the product's likely customer acceptability.

conciliation a form of intervention in collective and individual industrial disputes in which a third party assists the disputants in resolving their differences.

conglomerate a business that is engaged in a number of unrelated production activities.

consortium a group of independent companies or financial institutions which agree to work together jointly on some undertaking (eg, the construction of an electricity power plant or the provision of a range of financial services, each contributing some particular resource input or expertise).

constructive dismissal where the employee feels forced to leave because the employer acts unlawfully, unfairly or otherwise breaches the contract of employment.

consultation the process in which managers inform and seek the views of others before finally deciding what course of action to take.

consumer a buyer of a final good or service which is purchased to satisfy a personal consumption need.

consumer behaviour see **buyer behaviour**.

consumer durables consumer goods such as television sets, motorcars and microwave ovens which yield satisfaction to consumers over relatively long periods of time rather than immediately.

consumer goods products such as television sets, bread and clothing which are purchased by consumers for their own personal consumption.

consumerism an organized movement to protect the interests of consumers by forcing companies to behave in a more socially responsible manner.

consumer loyalty see **brand loyalty**.

contract a legally enforceable agreement between two or more parties. A contract involves obligations on the part of the contractors which may be expressed verbally or in writing.

contract of employment an agreement whereby a worker undertakes to work for an employer in return for a wage or salary.

contractor a person or firm which enters into a legal contract with another person or firm to supply goods or services.

contribution the difference between sales revenue and variable costs. If total contributions are just large enough to cover fixed costs then the producer breaks even; if contributions are less than fixed costs the producer makes a loss; while if contributions exceed fixed costs then the producer makes a profit.

control the process of ensuring that activities are carried out as intended. Control involves monitoring aspects of performance and taking corrective action where necessary.

convenience goods   products such as newspapers which consumers buy at frequent intervals with little comparison or buying effort.

copyright   the legal ownership by persons or businesses of certain kinds of material, in particular original literary, dramatic, musical and artistic work; sound recordings, films, broadcasts and cable programmes; the typographical arrangement or layout of a published edition; and computer programs.

correlation   a statistical term that describes the degree of association between two variables (such as sales and income). When two variables tend to change together then they are said to be correlated.

cost   the expenditure upon resources incurred by a firm in producing and selling its output.

cost-based pricing   pricing methods which determine the price of a product on the basis of its production, distribution and marketing costs.

cost of living   the general level of prices of goods and services in an economy as measured by a representative price-index.

cost of sales or **cost of goods sold**   the relevant cost that is compared with sales revenue in order to determine gross profit in the profit and loss account.

coupon   a voucher used as a means of promoting the sale of a product which is offered to buyers of the product to be redeemed for cash, gifts or other goods.

credit   a financial facility which enables a person or business to borrow money to purchase (ie, take immediate possession of) products, raw materials and components, etc and to pay for them over an extended time period.

creditors (accounts payable)   the money owed to individuals or firms because they have supplied goods, services or raw materials for which they have not yet been paid (trade creditors), or because they have made loans.

customer   a buyer of a good or service from a business.

delegation   the passing of certain duties or decisions by a manager or supervisor to a subordinate whilst still retaining overall authority for them.

demand   the amount of a product which is purchased at a particular price at a particular point in time. A *demand curve* is a line showing the relationship between the price of a product and the quantity demanded per time period over a range of possible prices.

demand forecasting   see **sales forecasting**.

demography   the analysis of human populations according to their total size, birth rates, death rates and migration; the age and sex distribution of populations and their geographical and occupational distributions; racial and religious profiles, etc.

department   a grouping of similar or closely related job roles into a discrete section within an organization (eg, the finance department).

department store   a large retail outlet. The distinctive charcteristic of a department store is the great variety of products it stocks, the term 'department' denoting the fact that a typical store will be divided up into a large number of sections each offering a particular kind of merchandise.

design   the process of translating a product idea into a product which can be produced and marketed on a commercial basis.

direct cost   the sum of the direct materials cost and the direct labour cost of a product. Direct costs tend to vary proportionately with the level of output.

direct labour   1.   that part of the labour force in a firm which is directly concerned with the manufacture of a good or the provision of a service.

2.   workers employed directly by local or central government to perform tasks rather than such tasks being contracted out to private sector companies.

direct mail   a form of direct marketing which involves posting information about a firm's goods and services direct to prospective/ existing customers.

direct marketing   forms of marketing a product that lead the customer to make an active response to the selling stimuli, rather than merely passively absorb advertising messages.

direct materials   raw materials which are incorporated in a product.

director   an official of a company elected by the shareholders at the company's annual general meeting and charged with certain powers and responsibilities to run the company on behalf of the shareholders.

directors's report   a report by the directors of a company to the shareholders which appears alongside the published annual accounts of the company to form the annual report and accounts.

direct selling a form of direct marketing which involves face-to-face contact between seller and buyer.

discount a deduction from the published list price of a product by a supplier to a customer.

discount store a self-service retail outlet. The term 'discount' derives from the fact that such stores compete primarily by offering customers highly competitive prices on manufacturers's branded products; additionally some also offer their own label brands at low prices.

discrimination inequitable treatment of employees on the basis of their sex or race for example.

disposable income the amount of income which a person has available after paying income tax, national insurance contributions and pension contributions.

distribution the process of storing and moving products to customers, often through intermediaries such as wholesalers and retailers.

distribution channel the route used in the physical distribution of a product from the manufacturer to the ultimate buyer of that product.

distributor a retailer or wholesaler who stocks and sells the products of particular manufacturers.

diversification the expansion of a firm into a range of different product areas which leads to it operating in a number of markets rather than a single market.

durable consumer goods goods used by consumers that have a life-span of more than one year; that is, goods that endure and can give utility over a longer period of time.

economics the study of the way in which countries endowed with only a *limited* availability of economic resources (natural resources, labour and capital) can best use these resources so as to gain the maximum fulfilment of society's *unlimited* demands for goods and services.

economy a country defined in terms of the total composition of its economic activities and the ultimate location of economic decision-making.

elastic demand demand for a product or service which changes greatly as a result of a small price change.

elastic supply supply of a product or service which changes greatly as a result of a small price change.

embargo a complete ban on all international trade with a particular country or group of countries, or on trade in particular products such as narcotics and defence equipment.

employee a person who is employed by an employer on a paid basis to perform a job or work task specified in his or her contract of employment.

employee participation the participation of employees in the affairs of the organization through (limited) participation in decision-making or acquisition of a stake in the company through employee share ownership schemes (financial participation).

employer an organization which engages employees to perform job tasks related to the types of good and service produced by the organization.

employers's association an organization of employers in an industry with the function of representing their mutual interests in the promotion of trade (for example, representation at trade fairs) and/or dealing with labour and industrial relations issues.

employment the use of labour and capital to produce goods and services.

employment agency a business which acts as an agent on behalf of firms seeking employees and of persons seeking work.

entrepreneur a person who undertakes the risks of establishing and running a new business.

equal pay the right for men and women to be paid the same rate of pay for performing the same job, established in the UK by the Equal Pay Act 1970.

ergonomics or **human engineering** the study of the interface between people and technology with the objective of achieving a better 'fit' between the two.

European Community (EC) or (formerly) European Economic Community (EEC), a regional bloc established by the Treaty of Rome in 1958 with the general objective of integrating the economies of member countries.

expense any expenditure which is chargeable to the trading activities of an accounting period.

factory a business premise used by a firm in the production of goods.

fast moving consumer goods (FMCG) low-priced goods in regular demand (eg, milk, tea, washing powder).

fee a payment to an agent or professional

person/firm such as an accountant or lawyer for performing particular services for clients.

fixed costs   any costs that do not vary with the level of output because they are linked to a time base rather than to a level of activity.

flexitime   a method of organizing hours of work which permits some flexibility in the times of starting and finishing each working day.

forward integration   when a firm engaged in assembly operations integrates forwards to distribute and retail its own products.

Four P's of marketing   product, price, promotion and place, the key variables of the marketing mix.

franchise   the granting by one company to another company (exclusive franchise) or a number of companies (non-exclusive franchise) of the right/s to supply its products. A franchise is a contractual arrangement which is entered into for a specified period of time, with the franchisee paying a royalty to the franchisor for the rights assigned.

free trade   the export and import of goods and services between countries totally unhindered by restrictions such as tariffs and quotas.

fringe benefit or **perk**   any benefit offered to employees in addition to their wage or salary (eg, luncheon vouchers, company car or mileage allowance, share option scheme, employer contributions to a pension scheme).

function   the separation of related activities in a business (eg, the accounting function, the production function).

good or **commodity**   an economic product which is produced to meet some personal or business demand. Goods which are purchased by individuals are called *consumer goods* or *final goods*, while goods purchased by businesses are referred to variously as *producer goods, capital goods, industrial goods* or *intermediate goods*.

graph   a means of portraying data in pictorial form that shows the relationship between an independent variable and a dependent variable by labelling and scaling the two axes of the graph to represent two variables; plotting joint values of the two in the space between the axes; and joining these values with a line.

grievance   a complaint by an employee arising out of his or her employment.

grievance procedure   a set of rules stipulating the procedures to be followed when an employee has a complaint arising out of his or her employment.

gross income/wage   an individual's earnings for work done before any deductions have been made for income tax, national insurance, etc.

group incentive scheme   a form of payment by results in which wages may be supplemented by additional payments based on the performance of the work group, the establishment or the enterprise as a whole rather than the performance of the individual worker.

guarantee or **warranty**   a legally binding promise by the seller of a product to the purchaser that in the event of the product failing to work properly the seller will either replace or repair it free of charge, or refund the purchase price.

'halo effect'   the regarding of an individual by others, especially his or her superiors, as especially good at his or her job. The reality may be different but, because the belief is strongly held, any shortcomings may not be perceived.

'hard sell'   a forceful and robust approach to marketing a brand or product.

health and safety   the regulation of organizations's working methods so as to discourage dangerous practices.

horizontal integration   the joining of firms that are producing or selling a similar product.

human relations   a concept of the management of human resources based on the belief that the character of social relationships at work has a profound effect on employee performance.

human resource planning   the process of determining the demand and supply of labour to ensure that the organization (or national economy) has the right people with the right skills at the right time.

hypermarket   see **supermarket**.

import   a good which is produced in a foreign country and which is then physically transported to and sold in the home market, leading to an outflow of foreign exchange from the home country (visible import).

incentive bonus scheme   a form of payment by results whereby an individual's wages may be supplemented by additional payments based on achievement of output or sales targets.

income   money received by individuals, firms and other organizations in the form of wages, salaries, rent, interest, commissions, fees and profit, together with grants, unemployment benefit, old age pensions, etc.

indirect cost   see **overhead cost**.

indirect labour   that part of the labour force in a firm which is not directly concerned with the manufacture of a good or the provision of a service.

indirect materials   any raw materials which, while they are not incorporated in a product, are nonetheless consumed in the production process (eg, lubricants and moulds for metal castings).

induction   the initial training an employee may receive at the commencement of employment to familiarize him or her with the workings of the organization.

industrial action   measures taken by one or more workers either to bring pressure to bear on employers during the course of an industrial dispute or as a response to their conditions of work and employment.

industrial buyer   a buyer whose function it is to acquire raw materials, bought-out finished components, services and equipment on behalf of his or her company.

industrial dispute   a dispute between an employer (or group of employers) and one or more workers usually arising over pay and conditions of employment, allocation of work, work discipline, etc.

industrial goods   raw materials, components, machinery, equipment, etc, which are used by firms as 'factor inputs' in the production of other goods.

industrial marketing   the marketing of goods and services to industrial buyers.

industrial relations   the general state of relationships between management, trade unions and workforce.

Industrial Tribunal   a 'labour court' which adjudicates on claims that individuals have been unlawfully treated by their employers.

industry   a branch of commercial enterprise concerned with the output of related goods or services. For example, the beer/brewing industry might be defined as all those firms that produce bitter and mild ales, lagers, stouts and ciders.

inelastic demand   demand for a product or service which does not change in spite of a large price change.

inflation   an increase in the general level of prices in an economy that is sustained over time.

inelastic supply   supply of a product or service offered for sale which changes very little in spite of a price change.

innovation   see **research and development**.

input   resources such as raw material, labour and capital which are used by a firm to produce goods and services (output).

intangible fixed assets   non-physical fixed assets, such as goodwill, patents and trademarks, which have a money value.

interest   the charge made for borrowing money in the form of a loan.

interest rate   the particular amount of interest which a borrower is required to pay to a lender for borrowing a particular sum of money to finance spending on consumption and the purchase of capital assets.

inventory   the stocks of finished goods, work in progress and raw materials held by businesses.

invoice   a document sent by a supplier to a customer that itemizes the products supplied to the customer, their prices, and the total amount of money owed by the customer for these products.

job   a work task or series of work tasks to be performed.

job analysis   a process of research to identify the tasks comprising a particular job and to determine whether they could be organized in a more productive or satisfying way.

job description   a statement of the work tasks which constitute a job and the responsibilities of the employee in performing that job.

job design and redesign   the process or outcome of grouping together work tasks to form individual jobs.

job enrichment   where workers are given greater scope in deciding how the tasks should be performed to enrich the quality of the job.

job evaluation   a set of procedures to assess the relative worth of groups of jobs in an organization so as to place them in a rank order. This can then provide the basis of a grading and pay structure.

job satisfaction   the satisfaction that an individual gains (or does not gain) from his or her job.

job security   the degree of certainty of continued employment with a particular organization.

job specification   the characteristics of a job.

joint consultation   where managers consult with employee representatives before deciding what course of action to take.

labour   the human input to work activity.

labour force or **workforce**   the total number of people employed by a firm or some other organization to produce goods and services.

labour-intensive   where an industry or particular system of production relies on the use of labour as a factor of production.

labour turnover   the proportion of an organization's labour force which leaves its employment over a given period.

launch   the introduction of a new product on to the market.

leadership   the process of influencing others to achieve certain goals.

legislation   the act or process of making laws; laws so made.

life cycle   see **product life cycle**.

life style   an individual's living pattern as expressed by his or her interests, values, activities and opinions.

line manager   a manager who has direct authority over other employees in the organization.

loss   the shortfall between a firm's sales revenues received from the sale of its products and the total costs incurred in producing the firm's output.

loss leading   the practice whereby a retailer sells a manufacturer's branded product at a price below bought-in cost. Loss leading is used by retailers to attract customers into their stores in the hope that buyers will then purchase a selection of full-price products in addition to cut-price items, thus making a profit on the purchases taken as a whole.

luxury product/service   any product or service which is above those needed for a normal standard of living (eg, jewellery, holidays).

mail order   a direct marketing means of retailing products to consumers through the post. Mail order firms supply catalogues to prospective customers who either themselves or through agents make purchases for delivery to their homes.

maintenance   the management process of repairing and maintaining buildings, plant, machinery and equipment to avoid breakdowns and disruption to production.

management   the process of organizing and directing human and physical resources within an organization so as to meet defined objectives.

management development   the preparation of managers for future work roles.

management style   the general character of management's approach to industrial relations.

managing director   the director of a company responsible for the day-to-day management of the company.

manual worker   a worker who mainly works with his or her hands.

manufacturer   see **producer**.

margin   the difference between selling price and cost price of a product or financial security.

marginal cost   the extra cost that is incurred by a firm in increasing output by one unit.

market   an exchange mechanism which brings together the sellers and buyers of a product.

market channel   see distribution channel.

marketing   the managerial process of identifying customer requirements and satisfying them by providing customers with appropriate products in order to achieve the organization's objectives.

marketing concept   a business philosophy which aims at the generation of profits by the recognition and satisfaction of customer needs.

marketing intelligence   information about developments in a firm's market environment that can assist executives in formulating marketing plans. Such intelligence could include details of new products being introduced by competitors, and price changes, or more general economic and social statistics published by government and other bodies.

marketing management   the process of setting objectives, formulating policy, analysis, planning, implementation and control of activities aimed at the effective selling of the firm's goods or services.

marketing mix   the range of measures used by firms to market their products to buyers.

marketing research   the systematic and objective classification, collection, analysis and reporting of information about a particular marketing problem.

marketing strategy   a strategy employed by a firm to attain its marketing objectives, which in turn is closely related to the achievement of the firm's overall business objectives.

market leader   the seller of a product who holds the largest market share. Generally firms become market leaders by establishing positions of competitive advantage over rival suppliers.

market penetration a business strategy pursued by a firm which is aimed at increasing the sales of the firm's *existing* products in its *present* markets thereby increasing its market share in those markets.

market penetration pricing a pricing policy that involves charging a comparatively low price for a product in order to secure growing sales and a high market share.

market potential the total size of the market for a product at a given time, measured in either volume or value terms.

market research the collection and analysis of information about a particular market.

market research agency a firm which carries out marketing research on behalf of clients.

market segmentation the division of a market into identifiable submarkets or segments each having its own particular customer profile and buyer characteristics.

market share the proportion of total sales of a product accounted for by an individual brand of the product or all brands of the product offered by a firm in a particular market.

mark-up the profit margin on a good or service which can be expressed as a percentage of the cost of the product or a percentage of its selling price.

mass production a method of organizing production whereby a component or product such as a motor car passes through a sequence of predetermined operations or processes which constitute a production line or assembly line. Mass production systems are used to make components or products in comparatively large quantities using specialized machines.

maternity rights the rights pregnant women and the mothers of very young children have in relation to their employment.

media the channels of communication available to a firm (or some other organization) through which the firm's products can be advertised to prospective buyers.

mediation a method of resolving industrial disputes in which a neutral third party acts as a go-between to the parties in dispute.

merchandising in-store promotional activity by manufacturers or retailers at the point of sale, designed to stimulate sales.

merger or **amalgamation** the combining together of two or more firms into a single business on a basis that is mutually agreed by the firms's managements and approved by their shareholders.

merit pay a one-off or regular payment used to reward work of a high quality.

method study an aspect of work study which involves the systematic recording and analysis of the way in which a job is performed, with a view to developing and applying easier and more efficient methods of performing the task.

middleman a person or firm which acts as an intermediary between a seller of a good or service and the buyer of that good or service.

minimum wage rate the stipulation by the government or by agreement between trade unions and employers of a minimum rate of pay for a specified job.

Monopolies and Mergers Commission (MMC) a regulatory body responsible, in part, for the implementation of UK competition policy.

monopoly a market structure characterized by a single supplier and high barriers to entry.

motivation the force or process which impels people to behave in the way that they do. In a work setting, motivation can be viewed as that which determines whether workers expend the degree of effort necessary to achieve required task objectives.

motivational research the measurement of attitudes and preferences likely to affect behaviour.

negotiation the process by which two or more parties attempt to achieve agreement on matters of mutual interest.

net profit the difference between a firm's sales revenue and all costs.

new-product development the process of creating new products by a firm as part of its ongoing product strategy.

non-profit-making organization an organization whose major objective is not to achieve a profit for distribution to its owners or investors.

obsolescence the tendency for products to become outmoded and to reach the end of their effective life.

office a business premise used by a firm in the provision of services.

Office of Fair Trading an authority established by the Fair Trading Act 1973 to administer all aspects of UK competition policy.

oligopoly a market structure characterized by a few large firms supplying the bulk of industry output.

operating profit/loss   the profit (or loss) arising from the manufacturing and trading operations of a business.

opportunity cost   when a decision is made in favour of one choice, the opportunity cost of that decision is the benefit that would have been gained from the next best alternative.

organization   a social grouping (eg, a business, company) arranged to achieve certain goals.

organizational behaviour   an umbrella term for theories and disciplines concerned with human behaviour in organizations and the influences upon it.

organization development (OD)   the process of improving organization performance by improving the pattern of interaction between members of the organization.

output   goods and services produced by a firm using resource inputs.

overhead or **indirect cost**   any cost that is not directly associated with a product, that is, all costs other than direct materials cost and direct labour cost.

overtime   extra hours of work undertaken by an employee that are additional to the number of hours specified as constituting the 'basic' working week, and for which employees are paid a wage rate higher than the 'basic' wage.

overtrading   a situation in which a firm expands its production and sales without making sufficient provision for additional funds to finance the extra working capital needed.

own-label brand   a product which is sold by a retailer bearing the retailer's own brand name.

packaging   the means of physically protecting and selling a product.

Pareto's law   a 'law' that suggests 20 per cent of items account for 80 per cent of the total amount of stock or sales or whatever.

partnership   a business owned and controlled by two or more persons who subscribe capital and share decision-taking as specified by a partnership agreement.

part-time work   employment where the hours of work are substantially fewer than the usual working week.

pay   the money paid to an employee for performing specified work tasks or jobs.

payment by results   a pay system in which a worker's wages and other payments received are related to the amount (or value) of output produced.

performance appraisal   the process of considering and evaluating the performance of an employee with the objective of improving job performance.

personal selling   a means of increasing the sales of a firm's product which involves direct contact between the firm's sales representatives and prospective customers.

personnel management   the branch of management concerned with administering the employment relationship and with achieving effective use of the human resources available to the organization.

Peter Principle   the principle formulated by the American management writer Laurence Peter, that in organizations people are promoted to the level of their incompetence.

picket   a person involved in a strike who seeks to prevent other persons from gaining access to a place of work during an industrial dispute.

piecework   a system of pay in which an individual's wage is related to his or her output.

point of sale display   promotional material, such as banners and posters or demonstrations of a product inside a shop or store, which is used as a means of stimulating sales.

price   the money value of a unit of a good, service, financial security or asset which a buyer is required to pay a seller to purchase the item.

price discrimination   the ability of a supplier to sell the *same* good or service in a number of *separate* markets at *different* prices.

price leadership   a situation where a particular supplier is generally accepted by other suppliers as the 'lead' firm in changing market prices.

price war   a situation of aggressive price cutting by a group of rival suppliers as a means of gaining sales at each other's expense.

producer or **manufacturer**   a business which is engaged in making consumer goods and capital goods using factor inputs such as raw materials, labour and capital.

product   a generic term which covers both goods and services.

product attributes   the various characteristics of a product which satisfy some particular consumer need.

product development   a business strategy pursued by a firm aimed at increasing sales by developing *new* products which can be sold in its *existing* markets (or new products which take the firm into *new* markets).

product differentiation   the means of which suppliers attempt to distinguish their own products from those offered by competitors.

production   the conversion process for transforming inputs such as materials, labour and capital into goods and services.

production management or **operations management**   the adminstration of the conversion process which transforms labour, materials and capital inputs into final goods.

product life cycle   the typical sales pattern of a product over time from its introduction on to the market and its eventual decline as it is displaced by new, more innovative products or until demand for it falls, due to a change in consumer tastes.

product line   a number of closely-related versions of a product (eg, variants of the Ford Escort car).

product range   the number of products and brands sold by a firm.

professional   a person with a recognized set of skills and knowledge which qualifies them to practise a certain occupation. Usually this knowledge is gained from lengthy training and is certified by examination, often by a professional association.

profit   the difference that arises when a firm's sales revenue is greater than its total costs.

profitability   the profit earned by a firm in relation to the size of the firm, measured in terms of total assets employed, long-term capital or number of employees.

profit margin   the difference between the selling price of a product and its production cost and selling cost.

profit sharing   the distribution of some portion of profits to the employees of a company.

promotion   the means of bringing products to the attention of consumers and persuading them to buy those products.

promotional mix   the means which a firm can use to inform prospective customers of the nature and attributes of its products and to persuade them to buy and repeat-purchase those products. The promotional mix is made up of advertising, sales promotion, merchandising, packaging, personal selling and public relations.

public relations (PR)   a general means of promoting a business's company image with a view to encouraging customers to buy its products and investors to buy its shares, as well, for example, as influencing government policies on issues relevant to the company.

purchasing   the business function which is involved in procuring raw materials, components, finished goods and capital equipment, ordering and acquiring supplies of these items at competitive prices.

quality control   the task of ensuring that the quality of a product or service meets specified performance criteria.

quantity discount   a price reduction from a supplier's list price given to buyers of products according to the quantities that they purchase.

questionnaire   a structure list of questions which is used to obtain information. It is frequently used in marketing research to help identify consumers's needs and motivations and to gauge their reactions to present product offerings.

quotation   the price and terms on which a firm is prepared to supply a good or service.

rate of return   the profits earned by a business, measured as percentage of the assets employed in the business.

raw materials   basic materials, such as iron ore, bauxite, wheat and coffee, which are converted into finished goods or components in the production process.

recruitment and selection   the process of filling job vacancies in an organization.

redundancy   the termination of an individual's employment when the employer ceases trading or the job ceases to be required.

repeat purchases   further purchases of a product by a buyer who, after having tried the product, is sufficiently satisfied with it to make additional purchases.

research and development (R&D)   the commitment of resources by a firm to scientific research (both 'pure' and 'applied') and the refinement and modification of research ideas and prototypes aimed at the ultimate development of commercially viable processes and products.

responsibility   the obligation to carry out specified duties and tasks.

retailer   a business which stocks a particular type of product (such as a shoe shop) or an extensive range of products (such as a department store) for sale to consumers.

retail outlet   business premises or facilities for selling products to consumers.

retirement   the termination of an individual's working career at a certain age with the expectation that he or she will no longer undertake paid employment.

risk   see **uncertainty and risk**.

risk analysis   the systematic analysis of the degree of risk attaching to capital projects.

royalties   payments made for the use of an intellectual property right (copyrights, patents, etc) or physical property rights (mineral extraction rights, etc).

salary   a payment made to employees for the use of their labour.

sale   the purchase of a good or service by a buyer from a seller at a stated price.

sales analysis   the recording, analysis and evaluation of a firm's sales data. Sales analysis is usually designed to give a breakdown of sales by product, by salesperson, by sales area, and by customer (age group, sex, etc).

salesforce   the salespeople employed by a firm to sell its goods or services.

sales forecasting   the process of predicting future product demand to help in making decisions about marketing expenditure, investment in production capacity and the scheduling of factory output.

sales promotion   the measures used by firms alongside other elements of the promotional mix (advertising, personal selling, etc) to increase the sales of their products.

sales revenue   the income generated from the sale of goods and services.

sales volume   the quantity of a firm's product or brand sold within a given time period.

sample   a small trial pack of a product or brand which is used to encourage buyers to try out.

scientific management   an approach to job design advocated by F W Taylor (1856–1915), an American work study engineer.

seasonal demand   when the purchase of a product by consumers varies according to the time of year.

self-service   a form of retailing wherby customers of retail outlets (shop, filling station, etc) select for themselves the goods they wish to purchase and pay for them at a check-out.

service   an economic activity which is performed to meet a personal or business demand.

shift work   a method of organizing work which enables production or services to be operated beyond normal working hours.

shop   a business premise which is engaged in the retailing of products to customers who visit the shop or store to make purchases.

shopping goods   products such as motor cars which represent a major purchasing decision and thus justify the buyer in 'shopping around' to compare suitability, price, quality and style.

shop steward   a shop-floor employee who represents his/her colleagues's interests in workplace negotiations with management.

sick pay   the payments made to an employee who is unable to work normally due to illness.

skill   any competence possessed by someone; in an employment context it often refers to a combination of knowledge and manual dexterity amongst manual workers.

social responsibility   a business philosophy which stresses the need for firms to behave as good corporate citizens, not merely obeying the law but conducting their production and marketing activities in a manner which avoids causing environmental pollution or exhausting finite world resources.

socioeconomic group   the potential buyers of a product grouped together in terms of certain common personal and economic characteristics.

span of control   the number of people a manager has formal authority over and is responsible for.

standard of living   the general level of economic prosperity in an economy as measured by, for example, the level of per capita income (gross national product divided by the size of the population).

statute law   the law laid down by government legislation (in the UK, an Act of Parliament).

stock   the part of a firm's assets that are held in the form of raw materials, work in progress and finished goods.

strategy   a unified set of plans and actions designed to secure the achievement of the basic objectives of a business or of some other organization.

strike   a stoppage of work by a group of workers as part of an industrial dispute with the aim of bringing pressure to bear on the employer.

suggestion scheme   a facility for employees to submit suggestions for revision of production equipment and working methods which will lead to improvements in efficiency or product quality.

supermarket   a large self-service retail outlet. Supermarkets may be under single-shop ownership or run as multiple chain-store businesses.

Hypermarkets are an extended form of supermarkets, usually located on the outskirts of town and cities where space is plentiful.

superstore a very large shop or store which is often located on the edge of a large town with extensive parking facilities, selling such products as groceries, furniture and do-it-yourself items.

supervisor an employee with responsibility for monitoring the work of others to ensure that they fulfil work targets generally established by managers.

SWOT analysis a framework of identifying the *internal* strengths (S) and weaknesses (W) of a firm, and the *external* opportunities (O) open to it and the threats (T) it faces, which can be used by corporate planners in formulating the firm's competitive strategy in individual product markets and its overall business strategy.

target market the market or market segments which form the focus of a firm's marketing efforts.

telephone selling a form of direct marketing in which a seller of a product contacts customers by telephone in order to establish an initial contact with them.

tender an invitation from a buyer who requires particular goods or services to prospective suppliers of those products to put in competing price bids.

test marketing a pre-launch trial run of a new product involving a representative sample of prospective buyers who are given the product to try.

Theory X and Theory Y two opposed philosophies of management and organization, so named by the American social psychologist Douglas McGregor (1906–64).

trade mark a symbol (a word or pictorial representation) which is used by a business as a means of identifying a particular good or service so that it may be readily distinguished by purchasers from similiar goods and services supplied by other businesses.

trade union an organization of employees whose primary objective is to protect and advance the economic interests of its members by negotiating wage rates and conditions of employment with employers or managers.

training the process of extending and improving the skills and knowledge of people so as to improve job performance.

transactions the activities of buying and selling in a market system.

turnover the speed at which a business can sell its product (the word is also sometimes used to mean sales revenue).

uncertainty and risk the comparative unpredictability of a firm's future business environment, bringing with it the possibility that the firm might incur losses if future economic and market conditions turn out to be radically different from those anticipated by the firm in, for example, pricing its products, moving into new activities, etc.

unemployment the non-utilization of part of the economy's available labour (and capital) resources.

unfair dismissal the unfair termination of a person's employment by the employer. Dismissal can be held to be unfair if the employer cannot show a 'fair' reason and acted 'unreasonably' in taking the decision to dismiss.

value the money worth of a product or asset.

value added the difference between the value of a firm's (or industry's) *output* (ie, the total revenues received from selling that output) and the cost of the *input* materials, components or services bought in to produce that output.

value analysis the evaluation and review of a product's design, with the aim of reducing its material or manufacturing cost without impairing its function or performance.

variable cost any costs that tend to vary directly with the level of output.

vendor the seller of a good or service.

vertical integration when companies from different levels of production join together to become one company.

voluntary group a business which operates as a wholesaler to a group of small retailers who undertake to place a certain volume of orders with the voluntary group, in return for price concessions on the purchases they make and various backup services (promotions, etc).

wage the money payment made to a worker, usually on a weekly basis, for the use of his or her labour.

wage rate the money payment made to a worker for each 'unit' of his or her labour input, usually measured either on an hourly time basis, or for each unit of output produced.

warehouse business premises used by a manufacturer to store both raw materials, components, etc (materials store) and final products (finished goods store), and by wholesalers and retailers to store finished products in the course of distribution to buyers.

warranty   see **guarantee**.

welfare   that aspect of management concerned with the well-being, both physical and emotional, of employees.

wholesaler   a business which buys products in relatively large quantities from manufacturers which it stocks and sells on in smaller quantities to retailers.

worker   a person employed by an organization to perform a job or work task either on a paid basis (as an employee) or on an unpaid basis (as, for example, a charity worker).

work in progress   any goods that are still in the process of being made up into their final form.

work measurement   an aspect of work study which involves the application of measurement techniques to establish the time it takes for a trained worker to carry out a particular job.

work study or **time and motion study**   an area of production management concerned with ensuring the best possible use of human and material resources in carrying out a specified activity.

Suggested Answers to Essays

Chapter One

Essay 1

The size of businesses can be measured in many ways. For example: by turnover, capital employed or number of employees.

Businesses vary in size for a number of reasons. For small businesses, it could be that their market is small – for example, a hairdresser in a village. Equally it could be that many competitors exist which prevents firms gaining a high market share. It may be that the firm is in an industry which requires it to offer a high level of personal service, which large organizations are unable to.

Large businesses may exist because economies of scale can be achieved or because huge capital investment is required (in the steel industry, for example). The market may be worldwide and so large businesses develop to meet this extensive demand. Other factors include the management style and objectives of the owners, the amount of capital to which they have access, the extent of government support and so on.

The simple answer to the second part is, 'yes'! Those industries which produce highly technical products, which require extensive research, tend to comprise large firms. Those that produce a perishable product tend to be smaller, etc. However, there are exceptions: industries exist which have both large and small firms – for example, the retail industry.

Chapter Two

Essay 1

Candidates should outline the techniques open to managers for motivation – many of which are included in the Volvo Case Study. For example, participation and consultation, job enrichment, quality circles, autonomous work groups, work place equality (clothing, canteens and other amenities). (This knowledge can earn up to 30 per cent of available marks.)

A balanced argument is required. The techniques mentioned can be supported from theories – Maslow's higher needs; Herzberg's satisfiers; Mayo's belonging; McGregor's Theory Y. On the other hand, some theories are difficult to apply in practice; it can depend upon the type of organization and its culture; different individuals react differently to different motivators; poor industrial relations cannot be cured by this means alone. (This analysis can earn up to 40 per cent of the available marks.)

The answer should be rounded off with some broader issues – for example, the effects of: the economic climate; the size of the firm; the industrial sectors and their industrial relations history; the values of the managers; the success of the firm; its ability to finance changes and so on. (This evaluation can earn up to 30 per cent of available marks.)

Essay 1

The candidate should outline the higher needs that result in motivation – for example, Maslow's higher needs or Herzberg's satisfiers (achievement, recognition, responsibility, etc). (Maximum 30 per cent of marks.)

An analysis of how these are incorporated in such techniques as job enrichment, participation, etc, and how McGregor's Theory Y assumptions and McClelland's achievement motive are essential ingredients. (Maximum 40 per cent of marks.)

Finally, individuals are unique and respond in different ways; theories are an attempt to understand patterns of behaviour; there are no certain ways; each firm will adopt a different approach depending upon its managers, size, position in the market and so on. (Maximum 30 per cent of marks.)

Chapter Three

Essay 1

(a) Candidates might start by giving an outline of the nature of job enrichment and the basic theories of motivation (approx. 7 marks). This could be followed by a discussion of how job enrichment put the theory into practice and the management style needed to ensure its success (approx. 8 marks).

(b) A short consideration of what is meant by 'assembly line' followed by a general description of steps similar to those taken by Volvo at Kalmar. Volvo and Borg Warner Automotive might be used as supporting examples.

Recognition should be given to the difficulties that might be experienced in such application, with suggestions of how those difficulties might be handled (for example, training and communication). (Maximum 10 marks.)

Essay 2

Candidates could give a brief outline of the communication process with an emphasis on the interpersonal aspects. This might be followed by some of the characteristics of IT – for example, impersonal, jargon, operating difficulties, physical problems. (Maximum 30 per cent of marks.)

A balanced argument about an organization's need for information and the ability of computers to provide it, with the difficulties of loss of social contact, the tendency to 'believe the computer', the danger of people relying on the computer and ceasing to listen or be imaginative or use initiative, and its overall impact upon effective communication. (Maximum 40 per cent of marks.)

A conclusion that firms are becoming more efficient in the use of computers and are getting them into a proper perspective. They are only a tool – the important thing is the information (not the channel) and the use to which the business puts the information. This is a human skill. However, the benefits of computers outweighs any disadvantages, and businesses are finding ways and means of exploiting them without loss of effectiveness in communication. (Maximum 30 per cent of marks.)

Chapter Four

Essay 1

Candidates should outline the functions of a personnel department – human resource planning, recruitment and selection and so on (30 per cent maximum).

This should be followed by an analysis of the effect of 'falling' unemployment on each of the functions. For example, human resource planning information might suggest that there will be a shortage in certain skills areas as a result. What might the firm do to preserve its position despite this shortage? Perhaps it could take on trainees in advance of the need and train them; or offer salaries sufficient to attract skilled people away from other firms. But what will other firms be doing? What about the cost? Will it affect the competitive position of the firm? Reputation and industrial relations history will matter. Will good people want to work for the firm? And what about satisfying or boring jobs? Similar consideration should be given to other functions in the personnel department. (Maximum 40 per cent of marks.)

Of course, the health of the economy may cause the position to change; some types of firm will be less affected than others; creative and innovative solutions will be found by some companies; the EC allows free movement of work people; there may be a greater willingness to move if there are more jobs available. (Maximum 30 per cent of marks.)

Essay 2

Candidates should outline the responses a firm might make. Such things as better liaison with schools; offering attractive training schemes; making full use of schemes such as YT; making jobs attractive and interesting to that age group; making provision for women returners (nurseries, working hours to suit school times); attracting older folks (retired service people, police officers, earlier retirers from elsewhere) and so on should be considered. (Up to 5 marks.)

Each of these 'responses' should be analysed to show how each would deal with the situation (maximum 5 marks). Fuller analyses should highlight some of the actions and changes that a firm would need to take to make these responses effective, and the likely costs and benefits they might bring in the short term and the longer term. (Further 6 marks.)

Candidates should attempt to identify the types of firm that will be affected, and the types of firm that will be little affected. Some of the 'responses' might suit some types of firm, other responses might be suitable for other types. Big firms might need different solutions from small firms. Some firms will find innovative solutions that give them an advantage over their competitors. It depends on the quality of the firm's management. (Up to 9 marks for evaluation.)

Chapter Five

Essay 1

Candidates would be expected to outline the purposes and benefits of training – for example, to change behaviour; to improve performance; to introduce change; to prepare people for promotion; to keep ahead of competitors; to avoid 'getting into a rut'. (Maximum 30 per cent of marks.)

Develop the notion that everyone in an organization, particularly managers, need these things. Examine why it is more important than the question implies. Learning should be focused on the needs of the firm now, and into the future – that cannot be left to chance. (Maximum 40 per cent of marks.)

Firms are only as good as the management. If the environment in which the firm exists is constantly changing, then the managers must be able to change with it. Winning firms will ensure they are geared up for change and be ahead of their competitors. The costs of training are not as great as the costs of ignorance or inefficiency. Without management training, people being promoted into management will be learning through trial and error – and errors can be expensive. Many managers feel that 'training' is an affront to their status. Sometimes there is not suitable training available for different levels of management. Some management training is poor and dissuades managers. There are new bodies formed by the government to tackle that problem – for example, Management Charter Initiative (MCI); National Vocational Qualifications (NVQ). (Maximum 30 per cent of marks.)

Essay 2

An outline of 'styles' should draw upon McGregor's Theory X and Theory Y and/or Tannenbaum's continuum of styles. (Maximum 30 per cent of marks.)

Candidates should analyse the likely effect of each style on the way people work, perhaps calling on Fiedler's Contingency Theory. (Maximum 40 per cent of marks.)

People are different. Some respond better to direction than they do to freedom. Situations change all the time – what is a suitable style for one will not be suitable for another. Good leaders analyse situations and lead accordingly. Some types of work call upon different styles – compare the job on a very paced assembly line with that of an office clerk, a teacher, a researcher and so on. Culture has a major impact on the way managers lead, and that is very difficult to define or change. (Maximum 30 per cent of marks.)

Essay 3

Candidates should outline situations of rapid growth compared with slower growth – for example, normal organic growth v mergers/take overs. Reference should be made briefly to the physical resource implications of growth, and the management problems that it might cause. But growth means change and people tend to fear or resist change – managing rapid change calls for skills that are different from those needed for normal change. Reference might be made to recruitment, training, industrial relations, communication, work load, staff development and availability of new managers. (Maximum 30 per cent of marks.)

Each of these should be analysed to show the difference in their application between normal and rapid growth. The 'managing change' skills should be highlighted – for example, distinguish-

ing between social and technical reasons, and the pressures to ignore the social during rapid change, and the likely consequences. (Maximum 40 per cent of marks.)

It seems that some people thrive on change whilst others prefer stability. Some jobs are subject to rapid change (oil exploration and extraction); others are very stable (teaching and accounting). Each attracts the appropriate sort of people. Present economic and market conditions seem to have increased rates of change. Therefore, managing skills in these conditions become more important for success. Technology – computers – make change more manageable, but people still have to be considered. (Maximum 30 per cent of marks.)

Chapter Six

Essay 1

Some brief reference to the changes in legislation during the 1980s, and to the effects of economic conditions on membership, should set the scene. An outline of reasons should follow – such as the benefits to members; strikes cost members in loss of pay; poor employer-union relations can cost jobs; more appropriate for the 1990s; more responsible role for unions; survival of unions depend on them changing; members do not want strikes and so on. (Maximum 30 per cent of marks.)

Are these reasons true? Do they just reflect weak unions? Or is it that some unions are greedy for members? How often do strikes occur anyway? Collective bargaining is weakened if there are no sanctions. Unions should get the best possible deal for members – and that means they must have power to hurt the employers. No strike agreements are 'Made in Japan' and are not appropriate here. (Maximum 40 per cent of marks.)

Candidates should bring the two together to show that there is a need to change as economic pressures and competitive pressures force changes that are necessary for survival. New technology and production methods make some union activities of the past inappropriate now. However, people still need to be represented in negotiations and possibly more so. (Maximum 30 per cent of marks.)

Essay 2

Candidates should outline: size of union; membership in workplace; militancy of members; political and legal position; skill of negotiators; public sympathy; state of the economy; public/private sector; financial strength of the employer; union funds available. (Maximum 30 per cent of marks.)

Each of these should be analysed in the light of prevailing conditions. Is the size of the union expanding or contracting? What if members do not support negotiators when it comes to the crunch (for example, miners in late 1980s)? What if the government has given priority to 'individual rights' rather than collective rights? Other factors to consider include: secret ballots; picketing laws; no secondary action; if public sympathy seems to ebb when strikes occur; unemployment is a weakener; if manufacturing jobs are decreasing and so on. (Maximum 40 per cent of marks.)

Fewer large-scale organizations and more technology removes some of the power. But many employers still recognize unions and value their activities. They can be a positive force and keep management on their toes. The changes imposed in the 1980s have made unions look for other areas of influence. Changes in working patterns have meant that unions have new roles and new situations to deal with and as they develop these they will regain their factors of success.

Chapter Seven

Essay 1

Candidates should say what marketing is. They should highlight the confusion in the question between marketing and selling. Outline that all products need some form of marketing – they need to be promoted by some means, priced and distributed. (Maximum 30 per cent of marks.)

Candidates should produce an argument that develops the following points and shows customers will only buy rubbish once; some firms who manufacture fine products are very marketing orientated (give some examples); good marketing can lead to economies of scale and benefit producer and customer; 4Ps are important to success; competition forces firms to become marketing orientated – otherwise people will forget; caring for the customer is the thing of the 90s. (Maximum 40 per cent of marks.)

Marketing does not just relate to external affairs, marketing is the responsibility of every member of staff. Marketing can be brought into disrepute because of a few abuses. British people do not respond to marketing in the same way as some of their international competitors. Economic conditions and state of the market are important. The costs of marketing have to be justified. Marketing applies to more than products and services – for example, charities, political parties, religion. (Maximum 30 per cent of marks.)

Essay 2

Candidates should give a clear outline of the stages of the life cycle, and draw them on a traditional graph. (Maximum 30 per cent of marks.)

Candidates should describe the strategies that managers can adopt to get the product successfully through each stage. The television examples used in this book, or something that achieves the same purpose, should be used. Discuss the cash flow and profit implications. Discuss the production implications and the administrative support needed as the life cycle progresses. (Maximum 40 per cent of marks.)

The concept is only a tool. It does not tell managers when each stage will occur, only that they will occur. Managers must use their skills and experience to ensure the product's success. It will not make decisions for them. It is only one tool and should be used in conjunction with others that are appropriate. Different products have different life cycle patterns. Different strategies would be used for different products. Different managers will make different decisions based on the same or similar information. (Maximum 30 per cent of marks.)

Essay 3

Candidates should state that the firm must gather data to explain what is happening to the products in the market-place – for example, marketing research with distributors and customers. State clearly the reasons for this. Examine the 4Ps. (Maximum 30 per cent of marks.)

Is the reduction happening to just this manufacturer, or to all furniture manufacturers? If all, is it the economy? If not, is it the product design, materials or what? Or is it the other Ps (examine them one at a time)? Based on good information the manufacturer can analyse the situation and make decisions about correcting it. (Maximum 40 per cent of marks.)

If management did not anticipate what was happening, would it be capable of an analytical approach? The cost of this sort of corrective action would be high – can the firm afford it? Other options from the above might be considered – for example, merge or be taken over. If they survive, management must ensure systems are in place that do not allow it to recur.

Chapter Eight

Essay 1

(a) Show how customers might change from one brand of a product to another – from Anchor Butter to Lurpac Butter, or from butter to low fat spread.

(b) 'Marketing strategy' should be explained. Using each of the 4Ps, explain how it would be used to bring about each type of change discussed in (a). For example, like brands would avoid using price as a major differentiation for fear of a price war, whereas a substitute may initially use price to attract customers away. Promotion would set out to create brand loyalty. A substitute would find positive benefits (better health, for example) for changing. AIDA would be a useful model to help the explanation.

Essay 2

Candidates should write as though they were marketing consultants. Firstly, confirm or otherwise the firm's beliefs using marketing research. Know the strategies of the originator clearly before deciding what actions to take. (Maximum 30 per cent of marks.)

Define niche and design strategy (4Ps) to exploit it. But the originator might react aggressively – explain the likely counter actions. However, if niche is of no interest to the originator, all will be at peace. Discuss the costs of such a venture and the risks. (Maximum 40 per cent of marks.)

There are seldom markets with only one supplier. The market structure allows for competitors. The originator may benefit from a competitor – more market education; keeps management on its toes and so on. Even though research showed an opportunity, it depends upon the effectiveness of marketing; reaction of distributors to product; reaction of customers to the product; any changes in the economy whilst all this was being developed. (Maximum 30 per cent of marks.)

Chapter Nine

Essay 1

Candidates should outline a variety of pricing tactics. Explain that demand and supply is a theory and does not reflect the real world. Price is only one element in the marketing mix. (Maximum 30 per cent of marks.)

Price is treated with care in the real world.

Price skimming and penetration should be explained and examples of the types of product and the situations that they suit should be given. Most manufacturers will not challenge the price makers. Sales promotion tactics are more common than straight price changes. Non-price competition is widely practised. Expand on ways that this can be done. (Maximum 40 per cent of marks.)

Often, there is an accepted price for a product that seems to satisfy customers and meet the manufacturer's objectives. Theories do not allow for such behaviour; nor do they allow for the individual preferences of managers. Such things as design, delivery dates and after-sales service often matter as much as or more than price. Customers cannot know all the prices being offered for a product, and therefore cannot choose the cheapest. Anyway, for some products, people would not be bothered chasing the cheapest. (Maximum 30 per cent of marks.)

Essay 2

Candidates should clearly state what mark-up is. They should be careful to focus on retail and not to discuss anything to do with manufacture. Highlight the difference between stocking and selling a fast moving convenience good and a slow moving speciality good. (Maximum 30 per cent of marks.)

Develop the points raised above. One make of soap has many competitors and most are fairly homogeneous. Demand is elastic; mark-up is low; self-service; stock turnover is fast. Whereas rings are inelastic; they are exclusive; their value is enhanced by high price and personal service; the stock turnover is low; and high costs (for insurance and stock holding, for example) means high mark-up. (Maximum 40 per cent of marks.)

There is a false market in diamonds that keeps the price high. There are 'cheap' diamond rings and 'expensive' soap. The location will have an influence – for example, soap in a department store; rings on a street market? Some jewellery stores are luxurious and this has to be paid for. Snob appeal costs! (Maximum 30 per cent of marks.)

Bibliography

Baker, M J (1974) *Marketing: An Introductory Text*, Macmillan.

Bell, K W (1979) *Management: An Experiential Approach*, McGraw-Hill Kogakusha Ltd.

Graham, H T and Bennett, R (1992) *Human Resources Management*, Pitman.

Green, G D (1991) *Industrial Relations*, Pitman.

Handy, C (1985) *Understanding Organisations*, Penguin.

Knell, A (Ed) (1993) *The Personnel Manager's Fact Book*, Professional Publishing Ltd.

Kolb, D A, Robin, I M and McIntyre, J M (1971) *Organizational Psychology: An Experiential Approach*, Prentice Hall.

Kotler, P (1988) *Marketing Management: Analysis, Planning, Implementation and Control*, Prentice Hall.

McDonald, M (1989) *Marketing Plans*, Heinemann.

Mullins, L J (1989) *Management and Organisational Behaviour*, Pitman.

Pride, W M and Ferrell, O C (1987) *Marketing*, Houghton Mifflin.

Schein, E (1980) *Organizational Psychology*, Prentice Hall.

Torrington, D and Hall, L (1987) *Personnel Management: A New Approach*, Prentice Hall.

Wilson, R M S (1973) *Management Controls in Marketing*, Heinemann.

Index